FAMOUS TRIALS

EDITED BY

HARRY HODGE AND JAMES H. HODGE

SELECTED AND INTRODUCED BY

JOHN MORTIMER

VIKING

VIKING

Penguin Books Ltd, Harmondsworth, Middlesex, England
Viking Penguin Inc., 40 West 23rd Street, New York, New York
10010, U.S.A.
Penguin Books Australia Ltd, Ringwood, Victoria, Australia
Penguin Books Canada Ltd, 2801 John Street, Markham, Ontario,
Canada L3R 1B4
Penguin Books (N.Z.) Ltd, 182–190 Wairau Road, Auckland 10,
New Zealand

ISBN 0–670–80320–0

Filmset in Baskerville
Printed in Great Britain by
Richard Clay (The Chaucer Press) Ltd, Bungay, Suffolk

These trials first published in unabridged form by William Hodge &
Co. Ltd in the Notable British Trials series (Rattenbury and Stoner,
1935; Hawley Harvey Crippen, 1920; Oscar Slater, 1929; Madeleine
Smith, 1927; Robert Wood, 1936; George Joseph Smith, 1922;
Ronald True, 1925; Herbert Rowse Armstrong, 1927;
William Joyce, 1946)

These abridged versions first published by Penguin Books in *Famous
Trials* volumes 1 (1941), 2 (1948), 4 (1954), 5 (1955), edited by
Harry Hodge and James H. Hodge
This selection first published in Penguin Books 1984
Published by Viking 1984

Contents

Introduction

Hɪɢʜ among the great British
contributions to world civilization, the plays of Shakespeare, the
full breakfast, the herbaceous border and the presumption of innocence, must rank our considerable achievement in having produced
most of the best murder trials in the long history of crime. It is a
talent that is not altogether lost to us. We may have surrendered
our pre-eminence in making motor cars, our cafés may no longer be
cleaner than those in Europe, many of the great dishes of our past,
such as boiled mutton and caper sauce, are no more than a memory,
but each summer the Old Bailey still contrives to mount, in time for
the tourist season, some crowd-pulling criminal attraction. Colour
supplements devoted to *nouvelle cuisine* have failed to make any great
change in the English Sunday, which goes with a joint in the oven,
the all-pervading smell of boiled cabbage, and an account of
charred remains found in a burnt-out Ford Popular as described on
page one of the *News of the World*.

But the great murders of the past, some of which are included in
this book, come from the vintage years before the last war. We have
not had, recently, a case as prosaically spine-chilling as that of the
'Brides in the Bath', nor as pathetically tragic as the life and death
of Alma Rattenbury. There is a school of writers on famous trials
which would attribute some decline in the quality of murder cases
to the abolition of the death penalty. 'It was the fatal question, and
as it was asked those in Court felt they saw the shadow of the
scaffold fall across the wretched Jones' was the sort of sentence
which figured often in their accounts. Indeed, the writers included

here sometimes rely on the outcome of a capital trial for their dramatic effects. 'Death was dealt to him [Armstrong, the poisoner],' writes Filson Young, 'on that May morning, while the birds in Cusop Dingle were singing about the house where his children were awaking, with the swift and merciful efficiency of modern methods; and for the sins that he committed he paid up to the full measure of his capacity to pay,' and Eric R. Watson signs off from the 'Brides in the Bath' case with 'fate, through the instrumentality of Messrs Pierpont and Ellis [the hangmen], made a most proper use of her running noose on 13 August 1915'. I have to say that it's not only the inelegant use of an internal rhyme that makes me find that sentence repulsive.

This is not the proper place to discuss the death penalty: that deliberate act of judicial killing, carried out by such curious proxies as Pierpont and Ellis, which stains us all, I believe, with the crime the murderer commits. No one can read William Roughead's brilliant account of the trial of Oscar Slater and see how a death sentence can be pronounced after an appalling series of false deductions, unreliable identifications, suppression of evidence by the police, misleading counsels' speeches and judicial misdirection, and feel content that something so unpredictable as a murder trial should be allowed to end in a mistake that might only have been rectified after the death of an innocent man. Oscar Slater, however, managed to survive the injustices heaped upon him. Timothy Evans, whom few can doubt was mistakenly hanged at the time of the Christie murders, unfortunately did not.

I don't think that it is only the shadow of the scaffold which gives such an extraordinary dramatic quality to the great criminal trials of the past. Murder, like farce, flourishes in the most respectable societies. If a Victorian husband, tied to the apron-strings of an impossible partner, loses his braces in a dubious hotel, or dismembers his wife, the result is far more dramatic than if such events took place in a colony of Los Angeles hippies. Murder, like prostitution and the music hall, was one of the great releases for Victorian and Edwardian society. Of course, not everyone had actually to do it. To read about murder in the Sunday papers, or the *Strand Magazine* where the Sherlock Holmes stories first made their

8

appearance, may have been catharsis enough. The violent outbursts, the dramatic escapes from convention, were done by proxy. Perhaps the bizarre conduct of Dr Crippen saved the lives of countless bossy suburban housewives, and when that respected country solicitor Herbert Rowse Armstrong resorted to poison he stood in for all those husbands whose spouses called them sharply in from a game of tennis to remind them that it was their bath night.

Murder, as is well known, like divorce and Christmas, mainly takes place in the family circle. It is an error to suppose that it is most often the result of violent and organized crime. It is an act of intimacy which occurs between husbands and wives, between lovers, between landlords and tenants, between those locked for years in the confines of a close and emotional association. And where society insists on making the bonds of such relationships almost unbreakable, by difficult divorce or rigorous convention, then it is small wonder that a number of quietly spoken, patient people go out to buy arsenic on the flimsy pretext of putting down rats, or killing dandelions, or merely improving their complexions.

Above all murder cases show the dark side of respectable middle-class England, the results of the repression of sexuality. As F. Tennyson Jesse, by far the best writer represented here, and the one with the deepest understanding of her subject, points out, both Alma Rattenbury and Madeleine Smith were modern women, born out of their time. Even in the thirties, the time of the Rattenbury trial, the prosecuting counsel was able to ask a doctor if regular sexual intercourse between an older woman and a boy of eighteen would not inevitably ruin the lad's health. Mr Justice Humphreys who otherwise conducted an extremely fair trial, told the jury that because Alma Rattenbury committed adultery 'they could not feel anything but disgust for her', a proposition which her own brilliant counsel felt himself bound to accept in his closing speech. And in Edinburgh the Judge referred to Madeleine Smith's love letters in terms which made it clear that he regarded sex between unmarried young people in approximately the same light as murder. When human nature is surrounded with such attitudes high farce or desperate tragedy is the almost inevitable result.

9

Again and again repressed sexuality is a theme of these trials. George Joseph Smith could never have lured his victims to the bath tub if he hadn't been blessed, or cursed, with some bright-eyed, physical magnetism which proved irresistible to young ladies with a small amount of money and no other avenue of sexual release. Murder investigations focused the public's attention on the dark side of respectable society, and with lip-smacking relish the *Daily Chronicle* was able to write, 'There are savages, as we call them, who would be ashamed to live the life that is led sometimes in Camden Town, and Camden Town is but the particular locality upon which this case has chanced to throw the flashlight revealing the seamy side of low life in London.'

Husbands and wives and lovers throng these pages, together with another recurring character of the vintage murder, the prostitute. Prostitutes had to put up with what many middle-class wives apparently couldn't or wouldn't accept. They not only took on the burden of sex for their more reputable sisters, they frequently died for them. Sickert, the great painter of Edwardian interiors where boredom seems to come seeping out of the fumed oak furniture, did the unforgettable pictures of the Camden Town murders. The prostitute lies with her throat cut on a brass bedstead in the position in which her husband found her when he returned, after a night away at his duties on one of the restaurant cars of the Midland Railway, to the little house in St Paul's Road. Beside the bed sits the shadowy and bulky figure of a man, perhaps someone else's husband, perhaps the murderer, no doubt not the young artist and engraver Robert Wood for whom Marshall Hall, in one of his greatest defences, secured an acquittal.

Another surrogate victim of our earlier respectability was Olive Young, alias Gertrude Yates, who carried on a quiet and orderly business as a prostitute in a basement flat in Fulham. She became the victim of the spoiled and wealthy young lunatic Ronald True, who roamed London's restaurants, hotels and music halls carrying a loaded revolver in a homicidal search for his other identity, a mythical man he said was also named Ronald True or Trew. When he met *him*, the eventual murderer of Gertrude Yates said, 'then there would be a "how d'ye do" '. Ronald True never found his alter ego, but contented himself with battering the inoffensive prostitute to death with a rolling-pin. She died as she lived and, in one of the most touching phrases in Donald Carswell's account of the case, she 'gave no trouble'.

The remarkable dramas called for great stars and Edward Marshall Hall, undoubtedly the greatest criminal defender, returns to Court in these pages. He comes on the stage, tall, good-looking, beautifully dressed and with a voice full of persuasion, in an attempt to save the life of George Joseph Smith, who always inquired about the bath when he brought a new wife to a boarding-house; and, more successfully, to protect Robert Wood in the Camden Town murder trial. Marshall Hall has a curious sort of immortality. Like all great advocates he remains a shadowy figure, his own personality packed away in the tin box which contained his wig and gown. He lives on only in the company of those accused of murders, such as Madame Fahmy and Smith and Ronald Light of the 'Green Bicycle' case. We can almost see him, if we read Edward Marjoribanks's great biography, standing in the cramped Edwardian courtrooms making his final speech to a hushed audience. The two arms were stretched to imitate the scales of justice, evenly balanced, and then into one well-manicured hand, protruding from a gleaming white cuff, Marshall Hall would place the invisible presumption of innocence, the small gold nugget of our criminal law, and the scales would tip inevitably in favour of the accused.

But anyone who thinks Marshall Hall was no more than a fine profile and a theatrically effective final speech should read his defence of Robert Wood. The picture is memorable, the great advocate taking every point with dogged persistence, the apparently unconcerned young client sitting in the dock sketching the Judge, and the Court packed with such theatrical stars as Pinero and George Alexander and Hall Caine. Most defenders accept police plans of streets around the scene of the crime as a matter of course, but Marshall Hall managed to prove that Sergeant Grosse had misrepresented the street lighting in St Paul's Road. In consequence the shop-worn cross-examination on identity, a cliché of many hopeless defences which depend on the amount of light on a subject's face, was an early success in the case. Later Marshall Hall had the delicate task of insisting on his client's innocence without obviously accusing the prosecution witnesses, some of whom were almost over-eager to show they couldn't have done the murder. He knew that it is fatal for a defendant to appear as a prosecutor, and left it to the prosecution to attempt to prove the innocence of other suspects in a way which, in the eyes of the jury, must have only made them appear more suspicious.

When Robert Wood was finally acquitted, Mrs Beerbohm Tree interrupted the play in which she was appearing to tell a cheering audience that the young man no longer stood in peril of his life. Fact and fiction, the theatre and the drama of the Court, seemed inextricable in those days, so when Oscar Slater, the enigmatic German Jew from Glasgow, was wrongly convicted of murdering an old lady for her jewellery, whom else should he choose to write to but the creator of Sherlock Holmes? It proved a wise choice and nowhere does that writer of genius appear in a more attractive light than in the account of the Slater injustice. Conan Doyle wrote endless letters of protest to the Scottish Secretary, to M.P.s and the newspapers. He spent his time and money without hesitation on lawyers and inquiries. After Slater had served fifteen years of an unjustifiable prison sentence, he smuggled out of prison a letter, written on paper stolen from the binding shop, which contained a last appeal to Sir Arthur, and in a final heroic effort the author helped to get the case reheard in the Scottish Court of Appeal. Conan Doyle sat in Court, heard Craigie Aitchison K.C. make his closely reasoned fourteen-hour speech to the five Appeal Judges and wrote an appreciation of a magnificent performance.

'Then there comes an objection from the judges. The blue eyes seem pained and surprised. Up fly the little plump hands. Once more the gentle voice takes up the tale. The wrinkle is smoothed out and the story goes on . . .'

It was as well that Conan Doyle was so delighted with Craigie Aitchison's advocacy for, after a somewhat stingy government compensation for Oscar Slater, he was left to pay the defendant's fees. Once more Sherlock Holmes helped the cause of justice.

Not many people, perhaps, will read this collection of famous trials because of the legal issues involved, and yet they do show the best and the worst sides of adversary trials, and must prevent any complacency, even though our system may be described as the best in the world. The most perfect judicial procedure has to be worked by fallible, prejudiced, inadequate and often mistaken human beings, for it would not be human to be able to avoid all the pitfalls of judgment. Certain trials, Rattenbury and Stoner for instance, or the case of Robert Woods, were conducted with conspicuous fairness. The Oscar Slater trial provides us with a manual of injustice, from the incompetent defence to the police who refused to admit their mistakes, from the passionately convinced prosecutor to the unfair Judge, no one emerges well from the proceedings except the prisoner. It is a cautionary tale which lawyers and Judges should never forget.

Before the Criminal Evidence Act of 1898 a prisoner was not allowed to give evidence in his or her own defence. This meant that defendants could not be cross-examined, and when the law was changed lawyers often said that more murderers lost their lives by giving evidence than had been saved by keeping silent. Madeleine Smith was not able to give evidence at her trial in the 1850s, although she was apparently anxious to do so. As her defence was based on the prosecution not being able to prove a final meeting with her lover, her enforced silence probably helped her. Had she been forced to explain the various reasons she gave for buying arsenic, had she been cross-examined about her love letters before a hostile Judge and a puritanical jury, the result of her trial might not have been so happy.

Now a prisoner can give evidence the decision as to whether or not to call your client is often a difficult one. A defendant in the box may be nothing but a help to the prosecution, on the other hand an innocent man or woman may win an acquittal by speaking directly to the jury. After Alma Rattenbury was persuaded by her own child, mercilessly sent to her by her astute lawyers, to give evidence, she no doubt saved her own, finally unwanted, life. The decision not to call Oscar Slater was a legal mistake which he lived to resent more and more during his long, undeserved years in prison.

So that the law may be seen warts and all, I have included the trial of William Joyce, 'Lord Haw-Haw', for treason. He was an unattractive character, a member of the British Union of Fascists when he was in England, and a very minor wheel in the Nazi propaganda machine. After the war he was hanged for treason, although the acts alleged were all committed abroad and he was never a British subject. Courts are sometimes tempted to come to decisions on the law, and to torture legal argument, in order to achieve a desired result; and the various judgments which upheld Lord Haw-Haw's conviction on the basis that he had once, and quite improperly, obtained a British passport, do our impartial judiciary no sort of credit. But then neither does the fact that many parents brought their young children to Wandsworth on the day William Joyce was hanged, and the excited crowd became uncontrollable.

Despite the legal issues, and for all the real and unhappy people involved, or perhaps because of them, it is hard to read these accounts without feeling gripped by the sort of excitement which marks the opening of a Conan Doyle story, with the growler making its way through the pea-souper, Lestrade puzzled, and the appalling discovery in the suburban villa. Now Robert Wood is meeting Ruby Young at Phit-Eesi's bootshop and begging her to supply him with an alibi. Now Ronald True is roaming the Hammersmith Palace of Varieties with his loaded revolver, telling great lies about his service in the Flying Corps and the Taquah Mining Company. Alma Rattenbury is tremulously making love to the handyman George Stoner (whom she obtained by means of an advertisement placed in the *Bournemouth Daily Echo* which read, 'Daily willing lad, 14–18, for housework. Scout-trained preferred.'). And Mr Armstrong the solicitor has invited his rival lawyer Mr Martin to tea, an occasion Mr Martin is trying desperately to avoid owing to his entirely justified suspicion of there being arsenic in the buttered scones. In short, English middle-class life is pursuing its usual placid and respectable course. Now read on.

JOHN MORTIMER

Rattenbury and Stoner 1935

F. TENNYSON JESSE

On 25 September 1934, the following advertisement appeared in the *Bournemouth Daily Echo*: 'Daily willing lad, 14–18, for housework. Scout-trained preferred.'

This advertisement had been inserted by a Mrs Rattenbury, of Villa Madeira, Manor Park Road, and was answered by a youth called George Percy Stoner. Since he was of an age to drive a car, and his previous employment had been in a garage, he was engaged as chauffeur-handyman.

On Monday, 27 May 1935, Alma Victoria Rattenbury and George Percy Stoner were charged at the Central Criminal Court with the murder of the woman's husband, Francis Mawson Rattenbury. Both the accused pleaded not guilty. Mrs Rattenbury was thirty-eight years old, and Stone had attained the age of eighteen in November of 1934. Mrs Rattenbury and Stoner had become lovers soon after Stoner was taken into Mr Rattenbury's employ.

Both Mr and Mrs Rattenbury had been previously married; he once and she twice. Mr Rattenbury had a grown-up son; and Mrs Rattenbury, a little boy called Christopher, born in 1922. The marriage of Francis Rattenbury and Alma Victoria took place about 1928, and a boy, John, was born a year after. Since the birth of this child Mr and Mrs Rattenbury had not lived together as husband and wife. Mr Rattenbury was sixty-seven years old and not a young man for his age. He was an architect of distinction, and had lived most of his working life in Canada, but when he retired in 1928, he and his wife came to live in Bournemouth. Eventually they took a little white house called Villa Madeira in a pleasant suburban road near the sea,

15

shaded by pines. A companion-help, Miss Irene Riggs, came to live with them. Little John went to school, but came home every week-end, and Christopher, the child of Mrs Rattenbury's second marriage, spent his holidays at Villa Madeira.

When Stoner was first employed at Villa Madeira, he lived at home and went to his work by day, but in November he took up his residence in the house. He had become Mrs Rattenbury's lover before that.

On the night of Sunday, 24 March 1935, Mr Rattenbury was attacked from behind as he sat sleeping in an armchair in the drawing-room. It was never in dispute that the weapon employed was a carpenter's mallet, which Stoner had fetched from his grandfather's house that afternoon.

The events that night, as they first were made known in the newspapers, were as follows:

Mrs Rattenbury declared that at about ten-thirty, after she had gone to bed, she heard a groan from the room below, that she went downstairs, and found her husband in the easychair, unconscious, with blood flowing from his head. She called Irene, her companion-maid, and told her to telephone for Dr O'Donnell, who was her doctor. Dr O'Donnell arrived and found Mrs Rattenbury very drunk, and Mr Rattenbury unconscious with blood flowing from his head. Mrs Rattenbury said: 'Look at him – look at the blood – someone has finished him.'

Dr O'Donnell telephoned for Mr Rooke, a well-known surgeon. Mr Rooke arrived and found it impossible to examine the patient as Mrs Rattenbury was very drunk and excitable, and kept getting in his way. The ambulance was sent for, and the patient removed to Strathallen Nursing Home. After his head had been shaved in the operating theatre, Mr Rooke and Dr O'Donnell saw three serious wounds on the head, that could not have been self-inflicted, and, accordingly, they communicated with the police.

Mr Rooke operated on Mr Rattenbury, and Dr O'Donnell between 3.30 and 4 a.m. returned to Villa Madeira. He found Mrs Rattenbury running about extremely intoxicated, four or five police officers in the house (some of whom she was trying to kiss), the radio-gramophone playing and all the lights on. He gave Mrs Rattenbury half a grain of morphia, and put her to bed. During the hours of progressive drunkenness Mrs Rattenbury had kept on making statements to the effect that she had killed her husband. The next morning she repeated her assertions in a slightly varied form and she was taken to the Bournemouth Police Station and charged with doing grievous bodily harm with intent to murder. When she was charged Mrs Rattenbury said: 'That is right – I did it deliberately, and would do it again.'

Such was the terrible case for the prosecution against Alma Victoria Rattenbury, and the picture that had inevitably formed itself before the public mind was revolting.

There was probably no one in England, and no one in Court when the trial opened, save Mrs Rattenbury, her solicitor and counsel, Stoner and his solicitor and counsel, and Irene Riggs, who did not think Mrs Rattenbury was guilty of the crime of murder. In everyone's mind, including that of this writer, there was a picture of Mrs Rattenbury as a coarse, brawling, drunken, and callous woman. But life is not as simple as that, and very often an accurate report fails to convey truth, because only certain things have been reported. The form of the English oath has been very wisely thought out – 'the truth, the whole truth, and nothing but the truth'. It is possible to give an erroneous impression by merely telling the truth and nothing but the truth. The 'whole truth' is a very important factor. The whole truth about Mrs Rattenbury came out during the trial, and the woman, who at first seemed so guilty, was seen to be undoubtedly innocent. This was not merely because there proved to be no evidence beyond her own drunken utterances, but because of her own attitude in the witness-box. For there is no test of truth so relentless as the witness-box – it is deadly to the guilty, and it may save the innocent.

In most criminal trials the pattern is set at the beginning and merely strengthens as the trial progresses. In the Rattenbury case the evidence – which seemed so damning on the first day – completely altered in character; what had seemed to be undoubted fact proved to be an airy nothing and the whole complex pattern shifted and changed much as the pattern of sand changes when it is shaken, and, like sand, it slipped away between the fingers, leaving a residue of grains of truth very different from the pile that the prosecution had originally built up. Even at the end of the trial, so rigid is the English fashion of thinking – or rather feeling, for it is not as careful or accurate a process as thought – on sexual matters, that many people still considered Mrs Rattenbury morally damned. That worst of all Anglo-Saxon attitudes, a contemptuous condemnation of the man and woman, but more particularly the woman, unfortunate enough to be found out in sexual delinquency, never had finer scope than was provided by the Rattenbury case.

Mrs Rattenbury was born Alma Victoria Clark, in Victoria, British Columbia, and was the daughter of a printer in quite humble circumstances. She was extremely talented musically. The cheap strain in her came out in the words of her lyrics, but she was a really fine pianist. She grew up to young womanhood just before the First World War, already well known in Western Canada as a musician, and, although not strictly speaking pretty, very attractive to men. In the witness-box she still showed as a very elegant woman. She was well and quietly dressed in dark blue. She had a pale face, with a beautiful egg-like line of the jaw, dark grey eyes, and a mouth with a very full lower lip. She was undoubtedly, and always must have been, a *femme aux hommes*. That is to say, that although she had women friends, and was a generous, easy, kindly, sentimental creature, she was first and foremost a woman to attract men and be attracted by them. She first married a young Englishman called Caledon Dolly, who joined the Canadian forces on the outbreak of war, and was transferred to England. She followed him and obtained employment in Whitehall. She was very devoted to her husband, but he was killed in action. This was the only completely happy relationship with a man which Mrs Rattenbury was ever to know. She joined a Scottish nursing unit, and then became a transport driver, and worked hard throughout the war. After the Armistice she married, for the second time, a man whose wife divorced him, citing Alma Victoria Dolly. She married this second husband in 1921, and the child of that union was born the following year. The marriage was unhappy, and she returned to the house of

18

an aunt in Victoria, and there she met Mr Rattenbury. Mr Rattenbury was married himself at the time, but fell very much in love with Alma Victoria, and his wife divorced him, citing her. At this time Mr Rattenbury was about sixty years of age, and Mrs Rattenbury thirty-one. Life was not too easy for Mr Rattenbury and his new wife in a country where everyone knew of the scandal of the divorce, and this was the chief reason why the Rattenburys came to England to settle in Bournemouth.

Mrs Rattenbury was a highly sexed woman, and six years of being deprived of sexual satisfaction had combined with the tuberculosis from which she suffered, to bring her to the verge of nymphomania. Now nymphomania is not admirable, but neither is it blameworthy. It is a disease. In spite of the urgency of her desires, which must have tormented her, Mrs Rattenbury had not, as far as is known, had a lover since the birth of little John. She certainly had had none the four years she had lived in Bournemouth, and she had no abnormal tendencies. She was fond of her husband in a friendly fashion, and he was devoted to her, very interested in her song-writing and anxious for her to succeed. He would often talk to Irene Riggs about his wife, and dwell on the unhappy life she had led, and he never in these conversations said anything against her. Miss Riggs, one of my informants as to these matters, also said that Mrs Rattenbury was very kind to her husband, that she was, indeed, kind to everyone. The household was not an unhappy one, but neither was it happy. For one thing, Mrs Rattenbury was a gregarious creature, and her husband was of an unsociable frame of mind. He knew hardly anyone of his own station in life, except Dr O'Donnell and Mr Jenks, a retired barrister who had an estate at Bridport. But Mrs Rattenbury was very different from her husband; she had that lavish, easy friendliness which one associates with music-hall artistes, and she could not live without affection. When she made a friend of Irene Riggs, she did so because it was her nature to be friendly with the people who surrounded her. She was fond of Irene Riggs, who, on her side, was devoted to her employer, in spite of the latter's impatient temper. Any little outing to London, any treat, such as a theatre, Mrs Rattenbury shared with Irene

Riggs, and the girl remained attached to the memory of the kindest person she ever met, who helped anyone in need that she came across. But the chief devotion of Mrs Rattenbury's life was for her children. No one denies that she was a good and loving mother. Dr O'Donnell and Miss Riggs both say that Mrs Rattenbury thought nothing too good for her children, and that there was nothing she would not have done for them. She was for ever thinking and talking about them, and occupying herself in practical ways for their welfare.

The Rattenburys lived peaceably as a rule, but sometimes they had quarrels – these were about money. Mr Rattenbury, like a great many men, was generous in big matters, but difficult in small ones. He allowed his wife £1,000 a year, and many newspapers reported this fact in such a manner that the reading public might easily have imagined that this sum was hers for herself alone. As a matter of fact, out of it she paid for the food for herself, her husband, the domestics and the children when at home, and for one of the boys' schooling. She also paid for Mr Rattenbury's clothes and for her own, and she paid the servants' wages. Mr Rattenbury was a heavy drinker of whisky, and every few weeks Mrs Rattenbury would drink more cocktails than would be good for her, so that the bill for drinks alone must have amounted to a good deal. It will be seen that £1,000 a year, even then, was not too large a sum out of which to support and clothe a household and educate a child. Mrs Rattenbury herself had very little money sense, and her husband had every reason to fear her lavish spending. About twice a year Mrs Rattenbury would coax an extra sum out of him; a large sum, over £100, but this he parted with much more easily than he would have parted with small sums more often. Mrs Rattenbury did not pretend that she told her husband true stories to induce him to give her this extra money. She admitted she invented whatever story would be the most likely to achieve the desired result. Mr Rattenbury was frequently very depressed about financial matters; like everyone else he had suffered in the slump, and he was apt, during his moods of depression, to threaten to commit suicide. One day in July 1934, he harped on this threat at greater length than usual, and his wife lost her temper, and told him it was a pity that he did not do it, instead of always talking about it. Mr Rattenbury in his turn then lost his temper and hit his wife, giving her a black eye. She sent for Dr O'Donnell, who found her very agitated and upset. Her husband had left the house, and she feared that he really had gone to kill himself. Mr Rattenbury did not, in fact, return till about two in the morning, by which time Dr O'Donnell also was extremely anxious. Mrs Rattenbury was by then so ill that he injected a quarter of a grain of morphia, and she slept for twelve hours. After that, life went on as usual with the Rattenburys. She bore him no grudge for having struck her. She was a person of quick temper herself, but generous in what children call 'making it up'. This was the only serious quarrel between the Rattenburys that Dr O'Donnell or Irene Riggs knew of in four years. In the box, Mrs Rattenbury was asked whether her married life was happy, and she answered: 'Like that . . .!' with a gesture of her hand. A gesture that sketched the married life of the larger part of muddled humanity.

Life might have gone on in the usual pedestrian fashion at Villa Madeira for ever, but George Percy Stoner joined the household, and Mrs Rattenbury fell in love with him.

The expression 'falling in love' is an attempt to define something which escapes definition. Mankind has a natural weakness for labels, for they simplify life, and though this particular label is one of the most pernicious which have been evolved, it must be remembered that it covers not only a multitude of sins, but of virtues. Perhaps no two people would give quite the same definition of its meaning. Very few people trouble to try. Mrs Rattenbury herself was a woman who dealt in labels, and she accepted the expression 'falling in love'. She wrote cheap little lyrics of the more obvious variety, and she herself would never have questioned what 'in love' meant. She was 'in love' with Stoner, who, except for his virility, was not a particularly interesting or attractive person. Indeed, lack of taste is one of the chief charges against Mrs Rattenbury, both in her work and in her life. She was very uncontrolled emotionally. Her lyrics were appalling. She was subject to drinking bouts, which added to her natural excitability. She had not scrupled, twice, to take other women's husbands away from them, and she seems to have been, to use a slang phrase, a natural-born bad picker. When she took Stoner as her lover, she said to Dr O'Donnell: 'There is something I want to tell you. I am afraid you will be shocked and never want to speak to me again.' Dr O'Donnell replied that there were very few things he had not been told in the course of his life, and that he was not easily shocked. She then told him the step she had taken, and he spoke to her seriously, warning her that she was probably being very unwise. But she was too far gone in love by then to heed any advice he gave her. She merely reiterated that she was in love with Stoner.

The obvious solution to the question as to what love meant for her is that it meant physical satisfaction. Yet, if it had meant only this, it would have deserted her when she stood in peril of her life. It did not do so, and neither did Stoner's love for her. Stoner refused to go into the box, and told his counsel he did not deny having attacked Mr Rattenbury. The woman for weeks insisted, to her solicitor and counsel, that she wished to take the blame, so as to save Stoner. Mr Lewis-Manning, her solicitor, made it clear to her that, if she lied, her story would not stand the test of the witness-box, and that she would only hang herself without saving Stoner. But not till Christopher, the little boy of her second marriage, was sent to her in prison to plead with her to tell the truth, did she give way. And, afterwards, in the witness-box, she said as little against her lover as possible, making light of certain alleged attacks of violence towards herself, attacks which had frightened her so much, that, long before the murder, she consulted Dr O'Donnell about them. Indeed, one of the most interesting points in this case is, that it is the only one, as far as I am aware, where two people have been charged together on the capital indictment when neither of the accused has abandoned the other in a scramble for safety. Milson and Fowler, Field and Gray, Gabrielle Bompard and Eyrand, Mr and Mrs Manning, Ruth Snyder and Judd Gray, to remember only a few at random, all tried to throw the blame on the partner in crime. Mrs Thompson, terrified and conscious of her own innocence of murder, never gave a thought to the safety of her lover, Bywaters. Mrs Rattenbury was willing and anxious to take the whole blame if by so doing she could save her lover. It is Mr Lewis-Manning's considered opinion that Mrs Rattenbury was not merely in a condition of exaltation that would have failed her at the last pass, but that she would have hanged without a tremor if by so doing she could have saved Stoner.

The story of Mrs Rattenbury's life is a mingling of tragedy and futility. It is easy to be sentimental and see only the tragedy. It is easy to be stupid and see only the futility. The truth is, that it is always easy to label people, but because a thing is easy, it is not necessarily accurate. No human being is simple. Stoner may have seemed simple enough to his family; he had always been a quiet boy who did not make friends, but his quiet appearance concealed stormy adolescent yearnings. He had the dramatic instincts natural to the young, and, unfortunately, circumstances thrust him into real drama before he could tell the difference between what was real and what was make-belief. Physically, he was very passionate, and nothing in his mental training had equipped him to cope with the extraordinary life to which it had pleased Mrs Rattenbury to call him.

Francis Rattenbury, that outwardly quiet man, is a pathetic figure in retrospect. Mr Justice Humphreys referred to him as being 'that very unpleasant character for which, I think, we have no suitable expression, but which the French call a *mari complaisant*. A man who knew that his wife was committing adultery, and had no objection to it.' Mrs Rattenbury said, in the box, that she thought her husband knew because she had told him she was living her own life. But she may well have told him that without his taking in the meaning of her words. He was completely incurious, and he lived not in the present, but in regrets for the past and anxieties for the future.

Irene Riggs, Dr O'Donnell, and, indeed, everyone acquainted with the household to whom the writer has spoken, was of the opinion that Mr Rattenbury was not aware that his wife and his chauffeur were lovers. But when I saw Villa Madeira, I thought this difficult to credit. It is so small as to be remarkable, small as the witch's cottage in 'Hansel and Gretel'. On the ground floor are the kitchen, drawing-room, dining-room, and a room that Mr

Rattenbury used as a bedroom, and which opened off the drawing-room. Is it possible that a man, in a house as small as Villa Madeira, would not hear the footsteps over his head whenever Stoner came into Mrs Rattenbury's room, and that he would not hear the occasionally loud quarrels which took place between them? Looking at Villa Madeira, the answer would seem to be that it would be quite impossible. And yet Mr Rattenbury's known character and habits supply a different answer. Every night Mr Rattenbury drank the best part of a bottle of whisky. He was a man brilliant in his profession, with many excellent qualities, and he was not a drunkard, but he was not a young man, and he was very deaf. The alcohol which he consumed every night explains why he no longer lived with his wife, why he was completely incurious as to her doings, and why he heard nothing of what was going on over his head. He was not, in the opinion of all who knew him, the doctor, his own relations, and Irene Riggs, who lived in the house, the character stigmatized by Mr Justice Humphreys as a '*mari complaisant*, not a nice character'. He was a quiet, pleasant man whose finances worried him, and whose emotional relationships had disappointed him.

A man in Mr Rattenbury's condition, and of his age, is apt to forget the power that the natural inclinations of the flesh had over him in youth and middle age, and he may fail to realize that it is still a factor in the life of anyone else. As far as Mr Rattenbury knew, he was a good husband to his wife. He admired her, was genuinely fond of her. There was nothing within his power that he would not have done for her, and Mrs Rattenbury was astute enough to take advantage of this whenever possible. In regard to his wife, his chief anxieties were financial, and after he had started to take his prolonged night-cap each evening, the rest of the world existed very little for him. The passions, the jealousies of a decade earlier, had ceased, not only in the present, but even as a memory of the past. The chief tragedy in life is, not what we are but what we have ceased to be, and Mr Rattenbury was an example of this truth. It is easy to say that a man who knows his wife is committing adultery and has no objection, is not a nice character. But it is not necessarily the truth. It is possible that a man who no longer leads a normal life with his wife, yet thinks of her, not as his property, but as a human being who belongs to herself, and has a right to a normal life. I do not say that this was Mr Rattenbury's attitude (although Mrs Rattenbury said that it was), I merely say that it would not necessarily have been a despicable attitude. But, of course, the judgement of the man in the street is the same as that of Mr Justice Humphreys. It is an Anglo-Saxon attitude. Another Anglo-Saxon attitude, accepted by the learned Judge, by counsel on both sides, and by the British public, was that, because of her greater age, Mrs Rattenbury dominated her young lover. It was this same assumption which hanged Mrs Thompson. There has been a growing consensus of public opinion ever since the Bywaters–Thompson trial, that the female prisoner was wrongly convicted; and the memory of the earlier trial haunted the Courtroom like a ghost. The Rattenbury case seemed like an echo of that tragedy, and it is not fanciful to say that Mrs Thompson's fate did much to save Mrs Rattenbury. A Judge who knew how to point out firmly and clearly to the jury that a woman must not, because of her moral character, be convicted of murder, and a jury, who were determined that no confusion of thought or prejudice should lead them into giving a wrong verdict, were two great safeguards for Mrs Rattenbury, and the uneasy memory of Edith Thompson was yet a third. Nevertheless, the assumption of the Bywaters–Thompson case, that an elderly woman dominates her young lover, still obtained at the Rattenbury trial. The actual truth is that there is no woman so under the dominion of her lover as the elderly mistress of a very much younger man. The great Benjamin Franklin knew this, and there is extant a letter of advice written by him to a young man, which is a model of clear thinking. The original belongs to the U.S. Government, and is in the custody of the Librarian of Congress at Washington, D.C.

June 25th, 1745.

My dear Friend,

I know of no medicine fit to diminish the violent nocturnal inclinations you mention, and if I did, I think I should not communicate it to you. Marriage is the proper remedy.

It is the most natural state of man, and therefore the state in which you are most likely to find solid happiness. Your reasons against entering it at present appear to me not well founded. The circumstantial advantages you have in view of postponing it are not only uncertain, but they are small in comparison with that of the thing itself – the being married and settled.

It is the man and woman united that make the complete human being. Separate, she wants his force of body and strength of reason; he, her softness, sensibility and acute discernment. Together they are most likely to succeed in the world. A single man has not nearly the value he would have in a state of union. He is an incomplete animal; he resembles the odd half of a pair of scissors. If you get a prudent healthy wife, your industry in your profession, with her good economy, will be a fortune sufficient.

But if you will not take this counsel, and persist in thinking a commerce with the sex inevitable, then I repeat my former advice, that in your amours you should prefer OLD WOMEN to YOUNG ONES. You call this a paradox, and demand reasons. They are these:

First. Because they have more knowledge of the World, and their minds are better stored with observations; their conversation is more improving and more lastingly agreeable.

Second. Because when women cease to be handsome, they study to be good. To maintain their influence over men they supply the diminution of beauty by an augmentation of utility. They learn to do a thousand services, small and great, and are the most tender and useful of all friends when you are sick. Thus they continue amiable, and hence there is scarcely such a thing to be found as an old woman who is not a good woman.

Third. Because there is no hazard of children, which irregularly produced, may be attended with much inconvenience.

Fourth. Because, through more experience, they are more prudent and discreet in conducting an intrigue to prevent suspicion. The commerce with them is therefore safe with regard to your reputation, and with regard to theirs. If the affair should happen to be known, considerate people might be rather inclined to excuse an old woman who would kindly take care of a young man, form his manners by her good counsels, and prevent his ruining his health and fortune among mercenary prostitutes.

Fifth. Because in every animal that walks upright the deficiency of the fluid that fills the muscles appears but on the highest part. The face first grows lank and wrinkled, then the neck, then the breast and arms – the lower parts continuing to the last as plump as ever; so that, covering all above with a basket, and regarding only what is below the girdle, it is impossible of two women, to know an old from a young one. And as in the dark all cats are grey, the pleasure of corporal enjoyment with an old woman is at least equal and frequently superior; every knack being, by practice, capable of improvement.

Sixth. Because the sin is less. The debauching a virgin may be her ruin and make her life unhappy.

Seventh. Because the compunction is less. The having made a young girl miserable may give you frequent bitter reflections, none of which can attend the making an Old woman Happy.

Eighth and Lastly. They are so grateful.

This much for my paradox, but still I advise you to marry immediately, being sincerely,

Your affectionate friend,
(Signed) B. Franklin

'Eighth and Lastly' is worthy of the consideration of English lawyers and the English public when a Thompson–Bywaters or Rattenbury–Stoner case is under consideration. Once Stoner had become Mrs Rattenbury's lover, she worshipped him. It was before the consummation of her desire that she was the dominating character, and to that extent she was responsible for the whole tragedy, but to that extent only. She felt this responsibility deeply, and it was remorse as well as love that made her eager and willing to save Stoner even at the cost of her own life. It was, indeed, a terrible responsibility in view of the events. She could not know that Stoner would be wild with jealousy, but she must have known, had she paused to think, that a lad of Stoner's age and antecedents would lose all sense of values when he became the lover of his social superior, who dazzled him with a whole new mode of life. If Stoner's first love-affair had been with a girl of his own class, no ill need have come of it. Nevertheless, another strange assumption was made – that it is somehow harmful for a young man of eighteen to have sexual connection. Dr Gillespie, physician for psycho-medicine at Guy's Hospital, a witness for the defence, was asked in cross-examination by Mr Croom-Johnson, whether 'regular sexual intercourse with a member of the opposite sex by a boy of eighteen or onwards, would be likely to do him good or harm?' Dr Gillespie replied that it would not do him good 'if a moral point of view were meant'. Mr Croom-Johnson said that he was not talking from a moral point of view, that he was asking him as a doctor. Still Dr Gillespie wisely refused to commit himself. 'Do you think it would likely be good for his constitution – a boy of eighteen – just think what you are saying, Doctor?' 'I am not saying that it is good for his constitution, but I am saying that if it were occurring with such frequency as my lord has said, namely such as nature would permit, it would not necessarily show the effects in his external appearance.' 'Take the ordinary case – the ordinary boy, not somebody very strong, talking about the ordinary English youth of eighteen – do you really find yourself in any difficulty in answering the question?' 'I find difficulty,' replied the Doctor, 'in answering the question as I believe you expect it to be answered.' Doctors, as a rule, make excellent witnesses, and in this little cross-examination, Dr Gillespie was no exception to the rule, but with what frank, Homeric laughter the question would have been greeted in a Latin country! In England it is apparently impossible to admit the simple truth that a young man of eighteen is an adult who would normally take a mate, were it not that economic conditions render it impossible.

Mrs Rattenbury was a good witness, and in nothing more notably so than in her simple acceptance of the values of life as she knew it. 'You have told us that on the Sunday night Stoner came into your bedroom and got into bed with you. Was that something that happened frequently?' asked Mr Croom-Johnson. 'Oh, yes,' replied Mrs Rattenbury simply. And later on: 'Did it occur to you that if you went to Bridport, Mr Rattenbury might want to treat you as his wife?' – 'No, if I had thought it was going to happen like that I would never have suggested going.' 'It never occurred to you?' – 'No.' 'You know what I mean by saying "treat you as his wife"?' – 'Yes, exactly,' replied Mrs Rattenbury, as though mildly surprised that there could be any mistake about it.

Mrs Rattenbury's vagueness about money matters and her lavish spending came out as clearly in the witness-box as her attitude towards sensual matters. In answering a question as to her habit of giving away cigarette holders, she said, 'That is nothing for me. If anyone sees a cigarette holder and likes it, I always say "take it". It is my disposition'; and later: 'I am very vague about money.' This was certainly true. Mr Croom-Johnson asked her in cross-examination how much money her husband let her have in the course of a year, to which she replied she 'really couldn't say'. 'Hundreds?' 'I suppose so,' said Mrs Rattenbury. 'About how much a year did he let you have?' 'He used to give me regularly £50 a month, and I was regularly overdrawn.' '£50 a month would be £600 a year?' 'I see,' said Mrs Rattenbury; and one received the impression she had not worked out this fairly simple sum for herself ever before. 'In addition to that,' went on Mr Croom-Johnson, 'about £150 on each of two occasions?' – 'Yes, I daresay.' Later, cross-examining her about the clothes she had lavished on Stoner in London, Mr Croom-Johnson said: 'You used the words "that he required clothes"?' – 'Yes, I considered so.' 'Silk pyjamas at 60s. a suit?' – 'That might seem absurd, but that is my disposition.' And certainly it was her disposition.

So, as we have seen, Mr Rattenbury was reserved, kindly, but rather mean in money matters. Mrs Rattenbury was unreserved, also kindly, but in a more indiscriminate fashion than her husband, and her generosity was indiscriminating also. Irene Riggs liked both of them, but her loyalty was naturally for the mistress who had been kinder to her than any human being she had ever met.

Irene Riggs was not as happy after Stoner's arrival as she had been before. Mrs Rattenbury told her about the liaison, and Irene was too fond of her to blame her, but nevertheless she felt uneasy about the affair, and sorry that Mrs Rattenbury could not have found happiness with someone more of her own age and class. Though Miss Riggs and Stoner did not like each other, they got on together well enough. He was a very quiet boy; she also was quiet, self-effacing, and efficient. She was shocked when Mrs Rattenbury first told her the truth, but human nature quickly adapts itself to knowledge, and Miss Riggs very rightly felt that it was not for her to praise or to blame. She stayed behind when, on 19 March, Mrs Rattenbury arranged to take Stoner with her on a trip to London, because Stoner was very jealous of any third person, and the charm of the little friendly expeditions that had been the highlights in Irene Riggs's life before the coming of Stoner was gone. In London Mrs Rattenbury and Stoner stayed at the Royal Palace Hotel, Kensington, and spent their days in shopping and going about London. Mrs Rattenbury explained the trip to her husband by saying she was going to have an operation (she had had several minor operations in the preceding years), and he gave her the generous sum of £250 for this purpose. Mrs Rattenbury used a large part of this sum to pay outstanding housekeeping bills, and the rest she spent wildly upon the London trip and presents for Stoner. The importance of the expedition to London lies in the fact that, for four or five days, Stoner was accepted by the little world about him as Mrs Rattenbury's social equal. He did not go to the Royal Palace Hotel as her chauffeur, but as her brother. They had two rooms opposite each other, and he had free access to his mistress. He was called 'Sir' by the servants, and every day Mrs Rattenbury bought him presents which to his simple mind must have appeared equivalent to Danae's golden shower. Crêpe-de-chine pyjamas at three guineas a pair and a made-to-measure suit, must have seemed to the young man, who was a labourer's son, most exciting luxuries.

The learned Judge referred to the 'orgy in London'. It is difficult to imagine an orgy at the Royal Palace Hotel at Kensington, and, indeed, I have never been able to discover of what an 'orgy' consists. It is associated, more or less vaguely, in the popular mind with the 'historical' productions of Mr C. de Mille; glasses of wine, dancing girls, tiger skins, and cushions are some of its component parts. The private coming together of a pair of lovers and their normal physical ecstasies, however reprehensible these may be morally, do not seem well described by the word 'orgy'. Even shopping at Harrods does not quite come under this heading. However, in this trial, as in all others of the same nature, the stock phrases were used of which most people are heartily tired. 'Adulterous intercourse', 'illicit union', 'this wretched woman' and the like, all have a very familiar ring. They are clichés, and come to the lips of those concerned in the administration of the law as inevitably as the adjective 'fashionably dressed' is attached to the noun 'woman' in any reporter's account of the female spectators at a murder trial. Leaving these clichés, the fact, nevertheless, remains that Stoner's trip to London must have thoroughly unsettled him. He was happy enough at Villa Madeira, where the social régime was easy and pleasant for such as he.

Mrs Rattenbury affected no superiority with anyone in humbler circumstances of life than her own, and Mr Rattenbury had lived for years of his life in the democratic country where Mrs Rattenbury was born. Stoner often played cards with him in the evening, and Mr Rattenbury, Stoner, and Miss Riggs took their meals together. Therefore, merely to have returned to Villa Madeira, to continue its pleasant, easy life, would not necessarily have upset Stoner. But this was not exactly what happened. The lovers arrived back late one Friday evening. Mr Rattenbury, already having imbibed his night-cap, asked no questions; even next day, according to Mrs Rattenbury, and as far as Irene Riggs's knowledge went, he never inquired about the operation his wife had ostensibly been to London to undergo. The Saturday found him in one of his worst fits of depression. A scheme for building some flats, of which he was to have been the architect, was hanging fire, owing to the financial depression, and Mrs Rattenbury tried to cheer him up in vain.

On the Sunday, Mr Rattenbury was still more depressed. In the morning Mrs Rattenbury took him for a drive. After lunch Mr Rattenbury slept. They had tea together, little John with them. Mr Rattenbury had been reading a book, a novel in which there was a perfect holocaust of suicides, and, according to Mrs Rattenbury, he expressed his admiration for anyone who had the courage to make an end of himself. Mrs Rattenbury suggested that she should ring up their friend, Mr Jenks, at Bridport, and ask whether they could go over on the Monday. She did indeed telephone, and Mr Jenks said he would be pleased to see them, and asked them to spend the night, an invitation which they accepted. The telephone was in Mr Rattenbury's bedroom, which opened off the drawing-room. Mr Rattenbury remained in the drawing-room, but Stoner came into the bedroom, and overheard the arrangements which Mrs Rattenbury was making. He was frightfully angry and threatened Mrs

Rattenbury with an air pistol, which he was carrying in his hand, and which she took to be a revolver. He told Mrs Rattenbury that he would kill her if they went to Bridport. Mrs Rattenbury, nervous lest Mr Rattenbury should overhear the conversation, though, as she said, 'He never really took very much notice,' urged Stoner into the dining-room, and went there with him. Once there he accused her of having had connection with her husband that afternoon – an accusation entirely baseless – and said that, if the Bridport plan were carried out, he would refuse to drive. Stoner said that at Mr Jenks's house the Rattenburys would have to share a bedroom, but Mrs Rattenbury assured him that would not be so, and what she said she knew to be the truth, for she and her husband had stayed with Mr Jenks before, and had had two rooms. Stoner, though he appeared to be pacified, continued to brood over the matter in his mind, and at about eight o'clock that evening, he went to the house of his grandparents, sat and chatted, apparently normally, with his grandmother for some time, and borrowed a carpenter's mallet, but borrowed it perfectly openly. He went back to Villa Madeira and Mrs Rattenbury noticed nothing abnormal about him.

That same evening Mrs Rattenbury sat and played cards with her husband, kissed him good night, and went upstairs. It was Irene's evening out, and Mrs Rattenbury passed the time by getting together her things for Bridport. She had already put out Mr Rattenbury's clothes in his bedroom downstairs. Irene came in at about ten-fifteen, and went straight to her room. Some ten minutes later she went downstairs, either to see if all was well or to get something to eat – there seems a slight discrepancy in her evidence here. When she was downstairs, in the hall, she heard a sound of heavy breathing, and putting her head into Mr Rattenbury's bedroom, she switched on the light. He was not there, and the sound of breathing came from the drawing-room, the door between that and the bedroom being open. Miss Riggs concluded that he had, as he so often did, fallen asleep in his chair, and she went upstairs again into her bedroom. A few moments later she went out again to go to the lavatory, and found Stoner leaning over the banisters at the head of the stairs, looking down. She said, 'What is the matter?' He replied,

'Nothing, I was looking to see if the lights were out.' Then about a quarter of an hour later Mrs Rattenbury came to Irene's room and told her about the expedition to Bridport. Mrs Rattenbury then went to her own room, and about ten minutes later Stoner came and slipped into her bed. He seemed very agitated and upset. She said, 'What is the matter, darling?' He replied that he was in trouble, but that he could not tell her what it was about. She replied that he must tell her, that she was strong enough to bear anything, and he then said, 'You won't be going to Bridport tomorrow.' He went on to say that he had hurt 'Ratz'. He said that he had hit him over the head with a mallet, which he had since hidden in the garden. Mrs Rattenbury definitely conveyed the impression from the box that it was possible that the idea in Stoner's head was merely to injure Mr Rattenbury, so that the proposed expedition could not take place. 'I thought,' she said, 'he was frightened at what he had done, because he had hurt Mr Rattenbury ... I thought he'd just hurt him badly enough to prevent him going to Bridport, and when I said "I'll go and see him," he said, "No, you must not; the sight will upset you," and I thought all I had to do was to fix Ratz up, and that would put him all right.'

It may be that this was the only idea in Stoner's unbalanced and ill-educated mind, but that he found it impossible to stop after the first blow, and administered two more. Or it may be that, in his disturbed and jealous state, he would have done anything sooner than allow the Bridport trip to take place. If Stoner had driven the Rattenburys to Bridport, he would have had to do so in his capacity of chauffeur. He would have stayed there in the same capacity, eaten in the servants' hall, not had access to his mistress, and ranked as a domestic with the other domestics. The thought of the expedition to Bridport, coming, as it would have, directly after the 'orgy' in London, was unbearable. It may be argued that as a motive, this distaste for going to Bridport was very inadequate. But all motives for murder are inadequate. Men have murdered for smaller sums than an embezzler would plot to obtain. Directly the sense of what Stoner was telling her penetrated to Mrs Rattenbury's mind, she jumped out of bed and ran downstairs as she was, in her pyjamas and bare feet. A minute later, Irene Riggs, who had not yet fallen asleep, heard her mistress shrieking for her. Miss Riggs ran downstairs and found Mr Rattenbury leaning back in an arm-chair, as though he were asleep. There was a large pool of blood on the floor, and one of his eyes was very swollen and discoloured, and she thought he had a black eye. Mrs Rattenbury asked Irene to telephone for the doctor at once, telling her to hurry and, to use Miss Riggs's own expression, went 'raving about the house'. 'Oh! poor Ratz. Poor Ratz!' she kept repeating. 'Can't somebody do something?' Mrs Rattenbury drank some whisky; she was violently sick, and drank more whisky. She kept on telling Miss Riggs to wipe up the blood because she said little John must not see any blood.

Now there is no doubt Mrs Rattenbury knew from the moment she set eyes on her husband that Stoner's talk upstairs had not been a mere attempt to attract her interest and attention. She knew that he had injured her husband in a terrible fashion, and that tragedy, which she could not control, had suddenly taken possession of her life. Her first thought was for her husband, her second for little John. Her third was for Stoner, and this thought persisted, and deepened in intensity, during the hours that followed.

Dr O'Donnell arrived at Villa Madeira at about eleven forty-five, in answer to the telephone call. Mrs Rattenbury was, in his opinion, already very drunk. Mr Rooke, the surgeon, arrived at the house about five minutes after midnight, and he also was of the opinion that Mrs Rattenbury was drunk. Dr O'Donnell and Mr Rooke decided that, largely owing to the excited condition of Mrs Rattenbury, the only proper place for her husband was in a nursing home. They took him there, shaved his head, and discovered three wounds, which were obviously the result of external violence, and of three separate blows. Dr O'Donnell telephoned the Central Police Station, about ten minutes' walk from the nursing home and two minutes by car, and said: 'Dr O'Donnell speaking from Strathallen Nursing Home, Manor Road. Mr Rooke and myself have just taken Mr Rattenbury from 5 Manor Road to the nursing home. On examination we find three serious wounds on the back of his skull, due to external violence, which will most probably prove fatal.' Central Police Station replied: 'You want an officer?' Dr O'Donnell said, 'Yes, at once.' But it was half an hour before the constable arrived. The constable then said he must get an inspector, and at about 3.15 a.m. Inspector Mills, who had already been at Villa Madeira, arrived. At three-thirty Inspector Mills, Mr Rooke, and Dr O'Donnell left the nursing home. Stoner was sleeping peacefully outside in the Rattenbury car, and he drove Dr O'Donnell back to Villa Madeira following the police car.

When Dr O'Donnell got out of the car, he was struck by the fact that every light in the Villa Madeira was on, the door was open, and the radio-gramophone was playing. There were four police officers in the house. Mrs Rattenbury was by now extremely drunk. A constable, who had arrived at three o'clock, had observed then that Mrs Rattenbury was under the influence of alcohol, but, as he put it, 'to a mild extent'. One has, of course, to realize that the police standard of drunkenness is very high; as Mr Justice Humphreys phrased it – 'drunk in the police sense seems to mean hopelessly drunk'.

At three-thirty, according to Dr O'Donnell, Mrs Rattenbury was past knowing what she was thinking or saying. Dr O'Donnell, very shocked, turned off the radio-gramophone, and tried to explain to Mrs Rattenbury the gravity of her husband's condition, but she could not take in what he was saying. Inspector Mills agreed that Mrs Rattenbury was more under the influence of drink than when he had seen her at 2 a.m. He said to her: 'Your husband has been seriously injured, and is now in the nursing home.' To which Mrs Rattenbury replied: 'Will that be against me?' Inspector Mills then cautioned her, and apparently was satisfied that she understood the meaning of the caution. Then she made a statement. 'I did it. He had lived too long. I will tell you in the morning where the mallet is. Have you told the Coroner yet? I shall make a better job of it next time. Irene does not know. I have made a proper muddle of it. I thought I was strong enough.' Dr O'Donnell, who considered that Mrs Rattenbury was unable to understand what was said to her, or to know what she was saying, pointed out that she was in no fit condition to be asked anything, and took her up to bed. He administered half a grain of morphia – a large dose – and went downstairs again. After a few minutes he went into the sitting-room and found that Mrs Rattenbury had managed to get downstairs again and was again being questioned by the police. Inspector Mills said to her: 'Do you suspect anyone?' and she replied: 'Yes. I think so. His son.'

Dr O'Donnell, who was aware that Mr Rattenbury's son lived abroad, knew that Mrs Rattenbury had no idea of what she was saying, and he said to the Inspector: 'Look at her condition – she is full of whisky, and I have just given her a large dose of morphia. She is in no condition to make any statement.' He then took her by the arm and helped her upstairs again. Then (it was by now after 4 a.m.), Dr O'Donnell went home. At 6 a.m. Inspector Carter arrived at the house, where some members of the police had remained all night. He went into Mrs Rattenbury's room and stated in evidence that she woke up. This was not unnatural, in view of the fact that the police had been in that very tiny house all night, perpetually going up and down stairs. Inspector Carter realized that Mrs Rattenbury was ill, and in no fit condition to make a statement, and he told Miss Riggs to prepare some coffee. When the coffee came the saucer shook so in Mrs Rattenbury's hand that she could not hold it. She managed to swallow it, but retched and said that she wanted to be sick. The Inspector telephoned for a police-matron, who arrived and helped Mrs Rattenbury downstairs to her bath and helped her to dress. This matron was not called as witness, but it is reasonable to conclude that she thought Mrs Rattenbury a sick woman. Yet, according to Inspector Carter, Mrs Rattenbury, who had been drinking steadily from about eleven o'clock the night before till three-thirty in the morning (quite undeterred by the police), who had then been given half a grain of morphia which she had not been allowed to sleep off, was by eight-fifteen competent to make a statement! The statement which she then made to him, after being duly cautioned, and which he wrote down in his notebook, read as follows: 'About 9 p.m. on the 24th March I was playing cards with my husband when he

dared me to kill him, as he wanted to die. I picked up a mallet and
he then said: "You have not the guts to do it!" I then hit him with
the mallet. I hid the mallet outside. I would have shot him if I had
had a gun.' Inspector Carter deposed that Mrs Rattenbury read
the statement over aloud and clearly and then signed it. He then
took her to Bournemouth Police Station, where she was charged.
Before she left the house she had a moment alone with Miss Riggs
and said: 'You must get Stoner to give me the mallet.' This is
important, and it will be found, on reading Mrs Rattenbury's progressive statements all through the night, that, even in her befogged
condition, there was one thread of continuity – a desire to help
Stoner, and to get hold of the mallet with which he told her he had
hit Mr Rattenbury, and then hidden in the garden. At the Police
Station, about eight forty-five, Mrs Rattenbury was formally
charged, and said: 'That is right. I did it deliberately, and would do
it again.' The police did not, at the hearing at Petty Sessions,
mention the fact that Mrs Rattenbury had been drunk, and Mr
Rooke, noticing this omission, communicated the fact to Mrs Rattenbury's solicitors. Had it not been for Mr Rooke and Dr O'Donnell, the fact that Mrs Rattenbury had been in no fit condition to
make a statement, to know what was said to her, or to know what
she herself was saying, would not have been given in evidence. Mr
O'Connor, in his cross-examination of Inspector Carter, said: 'Dr
O'Donnell has told us in his evidence that no reliance can be
placed on any statement made by Mrs Rattenbury at eight-fifteen
in the morning.' 'No,' agreed the Inspector. 'Do you say she was
normal at eight-fifteen?' – 'Yes. She was not normal when she first
woke up, but I waited till eight-fifteen.' 'Do you know that the
medical officer at Holloway Prison has reported that she was still
under the influence of drugs three days later?' – 'He has never
reported it to me.' 'Is your evidence to the jury that, from the time
you began to take her statement until she left your charge, she did
not appear to you to be under the influence of drugs?' – 'She did
not.' 'Not at any time?' – 'Not at any time.' Yet, Mrs Rattenbury
was, during the whole of the time Inspector Carter had to do with
her, *non compos mentis* from morphia!

Later in the trial Mr Justice Humphreys, turning over the pages of Inspector Carter's notebook, was struck by the fact that there was an entry that had not been put in evidence. This consisted of a statement that Mrs Rattenbury made directly she woke up at six o'clock. The learned Judge drew Mr O'Connor's attention to the fact that there was something which had not yet been observed in the notebook. Mr O'Connor was handed the notebook, read the entry through to himself, and expressed his gratitude to the learned Judge. Indeed, Mr Justice Humphreys had made one of the most important points for the defence that were made in the case, as was shown when Inspector Carter was recalled to the box.

By the Judge: 'Did Mrs Rattenbury make any statement to you about this alleged crime before eight-fifteen?' – 'No statement to me, my lord. Mrs Rattenbury said the words that I have written in that book, while she was lying on the bed, directly she woke up. I did not put them down in statement form. I did not refer to it in my evidence for this reason. When Mrs Rattenbury woke up, I said in my evidence that, in my opinion, she was not then in a normal condition and I did not caution her, and for that reason I made no reference at all to these remarks that I put down in my book that she said. That is why I omitted to say anything at all about it in my evidence in chief. I was not entitled, in my opinion, to give anything in evidence if I had not previously administered a caution, and, in my opinion, she was not in a condition normally to make a statement.' *By the Judge:* 'Then in your opinion she was not in a condition to make a statement at six-fifteen?' – 'At six-ten, no, my lord.' *By the Judge:* 'Then what was said at that time was something said by a woman who was not in a condition to make a statement that can be acted upon?' – 'Not in my opinion, my lord.'

There was no doubt that Inspector Carter was actuated by an admirable sense of fair play, and the learned Judge, in his summing up, said: 'I think there is no ground for complaining of his conduct or saying that he acted improperly here, although, I think, he was mistaken . . . he made a mistake in not informing the Director of Public Prosecutions that that statement had been made by the accused, and that he had it in his notebook. It is not for the police officers to decide . . . what is admissible in evidence and what is not, or what should be given or what not. Their duty is to give all material to the authorities, and let them decide.' Now, the important point about the first entry in Inspector Carter's notebook – the entry he did not put in evidence, that he wrote at six-fifteen – and the one which he wrote down after cautioning her at eight-fifteen, is this, the two statements are practically identical. At six-fifteen when, according to Inspector Carter, she was not fit to make a statement, she said: 'I picked up the mallet and he dared me to hit him. He said: "You have not guts enough to do it." I hit him. I hid the mallet. He is not dead, is he? Are you the Coroner?' At eight-fifteen she said: 'He dared me to kill him. He wanted to die. I picked up the mallet, and he said: "You have not guts enough to do it." I hid the mallet outside the house.' It will be seen at once that, with the exception of the words, 'He is not dead, is he? Are you the Coroner?' the statements are the same, except that at eight-fifteen she used the word 'kill', and at six-fifteen the word 'hit'! To put it concisely: she made the same statement when, according to the Inspector, she was fit to make a statement, that she had made two hours earlier, when even he had considered her totally unfit! It was to all intents and purposes the same statement. The importance of this is obvious – Mrs Rattenbury no more knew what she was saying at eight-fifteen than she did at six-fifteen, and the second statement was of no more value than the first. At one o'clock of that day, when Dr O'Donnell saw her at the police station, he says she was supported into the room, that she could not stand without swaying, that she looked dazed, and had contracted pupils as a result of the morphia. Three days later Dr Morton of Holloway Prison considered that she was still suffering from 'confusion of mind, a result of alcohol, and possibly a large dose of morphia. She kept repeating the same sentences over and over again.' From 28 March she was better and appeared to have forgotten what she had said and how she behaved on the previous days since her reception. It is perfectly obvious that police officers are not fit judges of when a person is under the influence of morphia or not. There is no reason why they should be. But they are judges of drunkenness, and

Mrs Rattenbury should not have been allowed to go on drinking, or have been questioned during the Sunday night. Dr O'Donnell, as the learned Judge pointed out, knew much more of these matters than the police officer, and much later on Monday, after she had been taken to the Police Court, he declared that it would still be unsafe to attach any importance to anything that Mrs Rattenbury said.

Now Mrs Rattenbury was not used to drugs, in spite of suggestions made to the contrary; she had, indeed, a horror of drugs, and the only time previously in her life that any had been administered to her was when Dr O'Donnell in July 1934 had administered a quarter of a grain of morphia, when she was ill and excited. On that occasion she was allowed to have her sleep out, and she had indeed slept for some twelve hours. When the stronger dose of half a grain of morphia was given to her on the night of Sunday, 24 March, she had no chance of sleep. It is not suggested for a moment that the police tried to awaken her. But Villa Madeira is a tiny house. Stoner and the police were up and down and about it all night long. Now, anyone who has had to have morphia knows that if he is not allowed to sleep off the effects his condition is far worse than if it had never been administered. This was the case with Mrs Rattenbury, and, according to the experienced Dr Morton, she still was suffering from the effects of the morphia three days later. Many people felt that even if Mrs Rattenbury did not know what she was saying when she was drunk and when she was drugged, yet what she said came from her subconscious self, and hence was true. This is an error, as any doctor knows. What does come through all her statements, if they are carefully analysed, is her anxiety for Stoner, and her wish to take the blame. Another strong point for the defence, besides the undoubted one that Mrs Rattenbury was quite unfit to make statements, was the complete blank in her memory when she emerged from her drugged state into ordinary consciousness at Holloway Prison. Mrs Rattenbury remembered nothing from the time when she began to drink after discovering her wounded husband, until 28 March at Holloway Prison. Many people, as a result of drinking, 'pass out' as it is called. Mrs Rattenbury did so, and the result of the morphia's effect being thwarted, was that she stayed 'out' for a very long time. Mrs Rattenbury remembered nothing from when she first became drunk on the Sunday night. As far as her mind was concerned, she knew nothing about the interrogations, nothing about the injection of morphia, nothing about the police-matron having helped to get her up. She did not remember being taken away from Villa Madeira in a car by the police; the only thing that swam up at all in her recollection was Stoner's farewell kiss in her room, and the face of little John at her door. Mr Croom-Johnson, in cross-examination, asked her: 'About conversations, your mind is a complete blank?' – 'Absolutely.' 'About incidents?' – 'Yes. It might be somebody else you are talking about.' 'Is your mind a complete blank about making the statement to Inspector Carter which he wrote down in this little book?' – 'I cannot remember that. I have tried and tried and tried yesterday, and last night I tried to remember again.' The notebook was handed to her, and Mr Croom-Johnson asked her whether the signature at the bottom of the statement was hers, and she said that it was. 'It is my signature, but I do not remember it.' Now it is natural for the layman to feel that loss of memory is a convenient form of defence, but Mrs Rattenbury could not have deceived medical men as highly trained and as astute as Mr Rooke, Dr O'Donnell, and Dr Morton – the last named accustomed to all the tricks of delinquent women.

The prosecution took the unusual step of allowing the defence to recall one of the Crown witnesses, Mr Rooke, and this courteous gesture was a great help to Mrs Rattenbury. Mr Rooke deposed that in his experience patients often talked long and lucidly when under morphia, but when the effects of the drug had worn off their minds were a complete blank regarding anything they had said. When it is considered that Mrs Rattenbury was not suffering from the morphia, but that before the morphia had been administered she had temporarily lost her mind through drink, I think it is clear that no reliance can be placed on anything that she said.

Mrs Rattenbury was removed to Holloway Prison in London, and Stoner and Miss Riggs were left in the house at Manor Road.

But Miss Riggs had no intention of being left alone with Stoner. She knew that Mrs Rattenbury was innocent, not only of striking the blows, but of complicity in the assault. One of Mrs Rattenbury's most striking characteristics was her horror of cruelty. She could not have hurt anything. Therefore Irene Riggs thought that either a burglar had broken in, or that Stoner must have been Mr Rattenbury's assailant. Irene's mother and brother moved into Villa Madeira and stayed there with her until Stoner was arrested on Thursday, 28 March. The story of those days between the commission of the crime and the arrest of Stoner is a curious one. Dr O'Donnell had been asked by relations of Mr Rattenbury to keep Villa Madeira under his eye, and the Doctor accordingly called there on the Monday, Tuesday, Wednesday, and Thursday. On the first three days he tried to see Miss Riggs alone, but found it impossible as Stoner did not leave them. On Wednesday Miss Riggs was nearly distracted with anxiety, and felt she must talk about the case to someone. She still felt herself the custodian of Mrs Rattenbury's secret love affair, and she never discussed her even with her relations. Although not a Catholic, she went to see a priest, because she knew that what she told a priest would be safe. She came back at about ten-thirty that night and her mother opened the door to her. Mrs Riggs told her that Stoner was very drunk, that he had been going up and down the road, shouting, 'Mrs Rattenbury is in jail, and I've put her there.' He had been brought back by two taxi-drivers. Irene Riggs telephoned to the police and two plain-clothes men arrived. Stoner was in bed and seemed very drunk. This was very unusual for him, for he not only never drank himself, but objected to Mrs Rattenbury drinking, and had a good influence on her in this respect. On the morning of Thursday, 28 March, Dr O'Donnell called at Villa Madeira. Irene Riggs opened the door. It had always been Stoner who had opened it up to them. Dr O'Donnell asked where Stoner was, and she told him that he had gone to Holloway to see Mrs Rattenbury. Dr O'Donnell then said that Mrs Rattenbury was the best mistress that Miss Riggs had ever had, or that she was ever likely to have, and if there was anything she could tell the police, it was her duty to do so. Poor Miss Riggs, still loyal to her employer, said she could not let Mrs Rattenbury's secret out, but Dr O'Donnell very sensibly said that a secret was nothing when a life was at stake. He pointed out that if she was put in the witness-box, and then had the story of Mrs Rattenbury's liaison dragged out of her, she herself would be implicated if she had concealed her knowledge. He asked Miss Riggs whether she thought Mrs Rattenbury had murdered her husband, and Irene Riggs replied: 'I know she did not do it.' Dr O'Donnell asked her how she knew, and she replied that Stoner had confessed it to her. He had told her that there would be no fingerprints on the mallet as he had worn gloves. Dr O'Donnell rang up Bournemouth Police Station, and said that Miss Riggs wished to make a statement, and that Stoner had confessed to her. Dr O'Donnell added that Stoner had left for London, and that no time should be lost in taking Irene Riggs's statement. At two-thirty the police arrived and Irene Riggs told them what she knew. Stoner was arrested at the station on his return to Bournemouth that evening, and this time the charge was murder, for Mr Rattenbury had died.

The very fact that both Stoner and Mrs Rattenbury refused to inculpate each other was a source of great difficulty to their defenders. Stoner further complicated his counsel's very difficult task, by injecting into his defence the curious suggestion that he was a cocaine addict, which there was no evidence to bear out, and which Mr Justice Humphreys disposed of in no uncertain fashion in his summing-up. The Judge pointed out that there was one human being, and one only, who knew whether Stoner was in the habit of taking cocaine, and whether he took it on the afternoon of Sunday, 24 March, and that was Stoner himself. Stoner was an available witness, and had he wished to prove that he had ever taken cocaine, or was under the influence of cocaine, he could have gone into the box to say so. 'What,' remarked the learned Judge, 'seems to me in the circumstances of this case a fact of the utmost significance, is that Stoner prefers not to give evidence.' Stoner had told Mrs Rattenbury a long time before the murder that he took drugs. She was so worried about this that she confided it to Dr O'Donnell, although she was not at all sure – for in spite of her headlong infatuation she had a certain shrewdness – that Stoner had not invented the whole thing so as to make himself interesting to her. Dr O'Donnell, at Mrs Rattenbury's request, had interviewed Stoner and asked him what drug he was taking. Stoner told him that it was cocaine, and that he had found it in his father's house. To anyone who had seen Stoner's father in the witness-box, the suggestion was not only cruel, but absurd. Mr Stoner was a self-respecting, honest, hard-working man. It detracts somewhat from what has been called the chivalry of Stoner's conduct that he should have been able to make such a suggestion about his father. Stoner was certainly not a drug addict. Whether he was a cinema addict I do not know, but this fantastic story might well have emanated from a cinema-nourished mind. Had he not confused his defence by insisting on this fairy tale, his counsel would have been able to present a much more sympathetic picture of a boy crazy with love and wild with unreasoning jealousy, who had hit without knowing what he did. The cocaine story was too far-fetched. When Stoner was asked to describe what cocaine looked like, he replied that it was brown with black specks in it, evidently describing the only sort of things he knew, such as household pepper or influenza snuff.

During the trial Stoner sat unmoved in his corner of the dock, with his elbow on the ledge, and his cheek on his hand. His eyes were downcast and his face remained immovable. Mrs Rattenbury also was perfectly calm, but it was a frozen, and not an apathetic calm. Her physical aspect changed, without any movement on her part, in a curious manner. By Friday she looked twenty years older than she had on Monday. On the last day even her hands changed colour, and were a livid greenish white. She was an excellent witness. Her voice was low and rich. She gave a great impression of truthfulness, and she was astonishingly self-controlled. Only a nervous tic in the side of her face, which jerked perpetually, betrayed the tension of her mind. Mr R. Lewis-Manning, her solicitor, was impressed throughout all his conversations with her, by her veracity. He, as did Mr O'Connor, felt a terrible responsibility. Mr Lewis-Manning was certain that Mrs Rattenbury was not pretending when for several weeks she insisted that she would not implicate

Stoner, but preferred to hang rather than he should come to any harm. Unlike Mrs Thompson, she had immense physical courage. It was the thought of her children, and what a fearful heritage would be theirs if she were found guilty, that eventually made her tell the truth. It is easy to say that all this could have been a pretence on her part, but it would not have been easy, indeed, it would not have been possible for her to make this pretence appear the truth to Mr Lewis-Manning and Mr O'Connor.

The behaviour of a certain section of the press during the course of the trial, had it been made public, which for obvious reasons it was not, would have caused an uneasy feeling in the public mind. Someone engaged in the case was telephoned to on the Monday when the case opened, and offered £500 as his 'rake-off', if he would get Mrs Rattenbury to write her life-story. Then, as the unexpected angle that the case was assuming became visible, the press raised its offer. By Thursday, this gentleman, engaged in the case, who was a man of honour, was offered £3,500 as his 'rake-off', and one paper was foolish enough to put this offer in writing! It is needless to say that none of the offers was considered for a moment, and would not have been if the wealth of the world had been offered.

Mr Casswell was handicapped in his defence of his client Stoner, by the fantastic nature of the story which Stoner had told. Mr O'Connor was in no such invidious position; he had a very clear notion of the mentality of his client, and he was able to give full play to his sympathetic interpretation of that mentality. There were cases, Mr O'Connor pointed out, when the accused person had a record and history which might inspire the jury with a revulsion against that person's character. 'It is in this case, perhaps,' he continued, 'that the task of the jury is most difficult of all – the task of separating from their minds the natural revulsion they feel against behaviour which nobody would seek to condone or commend. I am not here to condone, still less to commend, her conduct. I am not here to cast one stone against that wretched boy whose position there in the dock may be due to folly and self-indulgence on her part, to which he fell a victim.' Mr O'Connor went on to say that the jury must not imagine that the two defences had been arranged in concert – were connected in any way. Each defence was in its water-tight compartment. 'I will say no more,' continued Mr O'Connor, 'about what is past in Mrs Rattenbury's life. I would only say that if you may be tempted to feel that she has sinned, that her sin has been great and has involved others who would never otherwise have been involved, that you should ask yourselves whether you or anybody of you are prepared first to cast a stone.' Having pleaded one of the greatest of speeches for the defence ever uttered – and the deathless words 'cast a stone' sounded through a hushed Court – Mr O'Connor went on to give a very good description of the mentality of the accused person who was not his client. He said of Stoner: 'Can you doubt seduced; raised out of his sphere; taken away to London; given a very high time there; a lad who was melodramatic and went about with a dagger, violent sometimes, impulsive, jealous, his first love; a lad whose antecedents had been quiet, whose associations had been prosaic; never mixed with girls; flung into the vortex of this illicit love; unbalanced enough, and, in addition to all these things, either endeavouring to sustain his passion with cocaine or already an addict of drugs. You may as moral men and women, as citizens, condemn her in your souls for the part she has played in raising this position. She will bear to her grave the brand of reprobation, and men and women will know how she acted. That will be her sorrow and her disgrace so long as she lives. You may think of Mrs Rattenbury as a woman, self-indulgent and wilful, who by her own acts and folly had erected in this poor young man a Frankenstein of jealousy which she could not control.'

Mr Justice Humphreys's summing-up was a brilliant exposition of the law. There is no judge more capable of weighing evidence, and the right value was given to every piece of evidence that had come before the Court. But the Anglo-Saxon assumption, unfortunately, still is that women, whatever their circumstances, want to be married, and Mr Justice Humphreys was no exception to this assumption. He spoke, in his summing-up, of the period (the 'orgy') which Mrs Rattenbury and Stoner spent in Kensington. The learned Judge said: 'Do you believe that while they were in London, the future was not discussed? What they were going to do when they got back? Could life go on in the same way? Would not something have to be done with – or to – Mr Rattenbury? Would he not ask "What about my £250? How much did the operation cost you? Did you have the operation? If so, where? I hope you are better for it." Or, if he was so callous and disinterested a husband that he would not be expected even to ask about the operation, at least as a mean man would not you expect him, and would not they expect him – that is the point – to make some inquiries about the money? Do you think that these two persons in London imagined that life could go on just the same after their return, after an absence of four days, as before?'

The learned Judge went on to quote Mrs Rattenbury's account of the events of Saturday. He quoted Mrs Rattenbury's evidence: 'I think we played cards. I think it was just the same as any other night.' The learned Judge asked: 'Do you believe that? Do you believe that after an absence of four days Mr Rattenbury never asked a question as to what happened in London?'

Let us consider the history and mentality of these people as we know them through the medium of the trial. Ill-balanced as she was, Mrs Rattenbury was a woman of the world. The last thing she would have wanted was to have married a chauffeur, twenty years younger than herself; she was – again to use a slang expression, but slang fits Mrs Rattenbury's career – 'sitting pretty'. She had a kind husband who allowed her to live her own life. She had a young and ardent lover who satisfied her emotionally and physically. She had two children to whom she was passionately devoted. She was being supported as extravagantly as she could have hoped for, all the circumstances considered. She was, as she rather pathetically said in evidence, 'happy then'. For her husband, she had a maternal affection – it must be remembered that in all her loves Mrs Rattenbury was essentially maternal. She spoiled and protected Stoner; she adored her children; she comforted her husband; she tried to give Irene Riggs as good a life as possible; she was kind to every stranger who came within her gates. The one thing that would

have been impossible to Mrs Rattenbury, amoral, casual, unbalanced, and passionate as she was, would have been to have
taken part in harming another human being. Mrs Rattenbury,
both as a humane woman and a completely amoral woman, did
not desire her husband's death, and did not wish to marry her
lover, and there is no evidence, and none was ever brought forward,
that she had ever desired either of these things. The unfortunate
Stoner, with a much simpler experience of life and with that adolescent urge to heroics, which is a hangover from infantilism, could
not see that there was no need for any drama of jealousy at all. The
boundary line between drama and reality was obscure for him, and
living entirely in an unintelligent world of crude emotion, he hit
out almost blindly. And this gesture, conceived in an unreal world,
materialized in a world of actual facts. Our prisons are of course
full of sufferers from infantilism, and what goes on in their heads
bears no relation to real life, as it has to be lived, though it could
not possibly be said they were not sane.

The jury were out for forty-seven minutes, and they returned the
only possible verdict to which they had been admirably directed
upon the evidence. They found Mrs Rattenbury not guilty, and
Stoner, guilty, adding a recommendation to mercy. Mrs Rattenbury stood immovable while the verdict of not guilty was returned,
but when the foreman of the jury pronounced the word 'guilty' in
respect of Stoner, she gave a little moan and put out her hand. She
was led away, and Stoner received his sentence without flinching.
He spoke for the first time when asked by the Clerk of the Court
whether he had anything to say why the Court should not give him
judgment of death according to law. Stoner replied in a low voice,
'Nothing at all.' He was then taken below, and Mrs Rattenbury
was brought back to plead to the accusation of being an accessory
after the fact. She could not speak – she could not make any sound
at all, her mouth moved a little and that was all. The Clerk of the
Court informed the jury that the prisoner at the Bar had pleaded
not guilty. The prosecution said that they proposed to offer no
evidence, and Mr Justice Humphreys instructed the jury to return a
verdict of not guilty, which they did. Mrs Rattenbury was discharged.

Mrs Rattenbury had an admirably fair trial. She was not, of course, bullied by the prosecution, as she would have been in France or the United States. In fact, Mr Croom-Johnson could, even within the limits allowed to the Crown, have been more severe than he was. Mr Justice Humphreys told the jury unmistakably that even though they might feel they could not possibly have any sympathy for the woman, it should not make them any more ready to convict her of the crime. It should, if anything, make them less ready to accept evidence against her. This is admirable, and in the best tradition of the English law. Unfortunately, there is a custom in the Courts that is not nearly so admirable, to animadvert upon the moral qualities, or lack of them, in a person accused of a crime. I am, of course, using the word merely in the only sense Anglo-Saxons seem to use it, with reference to sexual morality. Mrs Rattenbury, at the time the learned Judge was making his remarks about her moral character, was a woman at the extreme edge of what it was possible to bear and go on living. But she had to listen to the dread voice of the Judge as he said: 'Members of the jury, having heard her learned counsel, having regard to the facts of this case, it may be that you will say that you cannot possibly feel any sympathy for that woman; *you cannot have any feeling except disgust for her.*' (My italics.) More could hardly be said of George Joseph Smith, or of a systematic poisoner, or a baby-farmer.

This may show a very lofty and moral viewpoint, but we are often told that a criminal Court is not a court of morals. In this trial apparently it was. And strange as it may seem, there are some of us, though apparently regrettably few, who are so constituted that we cannot see a fellow human being in the extreme of remorse, shame, and despair, without feeling pity as well as disgust. Indeed, it is quite possible for the disgust to cease to exist because of the over-whelming nature of the pity. Mrs Rattenbury was in some ways a vulgar and a silly woman, but she was a generous, kindly, lavish creature, capable of great self-sacrifice. She was innocent of the crime of which, entirely on the strength of her own drunken maunderings, she was accused, but, nevertheless, though her life was handed back to her, it was handed back to her in such a shape that it was of no use to her. 'People' – that dread judgement bar of daily life known as 'people' – would always say: 'Of course she told him to do it. And, anyway, she was a dreadful woman.' For the world has progressed very little since Ezekiel wrote: 'And I will judge thee as women that break wedlock and shed blood are judged, and I will give thee blood in fury and jealousy.' Such was the judgement of society on Mrs Rattenbury, and she knew it.

Her husband's relatives took her away with them, but the press besieged the flat where they gave her refuge. The doctor who had been called in to attend her, removed her to a nursing home, pursued by newspaper men, one of whom called out to the doctor escorting her: 'If you take her to Bournemouth we'll follow you.' A horrible example of what the demands of his newspaper can do to a young man who probably started as a decent human being.

Mrs Rattenbury was by now very ill, physically and mentally. And, in her fear and grief for Stoner, in her misery for her children, in her remorse and shame, she wanted to be alone. She left the nursing home; and of what she did during the nightmare hours that followed we only know from the tragedy that followed. She must have bought a knife and taken a train down to that part of the world where she had been happy in what was stigmatized as an 'adulterous intercourse'. And there, beside the placid waters of a little stream, she sat and wrote, feverishly and passionately, on the backs of envelopes and odd bits of paper, the reasons for the terrible deed that she was about to do. She referred to the assumption that she dominated Stoner, and declared that no one could dominate him, and that whatever he wanted to do he always did. She repeated that if she had not been made to tell the truth, she would never have given Stoner away. She complained about the press dogging her footsteps, and she wrote of the scathing attack on her character. How, indeed, was it possible for her ever to make a home for her little boys, to watch them at play, to invite other children to play with them? She must have known it would be worse for her children if she lived than if she died. Her writing finished, she thrust the knife six times into her breast. The blade penetrated her heart thrice. She fell forward into the water, dead. When an ancient Roman killed himself, he inserted the tip of the sword between two ribs, and fell upon it; he called it 'falling upon the sword'. He knew that the shrinking of the flesh was such that it was almost impossible to drive a knife steadily into the breast. Mrs Rattenbury drove it in six times.

The Rattenbury case had revealed a strange and unlovely mode of life, but the woman's last act raised it sharply to higher issues. Most people in England, especially women, seem easily able to feel superior to Mrs Rattenbury. She had had 'adulterous intercourse'; she had taken for her lover a boy young enough to be her son; and the boy was a servant. That out of this unpromising material she had created something that to her was beautiful and made her happy, was unforgivable to the people of England. Her life had been given back to her, but the whole world was too small a place, too bare of any sheltering rock, for her to find a refuge.

Stoner lost his appeal, but he was reprieved, and the sentence of death commuted to penal servitude. Blind and muddled humanity had been even more blind and muddled than usual, and everyone concerned had paid a terrible price for the sin of lack of intelligence.

Hawley Harvey Crippen
1910

FILSON YOUNG

MOST of the interest and part of
the terror of great crime are due not to what is abnormal, but to
what is normal in it; what we have in common with the criminal,
rather than that subtle insanity which differentiates him from us,
is what makes us view with so lively interest a fellow-being who
has wandered into these tragic and fatal fields. A mean crime,
like that of the brute who knocks an old woman on the head for
the sake of the few shillings in her store, has a mean motive; a
great crime, like that of the man who murders his wife and little
children and commits suicide because he can see only starvation
and misery before them, gathers desperately into itself in one wild
protest against destiny what is left of nobility and greatness in the
man's nature. It is not that his crime has any more legal justification
than that of the murdering robber; it has not. On the contrary,
it is more of an outrage upon life, and far more damaging in its
results upon the community. Yet we do not hate or execrate the
author; we profoundly pity him; it is even possible sometimes to
recognize a certain terrible beauty in the motive that made him
thus make a complete sweep of his little world when it could no
longer cope with the great world. There are, at the least, reasons
for a great crime; for a mean one there are, at the most, excuses.
The region of human mortality is not a flat plain; there are hills
and valleys in it, deep levels and high levels; there are also certain
wild, isolated crags, terrible in their desolation, wrapped in storms
and glooms, upon which, nevertheless, a slant of sunshine will

sometimes fall, and reveal the wild flowers and jewelled mosses that hide in their awful clefts.

Somewhere between these extremes, far below the highest, but far above the lowest, lies the case of Dr Crippen, who killed his wife in order to give his life to the woman he loved. His was that rare thing in English annals, a *crime passionnel*. True, the author of it was an American, and the victim a German-Russian-Polish-American, but the theatre and setting were those of the most commonplace and humdrum region of London life, and all the circumstances that contributed to its interest were such as are witnessed by thousands of people every day. The trial that followed it is in no sense remarkable from a legal point of view, except possibly with regard to the medical evidence; its chief interest lies in the story itself, in the characters of the people concerned, and in the dramatic flight and arrest at sea of Crippen and his mistress.

In the year 1900 there came to London an entirely unremarkable little man, describing himself as an American doctor, to find some place in that large industry that lies on the borderland between genuine healing and the commercial exploitation of the modern human passion for swallowing medicine. This was Dr Hawley Harvey Crippen, a native of Coldwater, Michigan, where he had been born in the year 1862, his father being a dry-goods merchant of that place. It was not his first visit to England; he had previously been here in the year 1883, when at the age of twenty-one he had come to pick up some medical training. His education had followed the ordinary course of studies for the medical profession in America. After receiving a general education at the California University, Michigan, he proceeded to the Hospital College of Cleveland, Ohio. After a little desultory attendance at various London hospitals in 1883, Dr Crippen had returned to New York, where in 1885 he took a diploma as an ear and eye specialist at the Ophthalmic Hospital there. He afterwards practised at Detroit for two years, at Santiago for two years, at Salt Lake City, at New York, St Louis, Philadelphia, and Toronto. These movements covered twelve years from 1885 to 1896.

In 1887 he had married at Santiago his first wife, Charlotte Bell; the following year was born a son, Otto Hawley Crippen, who at the time of the trial was living at Los Angeles. In the year 1890 or 1891 his wife died at Salt Lake City; and from there he returned to New York, where two years later he made the acquaintance of a girl of seventeen, whom he knew as Cora Turner. He fell in love with her, and although at the time he met her she was living as the mistress of another man, he married her and took her with him to St Louis, where he had an appointment as consulting physician to an optician. He had found out that his wife's real name had not been Cora Turner at all, but Kunigunde Mackamotzki, and that her father was a Russian Pole and her mother a German.

Mrs Crippen was the possessor of a singing voice, small but of a clear quality, her friends' appreciation of which led her to entertain ambitions with regard to it which afterwards did not turn out to have been justified. Crippen, however, who was nothing if not an indulgent husband, allowed her to have it trained. This was in the year 1899, when they were living in Philadelphia; but Crippen allowed his wife to stay in New York for the purpose of having lessons, for which, of course, he paid, her ambition being that she should be trained for grand opera. She was still there when in 1900 Dr Crippen came to London as manager for Munyon's advertising business in patent medicines, the offices of which were at that time in Shaftesbury Avenue. About four months later he was joined by his wife, who had given up her lessons in New York and abandoned the idea of going into grand opera. Her ambitions now lay in the direction of the music-hall stage, and she probably regarded England as a promising field for the development of her talents in that direction.

This part of the story may be very briefly dismissed. Although she came over with a sketch of her own design, and many obliging music-hall agents undertook to float her in this country, nothing ever came of it save profit to the agents. Her musical sketch turned out to be a thing of which the music and the words both remained yet to be written, and competent artists were hired by the obliging agents to fill these omissions. Mrs Crippen, who was assiduous in fulfilling all the external conditions of her proposed career, took a stage name of 'Belle Elmore', and provided herself with a quantity of dazzling dresses – all, of course, at her good-natured husband's expense. But in fact the only attributes of the music-hall artiste to which she ever attained were the stage name and the dresses. From star appearances in a first-rate London music-hall her ambitions dwindled down to appearances of any kind at any music-hall; and even these, when it came to the point, proved beyond the powers of the agents to secure. One or two feeble appearances were made at very minor music-halls; but Mrs Crippen's talents were so inadequate, and the failure was so obvious, that even these attempts (for which, of course, Dr Crippen had to pay) were abandoned. The truth was that Mrs Crippen never had any talent whatever for the stage – not even the very moderate kind that will suffice to make the performance of an attractive young woman with a voice, wearing pretty clothes, and with some financial backing, acceptable to a music-hall audience. Poor Mrs Crippen had to content herself with frequenting music-hall circles, reading *The Era*, retaining her 'stage' name of Belle Elmore, and adding to her already large stock of theatrical garments. Here was, indeed, a small tragedy. If the poor woman had had any kind of talent, and had really been the music-hall favourite that she loved to imagine herself, both she and her husband would probably have lived a normal life, each happy in a different sphere; but apparently she had nothing but vanity, no scrap of the ability or industry necessary even for her small purposes. The humblest English music-hall has its standards; and 'Belle Elmore', in spite of her personal attractions and her pretty clothes, could not attain to them.

People who met the Crippens at this time describe them as cultivating acquaintances among the Bohemian world of music-hall performers who meet in small restaurants and are always ready to welcome to their social circle those who are lively company and have money to spend. Her friends describe Belle Elmore at this period as being of an exceptional liveliness. A loud, clear voice with a strong New York twang would have called attention to her presence wherever she was; but her whole appearance corresponded with the vivacity of her character. She is described as good-looking, with large dark eyes, raven hair, always elaborately dressed, and in the brightest colours. Her appearance was likened by one enthusiast to that of a 'bird of paradise'. Strange paradise, indeed, from which this poor bird had flown, or whither she was flying.

Crippen was then the insignificant-looking little man he always remained, small and short and slight in stature, with a sandy moustache, prominent eyes that looked at you through gold-rimmed spectacles, and a large domed forehead. His rôle in the social life was that of a spectator. He was the silent member of the gay little companies that were entertained by him and the bird of paradise. He was always courteous, always hospitable; apparently contented to look on at and enjoy his wife's little social triumphs among her friends. Her clothes and her jewels were the recipients of a great deal of admiration, and Crippen, who paid for everything, was content to find his share of the enjoyment in the attention and applause which they excited. He often would give her money or a piece of jewellery in the presence of her friends; and was regarded, not surely without justification, as an ideal husband worthy of the good fortune that had befallen him in becoming the proprietor and companion of the bird of paradise.

He was undoubtedly at this time still very fond of his wife, very kind to her, very patient with her extravagances and the interminable calls which she made upon his time and his means. I do not mean that such things are sacrifices when they are given as Crippen gave them. His attitude to women was peculiar. He was not the type of man that likes to dominate women; he was of the type that loves to be dominated by them; and in his love for showering presents upon his wife in public, and in spending a quite ridiculous proportion of his income in the adorning of her plump little person, he exhibited the symptoms of the psychopathic type to which undoubtedly he belonged.

It is not my intention to trace in detail the lives of these people further than is necessary to discover their characters. The relations which existed between them at the time of which I have been writing did not continue. The inordinate vanity of the wife demanded more than a husband's admiration, and Crippen's affection for her, which had never been of a very spiritual type, died the natural death of all such passions. It is distasteful to speak of Mrs Crippen's relations with other men, but it is obvious that the avenue to her affections was not very narrow or difficult of access. This also had its effect on the relations of husband and wife. After two years in England Crippen had to pay a short visit to America, and when he came home he found that she had contracted a friendship with a Mr Bruce Miller, who was a witness at the trial. Crippen's own written statement is that 'she told me that this man visited her, had taken her about, and was very fond of her, also she was very fond of him . . . It is quite four years since she ever went out to sing, and although we apparently lived happily together, as a matter of fact there were frequent occasions when she got into most violent tempers, and even threatened she would leave me, saying she had a man she could go to, and she would end it all.' Is that a true or an untrue statement? As we cannot tell, we have to ask ourselves, is it likely or unlikely? Even a very moderate experience of the world would, I imagine, be enough to convince a student of this case that it is probably a very accurate description of the state to which affairs had drifted after several years of the life which I have been trying to indicate.

In the year 1905 the Crippens left the rooms in Shore Street, Bloomsbury, where they had been living, and established themselves in 39 Hilldrop Crescent – a small semi-detached house in a quiet, leafy crescent off the Camden Road. There had been recently a rather unpleasant trial in connection with the Drouet Institute, where Crippen worked, and he had severed his connection with it, and returned to the management of Munyon's where Ethel Le Neve was now engaged as book-keeper and secretary.

The life at Hilldrop Crescent, externally commonplace, reveals on a closer examination some peculiar characteristics. From a friend of the Crippens who lived near them, knew them well, and saw them constantly, we are able to get some interesting sidelights on the life of the household. Mrs Crippen's florid taste was reflected, so far as their means permitted, in the furniture and decorations. Having seen a green wallpaper in the drawing-room of her friend's house, Mrs Crippen expressed herself shocked, and said, 'Gee! you have got a hoo-doo here. Green paper! You'll have bad luck as sure as fate. When I have a house I won't have green in the house. It shall be pink right away through for luck.' And apparently nearly all the rooms in Hilldrop Crescent were decorated in this propitious colour.

I cannot do better than quote some notes of Mrs Harrison's on the life at Hilldrop Crescent. It is possible that some of her views are coloured by after-events, but they are so interesting that they should be told in her own words.

'Mrs Crippen was strictly economical in small matters in connection with their private living. In fact, to such an extent did she carry it that it suggested parsimony. She would search out the cheapest shops for meat, and go to the Caledonian Market and buy cheap fowls. She was always trying to save the pence, but scattering the pounds. It was a peculiar trait in her character . . . It was shortly after they took up their residence at Hilldrop Crescent (which was in the September of 1905) that the doctor was converted by his wife to Roman Catholicism. She, who had neglected her religion, so far as going to early Mass was concerned, started regularly attending the Roman Catholic church in Kentish Town.

'One Sunday morning they both called early, after Mass, to invite us to a little supper-party on the same evening, and it was then the doctor informed us that his wife had made him a Catholic. He always appeared subservient to her wishes. I seemed to think at that time that she appeared more contented and settled-down now she had a home to interest her and look after. He was delighted with the air up at Camden Road, and he chuckled with delight when he told us his clothes were becoming too small for him, and that he was getting quite fat. Within a few months he put on flesh and appeared quite jolly and lively. They were about a great deal together, and their garden and the embellishment of their house

seemed a source of great interest. He was a man with no apparent
surface vices, or even the usual weaknesses or foibles of the ordinary
man. Restraint was the one and only evidence of firmness in his
character. He was unable to smoke; it made him ill. He refrained
from the consumption of alcoholic liquor in the form of wines and
spirits, as it affected his heart and digestion. He drank light ale and
stout, and that only sparingly. He was not a man's man. No man
had ever known him to join in a convivial bout; he was always back
to time, and never came home with a meaningless grin on his face
at two o'clock in the morning attended by pals from a neighbouring
club. He never paid compliments to women, or flirted even in a
jocular spirit. His eccentric taste in the matter of neckties and dress
generally may be attributed to the fact that it represented feminine
taste. His wife purchased his ties, and decided on the pattern of his
clothing. She would discuss the colour of his trousers with the tailor
while he stood aside looking on, without venturing to give an opinion. The novelty of the new house employed her thoughts for a
time. Her next little harmless whim took the form of desiring to
receive paying guests for company. So she set to work to obtain
some, and advertised in the *Daily Telegraph*. Several German young
men, attracted by the newly furnished house and fascinating little
hostess, engaged rooms. Four young men took up their residence
with them. Still objecting to domestic servants, Mrs Crippen
undertook the domestic work, with the occasional assistance of a
woman to do the cleaning. The doctor had to do his part. He had
to rise at six o'clock in the morning to clean the boarders' boots,
shovel up the coal, lay the breakfast, and help generally. He was
always at his office before eight. It was a trying time, and quite
unnecessary exertion for both, as Crippen was earning well, and
gave his wife an ample supply of money; in fact, she had the strings
of the family purse, which will be revealed as this strange story
unfolds itself. She annexed the extra money from the boarders for
personal adornment, and he continued to pay the household bills.

'A Mr Richards, who was a member of their household for a
time, wrote from Paris to the effect that during his sojourn under
their roof he witnessed several domestic eruptions of rather a one-

sided nature. Mrs Crippen, excitable and irritable, chiding her husband; Crippen, pale, quiet, imperturbable.

'Ethel Le Neve, the quiet, ladylike, unassuming typist, always to time, neat in appearance, methodical, obedient, was interesting the man who employed her. Quietly, imperceptibly, she was creeping into his heart and dulling the affection for his wife. Crippen's home life, which could have been made happy with the means at their disposal, was not restful. Their Sunday was a strenuous day of unrest for a hard-working business man. Early morning Mass, boarders' breakfast to be prepared on their return, boots to clean, beds to make, crockery to wash, dinner for midday to be cooked and served, and all this to be done without domestic assistance. After dinner they played cards with their boarders, gave them tea at five o'clock and supper at nine. The novelty of the boarders' society, which entailed so much drudgery, soon wore off. Dr Crippen hinted that he objected to it. They left shortly afterwards, and the Crippens returned to their strange solitary mode of living. There was no system in the household. Mrs Crippen disliked fresh air and open windows. There was no regular house-cleaning. It was done in spasms. The windows in all the rooms, including the basement, were rarely opened. They had two cats, which were never permitted to roam for fear they should fall victims to the shafts of illicit love. At his wife's desire Crippen built a cage in the garden for them to take the air. Only when they received, were lights shown in the hall or living-rooms. They lived practically in the kitchen, which was generally in a state of dirt and disorder. The basement, owing to want of ventilation, smelt earthy and unpleasant. A strange "creepy" feeling always came over me when I descended – it was so dark and dreary, although it was on a level with the back garden.

'I followed her into the kitchen one morning when she was busy. It was a warm, humid day, and the grimy windows were all tightly closed. On the dresser was a heterogeneous mass, consisting of dirty crockery, edibles, collars of the doctor's, false curls of her own, hairpins, brushes, letters, a gold jewelled purse, and other articles. It reminded one of the contents of Mrs Jellyby's cupboard in

Dickens's *Bleak House*, when the cleaning operations were started for her daughter's wedding. The kitchener and gas stove were brown with rust and cooking stains. The table was littered with packages, saucepans, dirty knives, plates, flatirons, a washing basin, and a coffee-pot. Thrown carelessly across a chair was a lovely white chiffon gown embroidered with silk flowers and mounted over white *glacé*. The little lady cat, who was a prisoner, was scratching wildly at a window in a vain attempt to attract the attention of a passing Don Juan . . .'

It was at this period that Mrs Crippen made the acquaintance of several well-known people in the music-hall world, and became a member of the Music Hall Ladies' Guild – a society doing quiet, charitable work among the more unfortunate members of the profession. Mrs Crippen's enthusiasm for the work of this Guild was perhaps the best thing one knows of her. It had the double attraction of appealing to the impulsive kindness of heart which is characteristic of people of her type, and also of bringing her into a more interesting kind of society than would otherwise have been open to her. Mrs Martinetti, Mrs Ginnett, Mrs Eugene Stratton, Lil Hawthorne, and Mrs Harrison were among those with whom she was thus brought into intimate association. And in this, so to speak, posthumous way she was able to appear herself as a member of the great profession, call herself 'Belle Elmore', and appear to be enjoying the aftermath of those brilliant successes which, in fact, she had never enjoyed. She became honorary treasurer of the Guild, which she induced to rent one of the rooms of Dr Crippen's suite in Albion House, New Oxford Street. It is an ill wind that blows nobody any good; and the music-hall strike gave her an opportunity during the famine of actually appearing on the stage, although even in these propitious circumstances fate was against her. She was engaged for a week at the Bedford and Euston Palace, but on her appearance at the Euston (after an agitated week turning over all her most expensive gowns) the audience refused to listen to her, evidently regarding her as a 'blackleg', and she was hissed off the stage. The poor creature suffered great distress from this, and was only consoled by Crippen's sympathy and kindness. On this occasion there was an odd and sinister coincidence. An actor named Weldon Atherstone, who appeared on the same evening and had a similar reception, was able to sympathize with the weeping 'Belle Elmore'. Three years later, in July 1910, in the same week in which London was ringing with the discovery of the remains at Hilldrop Crescent, Atherstone was found shot in the garden of his flat in Battersea. The coincidence was commented upon by Dr Danford Thomas, the coroner, who a week later was himself dead.

In all this time the Crippens were keeping up a considerable appearance, spending money on entertaining at restaurants and little parties, while in private they were living the somewhat squalid existence described by Mrs Harrison. Also, Crippen's affection for Le Neve was developing. For this quiet, reserved, attractive girl the quiet and reserved Crippen was nourishing a genuine passion. From the strain and storm of existence at home he was finding something like repose and true companionship in his association with Miss Le Neve. His resources were further strained by his efforts to adorn her in the way he had adorned his wife – so much so that the doctor connected with Munyon's establishment objected to her too smart appearance, and requested her to return to a more sober habit of dress.

In short, the causes were now all assembled which were to produce such tragic results, and only some powerful agent was required to precipitate the tragedy from these ingredients. There was the life at home, sordid and quarrelsome. There was the outward appearance of affluence and display, coupled with the laboriously kept-up appearance of matrimonial felicity. There were the business interests and anxieties, and there was the secret growing passion for Miss Le Neve.

Here, then, was Crippen living, although not on affectionate, at any rate on endurable terms with his wife. That the relationship would, and indeed must, somehow at some time come to an end was probably in both their minds. They had no children to complicate the relationship, and Mrs Crippen's former manner of life and her popularity with a certain class of man must have familiarized her with ways in which she could be easily independent of her husband. But that the situation in January had become so intolerable that either thought of murdering the other I do not believe. Murder is, to say the least of it, an extreme step to take, even in marital disagreements; it is an extreme stage to which to carry them; it is an extreme method of solving them. There are thousands of men and women who daily carry the burden that Crippen was carrying, who wake up every morning to another day of a relationship of which bickering and distaste are the elements; who see stretching hopelessly before them a long and dreary vista of such days. But they do not resort to murder as an escape. Except to a maniac, or to a person beside himself with rage, jealousy, hatred, fear, or despair, the deliberate killing of a human companion is a difficult, disagreeable, and, indeed, abhorrent business. It is also highly dangerous, and (thanks to the law and to the machinery of justice) is almost certain to bring the offender into a situation in comparison with which the unhappiest married life would seem as charming as the memory of Eden must have been to our fallen parents. In such circumstances, tolerated for so long, and therefore tolerable for a little longer, something very acute, sudden, or final must occur to precipitate such an action. And something of the same character must have occurred in the Crippen household to make the doctor decide that he must not only escape from his wife, but murder her. What was it?

There are four theories, and only four, which can serve even approximately as a solution of the problem. Let us examine them.

The first theory, which may be called the official theory of the prosecution, is that Crippen murdered his wife simply that he might indulge his guilty passion for Ethel Le Neve. This is the kind of motive which is always good enough for a jury, especially when the facts of the murder are proved; but it will not stand intelligent examination. It is not reasonably in accordance either with the facts or with the characters of the people concerned. As for the guilty passion, Crippen had not only enjoyed it for a considerable time, but he obviously did not feel particularly guilty about it; it is even obvious that he took no more trouble to hide it than the dictates of elementary discretion and common sense demanded. It is pretty certain that all his friends and the people connected with him in business knew all about it, and had become so accustomed to it as to take it for granted. Ethel Le Neve was the companion of his business life and of his days; his wife was not even the companion of his nights; and much as he no doubt wished that he was married to Ethel Le Neve and not to Cora Crippen, that in itself could not have been a sufficient motive for him to commit murder. It was always possible for him simply to leave or desert his wife and live openly with Le Neve. But if he had been going to do that, he would have done it before. When a man is in love with a woman who is not his wife, the time at which he is most likely to desert his wife for the mistress is at the beginning of the new relationship; not when it has been going on for years and become, as it were, regularized. And if that is true of mere desertion, how much more true is it of murder, which requires so much stronger a motive, so much more impulsive a passion. If this theory as to motive were sound, Crippen would surely have committed the crime several years earlier, and not after he had settled down into a routine of existence which was, as I have suggested, if not happy, at any rate full of varied interests and had its private alleviations.

Another and most ingenious attempt to account for the sudden abolition of Mrs Crippen is, I think, the invention of Sir Edward Marshall Hall, who developed it at some length in a discussion before a private society in London. This was the theory upon which, if he had defended Crippen, his defence would have been founded; and it was because another line of defence had been opened at the police Court before the brief was offered to him that he ultimately declined it.

The theory is that, far from Crippen having ceased to cohabit with his wife, he was in fact something of a victim to her exigencies in that respect; that Mrs Crippen had an abnormal amative appetite – abnormal, that is to say, not in the nature but in the extent of the appetite; that her husband, devoted as he was to his mistress, found himself the victim of a double demand to which the poor little man's frail physique and advancing years rendered him unequal; and that he sought in the pharmacopoeia a remedy for this distressing state of affairs. That having known, from his former experience in lunatic asylums, that hyoscin is sometimes used as a sexual depressant in cases of acute nymphomania, he conceived the idea of administering a few doses of this drug in order to keep his wife quiet. That although he knew the drug was used he did not know what the dose was, and innocently went out and bought five grains, the whole of which he administered to his wife in a cup of coffee. And that when, instead of falling quietly asleep, Mrs Crippen, to the horror and surprise of her husband, incontinently died, he was so frightened at what he had done and foresaw such difficulty in explaining it that he cut up, burned, and otherwise disposed of the remains, and gave his friends the explanation of Mrs Crippen's disappearance which in fact he did give. That, in short, if when she died he had run out and told a policeman of his dreadful mistake, he would have been an object of sympathy rather than of legal vengeance.

The ingenuity of this theory cannot be denied; and there is a touch of true comedy in it, in spite of the grim facts, which makes one regret that it had not the chance of being fully developed in a criminal Court. Sir Edward Marshall Hall was not only convinced that he could have satisfied the jury and got the charge reduced to one of manslaughter, but (a much more extreme belief) he even thought this to be the true explanation of the facts. But I am afraid that it will not do either. There is the fact that, having occupied a common room and bed in their former homes, the Crippens had separate rooms at Hilldrop Crescent. It is all very well to represent Crippen as the victim of the inordinate concupiscence of his wife as well as of his own passion for his mistress; but these are two fires between which a man in his situation cannot really be forced to remain. Although Courts of law continue to make orders for the restitution of conjugal right, no method of enforcing them has so far been discovered; and relief from such a situation as this theory of the case presumes could be found in a purely negative line of conduct. Moreover (and here is the greatest weakness of this theory) it is almost unthinkable that a medical man who knew the properties of hydrobromide of hyoscin could be totally ignorant of the amount of the dose. It is quite possible that he would not know the minute variations of the dose for different cases; but that he should make such a wild mistake as lies in the difference between half a grain and five grains is unthinkable. That Crippen administered five grains is to be inferred not only from the amount discovered in the remains, but also from the fact that no residue of the drug was discovered in his possession; and it would have been of vital importance to him to produce such residue, in view of his own explanation as to his reason for purchasing hyoscin. So that this theory, ingenious as it is and profoundly interesting as its development would have been as a legal defence, must in my view be dismissed, not so much because it is unreasonable as because it is discordant with the revealed facts of the case.

There is a third theory to which, after full consideration of all the mysterious elements in the problem, I am driven as the most reasonable explanation of this extreme and violent act on the part of a man whose characteristics, as revealed to his associates through a number of years, were patience, kindness, and amiability. It is that the more or less sudden act which precipitated the tragedy came from Mrs Crippen herself, in the form of a definite decision to leave her husband and take with her the whole available capital of the family, including the money in the bank and the jewellery.

In regard to this there is a very important fact which did not come out at the trial, but goes far to explain what is otherwise almost inexplicable. It is known that Mrs Crippen had more than once in the month of January told one of her friends that if Crippen did not give up his association with Miss Le Neve she intended to leave him, and to take her money with her. It will be observed that she spoke of it as 'her' money, and it is clear that she so regarded it. What view Crippen himself took of this scheme I do not know, but it is at least strange that the bulk of their money was held in a joint account. It is not in accordance with the orderly and businesslike character of Crippen that he should have placed all his own resources, on which he depended not only for his household expenses, but also for the conduct of the various little businesses in which he from time to time engaged, at the mercy of a woman like his wife. He knew her character perfectly well – no one better; he must have known that, whatever qualities she possessed, she was not the sort of woman in whose hands it would be desirable to place the control of one's finances. In regard to the £600 on deposit in the Charing Cross Bank, some of this had been deposited in the joint names of husband and wife, and some in the name of Belle Elmore. Now, Mrs Crippen had no means of getting money unless it was given to her by her husband or someone else. She never earned any money during the five years which are the crucial period in this case. Crippen was, even on the admission of her own friends, liberal to her when he had money, and gave her whatever she required in accordance with his means. But the kind of salaries that Crippen earned did not entirely account for the sums of money that were from time to time in the possession of these two people, jointly or severally. It is true that in some of his businesses, although on a small salary (£3 or £4 a week), he was entitled to commission; but latterly, at any rate, that commission could not have amounted to anything considerable. In 1905, when he was manager of the Sovereign Remedy Company, it failed. From there he went as physician to the Drouet Company, and it failed; next he went to the Aural Clinic Company, and in six months it also failed. Then he returned to Munyon's as manager, and after some two years took it over as an agency – which seems to mean that the proprietors did not consider the branch sufficiently profitable to justify his salary, and allowed him to run it on an agent's commission. In November 1909 he had ceased to be manager of the agency, and was simply remaining on commission; and even this arrangement was to terminate on 31 January 1910. Undoubtedly he had various side lines of activity in the patent medicine business, but they were only side lines; and probably at the time of the murder his chief source of income was the partnership in a dental business which he had with

Dr Rylance at Albion House, New Oxford Street. But in all these affairs, having regard to the fact that he had a house to keep up and a wife to support who, for her station in life, was notoriously extravagant, there does not seem much room for the laying-by of money and the purchase of expensive jewellery. Where, then, did the money come from? And how far was Mrs Crippen justified in her claim to it as her own property?

We must remember what she had been and what she was. Undoubtedly she occasionally received 'presents' from various men; and whether these took the form of money or jewellery, or both, one can understand that she would regard them as entirely her own property and at her own disposal. What Crippen knew of their origin I cannot tell. The veil of mystery which surrounds so much of the character of this quiet and reserved man is not lifted to show any light on this aspect of the case. He was indifferent to his wife, who, by her vanity, her extravagance, her shrewishness, had long worn out the affection in which he had formerly held her and his pride in the kind of attention that she attracted. Crippen was not a robust man physically; his vitality was of a nervous sort. She, on the other hand, was robust and animal. Her vitality was of that loud, aggressive, and physical kind that seems to exhaust the atmosphere round it, and is undoubtedly exhausting to live with. In all probability, therefore, he did not ultimately care what she did, where she went, or whom she saw, as long as his life was allowed to go on without interruption. Of course, there were quarrels; 'Belle Elmore', who could be so pleasant and attractive to her music-hall friends, was not the sort of woman to withhold her words on provocation, or to take a philosophic view of her husband's liaison. It is true that she had ceased to care for him, and spared him neither in public nor in private before her friends; but, in the mean of soul, vanity takes the place of nobler passions, and though she did not want Crippen for herself, it was not in accordance with her vanity that he should enjoy the love of any other woman. She was probably getting bored with the Hilldrop Crescent existence; unless there was plenty of money to gild it, that was too dingy a life for the kind of woman she conceived herself to be. Also, she had reached that age – thirty-five years – when a woman of her race begins to realize that her youth is over, and that the time in which her attractions can still pass current in the world of men is growing short. She had any amount of clothes, plenty of jewellery, some money. Why not pick a quarrel with Crippen, and in the disguise of a virtuous and ill-used wife fly to the protection of some man who was, or whom she believed to be, ready to receive her?

I believe that somewhere about the middle of January 1910 she made this threat to Crippen, and perhaps began to look about her for the means to carry it out. I believe that he was worried, both on account of money and his business affairs, and possibly also through his love for Ethel Le Neve. It is possible that she, as well as Mrs Crippen, was discontented with the existing situation; it would be remarkable if she were not. Although she had given herself entirely to Crippen, and knew herself to be the object of his very real devotion, she was still working as an ordinary typist at Munyon's; and the contrast between her situation and that of the woman who had the official position of Crippen's wife and the spending of the money, the wearing of the clothes and jewellery, and the treasurer-ship of the Music Hall Ladies' Guild, and all the rest of it, must have been increasingly disagreeable. There is no evidence that she put any pressure of this nature on Crippen; it would not be fair to suggest that she did. But perhaps all the more for that reason would Crippen desire to give to the woman he loved what was at present being wasted on the woman he did not love. If his wife were to go away as she threatened, and take all her possessions with her, the situation would be worse instead of better. There would be a scandal in their little world; there would be no money just at the time when it was most needed; there would be none of the jewellery which Crippen longed to see adorning the person of his mistress. Remember Crippen's attitude to jewellery. Undoubtedly he had bought, and his wife possessed, jewellery of a value quite unusual for people in their circumstances; and there is no doubt that at the time when he was in love with his wife he found, as other men have found, an actual stimulus to his passion in seeing her hung about with precious and dazzling things. He greatly desired, now that his passion was centred on Ethel Le Neve, to give it some indulgence in the same way. If Mrs Crippen went away and took everything with her, there was an end to these hopes. But what if she were to die?

Here came the turning point in Crippen's life, when, from being a much-tried and much-enduring man, encoiled by circumstances and the consequences of his own actions, he became a criminal. It is a deep and unfathomable chasm that divides the two conditions, but it may be a very narrow one. Upon what plank he crossed or what exasperating word or deed goaded him to make the leap, I do not know or expect ever to learn. But from that moment he never wavered. He went and bought the hyoscin – always considerate, you see, even in the weapon he used to kill his wife. He had decided that it would be better that she should cease to exist; and his ingenuity and consideration combined hit upon what was at once the most merciful and the safest poison he could have used.

From 19 January, when the hyoscin came into his possession, he was probably considering the means and opportunity of using it. It is impossible to say whether its employment on the night of 31 January, when the Martinettis dined with them, was accidental or premeditated. It may have been in his mind to do it after an apparently amicable evening in the presence of friends, when he and his wife could be seen in an atmosphere of matrimonial amity. If so, that scheme was rather frustrated by the fact that Mrs Crippen rated him soundly in the presence of the Martinettis for allowing Mr Martinetti to go upstairs to the lavatory by himself, instead of escorted by his host. The matters into which one descends here are minute indeed, but who can say what bearing they may not have had on the destinies of those present? Mrs Crippen may have been anxious to have a word alone with Mrs Martinetti, and have been enraged with Crippen for not giving her the opportunity. Otherwise, seeing that Mr Martinetti knew the house well, and that they were in the habit of dining there at least once a week, Mrs Crippen's annoyance with her husband seems to have been excessive. However, it may have been enough; it may have been the spark that fired the train, and what is certain is that Mrs Crippen was never seen alive after that evening, and that her remains, containing traces of what had been a large dose of hydrobromide of hyoscin, were subsequently discovered beneath the floor of the coal cellar below the steps.

The only other theory with which the facts may be brought into accordance is one which would involve the collusion of an accomplice, and for obvious reasons cannot be discussed.

But taking the third theory as the one which is the most reasonable of those that are open to us, Crippen's subsequent conduct is all of a piece, and throws a profoundly interesting light on his character. Across the chasm which separates the ordinary citizen from the criminal, he had taken the fatal and decisive step; but having done so, instead of going off, like so many murderers, to wander in the wilderness as an outlaw, he resumed his ordinary course of life; he kept straight on; only now he walked on the far side of the narrow abyss. If the course of his life were to be marked on a chart one would not see it, as is usual in the case of criminals, turning suddenly at a right angle and continuing in that direction; it would appear as a straight course with one little step aside in the middle of it, and then continuing as before. It is certain that he showed no disturbance, remorse, or fright for the horrid deed that he had committed; and I believe that he did not feel any. In some obscure way he justified to himself what he had done without violating his conscience, because, as far as one can judge, his life was now happier than it had been before. But on the assumption that he committed this crime out of love for his mistress, his subsequent conduct was perfectly consistent. He took all the necessary steps, and took them with great skill and coolness, to conceal all traces of the crime. The bones, limbs, and head, as well as certain characteristic organs, had all been removed from the discovered remains, and the evidence was that they had been removed by a hand skilled in dissection. No one knows how they were disposed of; but it must have been a work of days. One theory is that it was done in the bath, and the bones and limbs burned in the kitchen grate, while the head was got rid of during Crippen's subsequent trip to Dieppe – dropped overboard in a handbag. But whatever the method, it must have involved labours physically exhausting, and of a nature horrible to contemplate.

He invented a story to account for his wife's disappearance. With a certain completeness of artistic circumstances he developed her disappearance into her death in far-away California; and he devoted himself to the girl for whose affections he was to pay such a price. It is characteristic of the inconsistency of human prejudice that half the indignation and horror aroused against him was because of the fact that he cut up his wife's remains, and that he wrote hypocritical letters to the music-hall ladies about her death in California. How absurd is such an attitude. The crime was in murdering his wife; it was a crime of such magnitude that nothing he could do afterwards could possibly aggravate it, unless it had involved cruelty or betrayal of someone who was alive. On the contrary, granting the crime and granting its enormity, what he did afterwards was technically admirable. It was his business to abolish all trace of it, and that he very nearly succeeded in doing. If he were going to tell a lie about his wife's death in California, he had better do it well than badly; and, in fact, he did it extremely well. If he had murdered his wife in order to be happy with Le Neve, the least he could do was to devote himself to her; and from that moment until the morning he was hanged in Pentonville Prison he had no other thought but of her welfare, no other object but to secure her safety and happiness, no other fear but that any consequence of his action should recoil upon her.

But human vanity, which is woven like a gaudy thread through the dark fabric of this story, was to prove his undoing. His wife gone, her disappearance explained and her death announced, with circumstantial details, including memorial cards and announcements in *The Era* – matters which occupied a couple of months – Crippen took Miss Le Neve more or less openly to live with him in Hilldrop Crescent (12 March). My theory as to the crime is supported by the fact that on 2 and 9 February Crippen pawned jewellery to the value of £195. He had now command of money;

Miss Le Neve was living with him, and he could begin to enjoy the fruits of his dreadful action. They became bolder and more open in the enjoyment of the situation. She was seen at a charity dinner and dance on 20 February, wearing some of the jewellery which had been Mrs Crippen's. This seems to have been too much for some of the lady friends of Mrs Crippen. Perhaps some of them felt that had she made a will she would have divided her treasured possessions among them. They knew that the last person whom she would have wished to enjoy them was Miss Le Neve. They talked, they wondered, they became suspicious; and on 30 June a Mr Nash went to Scotland Yard and raised the whole question of Mrs Crippen's disappearance.

A week later Inspector Dew and Sergeant Mitchell began their inquiries, visiting Crippen at his office. He then told them that the whole story of Mrs Crippen's death was untrue, that she had left him, he knew not with whom, and that to avoid scandal he had invented the story of her journey to California, her illness, and death. He gave a signed statement which was produced at the trial, and showed every desire to give them what assistance he could in discovering the whereabouts of his wife. This statement was given to Inspector Dew in Crippen's office, in the intervals between medical consultations and tooth-pulling; he would dictate a little of it, go out and extract a tooth, and return and dictate some more. It occupied the greater part of the day, and Crippen and Inspector Dew went out and had lunch together at the Holborn Restaurant in the middle of it. Crippen took the officers to Hilldrop Crescent, assisting them to examine everything. They went all over the house from attic to cellar, and found nothing whatever inconsistent with his story. Inspector Dew has told me that on this day, 8 July, having been almost continually with Crippen and having gone over the whole house, he had found nothing whatever to lead him to suppose that there was anything in the case other than what Crippen had told him. The investigation was to all intents and purposes finished.

And then something broke down. It was not the nerve of Crippen;

but it was not improbably the nerve of Miss Le Neve. It is impossible to be sure whether or not she knew the truth; it is quite possible, as both she and Crippen swore, that she did not. If she did, there would be little wonder that the situation had become too much for her. But even if she did not, she may have become uneasy and suspicious, and Crippen may have felt, now that there was an investigation afoot, that in some way her nerve would give way and her manner awake suspicion, and that the strain of further examination would prove altogether too much for her. He resolved on instant flight. Some very powerful influence must have been at work to induce Miss Le Neve to submit to the daring scheme of sudden flight disguised as a boy. If they had only known it, the worst was over; the probability is that if they had not gone away the matter would have been dropped, and Mrs Crippen's disappearance ranked among the many unsolved mysteries of London life. But they did not know it; and Crippen with masterly coolness arranged the details of the flight. He left his affairs in order; found time, even in this hurried hour of preparation, to write letters characterized by his usual courtesy which would enable his business associates to suffer the least possible embarrassment through his departure. Unsuspected and uninterrupted, they got away to Rotterdam and to Antwerp, where in the names of Mr and Master Robinson they took passage to Quebec on the s.s. *Montrose*, sailing on 20 July.

But in the meantime something had happened in London which renewed in a powerful and fatal form the almost extinct current of official suspicion. Inspector Dew, for no particular reason, decided to return on Monday 11 July to Albion House, Crippen's office, to ask some supplementary questions. There he heard that Crippen had gone away. His suspicions now thoroughly awakened, he returned to Hilldrop Crescent and made a further search of the house, taking up portions of the garden, examining the coal cellar, testing the bricks with his foot; but found nothing. With a fortunate pertinacity which won him his distinction in this case, he returned to the search on the next day, and again on the following day, the

74

13th, when, probing the bricks of the cellar floor with a poker, he discovered that one of them could be raised. Having got a few more out by the same process, he got a space and began to dig, and a few inches down came upon a compact mass of animal remains which, on expert investigation, proved to be the greater part of the contents of a human body from which the head, limbs, and bones were missing, as were also those particular organs which would have determined the sex of the body. On 16 July a warrant was issued for the arrest of Crippen and Miss Le Neve, but, as has been seen, they had successfully escaped, and were then, and during the four following days, waiting for the *Montrose* to sail from Antwerp.

The tragic chapters of the story succeeded one another with dramatic rapidity. There had been time for the sensational discovery at Hilldrop Crescent to be circularized, and the description of the two fugitives reached Antwerp before the ship sailed. The captain had read them, and he had not been at sea two days before he thought he had identified in Mr and Master Robinson the two people who were wanted by the police, and for information as to whom the *Daily Mail* had offered a reward of £100. Wireless telegraphy, then in its early commercial stages, was used for the first time in the science of criminal detection. Captain Kendall sent on the 22nd a long wireless message relating his discovery, and for nine days he kept his victims all unsuspicious of the dreadful part in their lives which the crackling discharge of the wireless played, coaxing them to talk and laugh, and luring them on to the exposure of their not very successful disguise. On 23 July Dew and Mitchell sailed from Liverpool, and on the 31st Crippen and Miss Le Neve were arrested when the ship was off Father Point, Dew coming on board disguised as a pilot, and, after extradition proceedings at Quebec, were brought back to London for trial.

The way in which, by the accidental inclusion of part of a pyjama jacket among the remains, the date at which they were buried – otherwise unascertainable – was absolutely fixed within certain limits; the brilliant and laborious analysis which proved that these few pieces of flesh and skin had been part of a body which had contained a fatal dose of hyoscin; the extraordinary contradiction and breakdown of the experts engaged for the defence – those are all discovered in the report of the trial. Sir Richard Muir was never in all his long career as a criminal prosecutor more formidable and unflinching than in his masterly weaving together of the web which bound Crippen to his ultimate fate. But the most amazing feature of the trial was the absolute coolness and imperturbability of Crippen in the long and terrible cross-examination to which he was subjected. The hideous moment in which the pieces of his dead wife's skin were handed round in a soup plate for inspection left him, alone of all the people in that crowded Court, quite unmoved. He peered at them with an intelligent curiosity as though they had been mere museum specimens. Not by one word or tremor did this frail little man betray any sign of his terrible position, to which, nevertheless, as we know from other evidence, he was acutely and tragically sensitive. This behaviour characterized him up to his very last moments of life. And just as the Crown, with all its resources, had not been able to produce a single person who could say otherwise than that in every relationship of life Crippen had always behaved with kindness, consideration, and unselfishness, so everyone who came in contact with him from his trial to his death – and some of them were fairly hardened prison officials – looked upon him not only with respect, but with something like affection.

He never gave any trouble, showed any concern, or asked for any benefit for himself; all his concern and all his requests were for the woman he loved. I have seen the tragic little book in which it was the duty of the warders who sat and watched with him day and night in the condemned cell to record his conduct from hour to hour, and although I do not feel myself free to quote from it, there is nothing in that record that shows any preoccupation whatever except anxiety on behalf of another. The only time he broke down was when, late on the night before his execution, the Governor of Pentonville prison brought him a telegram of farewell from Miss Le Neve, and his one request, when the Governor at this same midnight interview asked him if there was anything he could possibly do for him, was that the one or two letters he had received from her, and her photograph, should be buried in the prison grave with him on the morrow. This promise was given and kept.

No one will pretend to read in these pages any apology or justification for a proved murder. They are an attempt to trace the threads of motive throughout what is a very remarkable instance of good and bad influence acting on human conduct. Rightly read and understood this is an admonishing, sobering, and instructive story. We may consider Crippen a hateful man; but nobody who came in contact with him was able to say so. From those who, whether in business relations or as friends of his wife, had no reason to like or praise him, to the officials of the prison in which he was executed as a condemned murderer, there is but one chorus of testimony to his character as tested by daily intercourse with his fellow-men; even in regard to the very circumstances surrounding his crime, or at any rate following it, there is the same extraordinary feature; the very crime itself brought out in him high human qualities.

There are two sides to the story – the physical, which is sordid, dreadful, and revolting, and the spiritual, which is good and heroic; to the extent that most honest men, finding themselves in the situation in which he ultimately found himself, for whatever reason, and tried by the tests by which he was tried, would be glad to come out of them half so well. Such a story can only be understood by the aid of the imagination; and it should remind us, in the judgements that we pass on our fellow-men, never to forget the dual nature of human character and the mystery in virtue of which acts of great moral obliquity may march with conduct above the ordinary standards – conduct which, if we wish to be just, as we hope for justice to ourselves, should be remembered and recorded no less than the crime.

Oscar Slater
1909–28

WILLIAM ROUGHEAD

THE case of Oscar Slater, alike in
its inception, its developments, and its results, is altogether exceptional. In no other murder trial has the supposed right man been
got upon an admittedly wrong clue. In no other murder trial has a
conviction been secured on evidence of identity alone, unsupported
by other facts and circumstances inferring the accused's guilt. In no
other murder trial has the case been reopened and the verdict
quashed after well-nigh twenty years.

The conduct of criminal prosecutions by the police of this realm
was subjected to severe criticism, but recent revelations furnish no
incident more deplorable than what occurred here: the abandon-
ment by the Glasgow authorities of an obvious line of inquiry in
order to pursue, with uncommendable zeal, the object of official
suspicion. Another ugly aspect of the affair was the persistent refusal
of successive Scottish Secretaries to do anything to satisfy the
repeated demands for further investigation – the granting of the
secret inquiry of 1914 was hampered by such absurd restrictions as
to prevent, rather than facilitate, discovery of the truth. Firmly
entrenched behind its red-tape entanglements, the Circumlocution
Office repulsed all attacks, until the intensive campaign in the
autumn of 1927 resulted in sudden and complete surrender. The
convict was released, a special Act of Parliament was passed to
allow his case to be heard by the Scottish Court of Criminal Appeal,
and the man who had been reprieved within twenty-four hours of
the scaffold, and who had spent the best years of his life labouring
in the quarries of Peterhead, was found, after all, to have been

illegally convicted, and was given a solatium of £6,000, out of which he was expected to pay the costs of proving to the world the fact of his wrongous imprisonment.

Not the least striking episode in this long legal tragedy was the presence of Slater himself at the hearing of his appeal in the very courtroom where nineteen years before he had received sentence of death. That is a situation hardly to be bettered by our most sensational fictionists, and one which amply vindicates the superiority of truth. It is also a singular reflection that the man who was then formally doomed to die upon a certain specified date outlived the Judge who sentenced him, the Lord Advocate who prosecuted him, and most of the other actors who played their several parts in the drama of his condemnation.

Everybody must by this time know something about Miss Gilchrist's murder. No other case has been so fully and so frequently discussed in press and Parliament for such a long period of years. It is sufficient, therefore, here and now to recall only the more salient features of the affair.

At seven o'clock on the evening of Monday 21 December 1908 an old lady named Marion Gilchrist was slain in the dining-room of her flat at 15 Queen's Terrace, Glasgow, in circumstances of unexampled savagery, during the ten minutes' absence from the house of her servant girl Helen Lambie. The venerable victim was in two respects a singular woman – she kept concealed among her clothes in her wardrobe jewels to the value of £3,000; and so apprehensive was she of unauthorized intrusion that her house door was fortified with double locks, in addition to the customary defences. By arrangement with the Adams family, who lived in the flat below, she was to knock upon the floor should she at any time require assistance. That night the brother and sisters Adams heard 'a noise from above, and then a very heavy fall and then three sharp knocks'. Mr Adams went upstairs and rang the bell. He heard a sound 'as if it was someone chopping sticks', and returned to his own house. The strange noises continuing – 'the ceiling was like to crack' – his sisters sent him up again, and his hand was on the bell when he was joined by the maid, coming back from her errand. She opened the door with her two keys, and was making for the kitchen when a man emerged from the bedroom, passed behind her, and approaching Adams in the doorway 'quite pleasantly', rushed downstairs 'like greased lightning'. Now, it is remarkable that Lambie, in these suggestive circumstances, expressed neither surprise nor fear. She had left her aged and timid mistress alone; Adams had warned her that 'there was something seriously wrong'. She finds in the well-guarded house a stranger, who flees from it in haste; yet she says nothing, and, instead of at once running into the dining-room to see if the old lady was safe, she proceeds to inspect the kitchen and the bedroom; nor until Adams asks, 'Where is your mistress?' does she enter the fatal room. Her conduct has been characterized as inexplicable; but there is one hypothesis which would account for her behaviour, namely, that she knew the man. Mr Adams's impression was that he was a visitor familiar with the house. In the dining-room on the hearth-rug, lay the body of the old lady, her head horribly smashed, and the fireplace spattered with her blood. In the bedroom it appeared that the murderer had lit the gas – he left behind him for the assistance of the police his own 'Runaway' matches; and a wooden box in which Miss Gilchrist kept her private papers had been broken open by him and the contents scattered on the floor. Diamond and other rings, a gold bracelet, and a gold watch and chain lay exposed to view upon the dressing-table; yet the only jewel that this remarkable robber had seen fit to appropriate was a diamond crescent brooch, which, according to Lambie, had lain in the toilet dish with the other jewellery, though its presence there was not otherwise established. The expert in detective fiction will perceive in the methods of this inconsiderate burglar certain unusual features. Adams and Lambie in their turn now ran downstairs. They saw no one in the street – an important point in view of the evidence given later by the third person of the identifying trinity. Adams summoned his own doctor, who lived over the way; Lambie went to advise Miss Birrell, a cousin of Miss Gilchrist, of what had happened. The terms of her communication will be discussed hereafter. When Dr Adams – he was not related to the other Adams – came on the scene he examined the body, found that life was extinct, and communicated with the police by telephone. His observation of the dining-room led him to form a very definite opinion as to the means whereby the injuries had been inflicted, a theory of which we shall hear further in the sequel.

From the joint account given by Adams and Lambie the police were able to publish a description of the wanted man: 'A man between twenty-five and thirty years of age, five feet eight or nine inches in height, slim build, dark hair, clean-shaven; dressed in light grey overcoat and dark cloth cap. Cannot be further described.'

But that he could be further described presently appeared. A little message-girl of fourteen, named Mary Barrowman, returning home late on the evening of the crime, told her mother that as she passed the scene of the murder a man rushed from the house, knocked up against her, and ran out of her sight into West Cumberland Street, towards Woodlands Road. It was seven o'clock of a dark and rainy December night in a street indifferently lighted, and she had but a momentary glimpse of the fleeing man; yet this intelligent juvenile observer was able to supply much fuller particulars than were the two adults who had seen him walking quietly across the gas-lit hall. 'The man wanted is about twenty-eight or thirty years of age, tall and thin, with his face shaved clear of all hair, while a distinctive feature is that his nose is lightly turned to one side. The witness thinks the twist is to the right side. He wore one of the popular round tweed hats known as Donegal hats, and a fawn-coloured overcoat, which might have been a waterproof, also dark trousers and brown boots.'

While these several descriptions are fresh in the reader's mind, it were well that he keep in view the following facts. Slater was then in his thirty-ninth year, of medium height – five feet eight inches and heavy build, conspicuously broad-shouldered and deep-chested, with a short black moustache and a nose which, though high-bridged, turned neither to right nor left. But the arresting note of his personality, and that which struck the most casual observer of the man, was, despite his twenty years' residence as an involuntary stranger within our gates, his unmistakably foreign aspect; and this, oddly enough, each of these three witnesses failed to notice. In view of the discrepancies as to clothing, etc., the authorities at first naturally and properly assumed that these descriptions referred to two different men, and notices to that effect were issued to the various police stations throughout the city. But the course of events soon led them to change their minds, and, like Mr Pott's contributor, to 'combine their information'.

On Friday 25 December, a cycle-dealer named McLean informed the police that a 'German Jew' known to him as 'Oscar' had been offering for sale in the Sloper Club, India Street, a pawn ticket for a diamond crescent brooch. If this were indeed the murderer disposing of his spoil, he must have taken leave of his senses, for all Glasgow was agog about the missing brooch; but the authorities, abandoning the line they had hitherto adopted, namely, that the murderer was someone personally known to his victim, set off hotfoot upon this fresh scent. It appeared that Slater, under the name of Anderson, occupied a flat at 69 St George's Road; and, on inquiry, that he had left Glasgow with a lady friend and no less than nine trunks that very night for Liverpool. The order of their going was sufficiently open – a porter was employed to uplift their considerable baggage, a cab was hired to the Central Station, the luggage was labelled 'Liverpool', and tickets were taken for that place. The police afterwards maintained that, in furtherance of 'the flight from justice', Slater travelled with London tickets and changed carriages *en route*; but this, as we shall find, he was able to disprove. At the North Western Hotel, Liverpool, he registered himself in the hotel books as 'Oscar Slater, Glasgow', and the same day with his companion sailed in the *Lusitania* for New York.

Meanwhile the authorities had discovered to their dismay that their 'clue' brooch had been in continuous pawn since 18 November, five weeks before the murder, and, regrettably, therefore, had no connection with the crime. But the official mind, once made up, is not subject to change, so a reward of £200 was offered and a warrant obtained for Slater's apprehension, which was cabled to New York.

Before we too cross the Atlantic in pursuit, let us hear what little
is known about the antecedents of the wanted man. Oscar Joseph
Leschziner was born in the early 1870s of Jewish parents at Oppeln,
in Germany. His father, he tells us, was a baker, and carried on
business at Beuthen. He was one of six children. Apprenticed to a
timber merchant at fifteen, Oscar later became a bank clerk in
Hamburg; but on reaching military age, and being averse from
serving the Fatherland in the field, he forsook his fellow-countrymen
and came to England. London seems to have been his base, but
indeed he had no continuing city. He began as a bookmaker's
clerk, and became himself a bookmaker. We hear of him in London
and in Edinburgh, twice in New York and twice in Glasgow, before
his last ill-omened visit. His own name being unpronounceable by
Anglo-Saxon tongues, he adopted that of Slater as easier for all
parties, varying it, as occasion called, by those of George, Anderson,
and Sando. For ordinary business and professional folk one surname
usually suffices; but Slater was not of their company. He specialized
in the running of social clubs the sociability of which consisted in
facilities for gaming. In New York, for example, he ran successfully
such a popular resort in Sixth Avenue, known as the Italian American Gun Club, the sporting character of which is to be inferred
from its name. Of his private life all we know is that he married in
1902, that he subsequently separated from his wife, and that he
made in London, at the Empire, the acquaintance of a French lady
named Andrée Junio Antoine, professionally known as Madame
Junio, with whom he formed a left-handed alliance. She accompanied him to the Continent and later to America whither they
journeyed under the names of 'Mr and Mrs A. George'. In New
York, in association with a man named Devoto, he ran a club at
114 West Twenty-Sixth Street. They remained in America for a
year, and then returned to England. In the beginning of November
1908 the couple, with the lady's German maid Catherine Schmalz,
went to Glasgow, where, after a week in lodgings, they set up house
in the flat at St George's Road, which was furnished on the instalment system. The door-plate bore the legend 'Anderson', and the
ostensible designation of the occupier was, 'dentist'; but on other of

his cards he designated himself as 'dealer in diamonds and precious stones'. Whatever gems the house may have contained it certainly possessed none of the dread apparatus of dentistry. *Enfin*, he was a gambler, living by his wits and by the lack of them in others; and his chief places of resort were certain billiard-rooms in Sauchiehall and Renfield Streets, and the Motor and Sloper Clubs in India Street, of the latter of which he was a member. It is to be kept in mind that the police had up to this point nothing against the man, and that he had never been in what is technically termed 'trouble'. His original statement to his legal advisers, the truth of which he protested from the dock in the awful pause following upon the verdict, was that he never heard the name of Miss Gilchrist, that he was unaware of the existence either of herself or of her jewels, and that he knew not where she lived. And, surprising as it may seem in view of his condemnation for her murder, no evidence sufficient to disprove the truth of his story has even to this day been produced.

In order to procure the extradition of Slater from the 'Land of Freedom' the Glasgow authorities left no stone unturned. Unless Adams, Lambie, and Barrowman could identify him as the man they had seen leaving the house, the game, so far as Slater was concerned, was up. The precarious, and as is now recognized improper, course was followed of exhibiting a photograph of the suspect – an unnecessary precaution as regards Lambie, who on the night of the murder had told Detective Officers Gordon and Pyper that she would not be able to identify the man. Much labour was bestowed upon the preparation of the declarations or sworn statements of witnesses. Lambie says of the number of times her statement was taken, 'It was more than I could tell you'; Barrowman says she was examined every day for a fortnight. Such devotion to the cause of truth met with due reward, for Lambie now came into line with Barrowman as to the character of the man's hat and the colour and quality of his coat. So the two men of the police notice, as to whom official warning had been expressly given that they should not be confounded, were conveniently reduced to one; the

84

dark cloth cap became a tweed Donegal hat, and the light-grey overcoat a fawn-coloured waterproof – which made it much simpler for all concerned. Lambie and Barrowman occupied the same cabin on the voyage to New York, but swore that during its twelve days' duration they never once mentioned the object of their journey nor discussed the appearance of the man. No doubt they felt that the subject was already exhausted before they left Glasgow.

The extradition proceedings at New York were conducted with that efficiency and thoroughness which mark American judicial procedure. The interests of the defendant were in the capable and experienced hands of Mr Hugh Gordon Miller, of the New York Bar, assisted by Mr William A. Goodhart. Mr Commissioner Shields presided; and Mr Charles Fox appeared for the demanding Government. Before the case came on Mr Fox, Inspector Pyper, and the three Glasgow witnesses happened by a fortunate chance to be stationed outside the courtroom door when Slater was brought down the corridor between two officers of the Court – Messrs Chamberlain and Pinckley, deputy United States marshals. It was contended by Mr Miller that Slater was obviously in the custody of those officials, but the witnesses denied that they had noticed the fact or that they were prepared to see 'the man' where they did. As to what then occurred there is a conflict of evidence; according to that given at the trial in Edinburgh both girls simultaneously exclaimed to Pyper, 'That's the man!' Nineteen years later, however, Mr Pinckley himself crossed the ocean to bear witness in the Appeal Court that Slater was actually handcuffed to him at the time, and that as he passed the group he heard Fox, pointing to the prisoner, say, 'Is that the man?' It is therefore not surprising that afterwards in the courtroom the witnesses were able formally to identify him. Lambie gave as the reason for the faith that was in her, 'I saw the walk; it is not the face I went by, but the walk.' And, being pressed upon this point, she admitted, 'I could not tell his face; I never saw his face.' Yet at the trial in Edinburgh Lambie was able to swear, 'I did see his face.' And when there asked by Slater's counsel, 'Why did you not say so in America?' her retort was, 'I am saying it now', an answer more rude than reasoned. Again, in the extradition

Court, on Mr Miller venturing to inquire why she and the other witnesses were stationed in the corridor, she replied, 'That was my business and none of yours.' On hearing of the appeal in Edinburgh one of the Judges commented unfavourably upon American methods, as exemplified in the cross-examination of Lambie by Mr Miller, and, in the words of the Gilbertian baronet, 'paragraphs got into all the papers'. His lordship's observations ruffled the plumage of the great American Eagle, that susceptible fowl; and, indeed, seeing that Mr Miller believed that Lambie was, to put it mildly, mistaken, and in view of her impudent demeanour in the box, I do not, with due respect, think that she was unfairly treated. One illuminating statement was elicited from this witness as to the way in which the murderer got into the house – a matter of vital consequence, which, strange to say, was quite lost sight of at the trial. Questioned by Mr Miller upon this point Lambie said, 'Miss Gilchrist must have opened the door.' Now, as the old lady never opened the door in the maid's absence without first reconnoitring the visitor, it would seem that the man who rang the bell was known to, and may even have been expected by her. The foreign-looking and slightly sinister-seeming Slater of that day would have found the door slammed and bolted before he was half-way up the stair. Mr Adams more than once in his evidence referred to the stranger as, 'a most gentlemanly-looking man'; he took him, he says, to be 'a male relative'. We shall see the application of this later. Mr Adams, a man of education and culture – he was by profession a musician – whose opportunity of observation was much better than that of the others – he saw the intruder face to face – never went further than that the defendant 'resembled' the man. But these two ignorant and irresponsible girls – one of whom repeatedly said she 'never saw his face', while the other said he 'knocked up against' her in the dark – were confident in their identification. Mr Miller having successfully exposed the deception of the false clue by proving that the missing brooch had one row of diamonds, while that pledged by the defendant had three rows, which was the foundation of the case against him, there remained only the evidence of identity, which in the circumstances the learned counsel held to be wholly inconclusive. He, therefore, advised his client to resist the application for extradition; but Slater insisted on going back to Scotland to face the charge. The result of his appeal unto Caesar we are now to consider.

The widespread interest and intense excitement which the case aroused in Glasgow produced an effect not unusual on such occasions. Divers worthy folk, 'thinking back', as the phrase goes, recalled that they had seen for weeks before the murder a suspicious character haunting the street and watching Miss Gilchrist's house. An auger, found in the back green, had attached to it certain grey hairs, cemented, as was officially stated, with what was believed to be blood, but which unfortunately proved to be rust. On Slater's return from New York his nine boxes were unsealed, and, behold, among his carefully packed suits was discovered a small tin-tack hammer, which, together with other lethal weapons – screw-driver, pliers, gimlet, and bradawl – he had purchased from the Woolworth of that day on a card of household tools for 2s. 6d. So the auger was dropped and the hammer became the *pièce de résistance*, the deadly instrument with which the head of this old lady had been smashed to pulp. A further happy and suggestive find was a waterproof overcoat, which, owing to the operations of the Glasgow climate, was not unnaturally weather-stained; it well might be, however, that this was due to the victim's blood! The considerate behaviour of the murderer in thus preserving for production by the Crown the very weapon and garment used by him in doing the deed ought to have been appreciated by the police. Be that as it may, no other incriminating article was traced to his possession.

On Monday 3 May 1909 the great trial began at Edinburgh. Lord Guthrie was the Judge; Mr Alexander Ure, then Lord Advocate, and afterwards Lord Strathclyde, assisted by the two deputes, personally conducted the prosecution; Mr McClure, with a junior, appeared for the defence. Of the twelve witnesses professing to identify the accused as the man who, for convenience, I shall term 'the watcher', it may be generally observed that none of them knew either him or Slater by sight, nor, with a single exception, did they

87

ever hear him speak. All of them had, prior to identifying him, seen or been shown newspaper photographs of Slater as an obvious foreigner and had read the descriptions of the man furnished by Adams, Lambie, and Barrowman. The one witness who was privileged to hold converse with the watcher stated, in reply to the Court, that she noticed nothing about his accent; she did not think he was a foreigner. Now, whether or not the other eleven identifiers were right, this one was clearly wrong, for nobody possessed of normal faculties could fail to note, on hearing Slater speak, that he was patently and unmistakably an alien. The way in which the Glasgow police conducted the identification was, to use no stronger term, unsatisfactory. Slater, a German Jew, was exhibited to the witnesses among eleven other men, nine being policemen in plain clothes and two being railway officials, none of whom in any way resembled him, and all of whom were Scots. When Mr McClure asked one of the police witnesses whether it would not be fairer to an accused person to place him among men who were more or less like him, that officer significantly replied, 'It might be the fairest way, but is not the practice in Glasgow.'

One has difficulty in seeing what object the watcher had in so persistently perambulating this quiet street, thereby inviting the attention of the neighbours and of casual passers-by. The Lord Advocate's explanation to the jury was that the murderer 'required as part of his elaborate precautions to familiarize himself with the inmates of the house, with their movements and their habits, and also with the movements of the police. There was one method, and one only, by which that object could be accomplished, and that was by careful, prolonged, and steady watching with a skilled eye.' Why this expert reconnaissance should have led him to select for the execution of his fell design the casual and temporary absence of the maid instead of her regular afternoon and evening out twice a week, his lordship failed to explain. In one instance only did the watcher and the murderer apparently coalesce. Mrs Liddell, a married sister of Mr Adams, saw a man standing in front of the house at five minutes to seven on the fatal night – the assassin awaiting the appointed hour – whom she identified by his profile as the accused. Unfortunately she went on to add that the man was wearing a heavy tweed overcoat, not a waterproof, and 'had the appearance of a delicate man'. She was very much surprised at Slater's robust build when she saw him at the police station; doubtless his health had benefited by the voyage.

Of the three crucial witnesses, Mr Adams repeated his testimony with the fairness and moderation which marked his evidence throughout. With regard to his qualified recognition of the accused, it must be borne in mind that he said he was short-sighted, and had not on his eyeglasses when he saw the stranger in the hall. The two girls, however, were even more positive than before – distance, as appears, lending precision to their view. When shown the accused's waterproof, Lambie swore it was the identical coat worn by the murderer: 'That *is* the coat.' Barrowman swore: 'This is the man who knocked against me that night.'

Over and above the classic example of Adolf Beck, in appraising the value of evidence based on personal impressions, we must remember how such testimony in the Broughty Ferry case of November 1912 well-nigh resulted in a judicial miscarriage. The murder of Miss Milne by an unknown assailant in many respects resembled the slaying of Miss Gilchrist: the age and peculiarities of the victim, the wanton ruthlessness of attack, the apparent absence of motive, the disregard of available spoil – these features recall the crime of Queen's Terrace. There, too, a strange man had been seen about the house; a suspect was secured and photographed by the English police; his photograph exhibited to the local Scots witnesses, was recognized by them at once; they were conveyed to Maidstone, where they unanimously identified the prisoner, a Colonial 'down-and-outer' named Warner, as 'the man'. These five perfectly respectable and honest witnesses were all prepared positively to swear away his life, and had the case gone to trial might successfully have done so; yet mark the sequel. By the honourable intervention of Detective Trench it was proved beyond dispute that the accused had been in Antwerp, and, providentially for his neck, had pawned his waistcoat at the very time of the murder.

*

The movements of Slater, from his coming to Glasgow in the beginning of November until his departure from that city on Christmas Day, were minutely traced in the evidence adduced. Little, if any, suspicion of felonious intent attaches to his actings during this period. It was proved that early in December, being dissatisfied with the commercial possibilities of Glasgow, and finding its inhabitants inapt for what he termed 'business', he decided to resume practice among the guileless denizens of the United States. The only question is: was his declared intention accelerated by the happenings at Queen's Terrace on 21 December?

He set about his preparations for removal with openness and deliberation. Three weeks before the murder he announced to sundry persons his purpose of departure. He exhibited a letter from his old partner, Devoto, advising him to come out to San Francisco where 'business' was good, and said that he would go so soon as he could get rid of the flat and furniture. His friend Aumann inspected the house with a view to taking it over, but decided not to do so. Then through Rogers, a friend in London, it was arranged that a Mrs Freedman and her sister should come to Glasgow; they arrived on Christmas morning, and Slater left that night. So early as lunch-time on the day of the murder Slater gave Schmalz, the maid, a week's notice. He was collecting all his available assets, and that same forenoon he raised a further and final £30 upon the pawned brooch; he posted £5 as a Christmas gift to his old folks in Germany; it seems, therefore, unlikely that, in the Lord Advocate's dramatic phrase, he was 'gasping and panting for money'.

As to the doing of the deed in the time at his disposal, his alibi was as good as, nay, better than, might have been expected from one of his unconventional mode of life. The murder was committed between 7 and 7.10 p.m. At 6.12, from the Central Station, he sent a telegram in his own handwriting to London for his watch; at 6.30, remarking to Rattman that he was going home to dinner, he left Johnston's billiard-rooms in Renfield Street, which is a considerable way from Queen's Terrace. As Aumann says he was then wearing a waterproof and a bowler, he must have been something of a quick-change artist to gain his house and don the heavy brown tweed overcoat and tweed cap in which Mrs Liddell saw him at the railings at 6.55. Antoine and Schmalz both swore he dined at home that night as usual at 7 o'clock, and there was no reason to suppose that they were perjured. From the evidence of the ticket girl who swore that Slater between 7.30 and 8 o'clock rushed through her turnstile at Kelvinbridge Railway Station – 'the last witness to see the murderer' – the Lord Advocate drew a lurid picture of the guilty man, with the hammer hugged in his pocket, fleeing headlong from the scene of his crime to bury himself in the bowels of Glasgow, 'and to be taken by a train to some remote part of the city and then come strolling back to his house'. But this fancy portrait faded away in the light of the later testimony of MacBrayne, the grocer's assistant, as we shall in due course find.

I remember, after the trial, expressing to the late Sir Edward Marshall Hall my amazement at the Lord Advocate's feat in making this prodigious speech without written notes; upon which Sir Edward had the dry retort: 'Possibly that accounts for its manifold inaccuracies.' Be that as it may, his lordship was betrayed by his zeal as prosecutor into one serious and reiterated mis-statement, namely, that Slater fled on Christmas night because his name and description were that day published in the Glasgow evening newspapers. Now, as a matter of fact, it was not until that very night that the police first learned from McLean of Slater's existence, nor until he was half-way across the Atlantic did his name appear in any of the papers. Other inexactitudes, though none more grave, will call for notice in their place.

It was essential to the success of the Crown case to connect with the crime the hammer and waterproof found in Slater's luggage. Dr Adams, the first medical man to see the body, not only was not called as a witness, but his name was omitted from the Crown list. We shall have a guess at the reason later. Professor Glaister and Dr Galt, who performed the post-mortem examination, gave evidence for the prosecution. From forty to sixty blows delivered with the hammer could, in their opinion, have produced the extensive injuries observed. Dr Galt, on cross-examination, admitted that, *a priori*, he should have expected a heavier weapon. They found no bloodstains on the hammer produced, nor upon the accused's waterproof; and Professor Harvey Littlejohn, who also examined those articles, was equally unsuccessful. It is noteworthy that the Lord Advocate asked him no question about the hammer; which, as one happens to know, had, in the professor's considered judgement, nothing to do with the case. For the defence Drs Aitchison, Robertson and Veitch said that they deemed the hammer a most unlikely instrument to inflict such fearful injuries; they found no blood upon it or on the waterproof.

From the servant Schmalz the Lord Advocate, in cross-examination, obtained an admission that her mistress – and Slater's – 'received gentlemen in the evening', and frequented the local music-halls, and from Cameron, that the witness 'had it' that Slater lived on the proceeds of prostitution. The damning use of this hearsay evidence made to the prejudice of the panel by the Lord Advocate and by the presiding Judge was ultimately by the Appeal Court held alone sufficient to vitiate the conviction. The accused did not go into the witness-box. His agent afterwards stated 'that he was all along anxious to give evidence on his own behalf. He was advised by his counsel not to do so.' His purely negative testimony would, in their opinion, have served no purpose. But in so advising their client they underestimated the increased prejudice against him which such abstention might probably, and did in fact, produce.

Of the failure of the prosecution to adduce evidence known to them, favourable to the accused; of the conspicuous flaws which mar the fairness of the Lord Advocate's address; and of the shortcomings of the judicial charge, I now say nothing; we shall hear enough of these matters when we come to the inquiry and to the appeal. But a word may be said regarding the manner of the speech for the Crown. The dominating personality of Mr Ure, the unrivalled and irresistible force of his advocacy, the astonishing power of memory displayed by him in his two-hour address, delivered without pause or notes in a case of such complexity – these were of themselves apt to take captive the intelligence of a jury. I wrote of the speaker at the time: 'That he was convinced of the justice of his cause was manifest'; and upon this point we have an enlightening word in the tribute to Lord Strathclyde written on his death by his old friend and colleague, Lord Alness. His lordship observes: 'Some advocates are obsessed by doubts and by difficulties, Ure had none. Some are perturbed by considerations of the strength of the other side. For Ure there was no other side. He believed implicitly and invincibly in the strength of his own case; he could not see that any other view than his was possible.' Doubtless an invaluable gift, this, in a civil pleader; but one, I venture to think, dangerous and to be deprecated in a public prosecutor.

The speech for the defence suffered unduly in popular esteem by comparison with the perfervid rhetoric of the Lord Advocate, and posterity has not yet done justice to Mr McClure's handling of a most responsible and difficult case. The prejudice against his client was very bitter, the financial resources of the defence were negligible, and counsel was uninstructed upon many points, since brought to light, which, had he known of them, would immensely have strengthened his hand. But even with the imperfect material at his disposal, Mr McClure made a gallant and effective fight, and, but for the adverse conditions above referred to, would probably have obtained for his client a verdict of acquittal. The Lord Advocate, however, won the day; the jury by a majority found the panel Guilty, and, amid a scene rendered unspeakably painful by the prisoner's passionate protestations of innocence, the Court passed sentence of death. The voting was as follows: For Guilty, nine; for Not Proven, five; and for Not Guilty, one. Had two more jurymen been able to withstand the eloquence of the Lord Advocate, Slater would have been set free.

Public Opinion, that inconstant nymph, had from the first looked unfavourably on the accused's chances of escape. Now that he was safely condemned, this attitude was reversed. The atmosphere of excitement, rumour, and suspicion inseparable from a sensational murder case began to clear; and people realized that the weak links in the evidential chain by which the conviction had been secured were neither few nor far between. It was noted, for example, that nothing was said as to how the murderer got into the house, and that not the least knowledge by Slater of Miss Gilchrist and her hoard was even attempted to be shown. The Lord Advocate indeed had promised the jury to satisfy them upon this crucial point: 'We shall see in the sequel how it was that the prisoner came to know that she was possessed of these jewels'; but this was to beg the whole question, for his lordship said not another word on the subject, although, both for him and for the accused, it was one of paramount importance.

A petition for commutation of the extreme penalty was forthwith presented to the Secretary of Scotland (Lord Pentland) on the grounds that the evidence identifying the prisoner with the murderer was insufficient to justify the verdict, and that the accused's alleged immoral character was improperly brought before the jury and must have influenced their judgment. The petition bore over 20,000 signatures. A memorial was also prepared by the prisoner's law agent and forwarded to the Secretary, together with the deposition of Agnes Brown, a witness who was not called at the trial, though her name was included in the Crown list. The point of this lady's evidence is this: she was a school teacher, thirty years of age. At the hour of the murder, being in West Princes Street near Miss Gilchrist's house, two men rushed past her and disappeared down Rupert Street, towards Great Western Road. Neither of them was dressed like Barrowman's fugitive, who, it must be remembered, ran in a different direction. One of these men wore a navy-blue Melton overcoat with a velvet collar, and him Miss Brown afterwards identified with the accused. Beyond adding a new colour to the murderer's coat – which already in respect of hues resembled that of Joseph – the school mistress does not teach us much; but her testimony, if produced, would have been destructive of the message girl's evidence; so, as Mary Barrowman was the Crown's strongest card, Agnes Brown was suffered to remain in the seclusion of the witnesses' room, unsworn, unexamined, and unheard.

The execution was fixed for 27 May, and the usual preparations for that ceremony were duly made. Not until the night of the 25th did the Glasgow authorities receive official information that their labour was in vain. In deciding to commute the death sentence to penal servitude for life, the Scottish Secretary consulted the Lord Chancellor (Lord Loreburn), Mr (afterwards Lord) Haldane, then Minister for War, and Lord Guthrie, who tried the case. I am informed that, although his legal advisers were against a reprieve, Lord Pentland, a layman, was so dissatisfied with the conviction that he overruled their objections – which is not less creditable to his lordship's judgment than fortunate for Slater's neck. Questions were naturally asked in the House of Commons as to the grounds for this anomalous decision, but the Lord Advocate refused to give any information. The convict was sent to Peterhead, where he was to pass the next nineteen years of his life; and the £200 reward offered for his conviction was apportioned as follows: Mary Barrowman, £100; John Forsyth, £40; Allan McLean, £40; and Gordon Henderson, £20 – all witnesses for the prosecution.

The first edition of the report of the trial was published in April 1910, in the Notable British Trials series, affording to those who cared to study the peculiarities presented by the Crown case ample opportunity to do so. 'We march from puzzle to puzzle, and from perplexity we at no point escape,' wrote Andrew Lang, who twice reviewed the volume, and was greatly taken with the problem therein presented. 'One thing is clear: a legal case of the highest importance may be accepted as proved, in face of discrepancies of testimony which would leave a ghost story without a chance of acceptance by scientific minds.' And in a private letter he characteristically expressed the opinion that upon such evidence 'a cat would scarcely be whipped for stealing cream'.

Among other men of letters attracted by the subject was Sir Arthur Conan Doyle. That paladin of lost causes found in the dubious circumstances of the case matter after his own heart. *The Times* and the *Spectator* opened their columns to a discussion of the verdict, and many distinguished authorities, including Sir Herbert Stephen, supported Sir Arthur's contention that there had been a gross miscarriage of justice. Sir Arthur further contributed to the cause a little booklet, *The Case of Oscar Slater*, in which the ingenious and popular creator of Sherlock Holmes appealed to the wide audience at his command. Over and above what have long since become the stock features of the mystery, the author made the new and interesting point that some document, such as a will – not jewels – was the object of the murderer's quest, the abstraction of the brooch – if it in fact were stolen – being but a blind.

Edward Marshall Hall, who, as one happens to know, held very strong views on the subject, asked in the House of Commons on 10 December 1912 the following questions: Was the Scottish Secretary aware that the verdict upon which Slater was convicted was a majority verdict of three in a jury of fifteen? That certain witnesses to his identity whose precognitions had been taken by the Crown were not called at the trial? That the speech of the counsel for the prosecution contained inaccurate statements of fact? And, in view of the general uneasiness as to the justice of the verdict would he, the Secretary, state what steps he proposed to take? The Secretary for Scotland (Mr McKinnon Wood) replied (in Parliamentary language) that he proposed to take none.

The campaign in the press was continued; but no further development took place until March 1914, when Mr David Cook, writer, Glasgow, presented to the Scottish Secretary certain statements in support of an application for inquiry. The questions raised by these documents were as follows:

(1) Did any witness to the identification on the night of the murder name a person other than Oscar Slater?
(2) Were the police aware that such was the case? If so, why was the evidence not forthcoming at the trial?
(3) Did Slater fly from justice?
(4) Were the police in possession of information that Slater had disclosed his name at the North Western Hotel, Liverpool, stating where he came from and that he was travelling by the s.s. *Lusitania*?
(5) Did one of the witnesses make a mistake as to the date on which she stated she was in West Princes Street (Queen's Terrace)?

So serious were the allegations contained in these statements that not even a Secretary of State was able to ignore them, and it was intimated that Mr Gardner Millar, K.C., Sheriff of Lanarkshire, had been appointed as Commissioner to conduct an Inquiry into their truth and to report. This singular inquisition, known to history as 'The Secret Inquiry', was held in private in the County Buildings, Glasgow, on 23 to 25 April 1914, the only persons present through-out the proceedings being the Commissioner, his Clerk, and the several witnesses examined. The prisoner was not represented, but the Commissioner gratefully acknowledged the assistance given to him by the Chief Constable and the Procurator-Fiscal of Glasgow. As the original case against Slater had been got up – I use the term in no sinister sense – by those officials, it may be assumed that they were unlikely to be prejudiced in his favour. The purport of the evidence of each compearing witness was dictated by the Commissioner to his Clerk; and the result was afterwards issued as a Parliamentary Paper.

This being in effect a Court of Criminal Appeal, such as Scotland had still long to wait for, it is unfortunate that the conditions under which it was held can only be described as Gilbertian. The proceedings, we have seen, were conducted in secret without the presence personally, or by agent, of the prisoner; the witnesses were not upon oath; the Commissioner omitted from their evidence such passages as he deemed undesirable, whether in the interests of the Crown or of the prisoner does not appear; and it had been specifically ordained that his investigations 'should in no way relate to the conduct of the trial'. Compared with the restrictions by which this quest for truth was handicapped, the task set by Pharaoh to the captive Israelites was fair and reasonable. Before we consider the result of this inquisitional feat there is something to be said as to how it came to be performed.

John Thomson Trench, sometime detective-lieutenant in the City of Glasgow Police Force, and King's Medallist for meritorious services, had during his twenty-one years of duty deservedly enjoyed the reputation of a trustworthy, capable, and efficient officer. So signal was his fame that he was upon occasion 'borrowed' by the police of other towns – as in the Broughty Ferry affair – to advise in cases of especial difficulty. Now Trench, rightly or wrongly, but assuredly in all honesty, was from the first convinced that the Glasgow authorities were following a false trail in their pursuit of Slater as the assassin of Miss Gilchrist. He believed and averred that on the night of the crime Lambie had named another man, known to her as the 'stranger' she had seen in the lobby. But his chiefs, who originally held the view that the murderer was someone with whom his victim was acquainted, went off upon the false 'brooch' clue, which led to the wrong man: *hinc illae lacrymae*. Convinced that Slater had been unjustly condemned, his conscience gave him no rest; his experience of the Broughty Ferry business confirmed his distrust of identification based on personal impressions; he looked into the case again, and the more he looked the less he liked it. But his official duty was plain; Slater must be left for life in Peterhead. Finally, he felt unable to support the burden of his knowledge, and as it were vain to attempt to convince his superiors, he took counsel with Mr Cook, an experienced Glasgow writer, as to what he ought to do. The lawyer believed his tale and advised him in the interests of justice publicly to tell it. But Trench, justly fearing the consequences to himself which should follow any disclosure by him of the secrets of the prison-house, would not move in the matter without some guarantee of personal safety. Dr Devon, one of H.M. Prison Commissioners for Scotland, was approached, and that gentleman wrote to the Scottish Secretary (Mr McKinnon Wood), who replied on 13 February 1914: 'If the constable mentioned in your letter will send me a written statement of the evidence in his possession of which he spoke to you, I will give this matter my best consideration.' This letter was naturally regarded by Trench as authorizing him to give the information; he did so and the outcome of his action was 'The Secret Inquiry'.

Scholiasts differ as to the nature of the unforgivable sin: there is no such dubiety in Glasgow. 'It is contrary to all police practice for an officer to communicate to persons outside the police force information which he has acquired in the course of his duty'; and for this crime Trench was, on 14 September 1914, dismissed with ignominy from that constabulary of which he had been so long such a distinguished member. He enlisted in the Royal Scots Fusiliers; and at Stirling on 13 May 1915, the day before the regiment was to leave for Gallipoli, Provost-Sergeant Trench was arrested by the police on a charge of reset, i.e. receiving stolen goods. The same day Mr Cook was apprehended in Glasgow upon a like charge. They were not brought to trial till 17 August 1915, although the alleged offence had been committed on 19 January 1914! The charge arose out of the recovery by these gentlemen through an intermediary of certain articles of jewellery burglariously stolen from a Glasgow shop, the loss of which was covered by insurance. So grateful were the insurance company that they wrote to the Chief Constable, thanking him for 'the good offices of Detective Trench' in the matter, and suggesting that that officer should receive a reward! At the trial in Edinburgh before the Lord Justice-Clerk (Scott Dickson), the Judge told the jury it was clearly proved that Trench acted throughout with the knowledge of his superiors, and also with innocent or even meritorious intention. His lordship therefore directed them to acquit both prisoners, which was unanimously done, and the accused were discharged. Neither of the victims of this baseless and vindictive prosecution ever fully recovered from its effects. Trench rejoined his regiment, and served with distinction till the end of the war; he died on the fourth anniversary of his arrest. Mr Cook died two years later.

We must now return to 'The Street Inquiry'; and, knowing the evil which in this regard it so grievously wrought, let us see whether in other respects it was productive of any good.

As the result of the Commissioner's labours was issued in the form of a Government White Paper, it is here only necessary to direct the reader's attention to one or two points arising upon that singular publication. First, as regards the mysterious personage designated through the proceedings by the initials 'A. B.', whose identity was as scrupulously veiled as that of 'Mr A.', of the later *cause célèbre*, although there is no reason to believe that he was an oriental potentate. This, Trench declared, was the man named by Lambie to Miss Birrell, an acquaintance of Miss Gilchrist, on the night of the crime as the murderer of her mistress; and it is common ground that, whatever be his real name, it was not Oscar Slater. It will be noticed that when and wherever the witnesses touch upon this elusive personality there are always *lacunae* in their evidence, indicated, as the Commissioner informs us, by asterisks. So that even now we are not allowed to hear what they actually said about him. Both Miss Birrell and Lambie denied that the statements attributed to them by Trench were ever made: and his superior officers also denied that he was sent by them to Miss Birrell, or that he reported to them the result. But it is otherwise proved that Lambie did bring to Miss Birrell that night the news of the murder; that two police officers did interview that lady next day and took a statement from her; and that Trench did visit her for the like purpose. Chief Inspector Cameron corroborated Trench as to the latter's mission to Miss Birrell and stated that Trench told him at the time 'that Miss Birrell had said to him that the girl Lambie had said to her on the night of the murder that the man who had passed her in the lobby was like "A. B." '; and that Trench also told him (Cameron) that he had reported the matter to his superiors, who said it had been cleared up, and there was nothing in it. It appears from the evidence of three of the police chiefs that the movements of 'A. B.' were strictly inquired into after the murder. Why this was done when neither Trench, Miss Birrell, nor Lambie had mentioned his name we are not informed. There are surely some more asterisks here. And why was not one word of all this put to the witnesses at the trial, when they were on oath and could be cross-examined?

It is instructive to learn how this matter strikes an impartial observer; and the following excerpts from an article, 'But Who Killed Miss Gilchrist?' by Mr Philip Whitwell Wilson in the *North American Review* (November 1928), will be read with interest:

There is one question which has been for years in the mind of everyone who has studied the details of this case. Slater, though innocent, has suffered eighteen years of rigorous imprisonment. Trench, though disinterested, has been hounded into disgrace and death. Free use has been made of their names. Many men and women, unwillingly involved in this case, have had to face the music.

There is one man, among all these men and women, whose name must never be mentioned. Moslems of devout scruple are careful not to pronounce the awful syllables which indicate the Deity. A similar privilege has been extended by the authority of the law to the gentleman, whoever he may be, respectfully indicated by the letters 'A.B.' Approach this distinguished person, dead or alive, with all reverence. He is sacrosanct. Even Parliament must not dare to inquire into the identity of this carefully guarded and illustrious recluse. Who is 'A. B.'? Or who was he in the year 1908? Until the whole of the memorandum of John Trench is published, without either asterisks or other devices for hiding that to which the public opinion of two nations is entitled, the restless spirit of Miss Gilchrist will continue to haunt the halls where justice was denied to her memory.

With regard to 'the flight from justice' it was now proved that Slater travelled with Liverpool tickets and registered at the hotel there as 'Oscar Slater, Glasgow'. These facts were communicated to the Glasgow police on 4 January 1909, and Superintendent Ord at the inquiry stated: 'We passed on all this information to the Procurator-Fiscal.' Yet for some reason unexplained it failed to reach the jury at the trial. The next point dealt with was that raised by Trench respecting the contradictory statements of Mary Barrowman as to her movements on the night of the murder, from which he inferred that it was physically impossible she could have seen the fugitive. Agnes Brown, the lady who saw two men fleeing from the house, as already mentioned, was at last allowed to tell her story, which, if accepted, is subversive of little Mary's fairy tale.

There remains one new witness whose statement is not only in itself important, but has the merit, unique in this connection, of not being flatly contradicted by somebody else – Duncan Mac-Brayne. He was employed in a grocer's shop with which Slater dealt, and knew his customer personally. At 8.15 on the night of the murder – he was able satisfactorily to fix the date and hour – he passed Slater, calmly standing at the street door of his own house in St George's Road. Slater being extradited, MacBrayne informed the police, and was shown the suspect at the police station. Their recognition was mutual, Slater remarking, 'Oh, you are the man in the big shop in Sauchiehall Street.' Now, even a layman can see that this was real identification, very different from much of the stuff accepted as such at the trial; yet MacBrayne's name is not in the Crown list of witnesses, and the defence had at the time no knowledge of his existence. Put in the box, this witness would have confounded the girl at the turnstile and discounted the Motor Club master; and it is doubly unfortunate that, with MacBrayne's pre-cognition before him, the Lord Advocate should have allowed him-self to tell the jury: 'We know nothing of the man's movements until a quarter to ten at night, when he appears, excited, at the Motor Club in India Street.'

The White Paper, issued by the Government on 27 June 1914, two months after the close of the inquiry, had a bad press. The state of the new evidence only made the pristine darkness of the case more visible, and nobody was pleased – except the police. One journal petulantly complained that had the original programme for Slater's disposal but been carried out as arranged, 'there would have been no more about it'; which seems ungracious to one who had for so many years supplied the newspapers with copy. Questioned in the House, the Scottish Secretary replied: 'After careful consideration of the matter, I am satisfied that no case is established that would justify me in advising any interference with the sentence.' Nothing remained to be done, therefore, but to see that Messrs Trench and Cook, who had caused the Glasgow authorities so much unnecessary annoyance, should be punished for their presumption; and this, as we have seen, was adequately accomplished.

Before we take leave of Detective-Lieutenant Trench the reader may care to know the theory of so acute and able an officer touching what really happened in Queen's Terrace on that momentous De-cember night of 1908, as communicated by him to his friend, Wil-liam Park, who published it in his study of the case, *The Truth about Oscar Slater*:

The man who called at the house when the servant had gone out for the newspaper was on intimate terms of relationship with the victim. There was between them, however, a feud of some bitter sort. (A relative declared before the 1914 Commissioner that the deceased was not on friendly terms with certain people.) His object in coming to the house was to force her to yield up some document which she possessed and in which he was interested. He came without intention to murder, and he brought with him no weapon. His visit was to her unexpected. He rang the bell and was admitted by Miss Gilchrist . . .

A quarrel ensued; the visitor struck her, and she fell.

In the act of falling her head came in violent contact with the coal-box; the bone of the skull was penetrated on the side of the head. (The coal-box showed signs afterwards of blood, and was itself broken and displaced from its earlier position.) He saw she had been badly stunned and was making no signs to rise. He stooped down, quickly examined her, and judged there was a grave danger of fatal consequences, but not just at once. He was aware that if she survived beyond ten minutes, which seemed a certainty, and the maid were to reappear, his name would be disclosed, and, in the event of death ensuing, he would be accused of murder . . .

He lost his head, and decided to silence her for ever. 'He seized a chair and hacked at the prostrate woman, in his haste to extinguish life and get away before Lambie reappeared on the scene . . .'

When the bell rang, he knew that someone else had come to the door, Lambie having the keys, and so he went on, not desisting until satisfied she was far beyond the possibility of utterance. Even then he still delayed his exit. There was a paper in the box of which he wanted possession. If it were to remain, probably its contents would throw suspicion upon him. So he went into the bedroom where he knew she kept the documents, broke open the box, and removed the paper he desired. He then slipped out unchallenged – because the servant knew him, and his presence allayed rather than excited her suspicion.

It has often struck me how strangely certain features of this murder resemble the circumstances of that other most famous one in Dostoevsky's *Crime and Punishment*. The scene: the staircase, the empty flat – here above, there below; the victim: the strange old woman, Alyona Ivanovna; the situation of the murderer: Raskolnikov waiting breathless behind the bolted door, while the violent pealing of the bell rings through the silent house. I have sometimes wondered whether, had Lambie returned alone, she might not have shared the fate of hapless Lizaveta. But the parallel is incomplete, for Porfiry Petrovich, the Petersburg official, is rather better versed in criminal psychology and the arts of police detection than Superintendent Ord and the other Zametovs of Glasgow.

That the crime was unpremeditated and in some sort accidental, originating in personal animus and dispute, is probable enough. Trench's theory as to the weapon, too, is not only a likely one, but is supported by expert opinion. Dr Adams, the first medical man to see the body, who contrary to practice was not called as a witness for the Crown, was satisfied at the time, from the condition of the chair on which the old lady had been sitting, that the back leg thereof, then dripping as he observed with blood, had been used to inflict the injuries.

The years wore slowly on – terrible years for the convict in the compulsory peace of Peterhead, if he were really guiltless of shedding innocent blood; terrible years for his unconvicted fellows outside, suffering each in his own way the long agonies of the war. 'From time to time,' wrote Sir Arthur Conan Doyle, 'one hears some word of poor Slater from behind his prison walls, like the wail of some wayfarer who has fallen into a pit and implores aid from the passers-by.' But mankind had other things to think about; what mattered one individual wrong amid the huge welter of iniquities in which the world was plunged?

Not till the spring of 1925, when Slater had served over fifteen years of his commuted sentence, does the mass of press cuttings regarding the case which has accumulated yield anything of importance. In February of that year Slater contrived to send Sir Arthur a letter, begging him to make one more effort for the writer's release. Written upon a scrap of glazed paper from the prison bindery, it was smuggled outside by a discharged prisoner, in a tiny roll hidden under his tongue. This incident moved Sir Herbert Stephen, the eminent jurist who had so often championed Slater's cause, to write an article in which, after reviewing the facts, he observed: 'I still hold that no English judge would have allowed the case to go to the jury ... I do not doubt that he [Slater] was sentenced to death, and has been punished ever since, because he did not appear as a witness, upon evidence on which I suppose that no bench of magistrates in England would make an order for the destruction of a terrier which was alleged to have bitten somebody' – which is painful hearing for Scots lawyers. Fortified by this opinion, Sir Arthur wrote once more to the Secretary of State for Scotland (Sir John Gilmour) entreating his personal attention to the case, 'which,' he prophetically pronounced, 'is likely to live in the annals of criminology', and pointing out that 'the man has now served fifteen years, which is, as I understand, the usual limit of a life sentence in Scotland when the prisoner behaves well'. On 28 February the Scottish Office replied that the Secretary 'does not feel justified in advising any interference with Slater's sentence'. Sir Arthur, in acknowledging this letter, wrote: 'I have done my best to set this injustice right. The responsibility must now rest with you.' And again official silence fell upon the affair.

Future historians of the Slater case will date the turn of the tide in his favour from the publication, in July 1927, of William Park's book, *The Truth about Oscar Slater*. Mr Park, who unhappily did not live to share in the triumph of the cause to which he had devoted himself unsparingly for so many years, and of which the ultimate success was largely due to his indefatigable labours in the interests of justice, was a Glasgow journalist and a friend of Mr Trench. The first result was a strong leading article in the *Morning Post* of 1 August 1927, and a review of the book in that issue by Edgar Wallace. From his study of the case this expert in the mysteries of crime remarks of Lambie and the 'stranger' in the hall: 'Obviously she knew him. As obviously, to my mind, the murderer was in the house when she left, ostensibly to buy a newspaper.' And of the trial he writes: 'Nothing was said of the bloodstained chair, because it did not fit in with the case that had been manufactured against Slater. No questions were asked of Lambie that were in any way inconvenient to the prosecution.' A copy of the book had been sent to the Secretary of State for Scotland, and on 29 July the Lord Advocate (the Right Hon. William Watson, K.C.), questioned in the House regarding a press report that an inquiry was to be granted, replied that, if it were, he should be very much surprised. His lordship was destined to experience that sensation.

September saw the controversy revived with old-time vigour. The *Solicitors' Journal* took a hand, and other papers followed suit. 'Now, we all know that if anything is ever done in any way towards improvement in these days, the public press does it,' wrote Anthony Trollope in 1858; and seventy years later the saying still held good. As the Scottish Office refused or delayed to do anything, the *Daily News* decided to make its own investigation; and a special commissioner, familiar to the reading public by his pen-name of 'The Pilgrim', went up to Scotland for that purpose. The series of articles contributed by this gentleman to his journal, which began to appear on 16 September, written from first-hand knowledge, with admirable force and clearness, undoubtedly played no small part in bringing about Slater's liberation. They were continued daily till 19 October, and the editorial comment upon their completion was this: 'We do not think that anyone can have read our special correspondent's deadly analysis day by day of the evidence in the Oscar Slater case without being convinced that this unfortunate man is really the victim of a scandalous miscarriage of justice . . . that nothing should have been done in all these years, when the truth could have been so easily elicited through official channels, is a grave reflection on the British system of justice.'

On Sunday 23 October the *Empire News* published a document which was acclaimed as 'one of the most dramatic developments in a criminal case ever recorded'. This purported to be a statement by Helen Lambie, but no information was given as to the circumstances in which it was made. She admits that she knew the man in the hall as one who was in the habit of visiting her mistress; that she mentioned his name to the police, but was told that it was 'nonsense'; that the police persuaded her that she was mistaken; and that, as Slater was not unlike the man, she was led to identify him instead. She gives interesting particulars of former visits by other men whom her mistress did not allow her to see, Miss Gilchrist letting them in and out of the house herself; and on one occasion she overheard a quarrel between her mistress and one of the occult visitants. 'I am convinced that the man I saw was better dressed and of a better station of life than Slater. The only thing they had in common was that, when standing end on, the outlines of the faces from the left were much the same.' She says that her mistress sometimes sent her on unimportant errands when one of these covert callers was expected, and that it was not her regular custom to go out nightly for a newspaper. 'I have read the document, which, I understand, comes direct from Helen Lambie, and can be certified by an affidavit from the interviewer,' wrote Sir Arthur Conan Doyle. 'The matter is of enormous importance. Indeed, it is not too much to say that it must mark the end of the Oscar Slater case.' A copy of her statement was sent to the Scottish Office, where, it was announced, the matter would receive 'serious consideration'.

On 27 October the *Daily News* published an appeal to Lambie, begging her in the interests of justice 'to come forward and make a sworn statement'. All that was known of her was that she came of respectable parents in Holytown, Lanarkshire; that some time after the trial and before the 1914 inquiry she married a miner named Robert Gillon employed in the local coal pits; that shortly after the war they emigrated to the United States, and duly became American citizens. As she had already vouched for so many and various versions of the truth, it is odd that she should have scrupled to verify another; but Mrs Gillon took no notice of the *Daily News* appeal. She did not, however, disclaim or withdraw her statement, which on internal evidence may be accepted as genuine.

Meanwhile, by the enterprise of the same journal, Mary Barrowman, now a stout, married, middle-aged woman, was unearthed by 'The Pilgrim' from the backwoods of Glasgow; and, not to be outdone by the revelations of her former colleague, Mary averred that she never meant to go further than that Slater was 'very like the man', but was bullied into saying that he was the man by the Procurator-Fiscal, in whose office she had to rehearse her evidence every day for a fortnight before she was permitted to make oath to it at the trial. Her signed statement appeared in the *Daily News* of 5 November. When we recall that these two Crown witnesses were, at the time in question, the one an irresponsible servant maid of twenty-one, and the other a little errand girl of fourteen, the alleged methods by which the Glasgow authorities extracted from them 'the truth, the whole truth, and nothing but the truth' are sufficiently startling; and one ceases to wonder why it was expressly ordered that the secret inquiry 'should in no way relate to the conduct of the trial', or why the Commissioner received the official assistance which he so gratefully acknowledged.

The effect of these surprising statements was speedily apparent. On 10 November, in answering the time-honoured question as to what the Scottish Secretary proposed to do about Oscar Slater, Sir John Gilmour agreeably varied the regulation reply. 'Oscar Slater', said he, 'has now completed more than eighteen and a half years of his life sentence, and I have felt justified in deciding to authorize his release on licence as soon as suitable arrangements can be made.' This handsome pronouncement was not greeted with the enthusiasm which it deserved. The *Morning Post*, for instance, remarked: 'It almost looks as if the order of the release had been decided on as the readiest means of ending an agitation which it was inconvenient to meet.' Press editorial comment, both lay and legal, was unanimous that the release was an attempt to silence the demand for an inquiry, and that the matter could not be allowed to remain where it was left by the ingenious, rather than ingenuous, action of the Scottish Office.

At three o'clock on the afternoon of Monday 14 November 1927 the great gates of Peterhead were opened and the prisoner came forth again into the world of men. He was taken to Glasgow by the Rev. Mr Phillips, the Jewish Rabbi who had so loyally befriended him since the old days of the trial, and in whose home he now sought refuge from the ubiquitous emissaries of an energetic press. Never, excepting the vast bulk of the Tichborne claimant, had any figure in a famous case loomed more largely in the public eye; and every newspaper placard bore that week in its biggest and blackest capitals the familiar name of Oscar Slater. 'I am tired. I have not slept for the last five nights, since I heard I was coming back again. I want rest. I want rest.' Such were the first words of the enfranchised 'felon'; but rest was precisely the last thing the vigilant army of reporters beleaguering the Rabbi's house was willing to grant him. In the end he made good his escape, to Ayr, as afterwards appeared; and for a time contrived to baffle his pursuers.

Meanwhile Sir Arthur Conan Doyle had addressed to members of the House of Commons a circular letter, setting forth the facts of the case and invoking the powerful aid of Parliament to obtain a public and impartial inquiry. On 15 November the Secretary of State for Scotland, in reply to a question as to whether the Government would grant such an inquiry, announced his decision to remit all questions concerning the case to the Scottish Court of Criminal Appeal under the provisions of Section 16 of the Criminal Appeals (Scotland) Act, 1926, provided Parliament would pass a short Act giving retrospective effect to the section, which only applied to persons convicted after 31 October 1926. The official ice thus broken, the thaw set in: a special Bill was presented by Sir John Gilmour in the Commons on 16 November, and read a first time; on the 19th it was read a second time without a division and sent to a Committee of the whole House; and on the 30th it was read a third time in the House of Lords, cordially commended by Lord Buckmaster, and duly passed into law.

For the highly responsible duty of presenting Slater's case to the Scottish Court of Criminal Appeal, his law agents, Messrs Norman Macpherson & Dunlop, S.S.C., Edinburgh, selected a very strong team – Mr Craigie Aitchison, K.C., the unofficial leader of the Scots Criminal Bar; Mr J. C. Watson, Advocate; and Mr J. L. Clyde, Advocate – and in the hands of counsel of such ability Slater's interests were felt to be secure. Mr Aitchison may best be described for English readers unacquainted with his powers and prestige as the Marshall Hall of Scots advocacy. With the learned Judge in Gilbert's dramatic cantata he could justly boast—

> And many a burglar I've restored
> To his friends and his relations,

and the laurels were still fresh which he had won by his defence of John Donald Merrett, acquitted at Edinburgh in 1927 of the murder of his mother.

An immense amount of work required to be done before matters were sufficiently advanced to allow preparation of a detailed and definite statement of the grounds on which the appeal was based. Vanished witnesses had to be traced, lost documents had to be sought for, old statements had to be reviewed in the light of later evidence, and in all these manifold activities counsel and agents were, of course, heavily handicapped by the lapse of well-nigh twenty years since the events to be investigated. Not till 2 March 1928 was the requisite petition completed and sent to the Secretary of State for Scotland. In due course the Scottish Office referred the whole case to the High Court of Justiciary, under the amending Act already mentioned; and on 13 April the Lord Justice-General (Lord Clyde), the head of the Scots judiciary, directed the appellant to lodge not later than 19 May a supplementary note, containing such further specifications and particulars with regard to the grounds of appeal set forth in the petition, and such other grounds of appeal, if any, as he might desire to submit for the consideration of the Court. This supplementary note was duly prepared.

'Call the appeal of Oscar Slater against His Majesty's Advocate!' In these words were the proceedings opened at the preliminary hearing of this world-famous cause within the High Court at Edinburgh on 8 June 1928. The thronged benches, tiers of expectant faces, the formidable phalanx of the press, the goodly array of counsel, recalled, for such as had attended the original performance twenty years before, the strange drama of which that courtroom was once again the theatre. Though the setting was the same, there were many changes in the cast. On the Bench, instead of the single figure of Lord Guthrie, sat the five Judges of appeal: the Lord Justice-General (Lord Clyde), the Lord Justice-Clerk (Lord Alness), Lord Sands, Lord Blackburn, and Lord Fleming. For the appellant and former prisoner appeared Mr Craigie Aitchison, K.C., Mr Watson, and Mr Clyde; the Lord Advocate (the Right Hon. William Watson, K.C.), with Mr Alexander Maitland, senior advocate-depute, instructed by Sir John Prosser, W.S., Crown Agent, represented the Crown. In the dock, where of old the accused, cynosure of every eye, had watched that interesting game played by counsel with his life for stake, reporters were busy sharpening their pencils; while in the free seats, among the public spectators, bronzed, stalwart, and well-groomed, keenly following the fortunes of his cause, sat the sometime prisoner at the bar – Oscar Slater. What were his feelings in these unique circumstances may, as the cant phrase goes, be more easily imagined than described. Notable in the crowded audience was the familiar personality of Sir Arthur Conan Doyle, who had come north to witness the issue of his long warfare.

Mr Aitchison, having explained the legal position of his client under the statute, said that his application was for leave to lead further evidence and to recover certain documents. He proposed to adduce the appellant himself as a witness. Slater did not go into the box at the trial because of the violent and unprecedented attack upon his character made by the then Lord Advocate. He would now give evidence, denying all knowledge of the crime and answering any questions relative to the charge, but nothing more. He was not putting his character in issue. They also wished to recall the witness, Helen Lambie, if she could be made forthcoming.

'According to our information, a week before the crime, Helen Lambie, who was a maid in the service of Miss Gilchrist, went to her former mistress, who is still alive, without invitation and without any explanation whatever why she had come. She had not seen that lady for three and a half years. She told her former mistress that there were strange ongoings in the house of Miss Gilchrist; that jewels were being secreted in strange places; and that Miss Gilchrist said she was going to be murdered. The most significant thing of all that Helen Lambie said was in answer to a question by her former mistress whether anyone could obtain access to the house in the maid's absence. She replied that no one could get access to the house unless a prearranged signal was given. A week after the crime Helen Lambie returned to the same lady; and on that occasion, being asked how the man who committed the crime could have got access to the house, she did not answer the question, but volunteered the information, with very great emphasis, that she would not know the man again, and on being pressed as to how the man got in, and being reminded of her former statement that he could only get in in accordance with a prearranged signal, she became agitated and denied that she had ever made any such statement, and immediately left the house.

'Although that conversation took place twenty years ago, there could be no doubt as to its truth, for the lady consulted her law agent regarding the matter at the time. Unfortunately, it was not known to the accused's advisers at the trial; the information was only obtained last year. If it had been available at the trial Helen Lambie could have been most effectively cross-examined upon it; and they desired to do so now. Every possible step had been taken to find her, but without success; and they were going to ask the aid of the Crown to try to find her. Their information was that she was alive, and was hiding her whereabouts.

'They wished to put in the deposition of Duncan MacBrayne, who had since died, and whose evidence in Slater's favour was knowingly omitted by the prosecutor at the trial. With regard to "the flight from justice", the Crown had before them precognitions of ten witnesses who saw the prisoner after leaving Glasgow and before he sailed from Liverpool, and who noticed nothing suspicious in his manner; yet they selected one man, Forsyth, the Cunard booking-clerk, because he alleged that he did so. Counsel proposed to call the others, if they were now available. Failing that, he was going to maintain, on authority, that he should be allowed to use their evidence as given at the 1914 inquiry.

'As to the alleged identification in New York, which was attended by circumstances that entirely vitiate it, they desired to recover the Crown precognition of Inspector Warnock, who accompanied the three witnesses from Glasgow; and they proposed to call Messrs Miller and Goodhart, Slater's counsel and attorney in the extradition proceedings, and also Mr John W. Pinckley who had Slater in custody when he was identified by the girls in the corridor there.

'They wished to call a new witness, of whose existence the agents for the prisoner only became aware on the last day of the trial, when there was no time to test her evidence, which, if accepted, cut deeply into that of Barrowman.

'They desired that the medical aspect of the case should be reopened with regard to the alleged weapon. Dr John Adams, the first medical man to see the body, which he did a day before it was seen by Professor Glaister, then formed and had expressed a most decided opinion that the injuries were inflicted with the leg of a chair. Why Dr Adams's name did not appear in the Crown list of witnesses he [counsel] did not know; but their lordships would be unable to recall a case of homicide in which the Crown had gone to the jury without producing the doctor who first saw the body after death. They could prove the view of Dr Adams in two ways – by the evidence of his widow, and by that of Mr William Roughead, who had discussed the matter with Dr Adams at the time, and who could produce a letter from Dr Adams to himself, approving of the statement of his view as contained in Mr Roughead's introduction to the published report of the trial. According to their information, Professor Harvey Littlejohn declined to support the Crown view that the hammer had anything to do with the crime; they wanted to get the report by the professor upon that matter. They also desired leave to lead the evidence of Sir Bernard Spilsbury, which would be based, first, upon the view of Dr Adams, as communicated to him; secondly, on a description of the injuries sustained by the woman; and thirdly, on photographs of the head, taken at the time. Sir Bernard was accordingly in a good position to express an opinion, and he held a very strong one, namely, that there were features in this case which definitely and conclusively ruled the hammer out of consideration.'

The Court asked that a written list of the names and addresses of the witnesses whom counsel proposed to call be submitted, which Mr Aitchison undertook to have prepared forthwith.

The Lord Advocate, in reply, said he was anxious to assist legitimate inquiry in this appeal. There must be no attempt to re-try the case, and only new evidence could be allowed. Mere expert opinion was inadmissible, unless it arose out of fresh facts. Mr Aitchison asked leave to put the appellant in the box: this was not expedient, because it would mean that it was open to an accused not to go into the box at his trial, and when it came to his criminal appeal, then to go into the box. He opposed the motion that the appellant be allowed to give evidence. The proposed evidence touching the credibility of Lambie, if admitted, might involve a further extension of a matter which was debated at the trial. He opposed the production of precognitions and depositions as evidence; and argued that the identification at New York had been fully gone into at the trial. The Court then adjourned.

On the resumption of the hearing next day (9 June), the Lord Advocate continued his address. He objected to the admission of the new witness to identification, as the defence had known of her on the third day of the trial, and did not then ask leave to call her. He objected to the proposed evidence as to Dr Adams's theory of the crime. Professor Harvey Littlejohn made no formal report regarding the weapon, although it appeared that he considered the hammer too small and light. It had been the practice to indulge the defence with a sight of the Crown precognitions, but if this were demanded as a right, it would be difficult to continue that indulgence. He did not object to the Liverpool evidence, provided he was furnished with a list of the proposed witnesses.

On the conclusion of the Lord Advocate's address, their lordships retired to consider their decision, and returned fifteen minutes later, when the Lord Justice-General announced the findings of the Court. They were prepared to allow the evidence of Helen Lambie as to her alleged statement, and the evidence on that subject of her former mistress; also evidence of Mr Pinckley as to whether Slater was handcuffed when identified by Lambie and Barrowman in the corridor at New York; but they were not prepared to allow the examination of Slater's American lawyers, Messrs Miller and Goodhart. They made no order as to Inspector Warnock's precognition. The evidence of the new witness to identification would be received. With respect to the medical evidence, the Court would allow the evidence of Mr Roughead and of Dr Adams's widow regarding the opinion expressed by that gentleman to them; but the evidence of Sir Bernard Spilsbury, who never saw the body, could not be received. They made no order as to Professor Little-john's report. With regard to 'the flight from justice', they would allow the deposition of MacBrayne, and the evidence of Super-intendent Duckworth of Liverpool as to statements by witnesses taken there. With reference to the appellant himself, his counsel had stated that he had nothing new or additional to say, and that his evidence would amount to no more than a repetition of his plea of Not Guilty. 'In these circumstances,' continued his lordship, 'it would be quite unreasonable to spend time over his examination now, and the Court therefore is not prepared to allow his evidence to be received.' Monday 9 July, was fixed for the hearing of the appeal. The Court then rose.

The refusal of the Court to permit Slater to give evidence in his own behalf was bitterly resented by the appellant. He had become obsessed by the idea that he was still being made the subject of that conspiracy of silence of which, with good reason, he believed himself to have been so long the victim, and he left for Glasgow in dudgeon and despair. There, on 13 June, without having consulted his coun-sel or agents, Slater communicated to the press his intention to withdraw his appeal. He intimated his decision to his legal advisers in Edinburgh, and to his supporters, Sir Arthur Conan Doyle, Mr Park, and Rabbi Phillips, and he even wrote personally to the same effect to the Lord Justice-General. This bombshell, exploded next day in the newspapers, naturally caused the utmost vexation to all who had worked so loyally, and thus far successfully, for the appel-lant's interests. No time was lost in persuading him of the folly of his actions; and that night a fresh statement was issued to the press:

The appeal of Oscar Slater will proceed. The letter to the Lord Justice-General was written because of the appellant's great anxiety to enter the witness-box, and because his failure to do so would be misrepresented. The appellant has agreed to leave his case unreservedly in the hands of his advisers.

The question then arose whether in these circumstances Mr Ait-chison would consent to remain in the case; fortunately for the appellant he was prevailed upon to retain his brief. The episode – unique, like so much else in this unparalleled case – though it brought temporary consternation to those concerned, is eloquent of Slater's belief in the truth of his own story.

On Monday 9 July the resumed hearing of the appeal began with the new evidence which the Court had allowed to be led. Bench and Bar were as before; the same army of reporters occupied the front rows of what may irreverently be termed the stalls; Slater and Sir Arthur were again interested spectators; and Messrs Miller and Goodhart, who, though their evidence was not to be received, had come from America at their private charges to do what they could for their old client, were also present. The matters to which the new evidence related were: (1) Dr Adams's theory of the crime (2) the testimony of MacBrayne (3) the openness of Slater's proceedings at Liverpool, his signing the hotel register, etc. and (4) the 'identification' in the corridor at New York.

On the conclusion of the new evidence, Mr Aitchison said there were two other matters on which their lordships had allowed the appellant to lead proof. They were allowed to recall Helen Lambie. They had done everything in their power to get her. Through the courtesy of the Crown they were furnished with her address, and a representative was sent out to try to induce her to come. She declined to come. There was no machinery by which she could be brought, and accordingly the evidence which would have depended on her presence there could not be called. The only other point was the new witness, who alleged she saw the fugitive from the house. They had received from the Crown certain information as to that witness in view of which they felt unable to tender her evidence.

Mr Aitchison then began his address for the appellant, which, with suitable intervals for the rest and refreshment of the Court, occupied fourteen hours. Confronted by the task of giving by way of abridgement any conception of this masterly and comprehensive speech, I confess to feeling like a schoolboy set to write upon a postcard an epitome of *The Pickwick Papers*. All I can do in my allotted space is to attempt to give some notion of its scope and effect. The first thing, I think, that struck those who remembered the historic speech for the prosecution nineteen years before was the contrast between these two memorable addresses. We have heard something of the overwhelming and even passionate eloquence which marked or marred the one; the chief notes of the other were moderation and restraint. We have seen that the one was disfigured by mis-statements of fact and by the invocation of prejudice rather than of justice; the other was a reasoned argument, temperately stated, though logically unanswerable. One conceives how some counsel would have been loud upon their client's wrongs, the unfair methods of which he was the victim, and the twice-told tale of his misfortunes. Mr Aitchison's tone was almost conversational. He addressed the understanding rather than the feelings of his auditors, and to the emotions – for even Judges, being human, are susceptible of such – he made no appeal. But these negative virtues apart, perhaps his most positive achievement was the raising of this sensational and in some respects sordid case into an atmosphere of dignity, in which by reason of his impressive treatment it was sustained throughout the hearing.

Mr Aitchison, in opening his speech, said that he proposed first to deal with the evidence given at the trial in 1909; then with the new evidence which had been given that day. He would submit that the verdict of the jury was unreasonable and could not be supported, having regard to the evidence. In the second place, he proposed to deal with the Crown's conduct of the case, which he held was calculated to prevent, and did prevent, a fair trial. He proposed to deal with this part of the case under three heads: (1) mis-statements of facts, including prejudicial suggestions of the gravest kind, made by the Lord Advocate in the course of the trial, and in particular in his speech to the jury (2) the withholding of evidence by the Crown favourable to the prisoner and (3) the attack made on the character of the prisoner. The final matter was the Judge's charge with reference to (1) the attack on character (2) certain inadequacies in that charge as to questions of fact and (3) misdirections in law, both positive and negative. So far as the appeal rested on fact, it was obvious the crucial question was the

question of identification. The test to be applied was whether the
jury could reasonably reach the conclusion they did. He maintained
that the evidence of identification was altogether insufficient as a
basis for a jury's verdict in a case of murder.

Mr Aitchison then exhaustively reviewed the evidence relating
to 'the watcher', and analysed the various discrepancies and contradictions as regards clothing and appearance in the descriptions
of the man given by the several witnesses. Proceeding to examine
the evidence of the three crucial witnesses, Mr Aitchison suggested
that Helen Lambie knew the man who passed her in the hall that
night.

'If that man had been a stranger to her, for my part I cannot
understand why she did not at once go into the dining-room to
find out about the old lady of over eighty years whom she had
left a short time before ... I cannot understand why she did not
challenge the stranger. I think, making every allowance for the
situation by which she was confronted, her conduct is inexplicable, except on the view that she either left the man in the
house when she went out, or that she knew the man who met
her on her return.'

When counsel had concluded his reading of Lambie's examination-in-chief the Court rose.

On the resumption of the hearing next day (10 July) Mr Aitchison proceeded to deal with the cross-examination of Lambie in
America and at the trial; he characterized her in New York as an
untruthful and insolent witness, and in Edinburgh as one false and
unscrupulous. The incident in the corridor was, he maintained, an
outrage and a travesty of identification. Having read the evidence
of Mr Adams, whose fairness was commendable, counsel came next
to that of Mary Barrowman, and criticized the differing accounts of
the man's appearance given by her in Glasgow, in America, and at
the trial. As showing the value attached by these two girls to the
virtue of an oath, he instanced their sworn testimony that during
the voyage to New York they never talked about the case. 'Does
anybody believe that?' asked Mr Aitchison. 'It is simply a false-
hood.' With regard to the evidence of MacBrayne, it was admitted

that the Crown knew of its importance to the defence and did not call him at the trial.

'The effect was that a witness of the greatest possible materiality from the point of view of the defence was withheld from the jury. He was not in the Crown list, and accordingly no possible blame could attach to the defence in this matter. If there was nothing more in the case than that, he [counsel] submitted that the conviction ought not to stand.'

On 22 February 1909 MacBrayne went to the Central Police Office in Glasgow on the invitation of the Procurator-Fiscal.

'The fiscal knew about him and knew that his evidence was favourable to the defence. The information was transmitted to the Crown Office, yet the man was not put on the list of the Crown witnesses. This happened three months prior to the trial. If it is inadvertence, we will accept that explanation; if it is not, I would rather not characterize it.'

There could be no doubt that had MacBrayne's evidence been before the jury the Crown would never have obtained a conviction. As to 'the flight from justice', Mr Aitchison recalled that the police at the trial maintained that Slater had travelled to Liverpool with London tickets: that had now been disproved. The Crown were in possession of that information, and again it was withheld from the jury. It was just one more illustration of what they had got in this case from beginning to end – the putting aside of anything that told in the appellant's favour. Dealing with the medical evidence, counsel said he would found strongly on the opinion of Dr Adams and his absence from the witness-box. It was of the first importance to the defence that Dr Adams should have been called. For all they knew, the verdict against the prisoner may have turned on the evidence regarding the hammer, and had Dr Adams been called he might have inclined the jury to the other view. After all, the medical opinion was divided. Coming to the evidence regarding the appellant's character, improperly elicited by the Lord Advocate from the defence witnesses, Mr Aitchison observed: 'It is the duty of the Court to prevent improper evidence going to the jury. It was unfortunate that objection was not taken at the time. Even if it were legitimate cross-examination, the use made of it by the Crown was altogether illegitimate. The Lord Advocate missed no opportunity of rubbing it in, and when he came to address the jury made an entirely illegitimate use of it.'

Mr Aitchison having concluded his reading of the evidence, the Court adjourned.

Wednesday 11 July, the third day of the hearing, was in some respects the most interesting. The reading of the evidence was over; and Mr Aitchison, having laid the foundations of his case, was free to proceed with his argument upon the merits. The crux of the case, so far as the appeal was based on fact, was clearly the identification. If that broke down, the whole case broke down. But before making his submission on that matter there were two other matters to which he would refer: 'the flight from justice' and the medical evidence.

As to the first, the points negativing the suggestion of the Crown were (1) the intention to leave Glasgow and go abroad, definitely expressed long before the crime (2) the complete unconcern of Slater's movements prior to leaving Glasgow (3) the openness of his manner of departure and (4) his disclosure of his destination, the route he proposed to take, and the day on which he was going. That, counsel submitted, was almost conclusive against the idea of flight. And, lastly, the fact that he registered in the Liverpool hotel under the name of 'Oscar Slater, Glasgow'. He booked his passage under the name of Otto Sando; but he was a man in the habit of using different names: he sometimes called himself Slater and sometimes Anderson, and on his last visit to America he took the name of George. The Crown knew months before the trial that he had signed the register as Oscar Slater; if they were going to use the one fact against the man, surely in fairness they should have brought out the other fact in his favour.

With regard to the medical aspect of the case, he thought it impossible to say that the evidence of Dr Adams might not have impressed the jury. They had to take that evidence now at second hand, but it was clearly proved that in his view the hammer had nothing whatever to do with the murder. He (counsel) asked their lordships not to assume that the opinion of Dr Adams could not have been corroborated by expert testimony, had he been allowed to lead it. It was no answer for the Crown to say that the defence might have called Dr Adams; there was no excuse for the failure of the Crown to call him. If anything material was withheld from the jury, that, he submitted, was enough to justify the quashing of this conviction.

Upon the question of identification, Mr Aitchison referred to the unreliability of such evidence based on personal impressions. The three crucial witnesses had but a fleeting glance at the man; all the witnesses before they identified Slater had seen his photograph and had read his description, so there was present in that case every circumstance that increased the elements of uncertainty and liability to error. As to the quality of the evidence of the three crucial witnesses, Mr Aitchison contended that if it were unsatisfactory, the whole case had to go. Lambie's testimony was absolutely negligible. The learned Judge at the trial would have been more than warranted in directing the jury to leave it out of account. Her repeated contradictions in Glasgow, in New York, and at the trial, as to seeing and not seeing the man's face, were vital. The opportunity Barrowman had of observing the man was very limited: running at full speed past her on a dark, rainy, winter night. She said the man had a twisted nose; but none of the other witnesses, with better opportunities for observation, noticed it. Mr Adams was perfectly honest; he said he was near-sighted, and he would not swear to the man. He (counsel) could not conceive a more unsatisfactory basis for a verdict of murder. If Lambie were negligible, and Adams would not go the length of identifying, they were left with Barrowman upon this critical point; and, with the tremendous liability to mistake in this class of evidence, he submitted it was not sufficient. He argued that being in itself deficient, it could not be 'corroborated' by evidence that the appellant had been seen in the vicinity a week or two before the crime.

As regards Slater's movements that night, if a man was living in an underworld you could not rule out the evidence of people from that underworld; you could not brush it aside, as it was brushed aside at the trial. The evidence as to Slater's alibi had never been fairly put to the jury; the jury were told that they could not rely upon people of that kind. He founded strongly on the evidence of MacBrayne.

If there was nothing else in the case, he submitted, MacBrayne would carry him home. There could be no dispute as to the materiality of his evidence. Observe how the Lord Advocate presented the matter to the jury: 'We know nothing of the man's movements till a quarter to ten at night.' That simply was not true. The Crown were sitting there with the precognition. They knew that at 8.15 MacBrayne had seen Slater, and he could not be mistaken in his identification. It was the best identification in the case . . . The non-calling of MacBrayne might have been inadvertent; but, if not, it was a fraud on the prisoner and a fraud on the jury.

The next ground of appeal to be considered was the attack made by the Lord Advocate upon the character of the accused. The first inaccuracy was the statement that Slater knew that Miss Gilchrist was possessed of jewels, than which nothing could be more vital in a case where jewel robbery was the motive alleged; the second, that the prisoner was a jewel thief or a resetter (receiver) of jewels; the third, that he cleared out of Glasgow the day his name appeared in the papers. Mr Aitchison characterized the famous phrase: 'We shall see in the sequel how it was that the prisoner came to know that she was possessed of these jewels' – to which there was no sequel – as 'a damning mis-statement, without a scintilla of evidence to warrant it'. The Lord Advocate's 'six priceless inferences' were mere assumptions, e.g. that the murderer was on the hunt for jewels. There might well have been another motive: what about the scattered papers and the untouched jewellery? That was nothing but prejudicial suggestion, calculated from the very circumstances of the case to carry weight with the jury and induce a verdict. The use by the Crown of the evidence reflecting upon the accused's character was the most prejudicial that could possibly have been made. The Lord Advocate presented it to the jury as having removed a difficulty from his mind, and as something that would remove a difficulty from their minds, in dealing with the question of the prisoner's guilt or innocence. This struck at the very root of the criminal administration in Scotland, and he (counsel) hoped the Court would not hesitate to say so.

The last ground of appeal was the exceptions taken to Lord Guthrie's charge, as set forth in the supplementary note. 'He has maintained himself by the ruin of men and on the ruin of women, living for years past in a way that many blackguards would scorn to live.' That was not a very good preparation for the mind of a jury, and there was no evidence of the fact; the evidence was that the man was a gambler and lived with a mistress. 'I use the name "Oscar Slater". But this is not his name . . . We do not know where he was born, who his parents are, where he was brought up . . . The man remains a mystery.' These matters were no more relevant than was the question of where the jury was born. And his lordship further stated that Slater's life had been 'a living lie'. But the most vital thing Lord Guthrie said was this: 'A man of that kind has not the presumption of innocence in his favour which is a form in the case of every man, but a reality in the case of the ordinary man. Not only is every man presumed to be innocent, but the ordinary man, in a case of brutal ferocity like the present, has a strong presumption in his favour.'

He submitted that that direction to the jury could not be justified. It could not be supported either by principle or by authority. Lord Guthrie was confusing a presumption of innocence with a presumption of good character, which it is not. It is a presumption that a man is innocent *quoad* the particular crime with which he is charged. Mr Aitchison having cited a body of authorities upon the point, concluded his address as follows: 'That is the case for the appellant. I submit that individually the grounds of appeal here are strong, but collectively they are overwhelming. I submit that this conviction ought not to be allowed to stand. It is a grave thing to convict of murder, and no doubt a grave thing to quash a conviction for murder; but if any of the grounds I have ventured to urge upon your lordships should commend themselves to the Court, either individually or collectively, as grounds for setting aside this conviction, I am confident that, whatever the consequences, my lords will not hesitate for an instant to quash this conviction, and do what I humbly submit is in the whole circumstances of this case no more than an act of simple justice to the appellant.'

The Court then rose.

To afford the non-professional reader – who must be weary of these legal technicalities – a brief respite before conducting him to the Lord Advocate's reply, I shall quote a couple of paragraphs from an article contributed to the press at the time by Sir Arthur Conan Doyle, giving his impressions of the memorable scene:

'For three days I have sat in the well of a court. For three days a dignified row of five Scottish judges have sat at the back of me. For three days my whole vision has consisted of one man in front of me, and of the courtroom crowd behind him. But that one man is worth watching. It is well that it should be so, since I have watched him for fourteen hours . . . Yes, it is for fourteen hours exactly that he has been talking. He has been untangling the difficulties of a most intricate case. Deft, deft to the last degree has been that disentanglement. It is a miracle of analysis . . . He talks and talks with a gentle melodious voice, clearing up the difficulties. Those little plump hands accentuate the points. Then there comes an objection from the judges. The blue eyes seemed pained and surprised. Up fly the little plump hands. Once more the gentle voice takes up the tale. The wrinkle is smoothed out and the story goes on . . . Yes, the name of Craigie Aitchison will be known. He is a great counsel. One of his greatest points is his restraint. My friend Marshall Hall was a very great counsel. But he could not have argued a case without a jury and before a bench of judges as this man has done . . .

'And then suddenly one's eyes are arrested. One terrible face stands out among all those others. It is not an ill-favoured face, nor is it a wicked one, but it is terrible none the less for the brooding sadness that is in it. It is firm and immobile and might be cut from that Peterhead granite which has helped to make it what it is. A sculptor would choose it as the very type of tragedy. You feel that this is no ordinary man, but one who has been fashioned for some strange end. It is indeed the man whose misfortunes have echoed round the world. It is Slater.'

On Thursday 12 July, the last day of the hearing, the Lord Advocate rose to reply for the Crown. His task cannot have been a grateful one. He was called upon officially to condone the faults of his predecessor, to vindicate the conduct of the prosecution, and to justify the judgment of the Judge, for none of which things was he personally responsible. He began by reminding their lordships that the Crown had suffered as much as the appellant from the lapse of twenty years since the date of the trial. Many facts which might have been ascertained at the time were now impossible of determination. With regard to the new evidence, he could find no trace of any statement by, or communication with, Dr Adams. He submitted that Dr Adams's evidence was not of material value for the purpose of the appeal; his theory could never have stood the test of examination or investigation, and he asked the Court to disregard it. As to the incident in the corridor at New York, if Slater were actually handcuffed, he must have known it himself and might have informed his agent at the time. The same observation applied to Slater having signed the hotel register in his own name; had he thought it material he could have brought that out. His lordship could not tell the Court why MacBrayne's name was not put on the Crown list. They had a precognition from him containing the fact, material or not, that he saw Slater at 8.15. He had no reason to believe that the Lord Advocate knew anything about MacBrayne at all. With respect to the identification, people noticed that the man was dark; but it was the general look of the man that was so striking. The man must have had a face that impressed itself on people's memory; his own witnesses made that clear. Every point had been fully and fairly put before the jury, and he did not intend to go through all the evidence again. What mattered most was the identification in court in presence of the jury. The Appeal Court could never put itself in the same position as regards this question of identification as the Judge and jury who saw and heard the witnesses. There was certainly no insufficiency of evidence; they had Adams, Lambie, and Barrowman; and he submitted that the jury were entitled to believe any of the three. The jury were further entitled to take in association with that identification the evidence of loitering. There was no reason for the repeated presence of Slater in West Princes Street, with his gaze directed towards Miss Gilchrist's house. The local gossip as to Miss Gilchrist's jewels the jury were also entitled to consider as the forerunner of the watching of the house. He admitted that if Adams, Lambie, and Barrowman were struck out, the case was gone; one class of circumstantial evidence could not be used to corroborate another. With regard to 'the flight from justice', he submitted that it was proved that Slater's intention to leave Glasgow was undoubtedly hastened. As regards the Crown conduct of the case, he held that the Lord Advocate at the trial was entitled from the evidence to draw the inference that the appellant knew the murdered woman was possessed of jewels, and that he dealt dishonestly in jewels. As to the attack upon the accused's character, no objection was taken when questions regarding his mode of life were put. His lordship agreed that the phrase at the beginning of the Lord Advocate's speech was a melodramatic one, but in later parts of his address the point was fairly put. That was equally the case with regard to the Judge's charge. Where the Court heard but isolated phrases, the jury had heard continuous speeches; and their lordships had to consider whether, taking all the passages together, the jury were misled. He then proceeded to argue that the presumption of innocence was purely a negative presumption; there was no guilt until the Crown had proved it.

THE LORD JUSTICE-CLERK: In this case Slater made no attempt whatever to prove that he led a moral life, and for the very good reason that such evidence would have been irrelevant. Notwithstanding that fact, the Lord Advocate brought out that Slater did not in point of fact lead a moral life, and in his speech to the jury he used that in explicit support of proof of the charge of murder. Now, is that justifiable?

THE LORD ADVOCATE: If that is what your lordship holds it comes to, I am not going to attempt to justify it. I should be the last to say that that could be done.

The latter portion of the Lord Advocate's speech rather took the form of a discussion, as he had to answer a series of questions from the bench and to argue the points severally put to him by their lordships. On the conclusion of his address, which occupied over two hours, and was marked throughout by dignity and moderation in the discharge of a necessary duty, judgment was reserved and the Court adjourned.

On Friday 20 July the curtain rose upon the final scene of the great Slater drama. The proceedings, which lasted but twenty-five minutes, consisted solely in the reading by the Lord Justice-General of the written findings of the Court. The judgment was unanimous – probably the first occasion on which in this contested case unanimity of opinion has been achieved. The questions for the determination of the Court, as summarized by his lordship in the chair, were (1) whether the jury's verdict was unreasonable or unsupported by evidence (2) whether any new facts had been disclosed material to the issue (3) whether the appellant had suffered prejudice by non-disclosure of evidence known to the Crown and (4) whether the verdict was vitiated in respect of misdirection by the presiding Judge. On the first three heads the appeal failed; on the fourth, the Court held that the conviction must be quashed.

I watched Slater's face as, leaning forward in his place with his hand behind his ear, he strained every nerve in his anxiety to follow the low, rapid reading of the judgment; and as point after point was given against him, it was obvious that he believed his cause lost. Nor until the last words fell from his lordship's lips did the appellant realize that he had won the day.

Upon the crucial question of identification, the Lord Justice-General observed: 'The case was one of great difficulty.' And, again: 'In a department so notoriously delicate as proof of identity, these criticisms are most formidable.' But the Court was unable to hold that in the circumstances the verdict was either 'unreasonable' or 'unsupported by evidence'. With respect to the new evidence, their lordships thought the hearsay testimony of Dr Adams was of no materiality. They were unable to regard the Liverpool evidence as materially affecting the case. With regard to what happened in New York, the Court could not attach importance to the fresh evidence. MacBrayne's evidence was not inconsistent with the case for the prosecution, and his deposition was otherwise neutral; it did not appear to the Court to be material. As to non-disclosure of evidence by the Crown – the statements of Dr Adams, Inspector Duckworth, and MacBrayne – their lordships were of opinion that the appellant had no ground of complaint. The most difficult question raised by the appeal was the treatment of the appellant's character by the Lord Advocate and by the presiding Judge. With respect to the former: 'It was not only eminently capable of construction in the sense that the appellant's immoral life was evidence relevant for the consideration of the jury in deciding on his guilt of Miss Gilchrist's murder, but such was, *prima facie*, at any rate, its obvious import. And it was very possible that a jury might so understand it.' As the vital point of satisfactory proof of identity 'presented an unusually difficult and narrow issue, upon which the balance of judgment might easily be influenced', it was imperative that the jury should receive from the presiding Judge the clearest and most unambiguous warning against being influenced by considerations at once so irrelevant and so prejudicial as the relations of the appellant with his female associates. But the directions of the Judge not only did nothing to remove the erroneous impression which the opening passages of the speech for the Crown were likely to produce, but, on the contrary, they were calculated to confirm them. The direction that the appellant had not the benefit of the ordinary presumption of innocence amounted, in the opinion of the Court, to a clear misdirection in law. 'In these circumstances, we think that the instructions given in the charge amounted to misdirections in law, and that the judgment of the Court before whom the appellant was convicted should be set aside.'

The proceedings then terminated; and with them came also to an end the twenty years' contention.

While the decision of the appeal in Slater's favour was, except in official circles, generally welcomed, some surprise was expressed that the conviction had been quashed solely on a technical point of law – which might and ought to have been taken at the trial, or at any subsequent period by responsible authority – and that the Court did not see their way to give effect to any of those criticisms by Mr Aitchison upon the merits, which the judgment characterized as 'most formidable'. One regrets that the old-time custom of our Courts, beloved of Robert Louis Stevenson, was not on this occasion followed, by their lordships each delivering his individual opinion. 'We treat law as a fine art, and relish and digest a good distinction. There is no hurry: point after point must be rightly examined and reduced to principle; judge after judge must utter forth his *obiter dicta* to delighted brethren.' But doubtless the desirable unanimity attained was only compassed at the cost of some compromise. To take a single instance, the Lord Justice-Clerk at the hearing, with reference to MacBrayne's evidence, observed: 'To his mind far and away the most important part of the additional evidence – its importance was surely undeniable – was that a man who was alleged to have battered this old lady to death at 7.15 p.m. was seen to be standing unconcerned at 8.15 p.m. at the door of his house.' Yet that evidence is in the final judgment of the Court dismissed as 'immaterial'. It is noteworthy that their lordships accepted as proof of the appellant's abandoned moral character the hearsay evidence of Cameron and the answers by the servant to the leading questions of the Lord Advocate. The judgment brackets Schmalz, the German maid, with Antoine, the French mistress: 'his female associates', 'the appellant's disreputable relations with the female members of his household', etc. But this is, as regards Schmalz, an entirely new and original charge, and one not made even by the Lord Advocate at the trial; for the only thing against Schmalz was the fact of her employment in Slater's service. From personal recollection of this witness as she appeared in the box I can certify that she was unattractive enough to be virtuous. 'However, it is done now,' wrote Sir Arthur Conan Doyle in a last word to the press on the subject, 'and we must be thankful for what we have got.'

A Peoria, Illinois, correspondent telegraphed from America: 'Mrs Helen Lambie or Gillon said, when informed of the result of the Slater appeal, "I am glad it is all over." ' This, her final statement in the case, may at least be accepted for truth.

The sole remaining question was as to the 'compensation' to be made to Slater in respect of his illegal conviction and wrongous imprisonment. Questioned about this in Parliament on 23 July, the Secretary of State for Scotland replied: 'I think it is proper that the person concerned ought to have a reasonable opportunity of putting forward any claim he may wish to make.' To the further question, 'Would it not be more generous if the Government were to make a grant without waiting for a claim?' no answer was given. With reference to this matter, the appellant himself on 29 July made to the press the following communication: 'As far as I, Oscar Slater, am concerned, there will never be a bill for compensation sent in.' Questioned thereupon in the House on 1 August, Sir John Gilmour replied: 'I think it will be very unwise to take as conclusive fact any statement in the press appearing in that form.' On the 4th the Secretary wrote to Slater personally that the Lords of the Treasury 'have assented to an *ex gratia* payment to you of £6,000 in consequence of your wrongful conviction in May 1909, and subsequent imprisonment', and asking whether he wished that payment made to him direct or to the credit of his bank account. On the 7th Slater wrote desiring that the sum be paid into his account with a Glasgow bank.

In thus accepting the Government's offer the appellant acted entirely on his own responsibility and without consulting his legal advisers. Had he left the matter of compensation in the hands of his law agents, he would probably have obtained a much larger payment, and would certainly have avoided the unseemly situation which arose on the question of the costs of his appeal. The position as to these costs was this: Sir Arthur Conan Doyle had very generously guaranteed them before commencement of the proceedings. A defence fund, raised by public subscription and patronized by the Jewish community, had produced some £700, and the expenses of the appeal were estimated at about £1,500. How was the balance to be met? It was manifestly unfair that Sir Arthur, having fought the case for eighteen years and won it, should be called upon to pay; and not less inequitable that the appellant should be required out of his 'compassionate allowance' to meet the costs of proving the injustice of his conviction. Accordingly, on 14 November, several questions on the subject were asked in Parliament, to which Sir John Gilmour replied that 'the whole circumstances of the case were taken into consideration in fixing the amount of the *ex gratia* payment'. On the 21st the matter was again raised in the House, when the Secretary stated that the payment 'was made in full settlement of all claims, whether for costs or otherwise'. On the 28th the questions were repeated, with the like result. On 5 December Slater himself addressed Sir John Gilmour, pointing out that in the offer and acceptance of compensation nothing was said about costs. 'I should have thought,' he wrote, 'that the Government, in common fairness, ought not to expect me to bear the costs of this case.' The Scottish Office on the 13th replied: 'His Majesty's Government are not prepared to make any payment in addition to the *ex gratia* sum of £6,000 which was paid to you in August last.' The final word upon the subject was said in Committee in the Commons on 15 February, 1929, when a supplementary estimate for the £6,000 was, after discussion, agreed to without a division. The Lord Advocate pointed out that, even if the whole £1,500 were deducted, 'Mr Slater would be able to buy an annuity from the Post Office of £351 a year, or nearly £1 a day for the rest of his life.' Whether or not the appellant availed himself of this gratuitous legal advice is unrecorded. In the end Sir Arthur, having called the tune, had, as appears, to pay the piper.

On 31 January 1948 Oscar Slater died at his home in Ayr at the age of 76. For three years before his death he had been an invalid. He was happily married to a devoted wife, and had, since his release, lived quietly and respectably in Ayr, where he made many friends.

*

In concluding our survey of this strange and eventful history one or two remarks fall to be made. The Lord Justice-General, in pronouncing the judgment of the Court, justly observed of the case that there are mysteries about it on both sides, of which no explanation is now possible. Miss Gilchrist herself is a mysterious figure. We know not how she came by her wealth, for what reason she invested it in jewels, who were her familiars, or why she was afraid of being murdered. There may have been episodes in her eighty years' pilgrimage which would, if ascertained, throw some light on these matters, and upon the tragic issue of her fate. If Slater be in fact guiltless of her death, and if Trench's tale be true, it is a disquieting reflection that the murderer, unidentified and unpunished, may still be at large. He may even have attended the hearing of the appeal: an occasion which would be, for him, full of interest. And if, as I believe – and I am by no means singular in the persuasion – Helen Lambie holds the key to the mystery, her refusal to 'face the music' is, in the interests of justice, the most regrettable feature of the late proceedings.

And yet Miss Gilchrist must have been killed by somebody. Twenty years' reflection on the facts as proved in court confirms me in the view, to the likelihood of which I from the first inclined, that *two* men were concerned in the affair, one of whom either made off between Mr Adams's visits to the door, or waited – like Raskolnikov – in the empty flat above until the coast was clear. If the reader, who studies the evidence of the definitive edition of the Trial and Appeal published in the Notable British Trials series, will keep in mind this hypothesis – which I lack space to substantiate – he may find it helpful, as explaining the many difficulties created by the disparate accounts of the appearance and movements of 'the man'.

Madeleine Smith
1857

F. TENNYSON JESSE

On Thursday 9 July 1857 the trial of Madeleine Smith for the murder of her lover, Pierre Emile L'Angelier, by the administration of arsenic, ended in the verdict of 'Not Proven', and she left the High Court of Justiciary in Edinburgh, by a side door, a free woman.

Only twenty-one years of age, handsome, with a bright, hard, defiant beauty, a beauty unabashed by an experience that might well have ravaged it, she passed into obscurity from obscurity. For in spite of the fierce light that had beaten upon her and her doings, in spite of the way in which her past life had been examined and pored over, it remained mysterious then, and does so to this day. Little glimpses of her afterlife have been caught from time to time. It is known that she married four years later a young artist in London, and that she was interested in contemporary problems, and had become a Socialist. It has been stated that she eventually went to live in the United States of America; but her life since the trial is her own; it is those months which lie between April 1855 and June 1857 which present a riddle that has never lost its fascination.

In April 1855 the Smiths, who were a highly respected and extremely conventional family, were living in India Street, Glasgow. They had a country house called Rowaleyn at Row (or Rhu), on the Clyde, where they spent the summer months. Mr Smith was a prosperous architect, a man of position and some wealth, who 'kept his carriage'. Madeleine, the eldest of the family, possessed beauty, vivacity, and an adventurous spirit. She was a capable girl, and on her return from her genteel English boarding-school she took the cares of housekeeping and management off her mother's shoulders. Such a girl might be expected to make a good marriage, and Pierre Emile L'Angelier, a native of Jersey and a clerk at 10s. a week in the employ of Huggins & Company in Glasgow, was so hopelessly ineligible that even an introduction to Madeleine seemed beyond the bounds of possibility. Nevertheless, he was so struck by the sight of Madeleine that he determined to know her, and he succeeded in getting introduced to her in Sauchiehall Street by a mutual friend, a youth called Robert Baird. Madeleine's sister Bessie, two years younger than herself, was with Madeleine when the meeting took place, and it was to Bessie that L'Angelier confided his first note for Madeleine. The acquaintance begun thus clandestinely continued in the same manner, but it was discovered by Mr Smith. He forbade any further correspondence or meetings, and Madeleine wrote telling L'Angelier that everything between them had better be over.

L'Angelier, however, was not going to let the girl go so easily. He was determined to marry her, and not as the penniless cast-off daughter of an enraged parent, but as the bride of an accepted and welcomed son-in-law. A friend of his, a sentimental elderly maiden lady, called Mary Perry, had already been the *confidante* of the pair; she delivered letters and messages, and the lovers used to meet at her house. At the same time that Madeleine wrote to L'Angelier bidding him farewell, she wrote to Miss Perry, explaining the necessity of her action. But the sentimental Miss Perry threw all her weight on L'Angelier's side, and the meetings and correspondence began again. L'Angelier used to be admitted by Madeleine into the house in India Street after the rest of the family were asleep, and in the spring of 1856 he was meeting Madeleine at Rowaleyn after dark, and she had become his mistress.

In the winter of that year the Smith family moved from India Street to 7 Blythswood Square, and at this house also L'Angelier was received by Madeleine after dark. But the fierce fire of her passion was short-lived, and already it was nearly burnt out. She was tiring of him, and a more eligible suitor, though a much older one, Mr William Minnoch, began to court her; he was a friend of

Mr Smith's and lived next door to 7 Blythswood Square. Madeleine again broke off all connection with L'Angelier, and asked him to return her letters. This he refused to do, and threatened to blackmail her by showing them to her father. Madeleine implored for mercy, but he was relentless. She then apparently took him back in her favour and wrote him letters as passionate as before, begging him to come and see her.

Once in February and twice in March L'Angelier was taken extremely ill with internal pains and vomiting, and the third attack of this malady proved fatal. He died in his lodgings on the morning of 23 March, having returned thither in the small hours of the morning in a state of acute illness. This sudden death struck his employers and friends as peculiar, and a post-mortem examination was held which left no doubt that he had died from a large dose of arsenic, of which eighty-two grains were found in the stomach alone. Madeleine's letters were found in his room and at his place of business, with the inevitable result – she was arrested and stood her trial, accused of having administered poison to him on three occasions, the third time with fatal results.

All Great Britain was agitated over the trial, which lasted for nine days, and there were three points of view held by three different schools of thought. There were strong pro-Madeleineites who contested that she was innocent and that L'Angelier had committed suicide; equally strong anti-Madeleineites, convinced that murder had been committed and by her, and that she should pay the penalty; and a third school, in which probably most students of the case have found themselves ever since, which declared in effect 'probably she did it, but anyhow he deserved it'. Certainly very vital evidence necessary to prove her guilt was lacking. That evidence can never be forthcoming now, and so the riddle must remain for ever unsolved, but the great fascination of it still exists, and it is possible by examining and weighing not only all the evidence put forward in the court of law, but also documents which were not admitted as evidence, and by a careful study of Madeleine's own letters, to arrive at some slight knowledge of the various characters involved and the circumstances in which they lived, so that a living presentment of this tragic human drama can grow up in our minds today.

As is general with Scotsmen to this day, and was almost invariably so in the early fifties, Mr Smith was very much the head of the household. 'Papa', as Madeleine calls him, emerges from her letters as the very figure of the awful and august Victorian father. Even Madeleine, about whose courage and determination there can be no question, feared his anger. 'Mama', though a more shadowy figure, presents herself as the true type of Victorian mother – mild in comparison with 'Papa', yet inflexible in her very subservience to him. Both took to their beds when the disaster overwhelmed the house in Blythswood Square, and neither sat in the courtroom during the trial to encourage by look or smile the daughter who had so disgraced them.

Madeleine was the eldest child. Next to her in age was her sister Bessie, then came her brother Jack, and there were two much younger children, James and Janet. It is possible from Madeleine's letters to gain some notion of what these brothers and sisters were like, or, rather, what Madeleine thought they were like.

Madeleine and Bessie were not good friends, and it seems probable that the younger girl was jealous of Madeleine's stronger personality. The sisters made the acquaintance of Emile L'Angelier at the same time, and Madeleine in her first letter to the young man says: 'Bessie desires me to remember her to you.' But in her next letter she writes as follows: 'We are to be in town tomorrow, Wednesday. Bessie said I was not to let you know, but I must tell you why. Well, some friend was *kind* enough to tell Papa that you were in the habit of walking with us. Papa was very angry with me for walking with a Gentleman unknown to him. Bessie joins with Papa and blames me for the whole affair. She does not know I am writing you, so don't mention it. We are to call at our old quarters in the Square on Wednesday about a quarter past twelve o'clock, so if you could be in Mr McCall's lodgings – see us come out of Mrs Ramsay's – come after us – say you are astonished to see us in town without letting you know – and we shall see how Bessie acts. She says she is not going to write you.' Perhaps Bessie was tired of always playing second fiddle to Madeleine, who seems to have attracted most of the young men they met. Writing to L'Angelier of their projected marriage, Madeleine observes: 'We shall be the envy of many – of B. I know.' When Bessie had a new pink bonnet, Madeleine chooses a fawn one, as she knows that Emile would consider pink vulgar. In one of her passionate love-letters, when it still seems possible to her that they may be able to marry, she says: 'Bessie had an invitation to go to Edinburgh Castle next week. The Major knew I would not go, so did not invite me. I do not think she will go. Papa won't allow her by herself and I won't go, so I think she will have to stay at home – which is much better, don't you think so?' Whether Bessie thought so is, of course, another matter.

Jack appears at first to be rather a friend of Madeleine's. 'On Sunday I was at church, and in the afternoon Jack and I had a walk of four miles. Now when I can walk four with a brother I could walk eight with my own beloved husband and not be fatigued.' There is even at one time talk of her confiding in Jack and getting him to help her. 'I shall try to speak to Jack on Sunday,' she writes, and L'Angelier urges her thus: 'Do speak to your brother. Open your heart to him and try to win his friendship. Tell him if he loves you, to take your part.' There is no indication that Madeleine ever confided in her brother, and it seems very unlikely with her secretive temperament that she did so. It is not long before she is writing quite coldly about him to her lover. 'Jack is not near so nice as he was,' she complains, and – 'he has got a very fast look, Jack, of late. He is not improving and James is just a very bad little fellow and swears and goes on at a great rate.' Nevertheless, in spite of Jack's real or fancied deterioration, he was the only member of the family who met her after her acquittal, when he conducted her to the Smiths' country-house at Rowaleyn, where the rest of the family were stonily awaiting her.

As to Janet, the little girl frequently was a great nuisance to her sister, whose room she shared. 'I did, my love, so pity you standing in the cold last night,' writes Madeleine, 'but I could not get Janet to sleep, little stupid thing.' 'Janet is a good girl,' she writes at another time, 'but she is not very affectionate.' Now, Madeleine herself was undoubtedly very affectionate. People whom she loved were all that was perfect, at least for a short period. Any friend of L'Angelier's she considered must be perfection. Of some acquaintance of L'Angelier's she writes: 'I like Miss Williams' letter. I think she is very nice, and I like her ere I have seen her.' And of Miss Perry, of whom so much more was to be heard later, Madeleine writes: 'I am sorry I said anything about Mary. It was not kind of me. She is your kind and true friend. It was very bad of me, but I was vexed. She said she would not write to me . . . True love, do not say a word to her about my writing in an unkind way. No, sweet love, say nothing to her about it. She is your friend and that is enough. She shall be mine some day soon.' All Madeleine's likes and dislikes are apparently subject to fluctuations. In a burst of candour she says to Emile: 'I have come to the conclusion that you don't know me. If you were with me long you would know me better – it is only those I love that I am indifferent to – even my dog – which I love – sometimes I hate him for no reason – it is only a fancy which I cannot help. With strangers it is different.'

Letter after letter she poured out to L'Angelier, and it is in some of the letters in which she is dissimulating most that we get the truest glimpses of her nature. For the strange thing about Madeleine Smith is that, in spite of all the doubt that must for ever obscure certain of her actions, the girl herself stands revealed with a clarity that puts her nature almost beyond argument. Madeleine had intense vitality. A modern education might, almost undoubtedly would, have saved her. Games or a career, or both, would have occupied that restless mind and body. Her powers of will, not all turned back upon scheming and deception, could have carried her far. Even when all was over, when, with her life given back to her, but with nothing but shame and obloquy her portion, her nerve did not fail her. With intense languor and difficulty most women would have crawled back to any pleasure in life. Not so Madeleine. She takes her invincible spirit, her hard brightness, with her into the bosom of that family, every member of which must have wished she had never been born. Even her beauty was untarnished, that beauty which was of a bright darkness. She had a fair rosy skin, dark eyes, and hair of polished ebony that swept down beside her temples. Thus she appeared to the staring public in the courthouse, a little fashionable scooped bonnet set right at the back of her head, disengaging that clear-cut profile which had something of the eagle about its defiant contours.

Madeleine Smith was born before her time. She had all the profound physical passion with which the northern woman so often makes her southern sister seem insipid; and this passion, of the essence of her being, was a thing supposed at that particular date not to exist in a 'nice' woman. Nowadays Madeleine would have had various outlets for the violence of her personality. She could have become a business woman, or gone on the stage, or lived in a bachelor flat, and had love affairs, without the end of the world having resulted. In the fifties none of these solutions was available. In those days there was nothing for her to do but to get engaged, a very tame state of affairs for a character like hers, unless she could add to it a set of strange circumstances to give it interest. These circumstances she found in L'Angelier, for whom beyond a doubt she felt for some time a passion that was entirely sensual, of all forms of love the one which lays itself open the most to violent reaction. Desire, fulfilment, satiety, and disgust – these were the four phases through which Madeleine passed, and the last phase was foredoomed from the first moment.

She first met L'Angelier in April of 1855, and what love there was in the affair lasted only until the autumn of 1856, though outward expressions of it continue in her letters until the end of January 1857, when even simulated ardours wane perceptibly. Already for some time back she had been encouraging the attentions of another man whom she wished to accept. Madeleine had been educated at a genteel boarding-school at Clapton, near London. She was fond of music and fond of reading, fond of dancing, fond of pleasure, and fond of exerting consciously the power of her own personality. To pen a creature such as this in the respectable fastnesses of a Glasgow house, where her life consisted of a round of decorous visits paid with her mother and sister, and of dinner-parties given by her father's merchant acquaintances, was to court disaster. It was all right for a Bessie or a Janet, but it was disastrous for such as Madeleine.

Hers was a nature which had to have adventure. In the World War she would have been an admirable member of society. She would have driven an ambulance, had sentimental little affairs with the wounded officers, been thoroughly competent and completely occupied. Had she been a medieval Italian she might have been a successful intriguer and removed people who inconvenienced her from her path, and seduced those whom she wished to seduce without any loss of social standing. As it was, she was born in that period of the world's history which was the most hopeless for a nature such as hers. Strength, determination, passion, ruthlessness were a bad foundation to be overlaid with the Victorian sentimentality which was also hers in full measure, and which, living when she did, she could hardly have avoided. It was her only outlet, and she sentimentalized to the full. L'Angelier appeared to have a most romantic figure; he was practically a foreigner, he was poor, he was handsome, and above all, he was endowed with a great flow of words. He had been immensely taken with her from afar, and had urged a mutual acquaintance to bring about an introduction. This was a good beginning to make with any woman, and L'Angelier added to the irresistible appeal of the state of his feelings a charm of person new in her experience. Instead of the northern restraint and self-control, of the dour manliness to which she was accustomed, he possessed a small but pleasing person, with a pretty face and curly hair, and white hands with the art of love-making at the tip of their fingers. But as was the case with Madeleine herself, if the outside were soft and pleasing to the eye, there was relentless force concealed beneath. Pierre Emile L'Angelier had no notion of burdening himself with the cast-off daughter of a rich man. It seems that Madeleine, at the height of her love, was quite prepared to face poverty with a smile, but L'Angelier always refused. Parental approval was essential to his ambitious nature.

He was ten years older than Madeleine, and between the period when she met him and an earlier period when he had been employed by Dickson & Co., seed merchants, he lived in Paris, and as a member of the National Guard had been through some exciting times in the revolution of 1848 – another touch of the romantic which pleased her. Like Madeleine, he was primed with all the traditions of that generation as regards the nice conduct of love affairs. He had already adored a lady in Fife, had flattered himself that he had a broken heart, talked largely of suicide, but never committed it. He would boast of his successes with women and threaten to blow out his brains in almost the same breath, and, like most profligates, had an almost priggish standard for other people, particularly for any woman whom he might be debauching at the time.

And here in this very priggishness of his we find the characteristic which above all others seems to have enslaved Madeleine. Like many passionate girls, before they have attained sufficient know-ledge of human nature to enable them to acquire balance, she was an unconscious masochist. She saw herself in the position of L'An-gelier's slave. To that her letters bear indubitable testimony. This sordid little Abélard, playing the schoolmaster, this sensation-loving Héloïse, determined to be mastered into submission, were playing a game which he, with his greater experience, must have known was one which would land them in self-disgust, but which she found too alluring to be resisted. In her very first letter to L'Angelier Made-leine writes: 'I am trying to break myself of all my *very* bad habits. It is you I have to thank for this, which I do sincerely from my heart.' There are many passages in her letters which tell the same tale: 'If ever again I show temper, which I hope to God I won't, don't mind it . . . I ought never in any way to vex or annoy you.' 'I often think that I must be very, very stupid in your eyes. You must be disappointed in me. I wonder you like me in the least.' 'How I have reproached myself all the week for writing you such unkind letters. Will you, darling Emile, pardon me for them . . . How I look forward to our happy union. It cannot but be happy. We shall love each other so, and, believe me, it shall be quite different. I shall be beside you, so if I do anything wrong and you check me, I shall never, never do it again. I shall be all you could wish. You shall love me and I shall obey you.' 'I shall never cause you un-happiness again. I was cold and unloving, but it shall never be repeated: No, I am now a wife – a wife in every sense of the word, and it is my duty to conduct myself as such. Yes, I shall behave now more to your mind.' 'I do love you, fondly, truly. You will not leave me, your wife, with no guide, no friend, no protector, with no one to love me, no one to care for me, no one to tell me my faults.' 'Now, Emile, I shall keep all the promises I have made you. I shall love and obey you. It is my duty as your wife to do so. I shall do all you want me.' And writing to Mary Perry, the sentimental go-between of the pair, she gives away the relationship between her and L'Angelier with – 'As yet I fear I have done little to please him, but he has forgiven me all my faults.' L'Angelier played up to this aspect of himself as master. He would boast to a friend of his – 'I shall forbid Madeleine to do such a thing'; and early in the relationship, when she made her first effort to try and break away from him, he wrote: 'Madeleine, you have truly acted wrong . . . I leave your conscience to speak for itself.' But his finest effort he reserved until he had first succeeded in having connection with her, when he actually blamed her for the occurrence: 'I am sad at what you did,' he wrote; 'I regret it very much. Why, Mimi, did you give way after your promises? My pet, it is a pity . . . I was disappointed, my love, at the little you had to say, but I can understand why. You are not stupid, Mimi, but if you disappoint me in information, and I have cause to reproach you of it, you will have no one to blame but yourself, as I have given you warning long enough to improve yourself. Sometimes I do think you take no notice of my wishes and my desires, but say "yes" for a mere matter of form . . . We must not be separated all this winter, for I know, Mimi, you will be as giddy as last. You will be going to public balls, and that I cannot endure. On my honour, dearest, sooner than see you or hear of you running about as you did last, I would leave Glasgow myself. Though I have surely forgiven you, I do not forget the misery I endured for your sake . . . I cannot help doubting your word about flirting. You told me the same thing before you left for Edinburgh, and you did nothing else during your stay there. I do trust you will give me no cause to find fault again with you on that score, but I doubt very much the sincerity of your promise . . . Oh, Mimi, let your conduct make me happy.' It is no wonder that this sort of thing ended in weariness and disgust. When Madeleine is appealing to L'Angelier in February of 1857 to let her go, she admits as much: 'I did love you, and it was my soul's ambition to be your wife. I asked you to tell me my faults. You did so and made me cold towards you gradually. When you have found fault with me I have cooled. It was not love for another, for there is no one I love.'

Madeleine was correct in saying there was no one she loved. Her demure acceptance of Mr Minnoch's suit and her prim little letters leave no doubt that she was marrying the wealthy middle-aged merchant simply because she felt the time had come to put an end to her liaison with L'Angelier and to settle in an establishment of her own. What else could she do? She saw more and more clearly that there was no hope of a marriage sanctioned by her parents with L'Angelier, and she had no economic independence and no means of earning it. The months of gratified passion between April 1855 and February 1857 had probably exhausted her emotional capacity for some little time to come, for they had been full enough of excitement to please and eventually to weary even Madeleine. She had borne with a great deal from L'Angelier. His ardours, even those that savoured of the schoolmaster, she had undoubtedly wanted and encouraged, but his open and shameless scheming would have disgusted anyone less infatuated far earlier. In the same letter in which he reproaches her for having yielded to his desires, he poses the amazing question: 'Think of the consequences if I were never to marry you . . . Try your friends once more, tell your determination, say nothing will change you, that you have thought seriously of it, and on that I shall fix speaking to Huggins for September. Unless you do something of that sort heaven only knows when I shall marry you. Unless you do, dearest, I shall have to leave the country . . . It is your parents' fault if shame is the result. They are to blame for it all . . . Mimi, dearest, you must take a bold step to be my wife. I would treat you, pet, by the love you have for me. Mimi, do speak to your mother . . . Oh, Mimi, be bold for once. Do not fear them. Tell them you are my wife before God. Do not let them leave you without being married, for I cannot answer what would happen. My conscience reproaches me of a sin that marriage only can efface . . . I was not angry at your loving me, Mimi, but I am sad it happened. You had no resolution. It was very bad indeed. I shall look with regret at that night. No, nothing except our marriage will efface it from my memory. Mimi, only fancy if it was known!' This ineffable effusion was not admitted as evidence in the trial, as both it and another long letter which he wrote to Madeleine she had destroyed, and they only existed in drafts, which this cautious lover had kept in his own rooms. The defence argued that the admission of drafts as evidence was not allowable, and this objection was sustained. L'Angelier's letters, therefore, except for the few notes which were actually sent through the post and one press-copy which was admitted as evidence, remain merely unofficial proof of his peculiar frame of mind.

In the summers the Smith family stayed at their country-house at Rowaleyn, and here L'Angelier came several times and met Madeleine after dark by appointment. It was at Rowaleyn that the first connection between them took place in the summer of 1856, but that there must have been much love-making of an intimate nature in the months preceding this date there can be no doubt from a study of Madeleine's letters, which had been filled for months with the most ardent endearments. For a long time she had been signing herself 'his wife' and calling him 'her own darling husband', talking of the pleasure of being 'fondled' by her dear Emile. Complete intimacy once established between them, Madeleine let loose the pagan side of her nature, which was perhaps its most admirable quality, and which shocked most utterly her contemporaries when once it became known to them. She was quite frank about her enjoyment of physical pleasures: 'M. [mother] won't allow us to leave when we have friends in our own house, so I do not know where we may go. I do wish she would go, and then I could see you, be pressed to your heart, be kissed by you, my own, my beloved, my fond Emile. I am excited much tonight. Were you here I would love you with my heart and soul.' 'I must go to bed, for I feel cold, so goodnight. Would to God it were to be by your side. I would feel well and happy then. I think I would be wishing you to *love* me if I were with you, but I do not suppose you would refuse me, for I know you would like to *love* your Mimi.' And again: 'Emile, you are not pleased because I would not let you *love* me last night. Your last visit you said you would not do it again until we were married. I said to myself at the time, well, I shall not let Emile do this again. It was a punishment to me to be deprived of your loving me, for it is a pleasure, and no one can deny that. It is but human nature. Is not everyone who *loves* of the same mind? Yes.'

Candour such as this was felt to be perfectly shocking from a young woman, and to do the spirit of that time justice it would probably have been felt to be just as shocking had the parties been married. Love-making was a mysterious arrangement on the part of Providence, which was necessary to gentlemen and which a good wife accepted as her bounden duty. It was not a pagan festival such as Madeleine found it. The Lord Justice-Clerk (Lord Hope) expressed the feelings of everyone when he observed in his summing-up: 'The letters continued on her part in the same terms of passionate love for a very considerable time. I say "passionate love" because, unhappily, they are written without any sense of decency and in most licentious terms.' His lordship then read one of the letters, which ended – 'Oh, to be in thy embrace, my sweet love. Love again to thee from thy ever-loving and ever-devoted Mimi, thine own wife.' 'What,' asks his lordship, 'could she expect but sexual intercourse after thus presenting and inviting it?' The answer is, of course, that she did intend and wished sexual intercourse, and that had L'Angelier only let her go when she tired she would probably have never regretted it, in spite of the conventional expressions of remorse in her later letters – written when she was trying to soften L'Angelier's heart. Her candour seemed to the Judge almost incredible, and he continues as follows: 'Can you be surprised after such letters as those of the 29th April and the 3rd May that on the 6th of May, three days afterwards, he got possession of her person? On the 7th of May she writes to him, and in that letter is there the slightest appearance of grief or remorse? None whatever. It is the letter of a girl rejoicing in what had passed, and alluding to it, in one passage in particular, in terms which I will not read, for perhaps they were never previously committed to paper as having passed between a man and a woman. What passed must have passed out of doors, not in the house, and she talks of the act as hers as much as his.' These remarks, which at the time were considered the most severe condemnation, convey a truth which was Madeleine's only justification. The act was as much hers as his, and she never pretended otherwise. As to the satisfaction of her desire, she probably thought that it made small difference whether it took place respectably in a bedroom or beneath the trees at Rowaleyn. 'This is a letter from a girl,' continued the Judge, 'written at five in the morning just after she had submitted to his embraces. Can you conceive any worse state of mind than this letter exhibits? In other letters she uses the word "love" underscored, showing clearly what she meant by it . . .' Madeleine meant by it what most people mean by it, but she had the courage to say so.

Madeleine had been unashamed at the height of her fervent love, but when the force of her passion had subsided she felt very differently. There is no doubt that she did not show this change in her feelings to L'Angelier for some time. Mr Minnoch had been paying her attentions, the nature of which was quite understood by everyone concerned, the whole winter of 1856, and L'Angelier had been extremely jealous.

'I did tell you at one time that I did not like William Minnoch, but he was so pleasant that he quite raised himself in my estimation,' Madeleine writes to L'Angelier in the autumn of 1856; and again: 'Mr Minnoch has been here since Friday – he is most agreeable – I think – we shall see him very often this winter – he says we shall, and P. being so fond of him I am sure he shall ask him in often.' She knew that L'Angelier was bound to hear of Minnoch's attentions, and probably thought it better to write with an appearance of frankness. Not two weeks after the letter last quoted we find her writing a letter, beginning coldly 'My dear Emile', in which she says: 'Our meeting last night was peculiar. Emile, you are not reasonable; I do not wonder at your not loving me as you once did.

Emile, I am not worthy of you. You deserve a better wife than I. I see misery before me this winter. I would to God we were not to be so near Mr Minnoch. You shall hear all stories and believe them. You will say I am indifferent, because I shall not be able to see you much. I forgot to tell you last night that I shall not be able of an evening to let you in. My room is next to Bessie's and on the same floor as the front door. I shall never be able to spend the happy hours we did last winter.' Whether Madeleine hoped by suggesting frequently enough to L'Angelier that he no longer loved her, that he might come to believe so himself, we cannot tell, but if so she failed of her effect.

A servant called Christina Haggart, who had been wont to let L'Angelier in while the family still lived at the house in India Street, and who received L'Angelier's letters to Madeleine during the two summers at Rowaleyn, was again called into the service of the lovers in Blythswood Square, though apparently against Madeleine's wish, for in the letter posted on 20 October she wrote: 'Do you know I have taken a great dislike to C. H. I shall try and do without her aid in the winter. She has been with us four years, and I am tired of her, but I won't show it to her, so, dearest love, be easy on that point.' However, by November, when the family are back at Blythswood Square, Madeleine's letters are as ardent as ever, and she, who knew she was being courted by Minnoch, and who already tried to suggest a discontinuance of her relations with L'Angelier, was writing phrases like 'My own sweet darling husband, I long to be your wife.'

Minnoch was now a constant visitor at the house. 'It was Mr Minnoch that I was at the concert with. You see I would not hide that from you. Emile, he is Papa's friend, and I know he will have him at the house; but need you mind that, when I have told you that I have no regard for him? It is only you, my Emile, that I love. You should not mind public report.' In December she sends L'Angelier a portrait, saying: 'I hope ere long you will have the original, which I know you will like better than a glass likeness. Won't you, sweet love? I hope you got it safe. C. H. left it at the door for you.' Her letters during this period are full of references to her marriage with L'Angelier and her longing for it. She even goes so far as to discuss the different ways of getting married, when all the time she had determined to marry William Minnoch. She had, indeed, accepted his proposal of marriage on 28 January.

L'Angelier was in the habit of leaving notes for her on the sill of her bedroom window, which was below the street level. On one occasion at least he entered the house, for Christina Haggart admitted that she opened the back door and that she and the cook sat in the kitchen while L'Angelier and Madeleine occupied the servants' room, which was next to the back door. By the end of January the tone of her letters is still loving, but more despairing. She now talks of marriage as a beautiful impossibility: 'I never felt so restless and so unhappy as I have for some time past. I would do anything to keep sad thoughts from my mind . . . A dark spot is in the future. What can it be? Oh, God, keep it from us. Oh, may we be happy. Dear darling, pray for our happiness. I weep now, Emile, to think of our fate. If we could only get married all would be well. But alas, alas, I see no chance, no chance of happiness for me. I must speak with you. Yes, I must again be pressed to your loving bosom, be kissed by you, my only love, my dearest darling husband. Why were we fated to be so unhappy? Why were we fated to be kept separate? . . . If you are able I need not say it will give me pleasure to hear from you tomorrow night. If at 10 o'clock do not wait to see me, as Janet might not be asleep, and I may have to wait until she sleeps to take it in. Make no noise.'

Some letter that she wrote after this one was returned to her by L'Angelier, for quite at the beginning of February, the exact date is illegible, she writes: 'I felt truly astonished to have my last letter returned to me, but it shall be the last you shall have an opportunity of returning to me. When you are not pleased with the letters I send you, then our correspondence shall be at an end, and, as there is a coolness on both sides, our engagement had better be broken . . . Altogether I think, owing to coldness and indifference (nothing else), we had better in the future consider ourselves as strangers. I trust to your honour as a gentleman that you will not reveal anything that may have passed between us. I shall feel obliged by your bringing me my letters and my likeness on Thursday evening at seven. Be at the area gate and C. H. will take the parcel from you.' This letter was unanswered, and she writes again: 'I attribute it to your having cold that I had no answer to my last note. On Thursday evening you were, I suppose, afraid of the night air. I fear your cold is not better. I again appoint Thursday, same place, street gate, seven o'clock.'

L'Angelier evidently answered by threatening her, for the next letter begins: 'Monday night. Emile, I have just had your note. Emile, for the love you once had for me do nothing until I see you. For God's sake do not bring your once loved Mimi to an open shame. Emile, I have deceived you; I have deceived my mother ... I deceived you by telling you that she still knew of our engagement. She did not ... Emile, write to no one, Papa or any other. Oh, do not until I see you on Wednesday night.' The letter goes on madly imploring her lover not to drive her to despair and death. L'Angelier wrote her, but apparently nothing that would ease her mind, for in her next letter she says: 'No one can know the intense agony of mind I have suffered last night and today. Emile, my father's wrath would kill me. You little know his temper. Emile, for the love you once had for me do not denounce me to my P. Emile, if he should read my letters to you – he will put me from him, he will hold me as a guilty wretch. I loved you, and wrote to you in my first ardent love – it was with my deepest love I loved you. It was for your love I adored you. I put on paper what I should not. I was free, because I loved you with my heart. If he or any other one saw those fond letters to you, what would not be said of me? On my bended knees I write to you and ask you, as you hope for mercy at the judgement day, do not inform on me. Do not make me a public shame.' There is a postscript to this letter: 'I cannot get to the back stair. I never could see the way to it. I will take you within the door. The area gate will be open. I shall see you from my window at twelve o'clock. I will wait until one o'clock.' A meeting apparently took place, during which she must have been able to win him over by letting him think she would be his once more – perhaps even by becoming his once more – and on 14 February she writes, saying: 'Bring me all my cool letters back – the last four I have written – and I will give you others in their place.' L'Angelier, however, was not a man to give up anything, and Madeleine saw that there was no way out of her desperate position, and to gain time she continued to pour her ardours upon L'Angelier.

Now, on a day in the second week in February, just about the time when L'Angelier was threatening her with exposure, Madeleine had asked William Murray, a young boy employed at the house in Blythswood Square, to go to the apothecary's and get her a small phial of prussic acid. She wrote this request down on a piece of paper and gave it to him. The apothecary refused, and Madeleine, who had told the boy she wanted it to whiten her hands, said, 'Very well, never mind.' It was fortunate for Madeleine that the Lord Justice-Clerk did not make very much of this point in his summing-up. Even the Lord Advocate in his speech for the prosecution does not seem to have borne on it as heavily as he might have done. For Madeleine wrote L'Angelier a wildly imploring letter on 9 February, and William Murray and the doctor and apothecary in the shop to which he went for the prussic acid all agreed that the date when the purchase was attempted was in the second week of February. About 12 February a reconciliation between Madeleine and L'Angelier took place, and the ardent correspondence and meetings began again. All this time, it must be remembered, Madeleine was definitely engaged to Mr Minnoch, with the approval of her parents. She must have known that affairs could not possibly continue as they were.

On 17 February, which was a Tuesday, L'Angelier dined with Miss Perry, and, according to her, he said that he was seeing Madeleine on the 19th, but there is no evidence that he ever met Madeleine then (on the date in question). This day, on which, according to Miss Perry's evidence, he was to see Madeleine, was Thursday 19 February.

Now, in a note written by Madeleine after the breach between her and L'Angelier had been healed, and posted on 14 February, she says: 'I hope to see you very soon. Write me for next Thursday, and then I shall tell you when I can see you.' This is in the note in which she says she wants all her 'cool letters' back.

In the middle of the night of the 19th L'Angelier was taken violently ill in his lodgings, having gone out on that evening to a destination which will never be known. On the morning of the 20th he was found by Mrs Jenkins, his landlady, writhing in pain on the floor of his bedroom. He told her that on his way home he had been taken with a violent pain in his bowels and stomach. During the course of the morning he recovered somewhat, and between ten and eleven o'clock he dressed and went out. He returned in the afternoon, said he had seen a doctor, and brought a bottle of medicine with him, which he took. The symptoms of this, his first illness, were similar to those on the two following occasions, and this first illness occurred before Madeleine Smith could be shown to have purchased any arsenic or poison of any kind. Her first purchase of arsenic, as far as is known (and that purchase like her two succeeding ones was made quite openly), was on 21 February.

On Saturday 21 February Madeleine Smith went to the shop of a Mr Murdoch and bought arsenic. It was entered in Murdoch's book as follows: 'February 21st. Miss Smith, 7 Blythswood Square, six-pennyworth of arsenic. For garden and country house. M. H. Smith.' This arsenic was common white arsenic mixed with soot in the proportion required by the Act. Three days after the purchase Madeleine called in at the shop again and asked if arsenic should not be white, to which Mr Murdoch replied that the law required that it should be mixed with some colouring matter.

L'Angelier was taken ill with his second attack on the night of Sunday, the 22nd, having only just recovered from the attack of the previous Friday morning. There is no proof that he saw Madeleine on the night of Sunday, the 22nd. About four o'clock in the morning he called his landlady. He was vomiting the same sort of green substance as he had previously. She was unaware if he had been out the night before; he said nothing about it. Dr Thomson was called in by a friend of L'Angelier's in the afternoon, and left a prescription, which was duly made up. L'Angelier was about eight days in the house and away from his place of business. The prosecution did not allege any meeting to have taken place between Madeleine and L'Angelier during this period.

On 6 March Madeleine made a second purchase of arsenic from the shop of a Mr Currie. She got sixpennyworth, the same quantity as before. When she made this second purchase, Madeleine was accompanied by Mary Jane Buchanan, a girl friend. Miss Buchanan heard her ask for the arsenic and heard the shopman tell her she must sign the book. Miss Buchanan asked Madeleine why she needed the arsenic, a question not put by the shopman, and Madeleine replied that it was to kill rats. The shopman thereupon suggested phosphorus. Madeleine replied that she had tried that before and it had proved useless, and she added that the family were going to Bridge of Allan, and so there was no danger in leaving the arsenic lying about in the town house. 'On leaving the shop,' remarks Miss Buchanan naïvely, 'I laughed at the idea of a young lady buying arsenic. She said nothing, but laughed too.' Madeleine and her family left that day for Bridge of Allan. On 4 March Madeleine had written to L'Angelier suggesting that he should go to recover from his indisposition to the Isle of Wight: 'I hope you won't go to Bridge of Allan, as Papa and Mama would say it was I brought you there . . . Go to Isle of Wight. I am exceedingly sorry, love, I cannot see you where I go. It is impossible, but the first thing I do on my return will be to see you, sweet love.' L'Angelier wrote back: 'The doctor says I must go to Bridge of Allan. I cannot travel 500 miles to the Isle of Wight and 500 back. What is your object in wishing me so very much to go south?' What was Madeleine's object? The most probable solution of the riddle is that she felt that, if only L'Angelier could be got such a long way away, her marriage with Minnoch might be safely negotiated in his absence, and that, the dreaded event once a *fait accompli*, L'Angelier might cease to trouble her. L'Angelier's refusal, however, made this scheme, if she had intended it, of no avail. L'Angelier, angry and suspicious, once again expresses his belief in her engagement with Mr Minnoch. Madeleine wrote back soothingly two letters full of love and tender expressions. A letter written at the same time to William Minnoch contrasts rather strangely with those she was

writing to L'Angelier. 'My dearest William,' she wrote to Mr Minnoch, 'it is but fair after all your kindness to me that I should write
you a note. The day I part from friends I always feel sad; but to
part from one I love as I do you makes me feel truly sad and dull.
My only consolation is that we meet soon. Tomorrow we shall be
home. I do so wish you were here today. We might take a long
walk. Our walk to Dunblane I shall ever remember with pleasure.
That walk fixed the day on which we are to begin a new life – a life
which I hope may be of happiness and long duration to both of us.
My aim through life shall be to please you and study you. Dear
William, I must conclude, as Mama is ready to go to Stirling. I do
not go with the same pleasure as I did last time. I hope you got to
town safe and found your sisters well. Accept my kindest love, and
ever believe to be yours with affection, Madeleine.'

The Smith family returned to Blythswood Square on 17 March,
and L'Angelier went for a little holiday to Bridge of Allan on the
19th, entrusting M. Thuau, his fellow lodger, with the forwarding
of his letters. He had hardly left the house when a letter came for
him, which was forwarded on to Bridge of Allan, and in a letter
written to Miss Perry from there on the 20th he says: 'I should have
come to see someone last night, but the letter came too late.'

This letter, which was forwarded on to L'Angelier, was never
found, the envelope alone being in his bag when his effects were
examined. The subsequent letter, however, shows undoubtedly that
it had suggested an assignation, for Madeleine writes from Glasgow
on 21 March a letter beginning: 'Why, my beloved, did you not
come to me? Oh, beloved, are you well? Come to me, sweet one. I
waited and waited for you, but you came not. I shall wait again
tomorrow night, same hour and arrangement. Do come, sweet
love, my own dear love of a sweetheart. Come, beloved, and clasp
me to your heart. Come and we shall be happy. A kiss, fond love;
adieu, with tender embraces.' As the Lord Advocate said in his
address to the jury: 'That letter was posted in Glasgow, if at a box,
between 9 a.m. and 12.30 p.m., and if at the General Post Office,
between 11.45 a.m. and 1 p.m. That letter was found in the pocket
of a coat. About that letter and envelope there is no dispute or

question whatever. There was an appointment for Thursday, the 19th. On Wednesday, the 18th, she went back to Currie's shop, told him that the first rats had been killed, and that they had found a great many large ones lying in the house; and, as she had got arsenic before, appeared to be a respectable person, and told her story without hesitation, she got her third packet of arsenic. That letter was forwarded by Thuau to L'Angelier on the same day with the rest. He enclosed it in a letter of his own, in which he says that the letter came at half-past twelve, and that he hastens to put it in the post if there is time. L'Angelier got that letter after nine o'clock at Stirling on Sunday morning.'

In the evening L'Angelier arrived home at his lodgings and explained to his landlady that a letter forwarded on to him had brought him home. He looked well, said the landlady, and stated he was a great deal better, and almost well. He went out that night about nine o'clock, and before going out he said: 'If you please, give me the pass-key. I am not sure, but I may be late.'

'I saw him next at about half-past two on Monday morning,' affirmed his landlady. 'He did not use the pass-key. The bell rang with great violence. I rose and called, "Who's there?" He said, "It is I, Mrs Jenkins. Open the door if you please." I did so. He was standing with his arms crossed across his stomach. He said, "I am very bad. I am going to have another vomiting of that bile."'

L'Angelier did indeed have another vomiting, far worse than on the second occasion, worse even than on the first. By four o'clock he was very bad, and the landlady wished to go for the doctor, but he said it was too early. By five he was so bad that she insisted on fetching the doctor, and she went for a Dr Steven. The doctor himself was ill and could not come, but recommended twenty-five drops of laudanum and a mustard plaster on the stomach. L'Angelier refused both the laudanum and the plaster, and continued to retch. At seven o'clock Mrs Jenkins again went for Dr Steven, and this time he came with her. He evidently saw that the patient was very ill. The doctor put more blankets upon the bed and kept bottles of hot water round the patient's body. He gave him morphia and applied a poultice. Dr Steven called again at a quarter past eleven, and Mrs Jenkins met him telling him that L'Angelier had been quite as bad as earlier in the morning, but had just become quiet.

Dr Steven went into the room and found him lying dead, away from the light, in a comfortable position, his knees slightly drawn up, one arm outside the bedclothes as though he were asleep. At midday Dr Steven went again, and met Dr Thomson, who had attended L'Angelier in his previous illness. They decided it was impossible to give a certificate of death without making an examination. A second post-mortem examination was made later by Dr Frederick Penny, and it was proved beyond a doubt that L'Angelier had died as the result of arsenical poisoning. Now we have here, excluding the date of the first illness, two dates of the utmost importance in this case, 22 February and 22 March, both of them Sundays, and on neither of these dates is there the smallest proof that L'Angelier met Madeleine.

The Dean of Faculty naturally made the most of this: 'Observe, gentlemen,' he said, 'that unless you shall hold it to be true and proved by the evidence before you that these two persons met on the 22nd of February, which was a Sunday, or unless, in like manner, you hold it to be proved that they met again on the fatal night of the 22nd March, there never was a meeting at all after the prisoner had made any of her purchases of arsenic. I maintain that there not only was no meeting – that we have no evidence of any meeting – but that practically there was no possibility of any meeting. I say that unless you can believe on the evidence that there was a meeting on the 22nd of February, or again, on the 22nd of March, there is no possible occasion on which she either could have administered poison or could have proposed or intended to administer it.' Certainly Mrs Jenkins had no recollection of L'Angelier's going out on the evening of 22 February. As the Dean of Faculty went on to say: 'L'Angelier was not taken ill until late in the morning, and he did not come home ill. There is no evidence that he ever came home at all, or that he ever was out. All we know, as a matter of fact, is that he was taken ill in the morning about four or five o'clock.'

The argument of the prosecution that L'Angelier had indeed seen Madeleine on the evening of the 22nd was based on a letter posted in Glasgow on a Wednesday, but with an undecipherable date, in which Madeleine says: 'You did look bad Sunday night and Monday morning.' The argument of the prosecution was that this letter was written on 25 February, and that the writer was referring to the attack of the night of Sunday the 22nd. If this could have been proved it would, of course, have been a damning piece of evidence, but the postmark on the envelope was illegible. The defence maintained that it might have been written on any Wednesday during the intercourse between the accused and the deceased. The prosecution contended that they proved that it was written on 25 February, irrespective of the postmark. The letter went on to say: 'I think you got sick with walking home so late, and the long want of food, so the next time we meet I shall make you eat a loaf of bread before you go out. I am longing to meet you again, sweet love. My head aches so, and I am looking so bad, so I cannot sit up as I used to, but I am taking some stuff to bring back the colour, and I shall see you soon again.'

'Now, gentlemen,' said the Lord Advocate, 'if that was written on the 25th, it proves that he saw her on Sunday and Monday, the 22nd and 23rd. It proves that he was sick at the time, and was looking very bad. According to my statement, he was ill on the 19th. It proves that she was thinking about giving him food; that she was laying a foundation for seeing him; that she was taking stuff to bring back her colour. It proves that she was holding out a kind of explanation of the symptoms which he had, because she says she is ill herself; and it proves that all this took place the day after she bought the arsenic at Murdoch's.'

Now, Miss Perry stated in evidence that L'Angelier took tea with her on 9 March, this after his first two illnesses and before the third, and that he said to her, 'I cannot think why I was so unwell after getting that coffee and chocolate from her.' Miss Perry insisted that he referred to two separate occasions, and that 'her' meant Madeleine. She also added that he said, 'It is a perfect fascination, my attachment to that girl. If she were to poison me, I would forgive her.' As evidence, of course, this is valueless, and would have been rejected in an English court of law.

We now come to the all-important date of 22 March, the Sunday on which, after the receipt of a forwarded letter, L'Angelier hurried back to Glasgow. There is no question but that he went out on that evening, and the landlady concluded that he was going to see his young lady, as on these occasions he always asked for the pass-key. This in itself is, of course, in favour of the argument of the defence that he had not been to see Madeleine on the evening of 22 February, for the landlady stated that on that date he had not asked for the pass-key, and neither had she let him in. There seemed a good deal of justification for the Dean of Faculty's observation that the foundation of the prosecution's case was somewhat shaky. Until it came to dealing with the fatal events of the night of 22 March, it may be said that the defence had had rather the better of it. In spite of the most rigorous search no purchase of arsenic could be traced to Madeleine at the time of L'Angelier's first illness, and at the time of his second illness it could not even be proved that he had left the house.

By the date of the third illness three purchases of arsenic had been proved, and also the fact that L'Angelier had left his lodgings, taking the pass-key with him; but, again, we are confronted with the fact that no proof has ever been forthcoming that he and Madeleine met that night. Madeleine's own account of that evening in her declaration is simply: 'I went to bed on Sunday night about eleven o'clock, and remained in bed until the usual time of getting up the next morning, about eight or nine o'clock.' Her little sister Janet, who was called for the defence, said: 'I remember Sunday, the 22nd of March. We went to bed at the same time that night. I am quite sure. We went at 10.30 or after that. We went downstairs together from the dining-room. I don't remember which was in bed first. We were both undressing at the same time, and got into bed about the same time. We usually take about half an hour to undress. We were in no special hurry that night in undressing. My sister was in bed with me before I was asleep. I am sure of that. She was undressed as usual, and in her night-clothes.' Cross-examined by the Lord Advocate: 'I have seen my sister take cocoa; I never saw her make it in her room. She kept it in a paper in her room.' Re-examined: 'I have seen my sister taking cocoa in the dining-room. I don't know she had been recommended to take it. No other body in the house took it. She kept it in her room, and took it in the dining-room. On Monday morning, the 23rd of March, I found my sister in bed when I awoke.'

L'Angelier left his lodgings about nine o'clock. A man named James Galloway, who knew L'Angelier by sight, stated that on Sunday 22 March, he saw L'Angelier in Sauchiehall Street going east in the direction of Blythswood Square, and about four or five minutes from there. He was walking rather slowly. Mary Tweedle, a servant in a lodging-house in Terrace Street, who also knew L'Angelier by sight, stated that he called at the house of her employer, Mrs Parr, at about twenty minutes past nine that night, and asked for his friend, Mr McAlester, who was not at home. This house was about five minutes away from Blythswood Square. Thomas Kavan, a night constable in Glasgow, whose beat included the north and east sides of Blythswood Square, remembered seeing L'Angelier more than once passing along the garden side by the railings, but he swore positively that he had not seen him on the night of the 22nd.

No one will ever know exactly how L'Angelier spent the hours between nine o'clock and half-past two, when Mrs Jenkins was aroused by a violent ringing of the street-door bell. The only thing that is certain is that during that period of time he had swallowed a vast quantity of arsenic.

There is no doubt that Madeleine had a motive for wishing to be rid of L'Angelier. There is no doubt either that she could have had the opportunity had she chosen. There is also no doubt – it was never even denied by the defence – that she was in the possession of arsenic. Her own statement was that she had bought the poison as a cosmetic for washing her face and arms, and that she had used it all for that purpose – all the stories she told of needing it for the suppression of rats were proved false. The defence contended that it was impossible to administer such a large quantity of arsenic in any beverage so that it would remain undetected. 'Even supposing,' urged the Dean of Faculty, 'that anybody could swallow all that arsenic in a cup of cocoa, it was still impossible, with all that gritty undissolved powder passing over his throat, he should not become aware that he had swallowed something unusual. And yet,' he went on, 'instead of immediately calling medical aid or communicating his alarm or his suspicions to anybody, he staggers home in great pain; and through the long dreary hours of that fatal morning, amidst all his frightful sufferings, neither to the landlady nor to the doctor does he ever suggest that he might have been poisoned, or breathes a suspicion against her whom he had previously suspected of an attempt to poison him.'

And here we come to the most mysterious question in this mysterious case. Madeleine herself, innocent or guilty, is a comparatively straightforward proposition; it is L'Angelier, that little, scheming, sensual, iron-willed lady-killer, who is the insoluble riddle. There can be only four explanations, of which two cannot be entertained seriously, of the events of that night. The first is that the poison may have been administered to him by some person or persons accidentally, which is obviously not worth considering. The second is that he was murdered by some person other than Madeleine, which is equally untenable. No one had any cause to wish him ill. These two flights of fancy can therefore be laid aside. The third supposition is that Madeleine deliberately administered the poison, and the fourth is the one suggested by the defence, that he committed suicide. Now, this fourth suggestion is not beyond the bounds of possibility, but it may be observed that it is unlikely that he should have made several attempts on his life by the same very painful means. This, however, is not by any means a conclusive argument. Human nature holds so much that is strange, and L'Angelier in particular was a man of such devious ways that it is just possible he might have planned to revenge himself on Madeleine by suicide. He may have meant the moral blame for his self-killing to be laid at her door, or he may even – for nothing is too fantastic to happen in real life – have killed himself meaning her to be accused of his murder; but if either of these suppositions be true, it is strange that he failed to ensure that they should occur. He had only to let fall, when lying in his death agony, some remark as he had made to Miss Perry previously for the onus of the deed to be firmly fixed on Madeleine, but through all those hours of agonized consciousness he said no word of her. If, on the other hand, we can allow ourselves for a moment the supposition, for the sake of argument, that it was indeed Madeleine who had handed him the fatal draught, we are confronted with a riddle of equal strangeness, and we are driven into the belief that after all there was more good in this hitherto contemptible little man than had ever appeared. If he were attacked by his fatal illness after having accepted drink from Madeleine's hand, if there had, indeed, been anything in his remark to Miss Perry about his having been taken ill after receiving coffee and cocoa from that same hand before, then beyond a shadow of a doubt he must have known why he was lying there in agony. He had shown himself entirely relentless to Madeleine up to that time, he was prepared to ruin her life, and yet when, as he must have believed, she had committed the last betrayal of him, he closes his lips. There is nothing in the whole of the case so strange as the problem of L'Angelier's mind and soul during those last hours of his life. No possible solution to the riddle of his death provides any possible solution to the riddle of his life.

It may be mentioned, as against the theory of suicide, that when an exhaustive inquiry was being held into all the purchases of arsenic made in Glasgow and its environs there was no trace of any having been obtained by L'Angelier, any more than there was of any by Madeleine except the three amounts she bought openly.

L'Angelier died at about nine o'clock on Monday morning. He had previously asked his landlady to send for Miss Perry, but by the time she arrived he was already dead. L'Angelier may, of course, not have thought he was going to die so soon, and perhaps had Miss Perry arrived in time he would have confided to her the secret of the past night. But he does not seem to have been particularly urgent in his request, or agitated in his mind; indeed, the last words he addressed to his landlady were: 'If I could only get a little sleep I think I should be well.' It looks as though he did not realize that he had got his death, and is an argument against the possibility of suicide.

Miss Perry's next move was a curious one. She went to the house in Blythswood Square and asked to see Mrs Smith, whom she did not know and who, she knew, was unaware that Madeleine had not given L'Angelier up a couple of years before. Miss Perry's account in the witness-box is as follows: 'I called on Mrs Smith and intimated his death to her. I saw Miss Smith, but I did not mention it to her. She recognized me, shook hands, and asked me to go into the drawing-room if I wished to see her mamma. She also asked if anything was wrong. I said that I wanted to see her mamma, and that I would acquaint her with the object of my visit.' It is incredible, but true, that not only was Mrs Smith never called to give evidence about this singular occurrence, but Miss Perry herself was never asked why she asked for Mrs Smith instead of for Madeleine, or how Mrs Smith took the news, whether she asked why Miss Perry had come to her with it at all, or how Madeleine bore herself that morning. If the truth were only known about that interview it would be invaluable to a right understanding of the case. But there is no doubt that the Smith family were protected in every way throughout all the proceedings. The only member of the family who was called was little Janet, and that was by the defence.

In the afternoon of the same day M. Auguste de Mean, Chancellor to the French Consulate at Glasgow, called upon Mr Smith. He had been acquainted with L'Angelier about three years, and knew of the liaison with Madeleine. He knew that there would be letters of Madeleine's, which were bound to be discovered, and thought it better to go to Mr Smith and warn him, so that he might perhaps be able to prevent his daughter's letters falling into other hands. Mr Smith was not called, so there is no record of how he took this news from M. de Mean.

One day that week – it is impossible to fix the exact day – the Frenchman also had an interview with Madeleine in her mother's presence, in which he advised her very seriously to tell the truth if she had seen L'Angelier on Sunday night. He warned her that any casual passer-by might have seen her if she had done so, and in that case, if she denied it, it would tell seriously against her. Madeleine persisted in her denial, saying: 'I swear to you, Monsieur de Mean, I have not seen L'Angelier for three weeks.' 'I told her,' said M. de Mean, 'that my conviction of the moment was that she must have seen him on Sunday, that he had come on purpose from Bridge of Allan at her special invitation to see her, and I did not think it likely, admitting that he had committed suicide, that he had committed suicide without knowing why she had asked him to come to Glasgow.' Madeleine also denied to M. de Mean that L'Angelier had ever been into the Blythswood Square house.

On the evening of 25 March Madeleine dined at Mr Middleton's, a minister of the United Presbyterian Church. Mr Smith was ill in bed – bed seems to have been the great resort of the elder Smiths during this period of stress – and it was Mr Minnoch who called for Madeleine and took her to the dinner-party. He seems still to have been unaware that anything was wrong, and it is impossible not to admire the gallant way in which the Smith family were keeping up the fiction that nothing was the matter. The important point about this Wednesday is that something occurred on it which frightened Madeleine. Perhaps it was the day on which M. de Mean called to see her and her mother – surely Mrs Smith should have been questioned as to this – or perhaps the talk at the Middletons' dinner-party that evening was about the mysterious death of the young clerk. No one was questioned as to whether the subject came up in conversation that night or not, but next morning Madeleine rose early – if she had been to bed at all – and left the house. 'I remember the morning Madeleine went away,' said Janet in her evidence. 'I suppose she had been in bed that night. I was sleeping before she came to bed. She was away when I awoke.' All of which goes to show incidentally that little Janet was a very sound sleeper, and rather discounts the value of her evidence as to the night of the 22nd.

There must have been consternation in the Smith household when it was discovered that Madeleine had vanished, and here, again, we do not know nearly enough, since none of the family was questioned about the events of that morning. Only Mr Minnoch gave evidence to the effect that when he called on the Thursday morning he was told that she had left the house. He suggested that she might have gone to Rowaleyn, and he and her brother Jack went there to look for her. They found her on board the steamer which was going to Helensburgh and Row. They went to Rowaleyn with her in a carriage, and brought her back to Blythswood Square. Mr Minnoch seems to have treated her with great consideration. He was still unaware of the awful darkness of the shadow that was threatening her. He asked her why she had left her home and caused all her friends so much distress, and she replied that she was distressed to have caused her papa and mama so much annoyance. Mr Minnoch by now knew that there was some old love affair which was upsetting the Smith family, and concluded that she referred to that. Mr Minnoch saw her again on the Sunday, when she told him that she had written a letter to someone, the object of which was to get back some letters she had written to him previously. The trusting Mr Minnoch was there again on Monday, when they had no conversation on the subject. The pretence that nothing serious was wrong was still being kept up at 7 Blythswood Square. On Monday Mr Minnoch called to inquire for Mrs Smith, having heard she was unwell. On Tuesday morning he called again, and Madeleine referred of her own accord to the subject of L'Angelier's death, and spoke of the report that he had been poisoned with arsenic. She also remarked that she had been in the habit of buying arsenic, as she had learned at school that it was good for the complexion. This was the last time William Minnoch was to speak with Madeleine Smith, for that Tuesday afternoon she was arrested by the Procurator-Fiscal of Glasgow.

She emitted a declaration, all that a prisoner could do in those days when it was not allowable to go into the witness-box. Her manner was calm and unruffled, her gaze candid. She declared that she had not seen L'Angelier for about three weeks before his death, when she spoke to him through the bars of her bedroom window. She admitted giving him cocoa from her window on one occasion, a good time previously, on a date which she could not specify. She declared that the arsenic she had bought was for use as a cosmetic, and that she had so used it, that she had only said it was to kill rats because she did not wish anybody to know that she was using it for cosmetic purposes. She ended: 'I never administered, or caused to be administered, to Mr L'Angelier arsenic or anything injurious, and this I declare to be the truth.'

The trial, which was held in Edinburgh, lasted for nine days. It was presided over by three Judges, the Lord Justice-Clerk (Hope) and Lords Ivory and Handyside, and caused a tremendous sensation throughout the land. The speeches on both sides were brilliant, the defence in especial being a model of its kind. The onus of proof resting on the prosecution, the defence's strongest position was that no proof could be brought forward as to Madeleine having met L'Angelier before any of the three occasions on which he was taken ill. No such proof ever was forthcoming, and there cannot be the smallest doubt that it was this which enabled the jury to give a verdict of 'Not Guilty' as regards the accusation of administering the poison on the first occasion, and 'Not Proven' in answer to the accusation of administering it on the other two occasions.

The Lord Justice-Clerk, in his admirably reasoned and scrupulously fair summing-up, warned the jury of the difference between inference and proof. Speaking of the inference to be drawn from her letter asking him to see her, which brought L'Angelier back to Glasgow, Lord Hope asked them to put themselves the question: 'Is this a satisfactory and just inference? If you find it so, I cannot tell you that you are not at liberty to act upon it, because most of the matters occurring in life must depend upon circumstantial evidence, and upon the inference which a jury may feel bound to draw. But it is an inference of a very serious character – it is an inference upon which the death of this party by the hand of the prisoner really must depend. And then you will take all the other circumstances of the case into consideration and see whether you can from them infer that they met. If you think they met together that night, and he was seized and taken ill, and died of arsenic, the symptoms beginning shortly after the time he left her, it will be for you to say whether, in that case, there is any doubt as to whose hand administered the poison.' Towards the close of the summing-up he again warned them: 'You just keep in view that arsenic could only be administered by her if an interview took place with L'Angelier, and that interview, though it may be the result of an inference that may satisfy you morally that it did take place, still rests upon an inference alone; and that inference is to be the ground, and must be the ground, on which a verdict of "Guilty" is to rest. Gentlemen, you will see, therefore, the necessity of great caution and jealousy in dealing with an inference which you could draw from this.'

There were various excellent points for the defence which were made the most of, but put altogether they did not amount to the value of this failure of proof on the part of the prosecution. The Dean of Faculty argued very reasonably that L'Angelier's death only put Madeleine in a worse position, as her letters were then bound to be discovered, and the exposure and shame which she had dreaded bound to come upon her. The arsenic which she had bought at Murdoch's was mixed with soot; Currie's was mixed with waste indigo. Neither of the colouring matters was discovered in the stomach of the deceased. The prosecution argued, with medical evidence on their side, that the quantity of waste indigo in Currie's arsenic was very small, and that if a sufficient portion of that arsenic had been administered to cause death, and that prior to death a great vomiting had taken place, no colouring matter would remain, and that, if the arsenic containing carbonaceous particles had been administered long enough before death, traces of the carbon would not be found. The defence argued that it was impossible to suspend as much arsenic as the deceased must have taken in any fluid. The prosecution maintained that cocoa was an ideal vehicle to have held a large quantity of poison in suspension. There was, in fact, the usual conflict in the medical evidence.

The defence used the same arguments about L'Angelier's habits that were used later in reference to those of Mr Maybrick. It maintained that L'Angelier was fond of dosing himself, and was an arsenic eater, and he had certainly boasted of this habit to several people at one time in his life; but L'Angelier boasted of so much that it would have been rash to accept anything he said as necessarily being the truth. The defence also showed that L'Angelier was in the habit of doctoring himself, and that he had frequent and bad attacks of stomach trouble. The defence sought to prove that L'Angelier was already ill when, on Sunday 22 March, he started to go back to Glasgow from Bridge of Allan. Evidence was produced of a man, whom the defence declared to be L'Angelier, who entered various apothecary shops and demanded laudanum, and in one case a white powder, nature unknown. The prosecution produced evidence to show that L'Angelier had been in perfect health, and had not deflected from his way to make any purchases on the homeward journey. And, indeed, it seems unlikely that this fantastic story of a wandering stranger, alleged to be L'Angelier, was ever taken very seriously by the defence. The incontrovertible fact remains that the prosecution failed to adduce the smallest vestige of evidence that Madeleine met L'Angelier before any one of the three occasions on which he was taken ill. It is also incontrovertible that had the prosecution been able to adduce such proof, the jury would have been unable to bring in anything but an unfavourable verdict.

We now come to the most interesting point in the whole of this case. Amongst L'Angelier's effects was found a little pocket-book which he had started to keep on 11 November that year. There are various entries of no particular interest, then comes: 'Thursday, 19th February. Saw Mimi a few moments. Was very ill during the night. Friday, 20th February. Passed two pleasant hours with Mimi in the drawing-room. Saturday, 21st February. Did not feel well. Sunday, 22nd February. Saw Mimi in drawing-room. Promised me French Bible. Taken very ill.' These dates cover, it will be observed, the dates of the first two illnesses. The diary was not kept beyond 14 March.

The defence, quite rightly, fought hard to obtain the exclusion of this pocket-book from the evidence. The Lord Justice-Clerk, Lord Handyside, and Lord Ivory had to decide this vital question of the pocket-book. The Lord Justice-Clerk and Lord Handyside held that it was not admissible. Lord Ivory disagreed with them. The Lord Justice-Clerk said he was unable to admit such evidence. 'It might relax the sacred laws of evidence to an extent that the mind could hardly contemplate. One could not tell how many documents might exist and be found in the repositories of a deceased person. A man might have threatened another, he might have hatred against him and be determined to revenge himself, and what entries might he not make in a diary for this purpose?' Lord Handyside pointed out that, had the writer of the memoranda still been alive, they could not have been used for evidence. They might have been used in the witness-box to refresh the memory. It was generally felt dangerous to admit as evidence memoranda on which no examination could in the nature of things be possible. The pocket-book was therefore ruled out as evidence, and it is inspiring to observe the scrupulous manner in which the Lord Justice-Clerk kept his own knowledge of those entries, not only out of his summing-up, but apparently even out of his mind while he did so.

The prosecution contended, with every show of reason, that it was perfectly possible for Madeleine to slip upstairs, without waking either her little sister sleeping the sound sleep of childhood or the exhausted hard-worked servants, for her to open the front door and admit her lover into the drawing-room or dining-room of the house in Blythswood Square. That she did admit him on several occasions in spite of her denial there is no doubt. In a letter written to L'Angelier just before Christmas, Madeleine says: 'Beloved Emile, we must meet. If you love me you will come to me when P. and M. are away in Edinburgh, which I think will be the seventh or tenth of January.' We have Christina Haggart's word for it that he was at least on one occasion admitted to the back of the house. We have nothing but the knowledge that it was possible to lead us to infer that he was ever admitted by Madeleine herself at the front door.

Madeleine remained calm, the colour in her cheeks did not wither, during the hours when the prosecution and the defence were fighting over every inch of the ground – always excepting that part railed off and kept sacred to the Smith family, about which so much could have been learned.

It is not uninteresting to picture what might have transpired had it been possible in those days to put Madeleine Smith herself in the box. How would she have dealt with the question the prosecution must undoubtedly have put to her – the question as to why she wrote that last letter, in terms of passionate love, bidding L'Angelier come to her? She could not have denied she was wishing to get rid of him, that all her preparations for her marriage with Mr Minnoch were going forward ... What reason could she have given for writing in those terms except that she wanted an interview with him, and that those terms were the only ones which would bring him? And what answer could she have given as to why she wanted the interview? The dock protected her from the possibility of such questioning, and in the dock her poise never deserted her.

The verdict 'Not Proven' was received with wild enthusiasm in the Court; Madeleine Smith remained the calmest person there. In the division on the vote of the jury a minority of two cast their vote for 'Guilty', against the remaining thirteen, and it has been said that many of the majority felt convinced of Madeleine's guilt, but preferred to take the other way out of the dilemma in which they found themselves.

Madeleine was taken below, where she changed her dress of rich brown silk, put on a cloak and a bonnet with a dark veil, and she was then escorted by her brother out of a side door to a waiting carriage. They took the train to a station near Glasgow, where another cab was waiting to drive her home to Rowaleyn, which she reached after ten o'clock that night. Of that strange homecoming nothing is known, though much may be conjectured. Four days later she wrote a letter to Miss Aitken, the matron of Edinburgh Prison, which is far more profoundly shocking than any of her violent epistles to L'Angelier:

Dear Miss Aitken, You shall be glad to hear that I am well – in fact I am quite well, and my spirits are not in the least down. I left Edinburgh and went to Slateford, and got home to Rowaleyn during the night. But, alas, I found Mama in a bad state of health. But I trust in a short time all will be well with her. The others are all well. The feeling in the west is not so good towards me as you kind Edinburgh people showed me. I rather think it shall be necessary for me to leave Scotland for a few months, but Mama is so unwell we do not like to fix anything at present. If ever you see Mr C.

Combe, tell him that the panel was not at all pleased with the verdict. I was delighted with the loud cheer the Court gave. I did not feel in the least put about when the jury were out considering whether they would send me home or keep me. I think I must have had several hundred letters, all from gentlemen, some offering me consolation, and some their hearths and homes. My *friend* I know nothing of. I have not seen him. I hear he has been ill, which I don't much care. I hope you will give me a note. Thank Miss Bell and Agnes in my name for all their kindness and attention to me. I should like you to send me my Bible and watch to 124 St Vincent Street, Glasgow, to J. Smith. The country is looking most lovely. As soon as I know my arrangements I shall let you know where I am to be sent to. With kind love to yourself and Mr Smith, ever believe me, yours sincerely, Madeleine Smith.'

This is our last glimpse of Madeleine, not ravaged, not beaten down, merely slightly piqued because 'the feeling in the west is not so good towards me as you kind Edinburgh people showed me'. She even thinks it 'may' be necessary for her to go away for a few months!

Robert Wood
1907

BASIL HOGARTH

It has been said many times that the Camden Town Murder is the classic British crime of this century; and certainly a strong case for its pre-eminence over most other murders might easily be made out. The trial of Robert Wood at the Central Criminal Court, Old Bailey, in December 1907, for the alleged murder of a street prostitute, Emily Dimmock, in Camden Town is unique in many respects. To the layman interested in the psychological aspects of murder, the case must prove of abounding interest; while, to the purely legal mind, it furnishes a remarkable precedent of the first instance in which an accused murderer, availing himself of the facilities to give evidence on his own behalf bestowed by the Criminal Evidence Act of 1898, successfully maintained his plea of not guilty. Public opinion on the case – sane public opinion – was thus ably posited by a contemporary leader writer in the *Daily Chronicle*:

To the moralist and to every serious-minded citizen who considers the state of society, how terrible are the sidelights which the case throws on life in London! Of 'scandals in high life' we always hear much, and the publicity which they inevitably attract is perhaps out of proportion to their proper dimensions. Here in this case we have the limelight thrown upon scandals in low life, and it is a saddening and sickening spectacle that is revealed. How awful is the life-picture of the murdered woman – 'the lowest of the low', as they called her, passing at the end of the week as the wife of one man and for the rest of it consorting promiscuously, as the evidence showed; leading what is called a 'gay life', and ending it with her throat cut by some stray companion. We need not follow up the theme into the other byways of human folly, vice, depravity, and squalor which the evidence opened up to the public gaze. Englishmen are proud of their civilizing mission among the 'inferior races' in the 'dark' countries of the world. We are not among those who would ridicule or discourage such work. But is there not some civilizing to be done nearer home?

Camden Town is not beautiful. It possesses, in fact, a strong resemblance to a place once described by Arnold Bennett as:

A dingy and sordid neighbourhood where existence was a dangerous and difficult adventure in almost frantic quest for food and drink and shelter, where the familiar and beloved landmarks were public-houses, and where the immense majority of the population read nothing but sporting prognostications and results and, on Sunday mornings, accounts of bloody crimes and juicy sexual irregularities. A hell of noise and dust and dirt, with the County of London tramcars, and motor lorries, and heavy, horse-drawn vans sweeping north and south in a vast clangour of iron thudding and grating on iron and granite beneath the bedroom windows of a de-fenceless populace.

There is a street in Camden Town called St Paul's Road which, somehow, has become disentangled from the noisier streets in the neighbourhood. Traffic has almost ceased to circulate here, and in its shabby-genteel privacy it is like a forgotten garment, left faded and worn. At about a quarter past eleven on the morning of 12 September 1907 a rather elderly lady might have been seen knock-ing at the door of No. 29 in this street. Her name was Mrs Shaw, and she had travelled from Northampton by an early train to pay a visit to her son 'Bert', who had but recently married. She was admitted to the house by the landlady, Mrs Stocks – as yet the young couple could not afford a house of their own – who told her that, despite the lateness of the hour, her son's wife was still in bed. About a quarter of an hour later her son himself put in an appear-ance. He was a well-set-up young man, employed as a dining-car cook on one of the restaurant cars of the Midland Railway. It was his custom to return home each morning with the train leaving Sheffield at 7.20 a.m. bound for St Pancras, and he used to arrive at St Paul's Road between 11.30 a.m. and noon.

After greeting his mother and the landlady, Shaw went from the kitchen into his own apartments to rouse his wife. He knocked at the door, but received no response. When he tried to open the door, he found that it was locked. This unusual circumstance aroused his suspicions. Returning to the kitchen, he received a duplicate key from the landlady, who followed him through. In the parlour they saw around them evidence of a rapid search through the drawers, which had apparently all been hurriedly ransacked, as their contents were strewn about the floor in confusion. Folding doors led to the bedroom; in the lock of the door there was usually a key; but that too was missing this morning, and frantic knocking failed to elicit a response. Now thoroughly alarmed, the young man smashed in the wooden panels of the bedroom door. He stepped into the room and saw that the bedclothes were huddled together in a heap: on the floor a pool of blood had trickled down towards the skirting boards. Rushing to the bed, Shaw tore aside the sheets and discovered the dead body of his 'wife', completely nude, lying face downwards. A gaping wound had been inflicted in the throat, the fatal thrust having almost dismembered head from trunk. The bed was soaked with blood.

Although the venetian blinds were drawn, a few shutters had been half-opened, and through this aperture filtered a gleam of sunshine. This shaft of light was directed on to a sewing-machine on the top of which lay a postcard album, partly open, with some of its contents scattered on the floor. The presence of that postcard album in the bedroom, with some of the postcards torn out, puzzled Shaw, for it had always been kept on a small table in the front room, a treasure prized by the dead woman. He made a quick search through the bedroom and the parlour and found that a number of things had disappeared. So far as he could then remember, he found that a gold watch, a silver cigarette-case with his initials stamped on it, a silver 'curb' chain with a small glass charm, and a purse were among the things unaccounted for. Later he found that a wedding ring and keeper belonging to the murdered woman were missing also; yet on the top of the chest of drawers there were two gold rings. There was a washstand in the bedroom containing a jug of water and a basin, and on the back of a chair facing it there was cast a damp flannel petticoat which bore traces of blood. On the wooden rack of the washstand a white towel was folded, clean and dry. The remains of a meal, probably supper, stood on the table in the parlour. Four empty stout bottles, two plates, two knives, and two forks, and a few used dishes suggested a visitor at supper.

A murder is an unpleasant event to discover at any time. But it was especially distressing for young Shaw at this time. Perhaps it would not have been quite so awkward if his mother had not chosen to visit him that very morning; perhaps it would not have been so difficult if it had happened in his own house. As it was, he knew that there would have to be a lot of irksome explanations. What called for discreet explanation was the fact, as yet unknown to his mother and the landlady, that he was not really married in the legal sense. The girl who passed as his wife was in fact one he had picked up from the streets. Her name was Phyllis Dimmock and her past history, he knew, would not bear too close an inspection.

Shaw had known Phyllis for two years before she came to live with him. She was a street prostitute. When they arranged to live together, it was on the understanding that Phyllis, whose real name was the less euphonious Emily Elizabeth Dimmock, would abandon her calling and settle down to a liaison with him. They had lived together for nine months, and, so far as he knew, the arrangement had worked admirably. But Shaw, whose work took him away each night, did not know that Phyllis had never to any considerable extent altered her mode of living. Doubtless, from her point of view, the arrangement seemed perfect, because it combined the security of marriage with the varying rewards of freelance easy virtue. What could be more simple, during the absence of Shaw each night, than to slip out of their apartments and resume her profitable calling? There is no doubt that Shaw was genuinely surprised when he learned later from the police investigations the nature of the woman's duplicity.

Thus the true story of his association with Dimmock must now come to light. It was hardly a pleasant prospect for him; but he called a doctor and the police.

Dr John Thompson, the divisional surgeon of police, arrived at the house a little after one in the afternoon. The first thing that attracted his attention was the quantity of blood that had flowed from the wound. The bedclothes were saturated and a stream of blood had infiltrated the mattress, finding an outlet on to the floor, where hours of slow dripping had caused a large pool to settle in the direction of the fireplace. The reclining position of the body on the bed showed no evidence of a struggle. In fact, except in one remarkable particular, it was the position of one who had died painlessly in sleep. The one unusual feature was that the left arm was folded underneath the back, a position in which normal, comfortable sleep would have been impossible. He came to the conclusion that for some reason, never satisfactorily established afterwards, the arm must have been forced back into that unnatural position by the murderer. The nature of the wound, and the absence of a weapon, discounted any suggestion of suicide. The wound itself was very deep, an incised cut extending from beneath the lobe of the left ear to the lobe of the right. The carotid artery, the windpipe, and the jugular vein, as well as the pharynx down to the spine, had all been severed cleanly down to the dorsal vertebrae; the head was only held on to the trunk by a few muscles that had escaped the knife. Taking all these things into consideration, the surgeon advanced the opinion that the weapon employed must have been extremely sharp, powerful, and used with tremendous force and deliberation.

The body was cold and rigid, rigor mortis having set in. It is always a matter of difficulty to ascertain with precision, from the appearance of death-stiffening alone, the length of time which has intervened since death, and, as near as possible, Dr Thompson could only fix the time of death as having occurred between seven or eight, but not more than nine, hours previously. This would put the murder as having occurred some time between 4 and 6 o'clock in the morning. He carefully examined the room for other blood stains, and found two spots of congealed blood on the wash-hand stand and another spot on a jug. In the basin there were water and blood, and on the petticoat thrown over the chair back he also detected the presence of blood. A towel folded on the handrail of the wash-hand stand appeared to be free from blood stains, and later analysis in the laboratory confirmed this fact. Although the murderer must have utilized the jug of water, as the blood stains eloquently testified, there was not a trace of blood on the handle.

The police were extremely alert in their inquiries. Before nightfall they had acquired a stock of useful information concerning the movements of the murdered woman on the day before her death. She had passed the greater part of that day, which was Wednesday, in washing and ironing linen. A little while after 4 o'clock in the afternoon Shaw went out to catch his train to Sheffield, as was his regular habit. After he had gone Phyllis was seen in the yard at the back of the house taking down the clothes from the wash-line. Later in the evening, about half past seven, Phyllis came through into the kitchen and was seen to be wearing a light-brown skirt. She had curling pins in her hair. She returned to her own rooms, after a few minutes' casual conversation with the landlady, and half an hour later the latter and her husband heard the slam of the front door, indicating that Phyllis had gone out for the evening. As near as they could fix the time, she must have left the house at a quarter past eight.

In the same house there also lived a widow named Alice Lancaster, a clerkess. She could not say anything about the movements of the deceased woman on the Wednesday, but she was able to tell the police that on the same morning, shortly before 8 o'clock, she had taken two letters from the postman, addressed to 'Mrs B. Shaw, 29 St Paul's Road, Camden Town', and had slipped them under the door of Shaw's apartments.

No one had heard anything unusual or suspicious during the night. Mr Stocks had an alarm clock in his bedroom which was set to go off at twenty minutes to five, but he did not rise until forty minutes later. If there had been any strange sounds, then he would assuredly have heard them. Mrs Stocks knocked at Dimmock's door about 9 o'clock that morning. Receiving no response, she concluded that her boarder was having a 'lie-in', and thought no more of the matter until the arrival of Shaw and the episode of the missing keys. There were a number of keys in the possession of the dead girl: a key for the front door, which she always kept in her purse, one for the parlour, which was usually kept on the inside of the door, and one for the bedroom door, also kept in the lock, and the keys of the folding door. All these keys, except one that was later discovered, were missing.

At first the police were inclined to regard Shaw with suspicion. But he was able to account for every detail of his movements from the moment he left the house on the Wednesday afternoon at 4 o'clock until the time of his return at 11.30 the following morning. He had a complete alibi, corroborated by his employers. Whoever had committed the crime, it was established beyond a shadow of doubt that Shaw had had nothing to do with it.

In spite of the lack of material which the police had at their disposal, they were yet in possession of the main facts of the dead woman's history by the following day. They obtained in a few hours knowledge which she had successfully hidden from Shaw during the period of her cohabitation with him. And they found one man who furnished a valuable clue.

The history of Emily Elizabeth Dimmock provides another unfortunate instance of the familiar spectacle of real life plagiarizing fiction. George Moore, in his most imaginative mood, never penned a page of *Esther Waters* that was more vivid than the life story of this butterfly of the streets. She was twenty-three years old when she died, having been born at Walworth, the youngest in the family of fifteen. Later the family removed to Wellingborough, where, at an early age, the girl commenced work in a straw-hat factory. Soon she left this for domestic service, entering the house of a family in East Finchley as a general servant. She appears to have been a rather fascinating girl, and no doubt she felt the long hours of domestic service chafing and irksome. At any rate, she quickly slipped into an easier way of earning money, in which the glamour of paint and powder played a part. Tall and slim, always attractively dressed, with pleasant ingratiating manners, she was a favou-

rite among her associates, and before long she had consorted promiscuously with many men recruited from different classes. Phyllis
played the piano – rather well, if the testimony of her various
landladies, 'protectors', and stray associates is to be believed. She
was fond of collecting postcards, which she preserved in an album,
and her large collection, including as it did hundreds of postcards
posted in remote corners of the globe, indicated the extent and
variety of her paramours, many of whom were military and naval
men stationed in dismal barracks and obscure foreign ports. She
lived at many addresses in her short career, and at one time had
been the inmate of a brothel kept by a person named Crabtree, in
Bidborough Street. Other addresses at which she resided for brief
periods included Euston Road, Manchester Street, Gower Street,
Harrison Street, and Gray's Inn Road. All of which suggests that
her clientele was assembled in the main from the submerged depths
of London 'night life'.

When Shaw first suggested that she might come and stay under
his protection, he was fully aware of her previous history; but, as
has been mentioned, it was an implicit understanding between
them that, in return for his gift of board and shelter, she was to
abandon her former mode of livelihood. She kept up a pretence of
faithfulness to Shaw, but it was really her custom, after he had gone
to work each night, to slink to her old haunts in Euston Road and
pick up such stray admirers as were not averse to paying for a
night's adventure. If she found someone satisfactory, she would
return to the apartments in St Paul's Road late in the night, after
the landlady was safely in bed, and surreptitiously introduce her
visitor, who would retreat from the house in the early hours of the
morning. Her favourite rendezvous was the 'Rising Sun', a public-
house in Camden Town, where, with friends and associates, it was
her wont to beguile the hours of waiting for men of leisure and
ready money. It was in this 'Rising Sun' tavern that the police first
got in touch with a man named Robert Percival Roberts, who was
later to become a figure of considerable importance in the case.
Roberts was a ship's cook who had been paid off in the previous
month. On the Sunday before the crime he had met Phyllis in the

bar of the 'Rising Sun'. He was clearly a desirable companion for her, for he was then in the midst of the pleasant process of liquidating a sum of £38, his savings from a recent voyage. Roberts went with Dimmock to her apartments and stayed the night there. He left at half past seven on the Monday morning. The hospitality apparently delighted him so much that he spent the following two nights, Monday and Tuesday, in the same fashion, parting company with a couple of sovereigns and the price of a bottle of whisky for this pleasant lodging. He did not spend the Wednesday night with her as it happened that she had arranged to accommodate another guest that night. To the police this seemed a rather strange story, and doubtless would not have been believed but for the fact that Roberts, like Shaw, was able to produce a cast-iron alibi, proving conclusively that on the Wednesday evening he had slept at a temperance hotel. The proprietress of the hotel and a fellow-boarder corroborated this, and he was automatically eliminated in the search for the murderer.

Roberts was able, however, to give the police a valuable clue that proved the real starting-point in their investigations. On the Wednesday morning, just after he rose, he heard a knock at the door. Two letters were then pushed under and, picking them up, he handed them to Phyllis. One was from a lady's tailor, a circular advertisement; the other was a private letter. After reading it, she passed it over to Roberts, who read part of it. He was able to recall the contents. The tenor of the message was: 'Dear Phyllis, – Will you meet me at the "Eagle", Camden Town, 8.30 tonight, Wednesday? – Bert.' There was also a postscript to the letter, but he was not permitted to read this. When Roberts had finished reading, the woman rose, went to a chest of drawers, and took from out of one of the drawers a postcard which she handed to him. It was a picture postcard bearing on one side the portrait of a woman embracing an infant. The reverse side contained both the address and a message which read: 'Phillis [sic] darling, – If it pleases you, meet me, 8.15 p.m. at the [here there was a sketch showing a rising sun]. – Yours to a cinder, Alice.'

Roberts noticed that the letter and the postcard were both written in indelible lead, and from a comparison decided that the hand-writing was the same in both. The girl then took the letter and the tailor's circular, put them together in an envelope, and set fire to them with a match, throwing them into the empty fire-grate. She put the postcard back into the drawer. The reason for burning the one and keeping the other is obvious – the letter signed in a man's name would undoubtedly have aroused Shaw's suspicions had he come across it; the postcard, signed 'Alice', was innocuous – and, more-over, she was in the habit of collecting postcards.

In the fire-grate of the bedroom a detective had already found the charred remains of a letter, and although most of it had been destroyed, there still remained occasional letters and words which could be deciphered, corroborating Roberts's story in material re-spects. The postcard album and the hasty search were now ex-plained. The murderer had evidently been seeking the postcard. The police searched thoroughly for it, but in spite of their efforts nothing came to light. They interviewed hundreds of persons who had known the dead woman, and followed up innumerable clues that petered out; and for a while it looked as if the investigation would end in stalemate. Then it chanced that Shaw made an important discovery. In packing his things away, before leaving his rooms, he had to empty the chest of drawers. Each drawer had a lining covering the bottom improvised out of a folded sheet of newspaper. As he was removing one of these linings he came upon the missing postcard for which the police had searched so long in vain, and immediately communicated his discovery to them. The postcard was then exhibited to Roberts, who recog-nized it as the one that Dimmock had shown to him on the Wednesday morning.

With this tangible clue in the hands of Scotland Yard, the hunt was up, and efforts were redoubled to secure an arrest. As none of the intimate acquaintances of the dead woman could shed any light on the handwriting, the police had to fall back on other means of establishing the identity of the writer. There were three other post-cards in the album the handwriting on which bore a marked re-semblance to that on the 'Rising Sun' postcard, and so the Commissioner of Police ordered facsimiles of these four postcards to be sent to various prominent newspapers in the hope that their reproduction in the press would lead to the identification of the writing. Along with these facsimiles, the Commissioner sent a letter in which he remarked: 'The attached postcards are believed to have direct bearing on the case of Emily Dimmock who was found murdered at 29 St Paul's Road, Camden Town, on the night of 11th instant. Any person recognizing the handwriting should at once communicate with New Scotland Yard or any Metropolitan police station.'

Among the newspapers to which Scotland Yard supplied facsimiles of the 'Rising Sun' postcard was the *News of the World*. In the *News of the World* there appeared two facsimile reproductions of the 'Rising Sun' postcard, over which was the challenging caption 'Can You Recognize This Writing?' As a stimulus to detection the proprietors offered a reward of £100 to the person or persons who could give such information as would lead to the identification of the handwriting in the facsimile.

Thus it happened that on the morning of Sunday 29 September 1907 several million people from Land's End to John o'Groats saw the reproduction of the 'Rising Sun' postcard. Among these millions there was a young lady named Ruby Young who lived at Earl's Court and euphemistically designated herself an 'artist's model'. When she saw the facsimile she cut it from the paper and put the cutting into an envelope. She also wrote a letter, to which she attached the clipping, and laid the letter on a table with the intention of posting it later in the day. But the letter was never posted, for that same evening, between 8 and 9 o'clock, a young man called on her and saved her the trouble. The young man was an artist-engraver, and his name was Robert William Thomas George Cavers Wood. He had scarcely set foot inside her room when he burst out: 'Ruby, I'm in trouble.' Taking the envelope from the table, the girl opened it, drew the enclosed clipping out, and handed it to her visitor with the remark: 'That is your handwriting.' He did not deny this, but offered to explain.

The gist of this narrative was that one Friday evening in September, while in Camden Town, he was walking up Euston Road with a friend of his, and they called at a public-house known as the 'Rising Sun'. While he was in the bar, a girl came up to him and asked for a penny to insert in a mechanical organ. He gave her a coin, and later she asked for a drink in a friendly way. Meanwhile his friend went away, and the girl was left alone in the bar with him. While they were drinking an urchin came into the bar, offering picture postcards for sale. The girl, who called herself 'Phyllis', wanted to purchase a postcard from the boy, but the young artist stopped her, saying that they were common and that he had some which he had brought from Bruges. He showed her a selection. She chose one bearing a reprint of a picture in which a woman was fondling a child in her arms. She asked him to send it to her after he had written 'something nice' on it. He could not think of anything on the spur of the moment, but he recalled that he had arranged an appointment with his friend who had just left, so he wrote down a few words in the style of an appointment. He was about to sign it in his own name when she stopped him with a gesture of confusion, telling him to subscribe it 'Alice'. He promised to post it, but as he had no stamp at that moment he put it in his coat pocket. They had another drink, and then he left the 'Rising Sun'.

The matter, according to the young man's explanation, would have ended there had it not been for a strange coincidence. The next day he happened to be walking along Great College Street in Camden Town on his way to the office of the Gas Light and Coke Company when he came upon the girl who had been in the bar the night before. She was disappointed that he had not sent the card, and he again promised to do so. They walked a little way along the street and then parted. He posted the card on Sunday night and thought no more about the matter. Then he called at the 'Rising Sun' on the Monday night, and who should be there again but his acquaintance 'Phyllis', who came from the other side of the bar and greeted him. She left him, saying that she would come back shortly. As he had nothing better to do he hung about the bar, and waited some time. Eventually, as she did not reappear, he went outside and was about to go home, crossing the street for that purpose, when he saw her talking to a lame man. As soon as she caught sight of him she turned to her companion and said: 'I'll see you later when the "pub" closes.' She then came over to him and they went back to the bar and had a few drinks. He then left the bar. 'That,' said Wood, 'was the last time I ever saw the girl.' It was a plausible story, speciously told, and for the moment Ruby Young was satisfied. She did not therefore apply for the £100 reward, and she promised not to identify the handwriting.

There was another who recognized the elegant penmanship on the postcard; a foreman, called Tinkham, in the employment of a glass-works in Gray's Inn Road. When Mr Tinkham saw a placard exhibiting a large-size reproduction of the script, he immediately recognized it as that of an artist who worked for the same firm. The artist was, of course, Robert Wood, who had been employed for fourteen years along with Tinkham as a pattern designer. The foreman approached Wood and, when challenged, Wood admitted writing the postcard. He then gave an explanation that was in all material respects the same as that previously tendered to Ruby Young. Wood also added that his old father was in a poor way of health, and should it come to his knowledge that his son had been at all mixed up in such an unpleasant business there might well be disastrous results. He asked the foreman, as a personal favour, to keep the matter quiet. The latter, who had a great liking for the young man whose courteous manners and kind disposition had made him a general favourite in the works, promised to do so.

Thus the power of the press was defeated, and Fleet Street failed to recruit from its army of amateur detectives two persons who alone could shed light on the authorship of the 'Rising Sun' postcard.

The 'Rising Sun' after the murder became the rendezvous of morbid sightseers, as well as a place of increased interest to its old habitués, among whom were many ladies who had been friendly with Phyllis Dimmock. The police pursued their inquiries and elicited some interesting facts concerning the male friends of Phyllis Dimmock. The wife of a printer, a Mrs Emily Lawrence, whose friendship with Phyllis was so intimate as to extend as far back as 1899, described a young man whom she had often seen with Dimmock. She had occasionally seen them together in the 'Pindar of Wakefield', a public-house in Gray's Inn Road, and, a few nights before the murder, she had seen them together in the bar of the 'Rising Sun'. On Monday night 9 September Mrs Lawrence called at the 'Rising Sun' along with a friend, Mrs Smith. This young man was in the bar, and after he had inquired of them if they had seen Phyllis, he invited the two ladies to have a drink. Mrs Smith said to him, jocularly, 'Don't tell Phyllis we have had a drink with you or she will be jealous.' In a little while Phyllis came in, and the young man sat down with her. Eventually they left together, and the girl announced that they were going to the Holborn Empire. But Phyllis looked very nervous and confided to Mrs Lawrence that she did not like him at all. Later in the course of the evening the four met again in the bar, slightly before midnight. The girl said that they had not been to the variety show at all, but had spent the night in another public-house, the 'Adam and Eve'.

This information was very significant, for the police had been interviewing persons who had seen this strange young man in Phyllis Dimmock's company on the three nights immediately preceding the murder. Many witnesses came forward and, as in each case their accounts tallied, the authorities were able to circulate the following description of the mysterious companion: 'About thirty years of age. 5 feet 8 inches in height. Has a long thin blotchy face and sunken eyes. He was wearing a blue serge suit, a bowler hat with a somewhat high crown, a double collar, and a dark tie. He is a man of good education and of shabby-genteel appearance.'

They were also able to incorporate an important mark of identification into that description, for a carman named MacCowan came forward with a most remarkable story which, if true, would inevitably lead to an arrest. MacCowan, who lived in Chalk Farm, was out of work early in September, and he was in the habit of setting out early in the morning in search of employment. He used to wait for a friend of his, a man named Coleman, who was also out of work, and together they would set out on their quest. On the morning of the murder, at about twenty minutes to five, he left his house in Hawley Street and walked in the direction of Brewery Road. To get there he had to pass through St Paul's Road, and he arrived there about twelve minutes to five. As he was passing down the road he heard footsteps behind him. Turning round, he saw a man leaving the gate of No. 29. He watched the man go down the road in the opposite direction from Brewery Road. Although Mac-Cowan did not actually see the man's face, he noticed that he wore a dark overcoat, with the collar turned up, and a hard bowler hat. What particularly attracted his attention, however, was a peculiarity in the man's walk. There was a pronounced jerk of his shoulders as he moved. He carried his left hand in his pocket, and he was a stiff-built man of 5 feet 7 inches or 8 inches.

Of course, the police had kept in sight the fact that a prostitute's calling brings her into the company of many strange men, but what impressed them in the conduct of their investigations was that, although many of her male friends had been interviewed and had succeeded in proving to the police that they were not concerned in the murder, a number of persons, most of them habitués of the 'Rising Sun' inn, came forward and supplied a description of this man with the sunken eyes and the shabby-genteel appearance. The press day by day continued to supply the public with titbits about the Camden Town Murder; but, in spite of the optimistic assurances of several daily papers that an arrest was imminent, there was no concealing the fact that Scotland Yard were marking time. They possessed the description of their man, sufficiently circumstantial and precise in detail, but, among the thousands of people in London who were daily meeting with the suspect, there was no one so far who could supply information as to his whereabouts. And they could do little but continue to ask for the writer of the 'Rising Sun' postcard.

We must not, however, lose sight of Ruby Young, the artist's model, who plays an important role in this drama of Camden Town. For almost three years she had been on intimate terms with her artist friend Robert Wood, there being something in the nature of an irregular union between them.

Robert Wood was an artistic designer, who had risen from a very subordinate position in his firm to a responsible post. He was able to augment his salary with freelance cartoon drawing for the press, and seems to have had plenty of money. His father was an elderly Scot who had been a compositor for twenty-five years on the staff of the Edinburgh *Scotsman*. Shortly after the birth of their son Robert his wife died, and Wood went to London, where, with his large family of twenty, he settled in the St Pancras district. The father's employment in London with Messrs Eyre & Spottiswoode was excellent and secure, so he married again.

Robert was thus brought up in London. He went to the Thanet Church School, St Pancras, where he proved a clever and sociable boy, winning a number of school prizes. He attracted the favourable notice of a Dr Kent Hughes, then a house surgeon at St Bartholomew's Hospital and a friend of Wood's schoolmaster. When the boy was old enough to leave school, the physician secured a situation for him as an assistant steward at the Australian Medical Students' Club in Chancery Lane. Here the youngster showed considerable aptitude in sketching and reproducing illustrations from medical and surgical textbooks. In fact, so great was his skill, that he was frequently called upon by the students and medicos who frequented the club to draw diagrams and illustrations for them. Ultimately the club was disbanded owing to serious bank failures in Australia caused by improvident financial speculations. The number of Colonial students coming to London was suddenly restricted almost to *nil*, and among those who were in this country, many were compelled to return to Australia owing to serious losses.

In consequence Robert Wood was dismissed from his post at the club, and, in response to an advertisement, applied for a vacancy in the sand-glass works of Messrs J. R. Carson, a fairly large firm employing a hundred men, whose premises were then at 58A Gray's Inn Road, London. His work here consisted of designing figures and decorative patterns suitable for fancy glassware. In fourteen years he had risen from a humble position to that of one of the leading employees in the firm. He was of an exceptionally amiable disposition, kind and courteous to all who worked with him, and he won for himself a place in the affections of all, both his employers and his fellow-workmen having the highest regard for him. There was no doubt about his cleverness in drawing. Some two years before William Morris died, he had chanced to come across some of the young man's designs, and had been greatly impressed by their originality and the strong promise for the future of which they gave indication. Morris was introduced to Wood, and encouraged him to continue his creative work, giving him certain technical advice on decorative matters.

It may have been that he had too much money to spend, or that his tastes ran in a peculiar direction, but his relations with Ruby Young were of a very questionable nature. They had been for two years extremely intimate, and improper relations had habitually occurred between them. And although Wood was aware that his sweetheart was sometimes following the calling of a prostitute in the West End of London, he did not apparently consider this fact of sufficient importance to warrant a break in their relations. They did eventually separate, but for a reason unconnected with Ruby Young's profession.

Ruby Young lived with her mother, and when the latter removed from Liverpool Street, near King's Cross, to Earl's Court, it can only be supposed that Robert Wood found the distance from St Pancras rather trying. Hitherto, one of the most charming aspects of his relations with Ruby Young had been that she lived so near to his home – only a stone's throw away. At any rate, as months went by, Robert Wood's ardour began noticeably to cool. Where formerly he had met her at least twice during the week, and had spent the greater part of the weekend with her, he now found it difficult to meet her even once in a fortnight.

At the end of July 1907 there was a definite rupture, the cause being jealousy. For some time Ruby had caught stray wisps of gossip indicating that her young man's attentions were not wholly confined to herself, and one day she chanced to meet him with a female companion. There was, of course, a quarrel, and the two did not see each other again until August, when they met by chance in the street. Wood had been holidaying in Belgium – it was his custom to take his vacation abroad – and he had much to tell her. They talked for half an hour or so. What precisely happened at that meeting we do not know. But certainly no arrangements were made to renew their former relations. Apparently they were now little more than casual acquaintances, meeting only when chance should happen to bring about the encounter, and confining their conversation to superficial small talk.

Ruby Young did not see Wood again that month. But on Friday 20 September, a week after the discovery of the murder in Camden Town, she received a telegram from him in these words: 'Meet me at Phit-Eesi's tonight 6.30. – Bob.' Phit-Eesi's was a bootshop in Southampton Row, and in the old days of their intimacy they had frequently met there. Expectant and rather intrigued by the unexpected summons, Ruby Young went to their old meeting-place at the appointed hour. When she arrived at Phit-Eesi's, Wood was waiting. He had scarcely exchanged the usual polite greetings when he burst out, 'Ruby, I want you to help me. If any questions are ever asked you by any one, will you say that you always saw me on *Monday* and *Wednesday* nights?'

This was a strange request to make of a discarded sweetheart, and Wood's obvious anxiety aroused her curiosity. She asked for a reason, but he evaded the question. Ultimately, after a fruitless effort to try and extract the reason for this unusual request, and following upon much coaxing and persuasion, the girl agreed to his suggestion. They went to a teashop and had a little refreshment, during which the artist urged on Ruby the absolute necessity of saying, if ever she should be approached by anyone, that he always spent Monday and Wednesday nights in her company. When she had finally consented and her curiosity was to some extent assuaged, they left the restaurant. Wood explained that he had to see a Mr Lambert, a friend of his employed as an assistant in a bookseller's shop close by, and they parted at the Underground Station in Leicester Square.

If Ruby Young had possessed the novelist's omniscience and could have played the part of an eavesdropper, her curiosity would have been provoked even more than it was. For when Wood left

her he immediately went back to No. 106 Charing Cross Road,
where he saw his friend, Mr Lambert, a bookseller's assistant.
Wood's first remark was: 'I have seen Mr Moss, the head man at
the works, and he has been talking about the Camden Town
murder. If Mr Moss says anything to you, will you tell him that we
met and had a drink, but leave the girl out?' Lambert's mind
carried him back to the night of 11 September, which was the
Wednesday immediately preceding the murder of Phyllis Dimmock.
On that night, shortly after nine, Lambert had been in the bar of
the 'Eagle', a tavern situated opposite the Camden Town Station.
He was rather surprised to see there his friend Robert Wood, alone
with a young lady, whose rather untidy appearance impinged itself
on his memory. He noticed that she was still wearing Hinde curling-
pins in her hair, and the girl, in some confusion, seeing that Lambert
had observed her head-gear, proffered an apology, saying, 'Hope
you will excuse my dress as I have just run out.' When Lambert
asked Wood what brought him there, the latter's non-committal
reply was that he had business to attend to. The bookseller remembered that when he left the bar of the 'Eagle' that same night,
the girl and Wood, whose business, whatever it was, did not seem
to be of a pressing nature, remained behind. He had not noticed
the features particularly, and although some sort of formal introduction passed between them he had not registered a mental note
of her name at the time. But he realized now that this must have
been the girl who was murdered. No wonder the young artist,
whose family was so strait-laced in many respects, wished to avoid
all connection with the case. 'I tell you', Wood insisted, 'that I can
clear myself, only I don't want it to come to my father's ears. He is
an old man and in poor health.' Lambert agreed to keep silent, and
thereupon dismissed the matter from his mind.

As Ruby Young did not overhear the dialogue between Wood
and Lambert, she also gave the matter no further consideration.
The weekend passed with nothing particular to distinguish it. While
no further developments were recorded in the press, rumours were
circulating freely, and were accorded the fullest publicity. An old
man who had committed suicide in the Tottenham Marshes was

said to have been a bearded individual whose frequent visits to
Dimmock had aroused the suspicions of one of her many landladies.
This gentleman, who was passed off as 'Uncle', had a generous
habit of leaving the girl a sovereign after each visit. This was the
man, it was conjectured, who had murdered Emily Dimmock, and
who had then taken his own life in a fit of remorse. There was no
more truth in this catchpenny solution of the mystery than in any of
the other 'alleged confessions' and 'hourly arrests' so assiduously
discovered by the battalions of diligent reporters and special investigators who swarmed round Camden Town and New Scotland
Yard.

On Monday morning Ruby Young received a postcard from
Wood, which contained the following message: 'Sweetheart, – If it
is convenient for you, will you meet me as before at Phit-Eesi's,
6.30, and we will have tea together and then go to the theatre,
which I hope will be a little ray of sunshine in your life – Good-
bye.' They went to the Prince of Wales Theatre. When they came
out, and were separating to catch their respective homeward
vehicles, Wood suddenly said to her: 'Don't forget now. Mondays
and Wednesdays.' She did not see him again until he called at her
house on the following Sunday, which was 29 September, the day
on which the Sunday newspapers were flooding the country with
the facsimile reproductions of the 'Rising Sun' postcard. It was to
be seen on every hoarding and each newsboy carried enlarged
copies of the card.

We have already seen how Ruby Young first came to know that
Wood had previously become entangled in the Camden Town
affair. When she heard the story of Wood's encounter in the 'Rising
Sun', she divined the reason for his telegram and his strange requests; she realized then that she was being asked to assist in con-
cocting a false alibi. There was something about this which rather
stuck in Ruby Young's throat. She suggested to Wood that he
ought to go to the police, but he said: 'I cannot prove where I was
on the Wednesday night, that's why I can't go to them. On the
Tuesday night I was with my brother Charles the whole of the
evening, but on the Wednesday I was out alone, walking, and no

one was with me who could speak for me.' There was considerable discussion between them, and once again Wood asked the girl to stick to the story about Monday and Wednesday nights. After a while, not without misgivings, she gave way to his pleading. They put their heads together and formed their plan of campaign. The girl said: 'The best thing for me to do is to say that I met you at 6.30 at Phit-Eesi's, and we had tea at Lyons' Café, and then after tea we went down Kingsway to the Strand and straight on to Hyde Park Corner. Then we'd better say we walked along the park straight out to Brompton Oratory, and got there at half past ten. We will say that we parted there: you went back by tube to King's Cross and got back home just before midnight.' Wood thought this story was excellent. When he left that night, she travelled with him in the tube as far as Piccadilly Circus. In the train she confided to him that she was again feeling nervous about the story she was to tell, because it had now occurred to her that others might have seen her elsewhere on the Wednesday night. 'If my name gets into the newspapers,' she said finally, 'it will hurt my mother.' Wood assured her and once more she was mollified.

On the Tuesday following, at lunchtime, as she was passing through Museum Street, where Wood's elder brother Charles lived, she met Robert. He reminded her of her promise. The next day she saw him again, and once more he referred her to the arrangement. His insistence was now beginning to annoy her, and she replied tartly, 'Yes, I'll be true! Don't bother me! It's getting on my nerves.'

So Ruby Young was a woman entrusted with a secret; and, although she did not contemplate for a moment betraying Wood's trust, most of the pleasure in a secret for her, like many other women, was the illicit pleasure to be derived from its partial exposure to a confidential friend – not to be repeated, of course. That was exactly what Ruby Young did. Some days later she breathed a word of Wood's dilemma to a friend. That friend mentioned it, in confidence, to a journalist on the staff of the *Weekly Dispatch*. It was manna from heaven to him, and he immediately got into touch with Ruby Young. No doubt the pressman besprinkled his conversation with vague references to accessories after the act, and principals in the second degree, for, on 4 October, Inspector Neil, who was in charge of the inquiries into the case, received a message by telephone. The upshot of this was that he went to the Piccadilly Tube Station and saw outside the artist's model, Ruby Young. What she told him supplied the missing link in the police chain.

At 6.30 on the evening of 4 October, as Wood was leaving the premises of the London Sand Blast Glass Works in Gray's Inn Road, he was met by Ruby Young, who shook hands with him. As she did so, Inspector Neil approached them, made himself known to Wood, and asked him to step into a waiting cab. Before they drove off Wood said to Young: 'I have to go with this gentleman. If England wants me, she must have me. Don't cry, but be true!'

The destination of the cab was the police station at Highgate, and on the way Wood stated very emphatically that he had not made any secret about the postcard with the sketch of the rising sun. He said, after being cautioned: 'My young brother, or my stepbrother, called my attention to the handwriting of the postcard when it came out in the Sunday paper. I told them it was *like* my handwriting, but I knew at the same time that I wrote the card, and the same night I had a chat with my brother Charles, a conscientious sort of chap who lives at Museum Street, and his wife, Bessie. I was advised to go to Scotland Yard. But about that time I was very busy at the office with the work of the chief, who was away on holiday at the time. My brother then said that the next best thing to do was to write a letter, addressed to one of us, care of the poste restante at the G.P.O. We sent the letter, addressed to Charles, and it stated that I acknowledged writing the postcard, and giving my reasons for not coming forward. Now I want to get that letter, inspector, because it shows that I did not conceal the matter.' Neil took a note of the address. It was: 'Charles Carlyle Wood, Poste Restante, St Martin's le Grand.' Wood then went on to give an account of his relations with the dead woman, and this account was precisely the same story that he had already told Ruby Young. But he made one vital mistake. Not knowing that Ruby Young had been questioned, he thus explained his movements on the night of Wednesday 11 September: 'On Wednesday I left work about 6.20, and went straight home, and afterwards walked up to Holborn with my sweetheart, Ruby Young, who had called for me. We had tea in Lyons, remaining there until about 8 or 8.30 p.m. After strolling about the West End I bade her good-night at Brompton Oratory and returned by tube to Holborn. I then walked home from there, and arrived, as near as I can say, about midnight.'

Wood was detained at the police station, and on 5 October he was put up for an identification parade and identified by a number of persons, whose statements contradicted in several material essentials the statement made by Wood to Inspector Neil. He was identified as having been in the 'Eagle' tavern on the Wednesday night, and several women said that they knew Wood to have been acquainted with Dimmock for fifteen months before September 1907. Ruby Young also told the police about Wood's anxiety over the Mondays and Wednesdays matter; and they also became aware that he had attempted to close the mouths of Lambert and the works foreman. As a result, on 6 October he was formally charged with the murder.

From the police point of view the identification parade on 7 October clinched the matter. They had in attendance MacCowan – he who had told them about seeing a man leaving a house in St Paul's Road shortly before 5 o'clock on the morning of the tragedy. A number of men were assembled. MacCowan could not identify any one of them. Then a police official gave the order 'March', and MacCowan immediately noticed that one of the men in the parade had the same peculiar twitching of his shoulders as the man he saw emerging from the gateway. He identified Wood by his walk, without hesitation.

The inquest had commenced on 30 September before Dr Danford Thomas, the coroner for Central London, at St Pancras Coroner's Court. On 7 October Wood was brought before the magistrate at Clerkenwell Police Court, and charged with the murder. An application for bail at £2,000, put forward by his solicitor, Mr Arthur Newton, was objected to by the police, and refused by the magistrate. The verdict of the coroner's jury on 28 October was circumspect in wording. It was: 'We find that the deceased Emily Elizabeth Dimmock met her death by wilful murder, and that the evidence we have received is sufficient to commit the accused for trial.' Meanwhile, at the Police Court, the magisterial proceedings had been going on. The police knew that a conviction was going to be difficult to secure and, accordingly, after the first formal charge and evidence of arrest, the proceedings were directed by the Senior Counsel to the Treasury, Sir Charles Mathews. In spite of the clever defence of the accused's astute solicitor, and the indication of an alibi, Wood was sent forward for trial.

The accused's employers immediately put a sum of £1,000 at the disposal of the defending solicitor in order to brief counsel. Thus he was in a position to secure such leaders as he chose without regard to expense. The trial ought to have come before the November Sessions, but, as the Police Court proceedings had not then terminated, an application to postpone the trial was made on 20 November by Mr Huntly Jenkins before Mr Justice Ridley, who granted the extension of time craved for, and the trial was accordingly fixed for the December assize.

In December 1907 the Grand Jury, charged by Sir Forrest Fulton, K.C., had before them the depositions in the case of *Rex* v. *Wood*, and having considered them they returned a true bill against the prisoner. The trial commenced on 12 December at the Old Bailey, in the new building, which had been opened by King Edward in the preceding January.

The proceedings aroused unprecedented interest. The long delay before any arrest had been made, the 'gay' life of the murdered woman, the mystery surrounding the case, as well as the romantic interests involved and the apparent betrayal of a lover by his mistress – all these features combined to render the trial of overpowering interest for many people. On the opening day the courtroom was thronged. All the available space was occupied. Many famous novelists, dramatists, and society leaders were present. Prominent in the gangways reserved for distinguished visitors were such celebrities as G. R. Sims, H. B. Irving, A. E. W. Mason, Bart Kennedy, Sir George Alexander, Sir A. W. Pinero, Oscar Asche, Seymour Hicks, Mr Willard, and G. B. Huntley. At the solicitors' table, along with Mr Arthur Newton and the prisoner's elder brother, Charles, sat Sir Hall Caine, then fresh from his triumphs in the theatre. The trial opened before Mr Justice Grantham, and it was a common sight during the conduct of the proceedings to see Judges like Sir Albert Bosanquet and Judge Rentoul sitting on the Bench with the presiding Judge. Counsel for the Crown were Sir Charles W. Mathews, Senior Counsel to the Treasury, Mr (later Sir) A. H. Bodkin, and Mr I. A. Symmons; for the defence, Mr (later Sir) Edward Marshall Hall, K.C., led Mr Herman Cohen, Mr Huntly E. Jenkins, and Mr J. R. Lort-Williams.

An unusual incident occurred at the opening of the trial, Sir Edward Marshall Hall challenging two jurors, named Arnold and Reid. Both were compelled to leave the box, and as the challenges were peremptory, the leader for the defence was not bound to explain his objection to the gentlemen whom he challenged. (It is to be hoped that Sir Edward was not merely following the time-honoured principle of the Irish barrister who explained to a delighted Judge that he challenged any juryman who looked at all intelligent!)

The opening speech for the Crown was temperate, yet very closely reasoned. Sir Charles, in a voice that has been described as exceedingly grating and unpleasant to listen to for a number of hours consecutively, outlined the case against the accused; he stressed the fact that Wood had attempted to suborn a number of possible witnesses, and in many ways had tried to tamper with potential evidence, and stop evidence reaching the police through normal channels. Sir Charles put the character of the accused very fairly before the jury. He told them that Wood undoubtedly possessed a most excellent character and that he had served one firm, the London Sand Blast and Glass Company, for an uninterrupted period of fourteen years, during which time there had never been the slightest complaint made against him, either in his capacity as workman or in any moral way. But he submitted that, although he was to his fellow-workmen, as well as to his family at Frederick

Street, a model worker of an affectionate disposition, he was really living a double life and his spare time was spent in a very different fashion. Sir Charles also pointed out that it was an essential part of the structure of the Crown case that Wood had known Dimmock long before the day mentioned by him in his statement to Inspector Neil. He then elaborated the account already given of the request made by Wood to Ruby Young asking her to swear that on the nights of Monday and Wednesday he was always in her company. The Crown relied on this attempt to suborn witnesses and concoct a false alibi as a clear indication of guilt on Wood's part. Vital importance was attached to the similarity of handwriting between the decipherable remains of the charred fragments and the 'Rising Sun' postcard, which was admittedly in the handwriting of the accused. Clearly, if the jury were satisfied that the handwriting of the charred fragments was the identical handwriting of the post-card, then the letter received by Dimmock, and read by the ship's cook, Roberts, who had stayed there for two consecutive nights before the murder, must be in the handwriting of the accused. If so, it showed that he had made an appointment with her to meet him at the 'Eagle' tavern on the night of the murder.

The Crown attached great weight to the fact that Dimmock was not dressed on the Wednesday night as she would have been, smartly and attractively, if she had been going out to pick up a man from the streets that evening. She had her curling-pins in her hair. They were found still in her hair when the alarm was raised next morning, and were observed by three independent witnesses: (1) By the landlady, Mrs Stocks, who saw Dimmock with her hair in curling-pins at 7 o'clock on Wednesday evening just before she heard the front door slam (2) by a barmaid in the 'Eagle', who recognized Dimmock as being in the bar on the Wednesday night, and overheard her say to one of her male companions, 'Excuse me for being so untidy' and (3) by the bookseller, Lambert, who had seen Dimmock and Wood together in the 'Eagle', and who remembered that the girl made an apology for her apparent untidiness, saying something about having come out in a hurry. The inference to be drawn from these facts, according to the Crown, was that Wood, intending to murder Dimmock either late on Wednesday night or early on Thursday morning, sent her a letter making an appointment for a public-house where he thought he would not be known. As it chanced, however, he was observed. The hair-curlers pointed to the fact that the girl, having fixed an appointment for that night, did not trouble to dress up as she would have done had she been going out to attract a casual man.

The other important evidence in the Crown case was that of MacCowan, whose evidence and identification, if accepted, showed that Wood was in the neighbourhood of St Paul's Road at a time when, according to medical evidence, the murder had just been committed. Sir Charles Mathews strongly impressed upon the jury that the identification was excellent because it was a peculiarity of walk that had been described to the police long before any of the descriptions appeared in the newspapers, and because the witness unhesitatingly picked Wood out from a number of men merely by his walk and without reference to any facial characteristics. Moreover, his reference to the peculiarity in the accused's walk was corroborated by Ruby Young, who said that there was undoubtedly a peculiar feature in his walk, and agreed with MacCowan's description of it as a 'jerking or nervous twitching of the shoulder forward when walking'.

The state of the apartment on the morning when the discovery was made, in the belief of the Crown, pointed to certain obvious inferences which pressed onerously against the accused. The half-opened shutters of the venetian blind had been opened by the murderer in order to obtain a light sufficiently strong to enable him to search through the postcard album. What would there be in a postcard album that made it necessary to make so thorough a search at a time when every additional minute that the murderer stayed in the house was drawing nearer to the hour of possible detection? Clearly there was in that album something which, if left behind, was a valuable clue to the identity of the murderer. Wood had admittedly written a postcard, and the subterfuges he had subsequently resorted to in order to avoid his being known as the writer of it proved conclusively, in their opinion, that he realized what a dangerous clue it was. With regard to the missing articles, they had obviously been taken in order to simulate the appearance of a robbery and start the police on a false track. But robbery as a plausible motive could be discounted at the outset, for otherwise why should a thief leave behind him what were probably the most valuable of all Dimmock's possessions – the gold rings? In addition, the futile efforts made by the accused to suborn Ruby Young, the bookseller, Lambert, and others showed that he had something to conceal. The presumption raised by this conduct was that Wood was guilty of the crime of murder.

Any suspicion that might seem to fall on either Shaw or Roberts could be dispelled, as both men could prove beyond dispute where they were at the time of the murder. A suggestion had been made at the Police Court by Mr Arthur Newton, the solicitor for the defence, that the man responsible for the murder might be an associate of Dimmock known as 'Scotch Bob', who had been known to utter threats against the murdered woman. Sir Charles Mathews had caused exhaustive inquiries to be made, and, if required, he was prepared to put into the box this man, 'Scotch Bob', who could prove that at the time of the murder he was employed in a hotel in Scotland. There was a further point stressed by Sir Charles before he concluded his speech. Wood had always maintained the attitude that he knew nothing whatever about the crime; but a warder who had charge of him while in prison heard him say, after one of the identification parades, 'If it comes to a crisis, I shall have to open out.'

The plans prepared and produced by Sergeant Grosse were called in question by Marshall Hall, in cross-examination, his point being that the power of the lights that shone in the vicinity of 29 St Paul's Road had been tampered with to such an extent as to suggest that it was a brilliantly lit locality, when in fact it was very badly lighted. The whole of his cross-examination of this witness was directed towards laying a foundation for his subsequent cross-examination of MacCowan, who was the most damaging of all the Crown witnesses. Marshall Hall wished to show that, apart from the lights supplied by the local electricity company, there was no available light power in the neighbourhood; and that, as the street lights had been turned off at a time before MacCowan left the house, and as according to the evidence of MacCowan himself it was a morning of drizzling rain, it necessarily followed that the opportunities for intelligent and reliable identification were so small as to be practically negligible. It was Marshall Hall's determined and consistent attitude all through the trial that the case for the Crown was manufactured and bolstered up by rotten evidence, a glaring example, in his opinion, of what happens when 'vaulting ambition o'erleaps itself'.

His success with the first official police representative was a splendid augury. The officer was compelled to admit that the plan which was prepared by him gave the impression that St Paul's Road was in the full glare of a powerful row of lights coming from a railway siding, when in fact there was a fairly continuous row of houses in between. This row of houses was not shown clearly on the map. Thus anyone who looked at it would conclude, in the absence of any explanation to the contrary, that the side of St Paul's Road on which No. 29 was situated was lit up by a brilliant ray of light. Again, at the railway bridge, from which the light was said to come, a wall at least 9 feet high, which would prevent much light from escaping, was not marked on the plan. Marshall Hall did not hesitate to press the point home:

'Q: You know it was a dark, muggy morning. If the electric standards were extinguished at that time (4.37), they would be useless for the purpose of light at five to five? A: Yes. Q: Is it not the case that, this being so, you have been specially asked to prepare a map that would show, as your evidence suggests, a sufficiency of light coming from the railway forty feet below the road?' It is not surprising that no immediate answer was returned to that question.

It is of interest to notice that, although Marshall Hall often cross-examined Crown witnesses like Shaw and Roberts on their moral credit, with disastrous effect, the leading counsel for the defence did not try to bring home the guilt of the crime to any one. He was too shrewd an advocate to prejudice his client's case in that bungling fashion. If an accused sets up a defence that he is not guilty, but that either X, Y, or Z could be, he puts himself in a very perilous position, for, if he fails to prove the guilt of X, Y, or Z, the jury are apt to conclude that this very failure by itself is a proof of the accused's own guilt. Apart from the extreme technical difficulty involved when a defending counsel has to defend his own client with one hand and, with the other, prosecute some other individual (without the resources of the Crown), there can be no doubt that such a dual defence, if it fails, rebounds on the head of its author. An interesting example of the converse process occurred at the Old Bailey trial of 'Scotty' Mason, who was convicted in May 1923 of the murder of Jacob Dickey, a taxi-driver. In that case the Crown counsel, Sir Richard Muir, had to sustain the dual role of prosecuting the accused and defending his chief witness, Vivian, whom the defence accused of actually committing the murder. Although Sir Richard was successful in his onerous task, and the accused was convicted, the element of doubt that entered into the case resulted in the reprieve of Mason. Marshall Hall did not attempt to postulate: 'Wood cannot be guilty, because X or Y or Z is the guilty party, as I will now proceed to demonstrate to you.' He merely said: 'The facts which the Crown have brought forward are insufficient to enable you to condemn any one.'

Marshall Hall's questions often appeared on the surface to suggest that X or Y might have committed the crime. In reality, they were directed not to that end, but merely to show that things looked so black against X or Y that either, as a precautionary measure of self-protection, might well be prepared to take the opportunity of casting suspicion on someone else. Taken in this light, the cross-examination of the ship's cook, Roberts, was an inspired masterpiece of subtle forensic legerdemain. The damning feature of this witness's evidence was patently his identification of the handwriting on the charred fragments. According to Roberts, these charred fragments were the ashen remains of a letter which was received by Dimmock, who exhibited it to him, and which contained a specific assignation to meet the writer within the 'Eagle' bar, opposite Camden Town Station, on the Wednesday evening. This was very inculpatory evidence if once accepted by the jury. The cross-examination, therefore, was at first directed towards ascertaining Roberts's whereabouts on the night of the crime. Roberts was forced to admit that things looked very black against him – so black, in fact, that he would inferentially clutch any straw that would help him out of his danger. The rest was deceptively easy: a suggestion was put to Roberts that his identification of Wood had been obtained from a description supplied to him by a witness in the case, and was not a spontaneous identification, followed up by a suggestion that there had never been a letter of assignation at all but that it was a figment of his imagination invented in order to plant a false clue. Two curious facts came out in cross-examination: (1) The letter was signed 'Bert', and the accused always signed letters 'Bob' (2) the letter, according to Roberts, contained a message that was so brief that it would easily go on one page. Yet the charred remains prove conclusively that, whatever they were originally, there was writing on the four sides of the two leaves. Moreover, the writer was so cramped for space that he had to crush some of the words upside down into one of the corners.

It would be difficult to find a better illustration of a dangerous witness being disarmed by an adroit cross-examiner; it was a splendid example of the most polished technique of skilful cross-examination. This cross-examination was obviously piercing the armour of the Crown, for on the second day two witnesses were introduced to speak to Roberts's movements on the night of the murder. Strategically, this was an error, for in his closing speech Marshall Hall neatly turned the tables on this testimony by stigmatizing the Crown case as proving X to be guilty simply on the inference that A, B, C, and D had alibis that were satisfactory to the police, whereas X's alibi was not!

MacCowan's evidence had already been severely shaken at the magisterial proceedings by Mr Newton. At the Old Bailey, Marshall Hall drew out the following vitally significant points: (1) That the street lights were turned off at 4.37 and that as MacCowan did not, on his own admission, leave his house that morning until 4.40, the lights could not have been on. Therefore the opportunities for observation must have been very few, especially as, according to the witness, it was a thick, drizzly morning (2) the witness spoke of the morning as drizzly, but the weather records showed that the week of 7 September was the hottest of that year, and that no rain fell on either the day preceding the murder or on the day of the murder itself. Therefore, the witness's powers of recollection were demonstrably at fault (3) the witness admitted that he had not seen the man with the peculiar walk coming down the steps of the house in St Paul's Road. He had seen him on the road. Therefore it did not of a certainty follow that the person he saw had in fact emerged from No. 29. He might have been a casual passer-by.

The testimony of Inspector Neil was not much shaken, but, on the other hand, it was of an administrative nature and added little to the quota of substantial evidence at the disposal of the Crown.

Ruby Young's evidence was mainly connected with the attempts of Wood to concoct the false alibi. The manner in which Marshall Hall elegantly disposed of this point is instructive: 'With regard to that arrangement, have you ever thought that, having regard to the evidence of Dr Thompson, who places the time of the murder at three or four in the morning, the alibi Wood arranged with you from 6.30 to 10.30 on the evening previous to the murder, would be a useless alibi for the murder, but a perfect one for the meeting of the girl?' The witness confessed that, although it did not strike her in that light at the time, she saw the possibility of such an explanation when it was put to her.

A group of witnesses, including Mrs Lawrence, Mrs Smith, Gladys Warren, and a man named Crabtree, were called with the object of showing that Dimmock and Wood were intimate for months before the night of 6 September, which Wood adhered to as the date of his first meeting with Dimmock. It was on the evidence of these witnesses that the case against Wood really revolved, and as their testimony requires particular study, it will be better to deal separately with it later.

Towards the end of the fourth day the case for the prosecution was closed by the calling of their last witness, the mysterious 'Scotch Bob', who proved his alibi beyond dispute. After a fruitless appeal by Marshall Hall to the Judge to decide that there was no case to go to the jury, the leading counsel for the defence outlined his reply and indicated the nature of his defence. The mainstay of that defence was an alibi spoken to by the accused, and corroborated by a number of other witnesses, whose testimony was, in counsel's submission, not only credible, but incontrovertible. He hinted that the murder could only be the work of a maniac, a sadist such as used to prowl in the night haunts of Whitechapel a few years before. He relied on the excellent character borne by the accused to rebut the suggestion of any sexual mania.

There was no credible motive for Wood having committed the crime. None of the missing articles had ever been traced to him, and there was no sign of a weapon in his home at Frederick Street. The only factors that could possibly implicate Wood as a possible criminal were: (1) The charred remains alleged by the Crown to be a letter of assignation (2) the identification of Wood by MacCowan as the man he had seen in St Paul's Road on the morning of the murder (3) the attempts to suborn Lambert and Tinkham, the foreman at the glass-works (4) the untruthful statement made to the police and (5) the concocted alibi. Factors (3), (4), and (5) all bore a single construction susceptible of an innocent explanation. They were attempts made to conceal the fact of the accused's low relations with depraved persons. Being a young man, held in high esteem, he had in a sense been occasionally indulging in a double life. To his fellow-workmen and his family he appeared an upright and honourable young man leading a model life; the other side of the picture was that he had had intimate relations with Ruby Young and had met one or two undesirable women whom he would have been ashamed to acknowledge knowing to his father and colleagues. All that the so-called subornation of Lambert amounted to was a request to 'leave the girl out of it'. The alibi with Ruby Young was clearly useless if it was intended as an alibi to cover the time of the commission of the murder: it was only an alibi to get him out of a meeting on the Wednesday night with Dimmock. With regard to the false statement to the police, when he made that statement, he thought that it would clear him of the low association. Undoubtedly it was deception; but it was not the cunning deception of a callous, maniacal murderer. Marshall Hall maintained that it was the transparent duplicity of a young man of overweening vanity who was truly ashamed of his lapse from the virtuous path, and wished to conceal his association with an unfortunate of Dimmock's class.

The charred fragments were undoubtedly in Wood's handwriting. They were not, however, parts of a letter of assignation, but merely sketches and little notes drawn on scrap paper for his own amusement, which Dimmock by some means had secured. The letter relied on by the Crown was invented by Roberts to divert suspicion from himself – perhaps on to young Shaw. The signature 'Bert' was significant; if Wood had written the letter he would have signed 'Bob'. Factor (1) could be disposed of in this fashion.

The identification by MacCowan, factor (2), was in Marshall Hall's view 'the flimsiest and most unsatisfactory evidence of identity ever put before a jury in any Court of justice in the world'. If it were true, it turned solely on a peculiarity of walk described in circumstantial detail. Counsel was prepared to call sixty-five fellow-employees of Wood who would deny that there was the slightest peculiarity in Wood's walk. He did not suggest that MacCowan was lying. On the contrary, he agreed that MacCowan had seen a man, but that man was not even remotely connected with the murder. He was a railwayman, named Westcott, going to work. Westcott would be called, and the jury would see for themselves that he was a broad-shouldered young athlete, an amateur boxer, who walked with a noticeable swing.

Admittedly Wood had been on terms of intimate relationship with Ruby Young. He swore that he had not been immoral with Dimmock; but even the most casual association with a prostitute like Dimmock was disgusting in the eyes of good-living people like his father and brothers. So he had lied, more for their sake than for his own. He had been immoral and he had told a few lies, yet that was a long way from proving that he was necessarily a murderer on that account. The most that the lies could suggest was vague suspicion – and the jury were not entitled to convict on suspicion.

It was a splendid defence, the production of a marvellous forensic technique, and in architectonic structure Marshall Hall himself never improved on it. There was not a question that had not its appropriate answer, not a doubt but had its resolution on a perfect cadence.

When, towards the end of Mr Justice Grantham's summing-up, the learned Judge gave his own view of the case for the prosecution: 'In my judgment, strong as the suspicion in this case undoubtedly is, I do not think that the prosecution has brought the case home near enough to the accused,' his charge was interrupted for several minutes by a storm of applause which burst forth from spectators in Court, in spite of the stentorian rebukes of uniformed ushers. This was, of course, repeated when the jury brought in their not guilty verdict, and after the trial, when Robert Wood left the dock, there occurred such a 'scene' as has rarely, if ever, been paralleled in the records of our assizes. The Court sat until late in the evening of the final day and the verdict of the jury was not announced until close on 8 o'clock. Crowds thronged Newgate Street, and the streets in the vicinity of the Court were impassable: traffic was brought to a standstill. All London was waiting for the verdict, in the mean streets of Camden Town and in the palatial residences of Mayfair. Millions were engulfed in a colossal wave of mass hysteria. Theatrical performances were interrupted to announce the verdict when at last it was flashed through the telephone wires. At a West End theatre Mrs Beerbohm Tree (as she then was) rushed breathless on to the stage. 'I have just arrived from the Court,' she gasped, 'the Court where young Robert Wood stood in peril of his life. I am glad to be able to tell you that the jury found him not guilty.' When the cheers died away, she continued: 'I am pleased to hear the reception of the tidings I have brought. While the jury were out, we seemed to hold our breath, and we hoped, but we feared perhaps the jury would after all . . . I was one of those who burst into tears, others burst into cheers which were taken up, echoed and re-echoed by thousands on the streets . . .'

In its cheap sentiment and crude melodrama this farrago of maudlin emotions would be difficult to equal. It reads for all the world like one of the most boisterous pages of Sinclair Lewis or

Upton Sinclair pouring astringent satire on some criminal process of Gopher Prairie or Zenith City. After the trial a vast cordon of policemen escorted Wood and his relatives to a near-by restaurant. From the balcony of the teashop the appearance of the bearded figure of Wood's father was the signal for a furore of cheering. At length, amidst the applause the old man was heard to announce: 'I thank the public for their enthusiastic reception of me, and for the kindness which they have shown to me and my family in this very trying case . . .'

After the successful defence Marshall Hall was inundated with showers of letters and telegrams congratulating him on his splendid fight. He himself remarked afterwards: 'It has been a most extraordinary case. I have always been convinced of the innocence of Wood. He is certainly a remarkable young man, and his coolness and courage throughout have been beyond anything I have ever seen. He was actually engaged in sketching the judge during the absence of the jury. His ability, by the way, is wonderful. There was an unfortunate difference of opinion on the last day about the calling of witnesses Sharples and Harvey. Sir Charles Mathews did offer to call although I was not aware of it. I appreciate greatly the courtesy I received from Sir Charles; and the first to congratulate me were Mr Williamson of the Treasury, and Mr Bodkin. The conclusion of the case produced a very remarkable scene. I tried to get to the dock to congratulate Wood, but was unable to reach him on account of the crowd. I heard him several times attempting to thank me, and I received the profound thanks of his father and elder brother. Everyone shook hands all round when the verdict was given. The scene, especially the cheering outside, was more like an election than the end of a criminal trial. I must express my thanks to my juniors and to my solicitors for their great assistance in what has certainly been one of the most remarkable cases in modern times.'

In startling contrast was the attitude of the mob towards Ruby Young, who was generally regarded in the light of their popular hero's temptress. It was well known that, had that infuriated mob outside the Court laid hands on her, they would have killed her without compunction. The authorities managed, however, to get her out of the Court unnoticed. On the suggestion of Sir Herbert Austin she changed into the clothes of a charwoman, and, with two detective sergeants at her side, she escaped to Ludgate Hill, un-recognized by the prowling hordes of hooligans who were lying in wait for her. The majority of ill-informed people seemed to labour under an impression, perfectly erroneous, that Ruby Young had betrayed Wood for the sake of the £100 from the *News of the World*. Ruby Young said afterwards: 'It has come to my ears that I am supposed to have received £100 from the *News of the World* for information concerning the 'Rising Sun' postcard issued on 29 Sep-tember. I wish to contradict this statement as I have never received a penny from any one. It is against my nature to accept such a kind of reward. Perhaps the rumour arises in this way. My attention was first called to the facsimile of Robert Wood's handwriting in the postcard reproduced in the *News of the World*. On the Sunday it was published I received my copy in the ordinary way, being a regular reader. I was at once struck with the identical handwriting of my boy friend. I also noticed at that time that a reward of £100 was offered. I never thought for the moment of betraying Robert Wood for the sake of that money. On the same day he called on me and, as I have already stated at the trial and before the coroner, at the very time he called, my letter to him enclosing a cutting from the paper was on the table. I drew his attention to the matter. Later on I confided my secret to a friend and became the unhappy witness of his arrest. The stories about my accepting the reward – blood money as it is commonly called – have been most distressing to me.'

What happened to Ruby Young afterwards history does not record. She soon disappeared from the public eye. As for Robert Wood, he remained a nine days' wonder, and then his celebrity dwindled. He found it convenient to change his name, and in the passing of years he was forgotten, the mention of Camden Town, of Emily Dimmock, of Ruby Young awakening no responsive echo in the public ears. The man who had been for a brief moment a public idol soon was nothing more than a vague recollection, arousing only casual and indifferent comment.

Such is the ephemeral fame of a popular hero!

Many years have passed, and it is now possible to approach this case with a sense of that dispassionate objectivity which was so noticeably absent at the actual trial. One of the gravest objections that can be urged against the British system of trial by jury is the fact that it is impossible to disentangle from the circumstances of the case the surrounding elements of prejudice which the atmosphere and temper of the epoch necessarily breed. Nothing is more detrimental to the solution of a difficult judicial problem – especially where the solution of that problem depends on the correct statement of isolated facts from which inferences are derived, often trivial and meaningless in themselves, but convincing in cumulation – than the infusion of psychological elements which tend to banish impartiality.

There can be no doubt that at the trial of Robert Wood in 1907 there was a distinct leaning towards the accused; and the friendly attitude of the public eye at large was inevitably communicated to the members of the jury. Thus, in reconsidering this remarkable case after this lapse of time, we are in a position undeniably superior to that of the jury who sat in the Central Criminal Court in 1907. Admittedly we do not have the various witnesses before us to help us to decide the measure of credibility to be attached to their stories; but the lack of oral testimony will be more than compensated for by the avoidance of that unscientific party spirit and rancour which was in such obvious evidence at the trial.

The case for the Crown was purely circumstantial; its web of circumstance was spun with gossamer lightness, so fine as to be almost too weak to bear the structure of a prosecution. The argument was tenuous, it involved a reciprocal process of eliminating several potential murderers by exclusion and exhaustion, and it connected the prisoner with the crime by certain elements – scraps of evidence which, to yield a positive result, demanded the closest correlation. The case against Wood depended on the intersection of the following strands of evidence: (1) That a letter was written by him to Dimmock making an assignation for the Wednesday night at the 'Eagle' public-house (2) that the charred remains found in the fire-grate at 29 St Paul's Road were fragments of that letter (3) that Wood was seen by MacCowan emerging from the house after the murder had been committed.

It was desirable also to prove that Wood already knew and was intimate with Dimmock. While it was not imperative to know this – the murderer need not necessarily have known the woman at all – if it could be shown that Wood knew Dimmock before 6 September (the date at which he fixed the beginning of their acquaintance), the effect would be to strengthen the indictment in two vitally important respects. In the first place, it would establish a nexus between Dimmock and Wood, from which a glimmer of motive, whether jealousy or otherwise, might be invoked; and, secondly, it would follow that the accused in his statement to the police was deliberately lying on a material particular. This statement, containing vital untruths, might then be represented as a tissue of calculated lies; and the interpretation would be that the murderer was attempting to cover his traces.

For this purpose the Crown called an elaborate cycle of witnesses, whose testimony was intended to show that Dimmock and the accused were intimate over a period of some eighteen months before the woman died: (1) Gladys Warren is called to prove that she knew of their acquaintance, and she cites specific occasions when she saw the pair together (2) Crabtree, the keeper of a disorderly house, is called to prove that Wood was a constant visitor of Dimmock when she was an inmate of his brothel (3) Lindham is called to speak to occasions on which he saw Dimmock and Wood together in the 'Rising Sun' public-house (4) Mrs Lawrence is called to prove that she had seen them together in the 'Pindar of Wakefield' public-house. This quartet has seen evidence of intimacy between the artist and the dead woman on at least eight different occasions ranging over a period of eighteen months before the murder. The four witnesses are not known to one another. They have each individually identified Wood. If their testimony is to be rejected, these four witnesses, all strangers to one another, must be lying or mistaken. Reason revolts at either explanation. The law of parsimony in logic forbids us to invoke a remote solution when an obvious one is close at hand. True, the witnesses are all of a poor, and perhaps a depraved, class; but it has yet to be shown that truth, like love, flies out of the window when poverty comes in at the door.

Crabtree was admittedly a brothel-keeper and a convicted horse thief, but is his testimony automatically vitiated by that fact? In his eloquent speech to the jury, Marshall Hall argued that the appearance of such a disgusting specimen of humanity for the Crown was a tacit admission of the weakness of their case. The answer to that is painfully obvious. If Wood's associates were brothel-keepers and gin-sodden sluts, what could the Crown do but call them? The Crown were not, after all, responsible for Wood's friendships. Is there to be a yardstick of morality by which Crown witnesses alone are to be measured and rejected if they do not conform to a reasonable standard of purity? Even, however, if the evidence of Crabtree be discredited, there still remains that of the other three, whose standards of moral rectitude were not on a lower plane than that of the accused himself.

The 'Rising Sun' postcard, we have seen, played an important part in the early days of the mystery; but its function in the Crown case at the Old Bailey trial is not extremely important, except in this one particular: whoever committed the murder searched through the album in vain for a postcard. The inference is that he regarded the postcard at the time as a dangerous piece of evidence which he could not afford to leave behind. As we know, he did not find the card. The remarkable fact is that Wood later confessed to having sent a postcard, although his first steps were to conceal from the police all information that might lead to his being identified as the writer of it.

The charred letter is important, not so much because it proves a meeting at the 'Eagle' (for this could be, and was in fact, proved *aliunde* at the trial), but because it affords proof of a definite appointment made by letter. Wood's own explanation of this letter is worse than unconvincing; it is incredible. He admits that it is in his handwriting, but cannot explain its purport except as 'sketches and funny sayings'. He is quite certain that it is *not* a letter, but is unable to give any explanation *why* he is sure it is not a letter. On the charred fragments there is not the slightest indication of a sketch and there seems to be nothing in the nature of a funny saying. On the contrary, the fragments contain these syllables: 'ill . . . you . . . ar . . . of . . . the . . . e . . . Town . . . Wednes . . . if . . . rest . . . excuse . . . good . . . fond . . . Mon . . . from . . . the'. We have the evidence of Roberts, the ship's cook, who swore that he saw portions of a letter sent to Dimmock, on the Wednesday morning. The text, so far as he read it, was: 'Dear Phyllis, – Will you meet me at the bar of the "Eagle" at Camden Town 8.30 tonight, Wednesday. – Bert.' This certainly fits in with the decipherable words on the fragments.

The suggestion of Marshall Hall that Roberts was inventing this letter is untenable. The fact that two letters did arrive on the morning before the murder is corroborated by Mrs Lancaster, a lodger in the house at St Paul's Road, who slipped them under the bedroom door. There were charred fragments in the grate which contain words that will bear the construction of an assignation. These fragments are admittedly in the handwriting of the accused. Yet he can only suggest that they are sketches, which obviously they are not. So here Wood would appear to be concealing the truth. If Roberts had been lying, how could he have invented words almost identical to those which appeared on the charred fragments? Roberts supplied the police, be it remembered, with the text of this letter long before the charred fragments had been in fact deciphered. Roberts was not in the confidence of the police and could not have been aware that they had even discovered any fragments at all. It is unthinkable that he had invented such a letter and that the charred fragments discovered later contained words which by a mere coincidence, were similar to those invented by Roberts. Most investigators will therefore feel compelled to admit the truth of the first and second premises of the case for the Crown.

The third premise is MacCowan's identification of Wood, and here the patterned sequence of incriminating circumstances becomes involved. MacCowan's description of the peculiarity in the walk of the accused is corroborated by both Inspector Neil and

Ruby Young. Moreover, MacCowan certainly identified Wood at the parade on 7 October on this mannerism of gait. Identification is, however, one of the *quaestiones vexatae* of criminal jurisprudence. In all cases involving personal identification there is invariably abundant material present for founding cross-examination of the type so much to the forefront during the Wood trial. It depends on variable, inconstant factors, such as eyesight, climatic conditions, visibility and illumination, facial or bodily peculiarities, the possibility of a duplication of those peculiarities in other persons, ability of the identifier to describe accurately the mannerisms by which he is able to distinguish the particular person from others of similar build, the ability of that person to retain a clear mental vision of the person he has seen, the length of time between the identifier seeing the suspect and the identification parade, the possibility of external influences (photographs, newspaper descriptions, conversations with other witnesses, etc.), as well as the actual conditions under which the identification parade is conducted.

In the present case, not only were the witnesses divided as to whether or not Wood possessed a peculiarity of walk such as would impinge itself on MacCowan's memory, but a young man named Westcott was provided by the defence, who alleged that he was the man whom MacCowan actually saw. There are, however, grave objections against Westcott's testimony: (1) As Westcott could not identify MacCowan, there is no substantial, convincing proof that he saw MacCowan – he may have seen someone else, possibly the murderer (2) Westcott's evidence was not forthcoming spontaneously, whereas MacCowan's was (3) MacCowan, in his very first statement to the police, said that the man whom he saw in St Paul's Road was wearing a hard bowler hat. Westcott usually wore a cap. Therefore the man whom MacCowan saw was not Westcott, unless MacCowan was mistaken in his reference to the bowler hat. In a dispute as to the relative merits of the powers of observation of these two witnesses the honours must be awarded to MacCowan, who not only supplied a description of the man he saw but later picked him out at an identification parade; whereas Westcott, when asked to identify the man he had seen, failed.

It would seem, therefore, that we are on fairly safe ground in ignoring Westcott's contribution to the case. That favourite epithet of the defence – 'Lying or mistaken' – might be applied as well to Westcott as to any other witness of the trial.

It is not proposed to discuss at length the alibi put forward by Wood. From a legal point of view, the dictum of a famous Irish Judge on the alibi question might be quoted: 'An alibi, if it be true, is the best defence that can be put forward. But, on the contrary, if it turns out to be untrue, it amounts to a conviction';[1] and this from a later case: 'But from the facility with which it may be fabricated it is commonly regarded with suspicion and sometimes unjustly so.'[2] It is essential to fix the time within precise limits. In an interesting case tried in Scotland and reported by Alison, the jury were directed to disregard an alibi because it appeared that all it proved was that the accused went to bed at a certain hour and was found there the next morning. As the distance from the scene of the crime was only two miles, the alibi did not preclude the possibility of the accused having arisen in the night, returning to bed after he had dispatched his victim.[3] The possibility that the same thing happened in this case cannot be ruled out and must be taken into consideration in investigating Wood's alibi.

It will be noticed that the defence brought out the gentle disposition of the accused, stressing his refinement and good character. Still, the exemplary character of the accused, even if it be established, does not carry us one step further. A host of examples of murderers who led model private lives could be furnished. Evidence of good character in a capital charge counts for nothing. In any event, as Mr Justice Grantham pointed out, it was useless to put forward any claims to superlative character on Wood's behalf.

The last question is: How far can Wood's lies and efforts to conceal material evidence be reconciled with his attitude of innocence? The attempted suppression of evidence is properly regarded as a gravely prejudicial circumstance. Following the leading legal authorities on

---

1. Per Baron Daly in *Rex* v. *Killen*, 28 State Trials, 995, at p. 1040.
2. *Rex* v. *Robinson*, [1924] Old Bailey Session Papers 423.
3. *His Majesty's Advocate* v. *Frazer*, 2 Alison, 'Principles of the Criminal Law of Scotland', at p. 625.

this point, 'it is to be interpreted as a consciousness of guilt and a desire to evade justice'.[4] The fact that an accused tells lies to the police is not, of course, proof that he is guilty. Much depends on the enormity of the lies, and the question arises: Did the accused realize at the time of his lying that his position was really serious? Many people will tell a lie when they consider the occasion unimportant. There seems to have been a tendency, of recent years, to minimize the adverse effect of such lies on the principle *nemo adversarium armare tenet*. In the famous 'Green Bicycle' case (*Rex* v. *Ronald Light*, Leicester Assizes, 1920) the accused gave lying accounts to the police on several occasions. At the trial he admitted the falsehoods, but said that, not wishing to be implicated, and anxious to avoid causing his mother any worry, he simply told the lies in order to get out of the business. Light was acquitted. On the other hand, in the amazing Sacco–Vanzetti trial in America, the falsehoods told by both accused as to their whereabouts on the night of the crime for which they were indicted were founded on by the Commonwealth of Massachusetts as incriminating proof of their guilty minds, in spite of the fact that the accused, as illiterate aliens, might well have underestimated the seriousness of lying to the police.[5] The question to be decided is whether deliberate lies told to the authorities are evidence of a deep-rooted 'consciousness of guilt', or merely indicative of a mind that takes to lying as the line of least resistance. Wood's explanation, that his false alibi with Ruby Young was merely to conceal his association with an immoral person like Dimmock, and so avoid social ostracism, seems quite plausible until we remember the character of Ruby Young, who was in fact known to the police. It then becomes the proverbial route from the frying-pan into the fire.

Here, then, is an intricate problem calculated to provide mental gymnastics for every armchair detective. Who killed Emily Dimmock? The reader must evolve his own solution of this mystery of Camden Town since Time, despite the popular assurance to the contrary, cannot now be relied upon to tell.

4. *Rex* v. *Crossfield*, 26 State Trials, at p. 217; *Rex* v. *Donellan*, (1781), dictum of Puller, J.; *Regina* v. *Palmer*, 1856 Session Papers, Central Criminal Court.
5. *Commonwealth* v. *Sacco & Vanzetti*, 1921, before Thayer, Ju.

George Joseph Smith
1915

ERIC R. WATSON

$\mathbf{G}$EORGE JOSEPH SMITH, the most atrocious English criminal since Palmer, was born on 11 January 1872, at 92 Roman Road, Bethnal Green, his father being George Thomas Smith, an insurance agent, and his mother Louisa Smith, née Gibson. The son early displayed criminal tendencies, and seems to have been sent to the reformatory at Gravesend at the tender age of nine, remaining there till he was sixteen.

When he left the reformatory he went to live with his mother, but he speedily took to evil courses, and got seven days for a small theft. That would be about the year 1890. On 7 February 1891, he was sentenced to six months' hard labour at Lambeth Police Court, in the name of George Smith, for stealing a bicycle. He stated to Miss Thornhill, his only lawful wife, that he served three years in the Northamptonshire Regiment, and he referred to a service with it to Sergeant Page on his arrest, while to the witness Crabbe he referred in vaguer terms to a period of military service when he was a gymnasium instructor. The police attach little importance to this supposed devotion to Mars. What is incontrovertible is that on 24 July 1896, he received twelve months' hard labour at the North London Sessions for larceny and receiving – three cases in all – in the name of George Baker. At this time he was known to the police as an associate of a woman unknown, whom he placed in various situations and induced to steal for him.

After coming out of prison, he proceeded to Leicester, where he opened a baker's shop at 28 Russell Square. While residing there he met, towards the end of 1897, Caroline Beatrice Thornhill, and, after a short acquaintance, during which he suggested cohabitation without marriage, married her on 17 January 1898, at St Matthew's Church, her relatives, who strongly disapproved of the bridegroom, not attending the ceremony. The bride had previously been a friend of a girl he employed in his shop, and she was only eighteen or nineteen years of age at the time. On this occasion Smith gave the name of George Oliver Love, and described his father as a detective of the name of George Love. The business failed in about six months. 'Mrs Love' went to a cousin in Nottingham, where 'Mr Love' pursued her.

Bringing 'Mrs Love' with him to London, he forced her to take various situations in London, for which he supplied the reference – posing as her late employer. He himself did no work. He also obtained situations for her at various places on the south coast, such as Brighton, Hove and Hastings. At the last-mentioned resort the unhappy 'Mrs Love' fell into the hands of the police. Without going into particulars, it suffices to say that Smith succeeded in making his escape for a while from the clutches of the law, only, however, to be arrested in London on 11 November 1900, on a charge preferred by his wife, whereupon he was taken to Hastings, and on 9 January 1901, two days before his twenty-ninth birthday, he was sentenced to two years' imprisonment, with hard labour, for receiving stolen goods. He remained in durance until 10 October 1902, when he was released, and he was next heard of in Leicester trying to find 'Mrs Love', but he did not succeed, her brothers chasing him out of the town. 'Mrs Love' had reason to fear for her safety if she remained anywhere within the reach of her George, and she accordingly left the country, taking ship to Canada, where she continued to dwell, except for a brief visit to Leicester in 1912 and 1913, until summoned back to England by Scotland Yard authorities in 1915.

Smith was not, however, without a second wife, even at this early stage. Partly for the gratification of his strong animal propensities, and even more because he much preferred to exploit women rather than work for himself or them, he had availed himself some time during 1899 of a temporary absence from his Beatrice to cast his basilisk glances over Miss —, a very respectable and industrious boarding-house keeper in the metropolis. He went through a ceremony of marriage with her in 1899 at the register office, St George's, Hanover Square. From time to time he would return to her, demanding money, and sometimes showing her large sums of gold, for the possession of which he would account as later he did to Miss Pegler. I shall recur to his relations with this unhappy woman in the concluding part of my narrative. Her last glimpse of Smith was through a grating looking out upon the exercise yard at Pentonville Prison, where her 'husband', his sentence of death confirmed by the Court of Criminal Appeal, was in utter despondency pacing up and down, awaiting his removal to the gaol of Maidstone, the place appointed for him to expiate his iniquities.

Some time in 1908, in the name of George Love, he got some very subordinate employment in a West End club; he seems to have been dismissed for inefficiency, so far as can be judged from a letter written when awaiting his trial for murder in Brixton Prison in 1915. The letter, characteristic for its vile grammar and spelling, its incoherence, and its braggart assumption of 'my marked love of poetry and the fine arts', begged a favourable statement from the steward.

In June he was in Brighton, and he encountered on the front Mrs F. W., a widow. He gave the name of George Joseph Smith, posed as a man of means, and pursued Mrs W. to Worthing, where she was employed. The usual proposal of marriage followed; 'He insisted on seeing my bank book.' The amount was £33 13s. He professed to be a dealer in antiques; they remained at Worthing about three weeks, and the lady made arrangements to withdraw her balance. She introduced him to Mrs M—, a friend, but the lady took an instant and violent dislike to the antique dealer. On 3 July the happy pair went to Camden Town Post Office to withdraw the money. Smith would have appropriated the lot, but Mrs W. left in £3 13s.; so £20 in gold and two £5 notes were placed on the counter and snatched up by Smith. 'He knew I had no pocket,' said Mrs W.

The usual inexpensive jaunt followed – this time to the White

City – the usual excuse to leave the inamorata, the usual speedy return to the apartments, and the usual lying note about forwarding the box on. The total value of Mrs W.'s belongings that Smith took was about £80 to £90.

Now was about to begin the one romance of this sordid life. Smith, with Mrs W.'s money and effects, went to Bristol, where he set up a small shop at 389 Gloucester Road as a second-hand furniture dealer. At 368, in the same road, dwelt Edith Mabel Pegler with her mother. On 1 July 1908, she advertised for a situation as housekeeper, where a servant was kept. Smith replied to her advertisement, and she speedily consented to keep house for him, although he was not in a position to afford a servant. After a week's acquaintance, Smith had so captivated Miss Pegler's maiden heart that she consented to be his, although his means were very nebulous – a mythical aunt who allowed him money, and 'that he went about the country dealing'. The marriage was solemnized at St Peter's Register Office, Bristol, on 30 July by special licence, Smith being married for the first time in his real name, describing himself as thirty-three years of age, a bachelor and general dealer, son of George Smith, deceased, figure artist.

Smith's relations to the only woman to whom he did not behave with inhuman cruelty, although to her he lied and to her he begrudged the smallest sums of his ill-gotten wealth, sufficiently appear from her evidence at the trial. Two matters may here be noted, however. He gave poor Alice Reavil's modest trousseau to his Edith, saying he had been doing a deal in ladies' second-hand clothing. And it appeared from Miss Pegler's first statement to the police, taken by Detective-Inspector Cole and Sergeant Page in Bristol, that Smith only once during all the years she knew him had a bath, at Weston-super-Mare, and that he had never inquired at any of their various apartments for a bath, and that he had more than once remarked to her that he did not believe in using baths in apartment houses which other people had access to. At the trial, it will be noted, under the encouraging suggestions of Mr Marshall Hall, she was disposed to magnify somewhat the passion which ranks next to godliness, so far as it moved Mr Smith.

About June 1909, Smith was in Southampton with Miss Pegler, and using his customary licence of wandering forth o' nights without her, he encountered Miss S— A— F—. Posing as George Rose, bachelor and dealer in antiques, he laid immediate siege to her heart, but for a time they did not meet. In October he renewed his protestations; after a fortnight, during which he made play with the mythical moneyed and mysterious resources in the bank, of which, needless to say, Miss F— saw nothing, she capitulated, and they were married on 29 October at the local register office by special licence. The rest of Miss F—'s story is soon told.

They took the train to Clapham Junction, and put their belongings in the cloakroom, while they went to find apartments. 'Mr Rose' knew that his inamorata had £50 in cash before he married her, and he lost little time in ascertaining the full extent of her resources; he looked at her bank-book while she was unpacking, and was delighted to find that she was worth £260, without including about £30 of Government stock. By 2 or 3 November the whole £260 in notes and gold – he had asked for it all in gold – was in Mr Rose's possession – he denying to his yielding bride the price of a taxi fare. She had already given him the £50. On 5 November the proceeds of the sale of the Government stock were handed over to Mr Rose in his wife's presence, and, having now acquired everything but what she stood up in, the antique dealer and picture restorer was moved by a very natural desire to expand his bride's mind (as he was soon to enlarge her knowledge of human nature) by taking her to the National Gallery. Here, by a coincidence which befell him again in Miss Reavil's case, Mr Smith was obliged to retire and leave his submissive lady, promising to return in a moment. He did return – to their lodgings, where he packed up every stick of clothing the poor, deceived and betrayed girl possessed, and when, after waiting an hour at the Gallery, she returned to their apartments, she found only three empty boxes and his cycle, which was left in the cloakroom. As in Miss Reavil's case, he sent a lying letter and a further registered letter. Miss F—, with but a few pence left in the world, went to a friend's house for the night, and never saw Mr Rose again until he was in custody on a charge of murder, on 24 April 1915.

Smith, true to his invariable practice, now rejoined Miss Pegler, he writing to her to meet him at Southend. On 16 November he invested £240 of Miss F—'s fortune in buying 22 Glenmore Street, Southend, the price of which was £270, £30 remaining on mortgage. During his visit to the Gallery he had doubtless gazed at the masterpieces of our greatest land and seascape painter, and he told his confiding Edith that the funds he had so surprisingly become possessed of represented a fortunate deal in a seascape by Joseph Mallord William Turner.

After leaving Southend, the Smiths went to Ashley Down Road, Bristol, where he resided, maintaining himself on further loans until 2 September 1910, when the amount owing was about £93. He was still borrowing on the Southend house, for he sent a receipt for a loan received from the Woolwich Equitable Building Society, from which he had purchased the property.

Smith was now nearing the end of his resources, and he proceeded to search for another dupe. In the neighbourhood of Clifton – perhaps in those charming Leigh Woods dear to the memory of every old Cliftonian – he encountered Beatrice Constance Annie Mundy. She was the daughter of a deceased bank manager, and was at the time thirty-three years of age. Soon after her father's death her relatives persuaded her to execute a voluntary settlement of her property acquired under her father's will; her fortune amounted to some £2,500 in gilt-edged securities. Smith soon won Miss Mundy's confidence and affection, and they became engaged after a few days' acquaintance. He arrived on 22 August with Miss Mundy at 14 Rodwell Avenue, Weymouth, where they took two rooms, and on the 26th they were married at the register office, he giving the name of Henry Williams, thirty-five, bachelor, picture restorer, son of Henry John Williams, commercial traveller. Miss Mundy, of course, gave correct particulars.

'Mr Williams' was prompt in discovering that his bride received her income monthly from her trustees at the rate of £8 a month, and that there was due to her some £138, which they retained in hand to meet emergencies. On the very wedding day we find him instructing a Mr Wilkinson, solicitor, of Messrs Wilkinson & Eaton, Weymouth, to write to Mr Ponting, the Mundy family solicitor, of

Warminster, for a copy of the late bank manager's will. He then discovered the existence of the settlement, which protected the *corpus* of the property from his grasp; but still he could procure the £138, and he took the most energetic steps to obtain it. By 13 September, he had possession of all the accumulated arrears in gold, less about £3 for Mr Eaton's professional charges. He at once absconded, leaving Miss Mundy penniless, and almost without clothing, and he wrote her the cruel and disgusting letter which was read by Mrs Crabbe, the landlady, in her evidence, and in which he accused his temporary paramour of disease and immorality – both accusations, needless to say, were quite unfounded.

He returned to Miss Pegler, and arranged to pay off his debt to the Equitable, writing from Ashley Down Road, and on 21 September he called at the office and paid off the £93 mortgage. To account for his absence at Weymouth, he told his faithful Edith that he had 'been to London and round the country'. The pair did not stop long at Bristol, but moved to an address in Southend – not Glenmore Road – where they took premises and set up a small antique and general dealer's shop. There they remained for about four months, going thence to Barking Road, to Walthamstow, and once more to Bristol, Smith carrying on in each place the same sort of business in antiques. It was early in 1912 that they set up in Bristol, at Bath Road, Brislington.

For seven weeks life ran on uneventfully for Miss Pegler, when her husband began to show symptoms of restlessness. He said he would go to London and round the country dealing. He accordingly left her, with very little money, to run the small shop during his five months of absence, writing on the few occasions when he did write from the Woolwich Equitable Society's address. As Smith did not support her – he sent her only £2 in five months – and the business was not a thriving one, Miss Pegler sold it for a few pounds (about £5) and returned to her mother at 102 Ashley Down Road. When she next saw her husband she beheld the murderer of Beatrice Mundy.

By what the police believe to be the only genuine coincidence in the case, the errant footsteps of Smith took him in March to Weston-super-Mare, where Beatrice Mundy had been stopping since 2 February at the house of Mrs Tuckett, a boarding-house named Norwood. I will give the story of the reunion of 'Mr and Mrs Williams' in Mrs Tuckett's own words. On 14 March Miss Mundy went out about eleven to buy some flowers for Mrs Tuckett, who expected her back in half an hour. She, in fact, returned at one. 'She said' – I quote Mrs Tuckett – 'as soon as she went out she found her husband looking over the sea. She was very excited.' At three he arrived. I shall dwell later on the instantly unfavourable impression he made on Mrs Tuckett. The following passage is from her examination-in-chief:

MR BODKIN: After these questions that you put to the prisoner did he leave?

MRS TUCKETT: I told him it was my duty to wire to her aunt.

MR BODKIN: And did he remain in the house that night?

MRS TUCKETT: Oh no. She went with him. She said, 'I suppose I may go with my husband?' I said, 'I cannot hold you back; you are thirty!' She was over thirty; thirty-one or thirty-two. She left with him. She never took anything with her. In fact she had promised me to come back that night. I did not see her again.

Apparently it was not only the good Mrs Tuckett who read the sinister mind of the man, for in the letter of 15 March he refers to the 'heated arguments which would have occurred if my wife and self had to face you and your friends this evening'.

Incidentally he bilked Mrs Tuckett of about £2 10s., but any annoyance she felt at this was probably removed by the compliment the Judge paid her at the Central Criminal Court three years later.

MR JUSTICE SCRUTTON: I am obliged to you, Mrs Tuckett, for the clear and audible way you have given your evidence.

The next move of 'Mr Williams' was to get into touch with his wife's relations – with a view to an ostensible reconciliation and the extraction of more money. He accordingly dragged the submissive lady to the office of Mr Lillington, of Messrs Baker & Co., solicitors, of Waterloo Street. The visit was paid on the very day of the

apparently accidental meeting! With extraordinary effrontery Mr
Williams proceeded, in his wife's hearing, to give a totally untrue
account of the circumstances under which he had decamped with
her money in August 1910. He professed, too, to have 'borrowed'
£150 from her to repay a loan, and, on the solicitor's suggestion, he
gave his wife a note for that sum, with interest at 4 per cent. Mr
Lillington, perceiving that Mr Williams was doing all the talking
and that the wife was 'in an assenting demeanour', challenged her
as to the truth of every one of the husband's statements, and in
every instance she confirmed them. He strongly advised her to send
the promissory note to her uncle, but, of course, Mr Williams
frustrated any such intention. When Mr Lillington saw them for
the second and last time on 16 March, Mrs Williams still had the
note at their lodgings – and it never turned up again.

Leaving Weston-super-Mare, this singular couple travelled
about, staying at lodgings in different towns, and late in May they
left Ashley and came to Herne Bay. Here on 20 May, 'Bluebeard of
the Bath,' as Mr George R. Sims has dubbed him, walked into the
house of Mr F. H. Wilbee, J.P., of that town, a considerable owner
of small house property there. Within that house was a little office
where, at rather a high desk, there sat and had been sitting for
thirty-six-and-a-half years Miss Carrie Esther Rapley. He did not
know it – this cheap *accapareur de femmes* with the appearance of a
butcher and the breeding of a scavenger – but he had met one of
those women, and there were several in the case, whose feminine
instinct, like the protective antennae of insects, warned them that
here was a dangerous man. Miss Rapley was not a young woman,
but because she was a woman, Smith, without any friendships or
even acquaintanceships among men, immediately proceeded to
become expansive. I will let her admirably clear evidence speak for
itself, only regretting that I cannot give it word for word. She
becomes suspicious at the first interview. She asks for a banker's
reference, and he produces a Savings Bank book. She asks to see it;
he puts it back in his pocket. He is evasive about his means; but his
wife has money. 'I might just as well tell you she is a notch above
me,' and he grows more expansive. In the end he takes the house he

had come to inquire about, 80 High Street, on a yearly tenancy, at £18 a year, rent payable monthly. The agreement calls for little comment; it was, however, a yearly tenancy; Mr Williams wanted a monthly one, and he gave up the house, after paying two months' rent in advance, the second payment being at that singular interview with Miss Rapley which we shall come to later.

It will be recalled that soon after the marriage Mr Williams became aware of his wife's voluntary settlement; he had already obtained a copy of this about 5 September 1910, but he obtained another later, through her, about 10 June 1912, and this he brought to the office of Mr Annesley, solicitor, of Herne Bay, on 18 June. That he was in need of raising money at once appears from the evidence of Mr Hudgell, clerk to the Woolwich Equitable's solicitor, who produced a letter asking for the money due on the sale of the Southend house, 'as it is very urgently required'; the letter bore the date 12 May. A copy of the voluntary settlement was laid before Mr G. F. Spear, of the Inner Temple, to advise. Mr Williams, in short, wanted to know how he could get hold of the *corpus* of the wife's property. The trustees were very unlikely to consent to a revocation of the settlement in the circumstances; they were far from unlikely to exercise their discretion in buying the wife an annuity; if she died intestate, her estate would go to the next-of-kin under the Statute of Distributions, and the husband would get nothing; but if she, with £2,500, left a will in his favour, and he, without a shilling, executed a similiar will in her favour, and she died? Counsel's opinion came back on 2 July; it was Bessie Mundy's death warrant.

The mutual wills were drawn up by Mr Annesley and executed by the parties on 8 July. Next day Mr Williams came to the shop of Mr Hill, ironmonger, and 'cheapened' a £2 bath down to £1 17s. 6d.; he did not pay for it, but returned it on 15 July. Its dimensions were later carefully taken by Detective-Inspector Neil. It may here be said that it had no taps or fixings at all; it had to be filled and emptied by hand, and the inspector found exactly how many pails would be needed and how long it would take to carry them from the kitchen to the fatal room in order to fill that bath.

On the next day after that purchase Mr Williams took his wife to Dr French, who had been qualified about two years, and had set up in practice at Herne Bay, saying that she had had a fit. Being unaware of the symptoms of epileptic or any other fits, Mr Williams prudently forbore to enter into particulars, and Dr French put him 'leading questions', which enabled him to recall just what the doctor suggested and no more – limbs twitching, jaws moving, and so on; there was no suggestion of the dreadful scream which almost invariably heralds an epileptic seizure (as distinct from the *petit mal*), and Mr Williams said no word about a scream. The doctor prescribed bromide of potassium, a useful general sedative, a specific in epilepsy and an anaphrodisiac. In answer to the doctor's questions, Mrs Williams did not recollect anything about a fit; she had never had any, and only complained of a headache.

On Friday, 12 July, Williams fetched Dr French to see his wife in bed. The doctor saw nothing amiss, except that her hands were clammy, the weather being very hot, heart normal, tongue not very clean, face a little flushed; she looked like one awakened from sleep on a hot night. The doctor prescribed more bromide. At 3 p.m. he saw the pair again, when Mrs Williams looked 'in perfect health'; she complained of nothing worse than lassitude, the weather being so hot. Before she went to bed that night she wrote the following letter to her uncle, which she registered. It was produced by him at the trial.

Last Tuesday night I had a bad fit, and one again on Thursday night. It has left me weak and suffering from nerves and headache, and has evidently shaken my whole system. My husband has been extremely kind and done all he could for me. He has provided me with the attention of the best medical man here, who is constantly giving me medical treatment, and visiting me day and night.

I do not like to worry you with this, but my husband has strictly advised me to let all my relatives know and tell them of my breakdown. I have made out my will and have left all I have to my husband. That is only natural, as I love my husband.

At 8 a.m. next morning – Saturday 13 July[1] – Dr French was handed a note. It ran, 'Can you come at once? I am afraid my wife is dead.' The doctor hurried round to 80 High Street and found the door ajar; he entered and went upstairs with Williams, and saw Mrs Williams lying on her back in the bath. Particulars of her position will be found elsewhere in the narrative. Her head was beneath the water, and on removing her body the doctor found that the pulse had ceased to beat; the body was not yet cold, but all attempts at restoration proved useless. A square piece of Castile soap was clutched in the right hand. Williams assisted the doctor while he was trying artificial respiration by holding the woman's tongue, her false teeth having been removed. The face was dusky and congested with blood. Finding her beyond human aid, Dr French left the house, and about 10 a.m. Police Constable Kitchingham arrived, and saw the body lying quite naked; he also saw the bath three-parts full. He took a statement from Williams and went away. Williams now went out to arrange for the laying out of the body, and he first approached Mrs Millgate, with whom he afterwards boarded, and who lived next door. She said that she was too busy to come, but at 2 p.m. she called at 80 High Street, and learning from Williams that the woman the doctor was to send had not come, she went upstairs with him. What then happened I give in her own words:

MR BODKIN: What room did you go into?

MRS MILLGATE: The middle bedroom; and he said, 'She is in there.' He stayed outside on the landing and I went in, and I said, 'In here.' And I went in, and not seeing anything but the bath, I looked behind the door, and I saw Mrs Williams lying on the floor quite naked.

MR BODKIN: Quite naked?

MRS MILLGATE: Yes; that gave me a great shock, and I started back and turned suddenly round and said, 'Oh dear, it is not

1. All these brides died on a Friday night or a Saturday morning. Alice Burnham on Friday night, 12 December 1913, and Margaret Lofty on Friday night, 18 December 1914. The convenience of holding the inquest before the relatives could attend need hardly be pointed out.

covered over.' And he looked frightened as I started back. Mr Williams looked frightened as I started back.

MR BODKIN: Did you then cover the body up?

MRS MILLGATE: Yes; I went back again into the room, and I noticed she was lying on the edge of a sheet, and a lot of it was to her feet, and I picked it up and covered over the body . . . I asked him to fetch me a pillow, just to put under her head, as her head was on the bare floor, and he said to me . . .

Here the witness, who was rather deaf, was interrupted, and she did not give her reply. In her evidence at the police court she spoke of seeing blood near the corpse's waist. The medico-legal aspect of this I shall deal with at a further stage. Williams had early in the morning asked Mr Millgate for 'a few pieces of rag for the woman to wipe up some blood'. Alice Minter, who actually laid out the body about 4 p.m., asked for 'just the usual things – nightdress, brush and comb, bath sponge, and a towel'.

Whatever the explanation of the blood, it was Williams who wiped it up.

Mr Rutley Mowll, solicitor, of Dover, and coroner for East Kent, was informed of the death on the day it occurred by the police – probably by Kitchingham, who was coroner's officer. He was for holding his inquest forthwith, but he found the inquest could not be conveniently taken that day, so he gave directions to hold it at 4.30 p.m. on the Monday. The Mundy family had heard by wire from Williams of the death that Saturday morning, very shortly after receiving the last letter from Bessie, which has been set out. The wire ran, 'Bessie died in a fit this morning; letter following. – Williams.'

On the Monday, Herbert Mundy received a letter from Williams. 'Words cannot describe the great shock I suffered in the loss of my wife,' wrote the bereaved husband. No word was breathed by him as to the holding of any inquest, nor as to the date of it. When Herbert Mundy next heard, 'Crowner's Quest Law' had done its best – or worst – and Mr Mowll, displaying, as he said, 'more than ordinary perspicacity' and having 'taken very great care', and having 'thoroughly and carefully thrashed out' the case, returned through his jury a verdict that 'the cause of her death was that while taking a bath she had an epileptic seizure, causing her to fall back into the water of the bath and be drowned, and so the jurors say that the said deceased died from misadventure'.

The more than ordinary perspicacity of the coroner enabled him to state that, 'assuming the husband was fond of his wife – and there was no evidence to the contrary, but a great deal of evidence that he was – it was a terrible plight'. (I may pause to remark that Mr Williams had shed copious crocodile tears during the inquest, as next day he did over Miss Rapley's desk, but in the case of that shrewd lady the simulation of great grief was not successfully attempted.) Mr Mowll went on to say that 'a request had been made to have a post-mortem, and if he had had the request earlier – he had it by the earliest possible moment the Mundy family could make it – he should then with an abundance of caution have requested the doctor to make an examination'.

The first the Mundy family heard of any inquest was in a letter from Mr Williams, dated 15 July, the day of the inquest, running:

Dear Sir, I hope you received my letter this morning. The result of the inquest was misadventure by a fit in the bath. The burial takes place tomorrow at 2 p.m. I am naturally too sad to write any more today.

On the Sunday, 14 July, the dead woman's brother, G. H. Mundy, wrote two letters, one to Williams, the other to the coroner. They were substantially the same, but not identical; and the purpose of them was this, 'As Bessie's brother, I must insist that, as she died so suddenly, a post-mortem examination must be held before she is buried, for the satisfaction of all the family. Please see that this is carried out.'

Whatever the minute discrepancies between Mr Howard Mundy's letter to Williams and his letter to the coroner may have been, the coroner saw no reason to afford the Mundy family time to attend the inquest. The coroner and Williams compared their letters, and the result was that only Smith, *alias* Williams, *alias* Love, *alias* James, *alias* Baker, *alias* Lloyd, and Dr French – a Herne Bay practitioner of two years' standing, strangely described by his patient as 'the best medical man here, who is constantly giving me medical treatment' – gave the evidence upon which the verdict recorded was returned. The funeral was carried out by Mr Hogbin, who had also provided the furniture for 80 High Street. 'It was to be moderately carried out at an expense of seven guineas.'

MR BODKIN: And a grave?

MR HOGBIN: He said he would not purchase a grave. The grave was 8s. 6d., the interment fee.

The funeral, which had been provisionally fixed to take place on Tuesday 16 July, took place as arranged, as the inquest had gone 'favourably', and two days later Smith resold to the undertaker the piano and other furniture at 80 High Street for £20 4s. On the morning of the funeral, timed for 2.30 p.m., the bereaved husband walked into Miss Rapley's office, and, putting his arms and head on her high desk, he began to sob. 'She is dead,' he groaned. 'My wife; she had a fit during the week. I went out; she went to have a bath, and she must have had another fit, for when I came back I found her dead in the bath.' Miss Rapley was too shocked to make any comment, so Mr Williams proceeded, 'Was it not a jolly good job I got her to make a will?' Miss Rapley was more shocked. Mr Williams became angry. 'Well, is it not the correct thing when people marry for the wife to make her will and leave everything to her husband, and for him to make his and leave everything to her?' he snorted. 'Did you make yours?' asked Miss Rapley. 'Yes,' said Williams. 'I then looked him very straight in the face and I said,' so testified Miss Rapley, 'I thought you told me you had not got anything?' 'Oh, well, I made my will all the same,' was the weak reply.

He then told Miss Rapley of the previous day's inquest – the first she had heard of it. She persisted, 'Did you let her relatives know?' 'Yes, I did, and the brutes sent a letter to the coroner saying it was a very suspicious case.' Still Miss Rapley persisted, 'Let me see, where did you say her relatives lived?' 'I never told you where they lived,' snapped Mr Williams. Miss Rapley saw him once more at Herne Bay; he had come to pay the second and last instalment of rent; incidentally, he wanted her to find him a nice little place in the country – not more than £400. When she next saw Mr Williams he was in custody on three charges of murder.

On 17 July Mr Williams called on Mr Annesley, the solicitor who had drawn up the wills, and instructed him to obtain probate of his wife's will. A caveat was lodged by the Mundy family about the end of July, but was withdrawn by Ponting & Co. on 8 August, and in the course of the autumn of 1912 all the securities covered by the settlement (with the exception of £300 Cape of Good Hope stock retained until early in the following year against a liability of the estate for unpaid calls on shares in a moribund company) were handed over to Mr Williams. His exact dealings with the Mundy securities, which he turned into gold and notes and then into house property, and then again into cash and finally into an annuity, were traced in minute detail by Detective-Inspector Neil. Many different banking accounts were used by Smith all over the south and west of England, and he obtained by receipts £2,403 15s. against payments of £2,042 9s. 5d. The correspondence in relation to the winding-up of Mrs Williams' estate, carried on between Mr Annesley, Messrs Ponting, Smith, and others, is contained in no less than 215 letters and telegrams; the professional letters are very much like others, but the personal ones of Smith, from their spelling, style, and persistent inquiries after money, are very idiosyncratic.

Probate was granted about 11 September. Illness in the Mundy family and delays caused by Smith's own interference rendered the negotiations somewhat protracted, and 'Mr Williams' was very reluctant to pay Mr Annesley's bill, or to furnish Messrs Ponting with any particulars about himself. Under date 1 August 1912, he writes to Annesley, 'I was educated at Whitechurch, Glasgow [sic], after which I went to Canada – returned to London. I have always been of an extremely roaming disposition, never keeping a diary, but continually up and down the country buying and selling pictures, etc. I never remained in one particular town more than a week or so.' On 4 August he writes, 'Now, in regard to my history, which was requested by them, that also is bluff. It is not the matter of history inasmuch as the only proof required is whether I am the lawful husband of the deceased. If it was a matter of history, what on earth is the use of a will?'

The inspector was equally indefatigable in tracing the purchases and sales of house property. The net result was that Smith purchased the houses for £2,187 10s., and sold them for £1,455, a loss of over £600 in a few months. He invested £1,300 in an annuity in the North British and Mercantile Insurance Company, payable half-yearly in April and October, at a total charge of £76 1s. a year.

I will now pick up the threads of the story of Miss Pegler. That lady was never able to ascertain where her spouse resided when away from her. His rare letters came through the Woolwich Equitable or from some accommodation address. When he met her at Margate, as we shall presently see, and she told him that she had tried to find him at Woolwich and Ramsgate, he was very angry, and said he should never tell her his business again. He did not believe in women knowing his business and vehemently requested her to do no such thing again.

About the end of July or the beginning of August Miss Pegler received a letter from Smith asking her to join him at Margate; she did so. They stayed a week, and went on to Tunbridge Wells and other places mentioned in her evidence. She naturally asked him what he had been up to. He was angry, as has been said, but he condescended to inform her that he had just returned from Canada, where he had been very fortunate in buying a Chinese image for a song and selling it for £1,000. Mr and Mrs Smith appeared to have lived together for over a year, he leaving her early in October 1913, to go round the country; he explained that he had to do some dealing, as he had dropped £600 over his houses. When he returned after his calculated murder of Alice Burnham, he said he had just come from Spain, where he had bought some old-fashioned jewellery, which brought him in £200 eventually.

A very singular incident had occurred just before Smith went away to marry and murder Alice Burnham. He made the acquaintance, in August or September, while they were at Weston-super-Mare, of a young woman of twenty-eight or thirty years of age, of the name of Burdett, as far as Miss Pegler could recollect. She was a governess, and Miss Pegler several times saw the boy and two girls she had in charge. Some intimacy developed, and the Smiths asked her to tea. She came about four times, sometimes bringing the children. Smith told his Edith that he was going to insure the young lady as an 'investment', and an insurance agent actually called to discuss the matter, Smith taking Miss Burdett to see him. A policy for £500 was provisionally arranged. Miss Pegler, much against her inclination, accompanied Miss Burdett to see the insurance company's doctor, and Miss Burdett was passed as a first-class life. Miss Burdett knew quite well that the Smiths were married, and for some reason Smith cancelled the policy – if, indeed, it was ever issued – and recovered his premium.

When Smith left Miss Pegler he proceeded to Southsea, where he met Alice Burnham, his next victim, apparently at the chapel she attended. She was twenty-five years of age, and was nursing an old gentleman named Holt. She was a stout but healthy young woman, and had made a very good recovery from a somewhat serious operation. Within a very few days Smith had induced her to consent to an engagement. With that minute attention to matters of money so characteristic of him, 'George' brought his bank books and private papers when he came to propose, and from what we know of him we may be sure he lost no time in ascertaining from his new flame exactly how her financial affairs stood.

On 15 October the deluded girl wrote to her people announcing her engagement, whilst Smith on 22 October wrote to Mrs Burnham, Alice's mother, a letter expressing, in endearing terms, his affection for her daughter, and advising her that they were coming down to Aston Clinton to pay a visit. In accordance with the intention expressed in his letter, Smith and Alice Burnham journeyed to Aston Clinton, on Saturday 25 October, and were met at Tring station by her father, with his pony and trap. They remained until 31 October, the visit being cut short by the behaviour of Smith, which the family found so objectionable that Mr Burnham asked his daughter to leave. Indeed, from the first Mr Burnham felt the strongest dislike of Smith, whom he described as a man of 'very evil appearance, so much so that he could not sleep whilst Smith was in the house, as he feared Smith was a bad man and that something serious would happen'. Smith avoided Mr Burnham as much as possible.

Notwithstanding the chilling hostility of the family, Alice and Smith gave notice of their intended marriage at the church at Aston Clinton. That intention, however, they abandoned, and, returning to Southsea, they were married on 4 November at the Portsmouth Register Office, he giving his true name, describing his age as forty, and his condition as bachelor, of independent means, son of George Thomas Smith, deceased, artist, flowers and figure.

It may here be noted that Mr Burnham had inquired at Somerset House, but no trace of Smith's birth could be found.

Alice Burnham's means at the time of her marriage were these – in the Savings Bank, £27 19s. 5d.; due from her father £100 and interest on his promissory note; due from her sister, Mrs Pinchin, £10. She had also a quantity of jewellery and clothing.

It is best to tell the story of what happened in Inspector Neil's own words, as giving the reader an example of an official narrative, which presents the main facts with a telling succinctness.

20/10/13   she drew all her money from the bank, £27 19s. 5d., and on
3/11/13   prisoner introduced her to Mr Pleasance, an insurance agent, with the result that she was insured for £500. On the
4/11/13   the prisoner married her at Portsmouth Register Office in the name of George Joseph Smith. He immediately commenced application to Mr Burnham for the £100, which Mr Burnham declined to send as he was suspicious of the man and desired to know something of his antecedents, and for this purpose consulted Mr Redhead, solicitor, of Aylesbury, who wrote to the prisoner, asking him something about himself, and in reply Mr Burnham received an insulting postcard stating that his mother was a cab horse, etc. Every obstacle was put in the way of the money being sent, and the prisoner threatened to commence proceedings. Mr Burnham was eventually advised to part with the money, and on
29/11/13   he forwarded £104 1s. 1d. to his solicitor, who sent it on to the

prisoner through his solicitor. It is known that this money was paid by the prisoner into his own banking account. On

4/12/13 the insurance on Miss Burnham's life was completed and the premium of £24 17s. 1d. paid. This was no doubt the money drawn out of the P.O. On

8/12/13 Miss Burnham called on Mr March, solicitor, Portsmouth, and made a will in favour of her husband. On

10/12/13 prisoner and Miss Burnham went to Blackpool and called on Mrs Marsden at 35 Adelaide Street, but declined to take rooms there as there was no bath there, and they were recommended to go to Regent's Road where they took lodgings with Mrs Crossley. The same day they called on Dr Billing where the prisoner explained that his wife had a headache in consequence of a train journey. She was prescribed for. On

11/12/13 Miss Burnham asked for a bath, which was prepared by Mrs Crossley, and shortly after the prisoner went to Mrs Crossley and said he could not make his wife hear. She was found dead in her bath by prisoner and Mrs Crossley. Dr Billing was sent for, and on

13/12/13 an inquest was held and a verdict of death from drowning was returned. A funeral was arranged for to take place on

15/12/13 and on the day before Miss Burnham's mother and brother went to Blackpool to be present at the funeral. The same day Smith left them (immediately after the funeral) and said he had to get back to Portsmouth. They never saw him again though he promised to write. He went to 80 Kimberley Road, sold all Miss Burnham's belongings and then went to London where he approached Kingsbury & Turner, solicitors, Brixton, on

18/12/13 with a view to them obtaining probate. On

22/12/13 he returned to Miss Pegler at Bristol, when he said he had been to Spain and done fairly well. On the

19/1/14 he received the money from the insurance under Burnham's will through Heath & Eckersall, Cheltenham, to whom he had gone after Kingsbury & Turner had obtained probate. He resided in Cheltenham some time with Pegler. The money paid under the insurance was £506, and on

22/1/14 with this money he increased his annuity to the extent of £500. With Miss Pegler he then went back to Bristol.

Here for a time I will leave the Inspector and resume my narrative.

Smith had so completely estranged the affections and warped the mind of Alice Burnham during the brief period of their engagement that she actually brought herself to write two letters on 22 and 24 November to her father, in which she advised him on the former date that that was her last application for her £100 and interest on his promissory note, and finally on the 24th that she had instructed her solicitor to take 'extreme measures to obtain the money you have in your possession'. She also went so far as to instruct Mr Robinson, a solicitor, to write to her married sister, Annie Pinchin, demanding the return of £10 which she had lent her; later on, however, on the sister's marriage, she told her to regard it as a gift. The £10 was repaid on 28 November, by registered letter.

It is needless to anticipate the story of what happened at Blackpool; the medico-legal aspects are dealt with later. But one or two matters call for mention here, because the witnesses did not refer to them in their evidence.[2] On the afternoon following the murder of Alice Burnham, Smith returned with a full bottle of whisky; in the evening there was only a little drop left. He spent part of the afternoon playing the piano. He told Margaret Crossley that he had been in the Marines, and had shaved off his moustache a fortnight previously. He declined to pay the bill for the food supplied to Mrs Burnham and her son. Mrs Crossley had great difficulty in getting him to pay for his own board and lodging. He promised to recompense her for the trouble she had been put to, but he never did. To Joseph Crossley he said that he wanted a deal coffin, and on Crossley replying that he would not bury his wife like that, even if he had not a penny in the world, Smith retorted, 'When they are dead they are done with.'

A matter of some importance was noticed in Superintendent Wootton's letter from Aylesbury: 'I desire to draw your attention to Smith's letter to Mrs Burnham dated 13/12/13, giving an account of his wife's death, etc., in which he states that the inquest would be

2. For complete evidence in the cases of Mundy, Burnham and Lofty see *Trial of George Joseph Smith*, Notable British Trials series (Wm Hodge & Co. Ltd, London).

held early next week, whereas it was held on the day the letter was written.'

In consequence of this deception, the second inquest was of the same perfunctory character as the first. It was all over in half an hour, and many points of suspicion were never brought out – as that Valiant, the coroner's officer, noticed that the distracted 'husband' had carefully removed his coat and rolled up his right shirt sleeve before raising his 'bride's' head out of the water, and that Mrs Haynes, who resided next door, had noticed a very considerable quantity of hair at the sloping end of the bath (the deceased had been sitting facing that end) on the Sunday morning, when she went to clean the bath.

Again, Smith was a transparently uneducated man. Yet his statement that, 'I am a gentleman of independent means, and have never followed any occupation,' aroused no incredulity – though he had told his very landlady that he had been a marine! The only witnesses were Dr Billing, Mrs M. Crossley, Valiant and another sergeant, and Smith himself. He duly contrived – assisted, maybe, by the bottle of whisky he had consumed – to make his lachrymal glands perform their function, and his freely flowing crocodile tears moved all hearts except Mrs Crossley's.

The coroner had another inquest to hold and the 8 p.m. train to catch – all between 6.30 and 8, so with little ado the jurors of Our Lord the King found that 'the deceased Alice Smith came to her death at Blackpool aforesaid on the 12th day of December, 1913. The deceased suffered from heart disease, and was found drowned in a hot bath, probably through being seized with a fit or faint. The cause of death was accidental.'

The deception as to the letting off of the water in Smith's letter to Mrs Burnham is truly remarkable. When Dr Billing arrived on the scene he asked Smith why he had not lifted his wife out; he said he could not. He was then asked why he could not pull the plug; he said he never thought of it! And yet in the letter he says – 'I held her head out of the water and let the water run off away from her; when the doctor came we lifted her out of the bath.' His lying hypocrisy can be estimated even better when one reads that in the same letter he describes the death as 'the greatest and most cruel shock that ever a man could have suffered'.

Smith fled hastily from the scene of his crime. He left his address with Mrs M. Crossley on a postcard. On the back she wrote, 'Wife died in bath. We shall see him again.' When the card was shown to her at the Old Bailey two years later, the usher was directed to show her and the jury only the address side of that card. What Mrs Crossley wrote – like what the soldier said – was not evidence. As he sped down the street she hurled after him an opprobrious name – 'Crippen'.

With that sordid love of money which never forsook him, he realized all his wife's wardrobe and jewellery just as he had sold Bessie Mundy's linen to a Margate dealer before Mrs Millgate, his landlady, had got it back from the laundry.

He returned to Edith Pegler, and with her recommenced those aimless wanderings from place to place – Bournemouth, Torquay, etc., until about 14 August, when, once more in Bournemouth, he marked down his penultimate victim in the person of Alice Reavil, a domestic servant.

She gave evidence at Bow Street, and her statement, as taken by Inspector Cole and P. S. Page, reads as follows:

On 7th or 8th September I was in the garden on the front, sitting on a seat, when a man came and spoke to me . . . We had some conversation, in which he said he admired my figure. After an hour's conversation, in which he informed me he was an artist, and had £2 a week from some land in Canada, he made an appointment for 6 p.m. the same evening. I met him as arranged; he did not tell me where he was staying; I never knew. Next day I met him as arranged, and he then told me his name was 'Charles Oliver James'. He said he had been to Canada and his agents sent him his money. He also said he understood I had some money. I met him every evening, and I returned to Woolwich on the 14th or 15th September. After the third or fourth day of our acquaintance he asked me to marry him, and I consented, and he said he would put his money with mine and he would open an antique shop . . . He asked me how much money I had, and I said about £70 odd, and some furniture, including a piano. He asked me to sell them, and I decided to . . . We went to the Register Office and were married by special licence [this was on September 17]. In the meantime I had sold my belongings, and they realized £14. After we married we left Woolwich for Waterloo, and went to 8 Hafer Road, Battersea Rise, where he had taken two furnished rooms . . . On the way he showed me a lot of bank-notes, and he asked me for my £14 to put in the bank with his. I gave it to him. When we got to our lodgings . . . he produced a Post Office withdrawal form for me to fill up to draw all my money from the bank. I filled it up, and added, 'with interest to close account', and we went out together to post it . . . He put it in the box. I signed the withdrawal form in my maiden name, and he gave instructions to the landlady to take it in . . . About three days later the warrant for withdrawal was delivered, and he took it in. This was on Saturday, September 19, 1914. He kept the warrant. All my clothing was at this address, and was kept in four boxes. On September 21 we went to the Post Office, Lavender Hill, to obtain the money . . . He told me to ask for all £1 notes, but they gave me four £10 notes and two £5 notes, and the remainder in £1 notes and cash. In all I received £75 6s. and some coppers. He picked up the notes and I the cash – the odd 6s. I never saw the notes again . . . The same evening we packed our belongings, with the intention of getting another house. He went out to get a man to take the luggage to Clapham station, and later a man arrived with a barrow to take it away – as I thought, to the station . . . He told the landlady we should go away next day; he paid the bill – I think 10s.; I had bought all the food we had. On September 22 we left the house . . . We got on a tram-car, and on the way he spoke of Halifax, Nova Scotia, and asked me if I would like to go. He took penny fares and we got off at some gardens. We walked through the gardens and on getting to the other end he said he was going to the lavatory and asked me to wait. I did so, and waited about an hour. He did not return so I returned to 8 Hafer Road, and found the attached telegram waiting for me. [It ran, 'Wait home for letter. Next post – James.'] I remained as requested and some hours later received a letter (registered), posted at Battersea. I stayed at Hafer Road the same night, and returned to 39 Plumstead Common Road next day. None of my boxes arrived, and I have not seen them since. On February 22 . . . I attended Bow Street, and I identified a man known as George Smith as my husband . . . I communicated with the Post Office, and obtained the numbers of the notes paid on the warrant. When I married the prisoner he was clean-shaven. I value my clothing, jewellery, etc., at about £50. The result of my meeting with prisoner was that I was left with only a few shillings and the clothes I was actually wearing. What he had taken consisted of the whole of my life savings.

237

Smith now for the last time rejoined Edith Pegler, taking with him Alice Reavil's modest trousseau. This – or, rather, what remained of it – he gave to her, remarking that 'he had been to a sale in London and had bought some lady's clothing. He had some left, and gave it to me. It was kept in a black trunk, which I had not seen before. The lady's clothing taken away by the police was brought to Weston-super-Mare by Smith.'

During the period between the Reavil marriage and the Lofty murder, Miss Pegler thought about November 1914. 'He remarked to me that, if I interfered with his business, I should never have another happy day, as the world was wide, and he would forfeit it all. This was because I had spoken about his annuity. Just after Christmas 1914, we were living in apartments at 10 Kennington Avenue, Bristol, and I said I was going to have a bath. He said, "In that bath there?" – referring to the bathroom – "I should advise you to be careful of those things, as it is known that women often lose their lives through weak hearts and fainting in a bath." '

Towards the end of 1914 the Smiths were in Bristol, when a mood of restlessness once more swept over George Joseph, and he said he 'would have a run round again before Christmas with another "young fellow" – he had met in Clifton'. The 'young fellow' was Margaret Elizabeth Lofty, spinster, aged thirty-eight, daughter of the late Rev. Fitzroy Fuller Lofty, who had died in 1892, leaving a widow, one son and three daughters. Miss Lofty soon responded to Smith's overtures; a disappointment in love a year before – it turned out that the man had a wife already – had rather unsettled her for her vocation as companion to elderly ladies in quiet cathedral cities; and Smith, whatever he lacked in address or education, left nothing to be desired from the point of uxoriousness or virility. She seems to have perceived that her mother and sisters would be critical of her *fiancé*; so she writes them pious untruths; she is going away to be clandestinely married, and she writes, under date 15 December 1914, Bristol station:

Dear Elsie, I am off to a situation and meet my lady here. We go, I believe, to London for a day or two. Don't worry . . . Your affectionate sister, Peggy.

And she encloses a note for her mother in similar vein – all untrue.

As she had but about £19 in the Savings Bank, a life policy became imperatively necessary from Smith's point of view. He is 'John Lloyd' now. He has ceased to be of independent means, and has become a land agent, like his father before him, one John Arthur Lloyd. Accordingly, the unsuspecting victim is sent to the office of the Yorkshire Insurance Company, 4 St Stephen's Avenue, Bristol. She did not strike Mr Cooper, of that office, as at all a good business woman when he first saw her on November 24. She called again next day, and filled in a proposal form for a £700 endowment policy. One regrets to note that she told several untruths when applying; it is needless to suggest who inspired them. She said she was of independent means, whereas she had but £19 odd; she said that she did not contemplate matrimony, whereas she was bent on nothing else; she said that she had brought her birth certificate because Mr Cooper had suggested it, whereas he had done no such thing; the question of proving her age had never been mentioned by him. She wished the issue of the policy to be expedited as much as possible, and the insurance was completed on 4 December, when she paid the premium, no doubt with money supplied by Smith – it was in the form of new Treasury notes obtained from the unfortunate Alice Reavil – because she had not enough of her own in the bank. She struck Mr Cooper as having learnt a good deal – 'had the business at her finger-ends' – about insurance matters since her first visit, and he thought she must have been prompted by someone.

On 17 December the parties were married, Smith of the occupation of land agent and in the name of John Lloyd, aged thirty-eight, his bride of the same age; she gave, of course, a correct account of her parentage. They left Dalkeith House, 4 Stanley Road, Bath, from which they had been married, the same day, and, with no luggage beyond a hold-all and a gladstone bag, took the train to London, and went to 16 Orchard Road, Highgate, where Lloyd had booked rooms on the previous Monday, paying

6s. deposit. The house was owned by a Miss Lokker, and a Mrs Heiss managed it in her absence; there were reasons why they had to be especially careful, in 1915, and that they did not take in undesirable lodgers without references; in fact, they had had such lodgers, and they had been robbed. The facts were that Miss Lokker was a Dutch subject and Mrs Heiss a German. At Bow Street Mrs Heiss stated, 'I did not like the way he asked about the bath.'

Lloyd, when he called on the Monday, had asked to see the bath. He looked at it 'as if he was measuring it with his eyes', and said to Mrs Heiss, 'This is rather a small bath, but I dare say it is large enough for someone to lie in.' He looked at her and smiled, and she said, 'It is.' He decided to take the rooms, paid his deposit, and left. But he had made so bad an impression by his manner that Miss Lokker had decided by Thursday that she would not let him the rooms. When he arrived with his bride, about 3 p.m. on that day, the door was opened to him by a Mr Van Rhym, who said, 'You cannot have the rooms now; they are not ready,' and told him to return at 6 p.m. Lloyd appeared annoyed and nasty, and left his luggage in the passage and went away. Detective-Sergeant Dennison had so advised when he visited the house at 2.30, at Miss Lokker's request; he had acted for her in the matter of the other undesirable lodgers. Lloyd returned a little after 5 p.m., but Mrs Heiss was so frightened by his evil appearance that she would not let him in; he kept knocking and calling out to people in the road that, if it were not for his wife, he would have knocked the man (Mr Van Rhym) down.

Dennison had arranged to call again at six, and Miss Lokker, in some alarm, went through a neighbour's house to look for him. Lloyd was at the door. 'He was in a temper, and asked me if I had anything to do with the house. I said "No." He said a lot I do not remember, but I know I asked if he had given a reference. He said, "I have never heard of such a thing. I have plenty of money and a banker; that is good enough." He said he had been everywhere abroad, but had never been treated as he was being treated. He said "I can see it is all planned. All I want is my money and luggage back; I have taken rooms somewhere else." He did not know I was the landlady, and all the time he was talking to me he was running the place down.'

At six o'clock Dennison opened the door to Mr and Mrs Lloyd, and said, 'You cannot have the rooms, because you cannot furnish references.' In reply to Lloyd's question, 'Who are you?' the officer cautiously replied, 'I am acting on behalf of the landlady.' Mr Lloyd turned to his bride, exclaimed, 'They don't want us,' and having been given back his deposit, was shown the door by the detective; he departed in a passion.

Mr Lloyd sought apartments next at 14 Bismarck Road, Highgate (now Waterloo Road), where Miss Blatch had a furnished room to let. He came with his bride, without luggage, paid seven shillings deposit, and went away, as he said, to fetch the luggage. Before agreeing to take the room, Mrs Lloyd had inquired if there was a bath; the answer was in the affirmative. During her husband's absence, Mrs Lloyd told Miss Blatch that she did not know her husband's plans, but they were going to Scotland for their honeymoon. It is needless to travel in detail over the evidence of the witnesses as to the death at Bismarck Road. I will condense the narrative in the Inspector's style. About 5 p.m. on

17/12/14	Smith in the name of Lloyd arrives at 14 Bismarck Road, and takes a room after inquiring if there is a bath, and at 8 p.m., on
17/12/14	he takes 'Mrs Lloyd' to see Dr Bates at 30 Archway Road, who prescribes for her, and on
18/12/14	Mrs Lloyd goes to the office of Mr Lewis, solicitor, 84 High Street, Islington, and makes her will, bequeathing everything to her husband, who was appointed sole executor. On the same day she draws out her whole balance in the savings bank from Muswell Hill Post Office, £19 9s. 5d., having given notice of withdrawal on the fifteenth, and on
18/12/14	she returns to Bismarck Road, and at 7.30 p.m. on
18/12/14	Mrs Lloyd asks for a hot bath, and at 8.15 p.m. on
18/12/14	P.C. Heath is called to the house and he finds Mrs Lloyd dead, and on
20/12/14	Mr Lloyd calls on Mrs Beckett and desires to have the funeral next day, and on
22/12/14	Mr Schroder holds an inquest, which he adjourns to

1/1/15   when the jury finds that Mrs Lloyd died from suffocation by drowning in the water, Mr Dale, instructed by Mr Aylwin, appearing for Lloyd, and on

4/1/15   Smith, as John Lloyd, calls on Mr W. P. Davies, solicitor, of 60 Uxbridge Road, Shepherd's Bush, and produces the will of Mrs Lloyd, née Lofty, and her marriage certificate and her life policy and instructs him to obtain probate. On

19/1/15   in consequence of information received, Detective-Inspector Neil communicates with the Aylesbury police and with the G.P.O., and on

21/1/15   Inspector Wootton replies from Aylesbury, and reports are received the same day from Bath and Bristol. On

22/1/15   three documents reach the police, Mrs Lloyd's bank book, her withdrawal order, and receipt for £19 9s. 5d., and on

22/1/15   Inspector Neil submits his first report, subject 'Suspicious deaths', from Kentish Town, and on

1/2/15   having kept daily observation on Mr Davies's premises the police see Mr Lloyd enter the office. On leaving he is stopped by Detective-Inspector Neil and Police-Sergeants Page and Reed, when he admits he is also George Smith, who married Alice Burnham, who died in her bath at Blackpool. 'As it was thought he might be in possession of fire-arms he was searched but none were found.' He was not dressed in mourning, and the only evidence of such found was a black tie in his bedroom at his new address – 14 Richmond Road – where was found a hold-all with a quantity of ladies' clothing. Lloyd was identified as Smith the same night by Mr Burnham and Mrs Pinchin, and on

2/2/15   he is charged with causing a false entry to be made in the marriage register at Bath. (It was false not only as to his name, etc., but as to his and his wife's period of residence in Bath previous to the marriage.) He is remanded at Bow Street and on

23/3/15   he is further charged with the wilful murder of Bessie Mundy, Alice Burnham, and Margaret Lofty, and after several remands is committed on all three charges on

12/5/15   and on

9/6/15   a true bill is returned against him at Lancaster Assizes for the murder of Alice Burnham, and on

15/6/15   a true bill is returned at the Central Criminal Court in respect of Miss Lofty. On

16/6/15   a true bill is returned at Maidstone in respect of Miss Mundy, and the two country indictments are removed to the C.C.C. under 'Palmer's Act'.

Alice Reavil alone of the women defrauded and deserted gave evidence during the proceedings at Bow Street. Smith, on almost every occasion, lost all command over himself, hurling imprecations at Inspector Neil and Mr Bodkin, who appeared for the Crown and was reviled by the man in the dock as a 'criminal and a manufacturer of criminals'. Mrs Crossley was, as at the Old Bailey, denounced as a lunatic. After the prisoner's committal, Mr Montague Shearman apologized for his client's outbreaks, but he behaved little better on his trial until a withering rebuke from the Judge put an end to his ill-timed and ill-bred interruptions, betraying, as they did, the wreckage of his nervous system, the not unnatural consequence of forty-three years of life mis-spent in crime and debauchery.

As some little mystery has prevailed as to the manner in which Scotland Yard was first put on the track of the murderer, it may be said that Mr Charles Burnham noticed an account of the Highgate inquest in the *News of the World*, and forwarded it through Mr Redhead to the Aylesbury police. Mr Joseph Crossley had also seen some report of it, and he sent it to the C.I.D. with a cutting reporting the Blackpool inquest. The Aylesbury police communicated with the Blackpool police and with headquarters, which then, through Detective-Inspector Neil and Inspector Cole and P.S. Page, commenced elaborate investigations in over forty towns in England, taking statements from 150 witnesses, of whom 112 were called at the trial, and examining the details of one account at Parr's Bank, Herne Bay, of accounts at three branches of the London City and Midland Bank, at Tunbridge Wells, Bath, and Portsmouth; of accounts at the Capital and Counties Bank at Bristol, Cheltenham, and Weston-super-Mare; of one account of the National Provincial Bank at Weston-super-Mare; of another of the Wilts and Dorset Bank; and of two of the London and South-

Western Bank at Highgate and Shepherd's Bush, to say nothing of six Savings Bank accounts, of which four were in the names of Smith's victims and the other two in the names of John Lloyd and George Smith.

The police communications between Highgate, Blackpool, Aylesbury, Bath, Bristol, and to the C.I.D. have been placed at my disposal by Mr Neil. As they are documents of a confidential nature, I have so handled them, quoting here and there to make a point that does not appear in the evidence. It seems that Mr Schroder was not satisfied about the Highgate death, and would have preferred an open verdict. Mr Kilvington, for the Lofty family, was, however, satisfied. Mr Burnham had always suspected foul play, but felt he could do nothing in the face of the Blackpool verdict. The astute Mr Neil, even as late as 19 January 1915, went so far as to write, 'Although we have no real grounds for suspicion that the death was otherwise than accidental . . . it is desirable that he should not have the money in question for a while.' Great precautions were used to prevent Smith suspecting that he was under observation, and that inquiries were being pursued about him.

The police did not receive information from Herne Bay until Mr Lloyd was already charged with the two later murders. It was on 15 February 1915, that Inspector Neil told the prisoner that he had reason to believe he was identical with Mr Williams, whose wife had died in her bath at Herne Bay. On the 19th of that month her body was exhumed, examined by Dr Spilsbury, and reinterred. In his report of 20 February the Inspector adds, 'I am of opinion that we have not, so far, discovered the full list of this man's crimes.'

A feature of the proceedings at the Police Court was the inordinate interest taken by women in the accused; they would, as early as eight o'clock in the morning, take up their station in queues outside the Court, bringing lunch with them, and they literally hemmed the prisoner in, by pressing so closely around the dock that they actually touched him.

The verdict at the inquest was the subject of Parliamentary inquiry, and on 14 July 1915, Mr Raffan asked the Home Secretary whether he would institute an inquiry into the circumstances which led to the verdict of accidental death being returned at the Coroner's inquests on the bodies of Bessie Mundy, Alice Burnham, and Margaret Lofty, whose deaths were subsequently shown to have been caused by murder, and whether he can state the legal and medical qualifications of the Coroner who held the inquests. Sir John Simon, 'I will look into this matter, but its consideration must stand over until the Court of Criminal Appeal has dealt with the prisoner's appeal against his conviction which is now pending'; and on 22 July Mr Booth asked an identical question. Sir John Simon merely referred him to his previous answer.

The trial at the Central Criminal Court opened on 22 June 1915, and lasted until 1 July. It was the longest and the most important murder case tried in England since Palmer's, sixty years before; in one respect it constituted a record – no fewer than 264 exhibits were put in; the witnesses came from over forty different towns, and numbered 112, of whom eighteen were solicitors, or solicitors' clerks, and fourteen were officials from banks.

The legal and medico-legal aspects of the trial receive special consideration in the next section; the full report of the story cannot be given here, but the entire eight days of its consideration abounded with dramatic incidents. To the horror of Mrs Millgate, when she saw the naked corpse behind the door, and the amazement of Miss Rapley at Mr Williams's appalling callousness, may be added the dramatic incidents, when Mrs Crossley, of Blackpool, and Miss Blatch, of Highgate, were taken by counsel over the very moments when, unknown to them at the time, the murderer was at his dreadful work in the little bathrooms above where they were sitting in the peaceful pursuit of household duties.

Not even a verbatim report can convey their emotional distress, but I will quote a few words from the official report kindly lent by Sir Edward Marshall Hall.

MR BODKIN: Whilst you and your daughter and son-in-law were in the kitchen, did you notice anything about the kitchen?
MRS CROSSLEY: I noticed the ceiling.
MR BODKIN: What did you notice about the ceiling?

MRS CROSSLEY: The water was coming through.

MR BODKIN: Would you like a little water?

MRS CROSSLEY: No, it worries me to think of the time.

MR MARSHALL HALL: Did you think he had something to do
with his wife's death? Now then, answer me the question. (The
witness mumbled something.) I cannot hear a syllable.

MR JUSTICE SCRUTTON: Ask the question again! Somebody
moved or coughed just at the time we wanted to hear.

MRS CROSSLEY: I shall not answer the question, what I thought.

MR HALL: You won't answer the question?

MRS CROSSLEY: No.

MR HALL: If you won't answer it –

MRS CROSSLEY: I cannot answer it, what I think about that.

But she had already answered what she thought about it, by what
she wrote on the back of exhibit 175. The postcard on which Smith
had left his address, 'Wife died in bath, we shall see him again!'

Miss Blatch, after that terribly grim story of the splashing heard
above, the wet arms on the side of the bath, and the final sigh, the
organ pealing forth its funeral notes for full ten minutes from the
sitting-room, the slamming of the front door, the ring at the bell,
the calling out to the dead woman, was asked, 'Where were you
when he so called out?' 'At the bottom of the stairs.' 'Did you go up
then?' 'I said, "I cannot come, Mr Lloyd." '

'I rushed upstairs to another gentleman I thought was in the
house . . . I rushed to the door. I did not notice anything . . . He
said he would go for the police. I said I would go myself . . .'

MR JUSTICE SCRUTTON: Did you put on your hat before you
went out?

MISS BLATCH: I put no hat on.

MR JUSTICE SCRUTTON: When you saw the prisoner with the
body in his arms and the legs in the bath, did you look for any
time?

MISS BLATCH: No, I looked for no time; I felt her arms and went
downstairs.

The defence was, as in Palmer's case, the least impressive part of the trial. Never, except in the Sandhills crime,[3] was Mr Marshall Hall so destitute of material; his miserable client – all the bravado knocked out of him, and speaking, when he interrupted to his own detriment, in a voice which a lady present likened to a patient's when only partly under chloroform – was an impossible witness, damning though his absence from the box necessarily was. Counsel combated the theories of Drs Spilsbury and Willcox, and employed a favourite argument with him, namely, that one would have to go back to the days of the Borgias to find such depths of wickedness as the prosecution alleged. One substantial point he made – Would Smith, if he had intended to murder Miss Burnham or Miss Lofty, have gone to the expense of an endowment policy, when for about half the premium he could have got an all-life policy, which would have served his purpose just as well? As will be seen, Smith only abandoned the all-life policy on Miss Burnham when a further premium was demanded from him to cover the risk of marriage; and he probably found that an endowment policy masked his designs better from his two brides, besides furnishing his advocate with a plausible argument. Still, it must have cost Mr Smith a pang to forgo £500!

The inevitable verdict was reached on the final day in a very few minutes. Some reporters, who must have been poorly accommodated, said that the prisoner heard it unmoved; in truth he collapsed, so that a doctor stood near him. He was 'very pale – almost livid. That tell-tale patch of red on his high cheekbones flushed angrily.' Called upon by the Clerk of Court, his lips refused their office. 'Then, with an effort, he gasped, "I can only say I am not guilty." '

Like Baron Bramwell in sentencing the *Flowery Land* pirates a half-century before, the Judge forbore to add anything to the words of his sentence, but, unlike the Baron, he concluded with the usual invocation of heaven to be merciful to the doomed man's soul. It is

3. The murder by Holt, between Blackpool and St Anne's, of Mrs Elsie Breaks, who had just made a will in his favour, bequeathing him the amount of her life policy. It well illustrates 'the desperate and short-sighted wickedness' of murderers that Holt committed his murder within four miles of the similar murder by Smith, by whose fate he was unwarned.

no part of a Judge's statutory or other duty to add these words. Smith thanked his counsel, the Judge thanked the jury, and Inspector Neil, and thus ended one of the most remarkable murder trials, both from the atrocities of the criminal and the ingenuity with which the net was spread around him by the C.I.D., in the annals of British crime.

Smith was removed to Pentonville, pending his appeal, which was heard on 29 July. A violent thunderstorm raged during the proceedings, and, after a peculiarly loud peal of thunder, the accused man looked nervously at the roof of the Court, as if he seemed to read his destiny in the wrath of the heavens. Mr Marshall Hall traversed much the same ground in his main argument as at the Old Bailey – that there was no *prima facie* case of the murder of Bessie Mundy apart from evidence of system; that such evidence was not admissible until a case to go to a jury had been built up *aliunde*. If the prisoner had given evidence that the death was accidental, then such evidence of system was admissible in rebuttal, but was not admissible in chief; there was no evidence of any physical fact by the prisoner causing Bessie Mundy's death, and no evidence as to surrounding circumstances ought to have been given in respect of the deaths at Blackpool and Highgate; that evidence of what took place at Mr Annesley's was improperly admitted, as it was an interview between solicitor and client, and therefore there was a privilege not to disclose it; that the question put to both Dr Spilsbury and Dr Willcox, was the death consistent with accident? was *the* question for the jury, that the suggestions of the judge that the prisoner might have lifted the bride into the bath and that he might have employed drugs were improper, as supported by no evidence; and that Mrs Thornhill's twice-repeated remark about the prisoner's sentence of two years had improperly influenced the jury. Mr Bodkin shortly replied on the circumstantial evidence of an act of murder followed by evidence to show design, and he commented on the position of the body as inconsistent with epilepsy, which was very unlikely to begin at thirty-five years of age. Mr Hall did not reply. The Court, after the Lord Chief Justice had paid a compliment to the powerful and able argument of counsel –

none the less forcible for being condensed so as to deal with the real points of the case – dismissed the appeal. The prisoner, who had only once taken his gaze from the faces of his Judges, turned ghastly white, and was at once removed.

He remained at Pentonville until 4 August, when, pursuant to his sentence under Palmer's Act, he was removed to Maidstone. The few remaining days of his life he passed in great prostration and almost constant tears. On 9 August he wrote a letter to Edith Pegler. He listened to the Wesleyan minister who was sent to comfort him and to the chaplain; but he discovered no trace of penitence, and made no confession. His execution was fixed for 13 August, at eight o'clock, Pierpont and Ellis being the executioners. The last morning found him in a painful state of collapse; he was assisted to the scaffold, which it took three minutes to reach – thrice the usual time – from the moment the executioners entered the condemned cell. Outside a large crowd had collected, many of whom were women – and many women of all ranks gazed from the windows of neighbouring houses – and the loud babble of their voices could be heard in the cell while the preparations were being made, and the voice of the chaplain was drowned as he recited the opening words of the burial service. As eight o'clock struck a great silence fell on the multitude, and it lasted while the helpless man was almost carried in a blaze of summer sunshine across the prison yard to the fatal shed. He had to be supported on the drop.

What were his thoughts? It is idle to speculate. Had he ever heard of Nero and his cunning and cruel attempt to drown his mother Agrippina? Had he, with his smattering of book knowledge, ever heard of the last recorded utterance of the most infamous of the Imperial Caesars – *Qualis artifex pereo*? If, stupefied and terrified as he was, he was incapable of coherent reflection, we may be sure his last thought was one of self-pity – what an artist to perish, to have thought out a new mode of murder, and only to end like any common cut-purse of the old hanging days!

At the inquest held the same day in the prison, evidence was given that death was instantaneous and painless from fracture of the cervical vertebrae; the body was formally identified by Inspector

Neil, and then consigned to the destroying quicklime – naked as his
brides had lain naked – exposed to the gaze of strangers.

> Deep down below a prison yard
> Naked for greater shame,
> He lies, with fetters on each foot,
> Wrapt in a sheet of flame.

The principles regulating the admission of evidence at the trial of
other acts than that charged, in order to show system, turned on
the case of *A.G.* v. *Makin.*

This was one of the points of law raised at the subsequent Appeal,
when the principles enunciated in a number of authorities were
discussed in full, and are somewhat too technical for a full analysis
in a book intended mainly for the general public.

When such evidence is admitted, it is admitted to show, 'not that
the defendant did the acts which form the basis of the charge, but
that, if he did such acts, he did them intentionally and not accidentally, or inadvertently, or innocently'. Only a minority of the
cases illustrating the principle were murder cases. Palmer's case is
often put forward by legal purists as a case where, though there
were other indictments against the prisoner for the murder of his
wife and brother, the suggestion of the murder of these 'was never
made or hinted at'. A broad distinction between a case like Palmer's, on the one hand, and Smith's or Armstrong's, on the other,
is that in Palmer's case the defence was that Cook's death was due
to natural causes, and not to misadventure or suicide. That other
persons Palmer had access to had died mysteriously was, therefore,
regarded professionally as a matter of prejudice. Of well-known
murder cases, in which such evidence was admitted, *R.* v. *Geering*
was a charge of the poisoning by arsenic of the prisoner's husband
in September 1848; there were three other indictments against the
prisoner charging her with the murder of her son, George, in December 1848; with the murder of her son, James, in March 1849;
and with the attempted murder of her son, Benjamin, in the following month, all by the administration of arsenic. The evidence of the
circumstances of the later death and of the illness in the last case

was admitted by Lord Chief Baron Pollock on two grounds (1) to show that the death of the husband, whether felonious or not, was occasioned by arsenic and (2) to enable the jury to determine whether the taking of the arsenic was accidental or not. It was not admissible as tending to prove a subsequent felony.

Neill Cream's case was another of murder by arsenic poisoning. It was a very celebrated trial, but it did not figure in the law reports, nor did Mr Justice Hawkins give any reason for admitting the evidence, because, as he stated in a letter to Mr Justice Windeyer, any comments he might have made in pointing out the relevancy of the evidence would have been very prejudicial to the prisoner. The murder of which Cream was convicted was of an unfortunate named Matilda Clover, and, the defence suggesting in cross-examination death from delirium tremens, evidence was given, after the close of the direct evidence relating to Clover, of the death of three other unfortunates with the same symptoms, and of the attempted administration of a pill to a fourth, who, however, evaded taking it. In the letter referred to Mr Justice Hawkins goes, I think, rather further than any British authority has gone, when speaking judicially. 'I dissent,' he wrote, 'from the suggestion that such evidence . . . can only be admitted in corroboration of a *prima facie* case which a Judge would be justified in leaving to a jury if it stood alone. The admissibility of evidence in itself material and relevant to the inquiry can never be dependent on whether it is used to corroborate evidence already given, or is offered as an independent piece of evidence.'

The principle has been well stated in *R*. v. *Francis* (false pretences) by Lord Chief Justice Coleridge – 'It seems clear . . . that when the fact of the prisoner having done the thing he is charged with is proved and the only remaining question is, whether at the time he did it he had guilty knowledge of the quality of his act or acted under a mistake, evidence of the class received must be admissible. It tends to show that he was pursuing a course of similar acts, and thereby raises a presumption that he was not acting under a mistake.'

This was applied in the New Zealand case of *R*. v. *Hall*, where the prisoner was tried for the murder by antimony of Henry Cain on 29 January 1886. The hypothesis of accidental administration was distinctly before the jury. The Judge, wrongly as it was held, admitted evidence to show that from June to 15 August of that year the prisoner was in attendance on his wife, and that antimony was found in his possession and in her excreta. In holding the evidence improperly admitted, the Court said – 'The evidence is admissible as proof of the intent, where the prior fact of administration has been sufficiently established by independent testimony . . . by prior proof must be understood that there was sufficient evidence of the fact to go to a jury. This preliminary question the presiding Judge must determine.'

In the case before them the New Zealand Court of Appeal saw no satisfactory evidence of a design, which required for its achievement the deaths of Cain and Mrs Hall – in other words, there was no *nexus* between the two deaths.

A.G. v. *Makin* is now generally regarded as the leading case, and the instructive judgments of the New South Wales Court of Crown Cases Reserved are quite as valuable as the report of the case in the Privy Council. Its resemblance to Smith's case lies in the presumption of the physical fact constituting the murder charged from the evidence as to the other deaths; in other words, of the facts showing system. Just as Smith was never proved to have been in the bathroom at Herne Bay when Bessie Mundy was expiring there, so the Makins were never proved to have done any physical act to Horace Amber Murray by which he could have been deprived of life. The homicidal act – its manner unknown – was inferred from the facts showing system, the other bodies found, and the overwhelming evidence of motive. The state of the law will be found clearly summarized in Mr Herman Cohen's edition of Roscoe's *Criminal Evidence*.

The law appears as a result of the authorities to be this:

1. No direct rule can be laid down as to the moment at which evidence of facts showing system becomes admissible. Roughly, the moment is when its relevance appears clear to the presiding Judge.

2. Direct evidence of the physical act constituting the crime is not necessary before evidence of system becomes admissible.

3. The introduction of such evidence, tending to prejudice the accused, is not permissible before an issue has been raised in substance, if not in words, to which it is relevant, e.g. in Smith's case, that he was absent from the bathroom at all material times.

4. The evidence, to be admissible, must be (a) to prove a course of conduct; or (b) to rebut a defence of accident or mistake; or (c) to prove knowledge by the prisoner of some fact.

5. Whether such evidence would be admissible if there were no *prima facie* case without it, *quoere*.

This was the matter left in doubt in Smith's case; as the Court expressly said, 'We have come to the conclusion that there was . . . *prima facie* evidence that the appellant committed the act charged quite apart from the other cases.' Mr Justice Windeyer had said in the Makins' case, 'it appears to me that the evidence . . . need not amount to such a case as would be required to justify the Judge in leaving it to a jury'.

Mr Marshall Hall's contention that the Judge should not have put to Drs Spilsbury and Willcox the question whether the deaths could be consistent with accident, as that was *the* question for the jury, recalls a conversation between Lord Brougham and Lyndhurst in old age; they were discussing Sir Francis Buller's oft-criticized question – whether the laurel water, in his opinion, was the cause of Broughton's death – to the great Hunter in Donellan's case. Lyndhurst – 'I think that Buller had no right to put the question. The point was not in the province of any witness – it was the very question which was to go to the jury. What do you say, Brougham?' Brougham – 'Buller was wrong; there can be no doubt of it whatever.'

All cases of death from asphyxiation, whether proceeding from drowning, hanging, strangulation, or suffocation, present certain characteristic post-mortem appearances. Shakespeare has given an enumeration of them in language of which all men have long recognized the beauty, while medical men have recognized its fidelity.

Warwick, gazing on the corpse of Gloucester in the second part of King Henry VI, Act III, Sc. II, exclaims:

See how the blood is settled in his face.
Oft have I seen a timely parted ghost,
Of ashy semblance, meagre, pale and bloodless
Being all descended to the labouring heart,
Who in the conflict that it holds with death,
Attracts the same for aidance 'gainst the enemy;
Which with the heart there cools the ne'er returneth
To blush and beautify the cheek again,
But see, his face is black and full of blood,
His eyeballs further out than when he lived,
Staring full ghastly like a strangled man;
His hair uprear'd, his nostrils stretched with struggling,
His hands abroad display'd, as one that grasp'd
And tugged for life and was by strength subdued.
Look on the sheets, his hair, you see, is sticking;
His well-proportioned beard made rough and rugged,
Like to the summer's corn by tempest lodged.
It cannot be that he was murder'd here,
The least of all these signs were probable.

Where, however, a death is due to drowning – and many bodies die in the water from other causes, such as syncope, shock, or a stroke – only about 25 per cent, according to Ferrier, die of pure asphyxia, while in 12·5 per cent of deaths in the water there is no asphyxia at all. Suspension of efforts at respiration due to early loss of consciousness effect the post-mortem appearances, both internal and external. Less water is swallowed; there is congestion of blood in the face, and less bloody froth in the lungs and mouth.

Death may occur from drowning without any water being found in the stomach. As to the time sufficient to produce death, where there is complete submersion, if the efforts to breathe are continuous – in other words, if consciousness is not lost from some independent cause – one minute and a half will suffice. In one case there was complete insensibility within a minute. Where a girl fell into the water in a state of syncope, she recovered after six minutes' immersion; and trained divers, who, of course, do not attempt to breathe under the water, can remain submerged for two or more minutes, but of two divers going under water with apparatus whose air supply was cut off, one who was brought to the surface within a minute and a half survived, while the other, who was not brought to the surface under two minutes, did not survive.

As to the degree of violence necessary to overcome the resistance of an adult who is being murdered in this manner, Taylor says in the *Dublin Quarterly Journal of Medical Science*, 1853: 'It is the result of twenty years' experience of these cases that the resistance which a healthy and vigorous person can offer to the assault of a murderer intent upon drowning . . . her, is in general such as to lead to the infliction of a greater amount of violence than is necessary to ensure the death of the victim.' Apart from the mysterious blood in the Mundy case, there was no evidence of violence in any of the three cases, except slight bruising of an arm in the Lofty case.

But this authority, high as it is, needs to be profoundly modified where the struggles of the victim are confined by the sides of a bath. There being no example of a similar murder to those alleged against Smith to be found in any works on forensic medicine, one of the detectives engaged on the case persuaded a young lady of his acquaintance, who was a practised swimmer, to sit in a bath, in a swimming costume, which was filled to the same height as the Herne Bay bath. She was aware that the experimenter was about to submerge her if he could; she was aware that his intentions were not felonious, and she was accustomed to having her head under water; yet with all these circumstances in her favour as compared with Smith's victims, she was unable to get her head above water, after it was once submerged, and consequently unable to cry out, and she almost instantaneously ceased to struggle, whereupon the experiment was at once discontinued; but not before the experimenter had satisfied himself not merely of the possibility, but of the ease, with which an ordinarily vigorous man could destroy life in the manner in which Drs Spilsbury and Willcox opined Smith might have murdered Miss Mundy.

Other experiments carried out in empty baths satisfied several detectives that, using certain means, a woman might be held under water without inflicting any bruises upon her.

I will now proceed to a separate consideration of the three cases. The Herne Bay bath was five feet long, inside, at the top; three feet eight inches along the flat bottom; the width at the sloping end was two feet at the top and one foot six inches at the bottom; at the other end it was one foot seven inches and one foot one and a half inches. Its depth was one foot four inches at the sloping end, and a quarter-inch more at the other end. The deceased was five feet nine inches high, and this was the position in which Dr French found her – 'The face was upwards, the trunk at the sloping end, the feet out of the water resting on the side of the bath a little below the edge. The position of the body kept the legs from slipping down. The head was submerged and the trunk partially so. The mouth was under water; her arms rested by her side. The right hand contained a piece of soap. The bath was just over three-parts full. (In other words there was at least twelve inches of water in the bath.) The legs were out straight – straight from the trunk.'

As to the theory of epilepsy, which was accepted by the jury, I will let Dr French speak for himself – 'Further than his saying that she had temporarily lost consciousness, he could not get anything very definite out of him.' Although the grounds for regarding it as an epileptic fit were very slight, he prescribed bromide of potassium (not only a specific in epilepsy but a general sedative). The probability of a woman having her first epileptic fit at thirty-five appears to be over twelve to one. Quain stated that only 6 per cent of cases first occur after thirty years of age. The probability of a person having a fit of this sort and not giving the warning scream, which is so characteristic as once heard never to be forgotten, is about three to one.

The probability of a person having such a fit and getting into the position described, the lay as well as the medical reader can judge for himself.

Mr Mowll and his jury did not see the bath nor ascertain the position of the body in it; they had no measurements, and they never tested, as Inspector Neil did, the possibility of the bath being filled by the deceased woman in the half-hour that Smith said he was out of the house.

The theory of epilepsy finds little support, again, from the post-mortem appearances; the face was dusky – blue all over – and much congested with blood; there was froth, which flowed out of the mouth, and on pressing the chest water flowed out of the mouth, facts indicating continued efforts at respiration after the face was submerged, and negativing the notion of a fit.

The piece of soap clutched in the right hand was a matter of some comment. Counsel spoke of the expression that 'drowning men clutch at a straw' as figurative. In a sense it is; but the figure of speech rests on a well-known truth of forensic medicine. There is unusual unanimity among the authorities on this point: Professor Glaister refers to 'the presence of objects in the firmly clenched hand – as weeds, grass, sticks, or other objects', as a safe indication that death was due to drowning.

'It is certain,' says Poore, 'that a man who is drowning does clutch at anything with which his hands come in contact.' 'The presence of substances clutched in the fingers – due, in the first instance, to a vital act subsequently rendered permanent by in-stantaneous cadaveric rigidity – is evidence of submersion during life' (Dixon Mann). 'Vain clutchings are made at whatsoever comes within reach. The indications of such instinctive efforts form the most important evidence of submersion during life' (Ferrier). It is also generally stated by the authorities that instant *rigor mortis*, lasting until putrefaction, is more common in drowning than in any other form of violent death met with in civil life.

Re-examined as to the soap, Dr French said that if a person died suddenly with a piece of soap in her hand the grasp would be continued after death; and Dr Spilsbury, recalled, said, 'If only consciousness is lost, the soap would probably drop out of the hand by the relaxation, but if death occurred immediately, then the object might be retained owing to this condition of instantaneous death stiffening,' and the body would retain its ante-mortem position. Taylor has stated that some of the bodies after the Regent's Park disaster of 1867 were 'stiffened in the attitude of active exertion, the hands and arms being thrown forward as if sliding or skating'. In that case, however, the cold may have produced stiffening by solidification of subcutaneous fat, which may have been confounded with true *rigor mortis*.

A difficulty that remains as to the piece of soap is that if Dr French's memory was to be trusted after three years, cadaveric rigidity had not set in when he saw the soap in the hand. 'I do not think it was stiff . . . It was limp.' 'Any part of it was not stiff?' 'No.' [4]

A word as to the blood seen by Mrs Millgate about the waist of the body. As Mr Marshall Hall seems to have suggested that each fatal seizure occurred during a period – a suggestion that renders Smith's conduct in each case still more astounding and revolting – it may, with diffidence, be suggested that this blood, the nature of which was never explained, may have been due to post-mortem bleeding from the vagina. In the case of the 'Ireland's eye' murder, Mrs Kirwan was found to be bleeding from the ears and private parts. After the conviction of Kirwan, Dr Alfred Taylor contributed a paper and Dr Thomas Geoghegan another on the medico-legal aspects of the case. Dr Taylor wrote: 'It is a rare condition of asphyxia and not a constant accompaniment or sign of the suffocation or strangulation of females.' And he adds, 'I have not known it to occur in drowning.' Dr Geoghegan, from the experience of colleagues, found it quite common in the strangulation of women in judicial and suicidal hanging. 'Vaginal bleeding has been frequently noticed in hanging and strangulation,' he says, but while admitting that the 'subject appears not to have sufficiently attracted the attention of

4. The firm clutching in the hand after death of articles retained by it *in articulo mortis* is common to all cases of asphyxia. Mary Patterson, Burke and Hare's beautiful victim, had twopence halfpenny, which she held fast in her hand. Mrs Hostler, another victim, had ninepence halfpenny in her hand, which they could scarcely get out of it after she was dead, so firmly was it grasped. – Burke's *Courant* Confession, Appendix I, *Trial of Burke and Hare*, Notable British Trials series.

medical jurists,' he seems to regard it as peculiar to death from strangulation, as apart from other forms of asphyxia.

It will probably suggest itself to medical readers that the great venous congestion in all cases of asphyxia may render such post-mortem bleeding no less likely in asphyxia from drowning as from other causes of death of the like sort. In the few cases in our reported criminal trials there were other things to account for the bleeding that was observed, and authority is very scanty in the treatises on legal medicine.

The *cutis anserina*, which Dr Spilsbury found, was of little import-ance in determining the cause of death. It is a sign of exposure to water at the time of death, and not of death from the immersion in water. Dr Spilsbury agreed that it was found in sudden deaths, other than from drowning, but the weight of authority seems to be that *cutis anserina* has no value bearing as on the cause of death occurring in water.

A last word on the Mundy case. Smith, it will have been noted, informed the relatives that 'Bessie died of a fit in a bath.' That is not what Dr French said – he was always clear that death was due to drowning – but the appearances in the case of a body of a man of thirty who died of an epileptic seizure in a bath and not from drowning have been recorded by Taylor. Much congestion of the brain was noted, in the right ventricle only a small clot of blood, otherwise the cavities of the heart were quite empty. The body of Miss Mundy was so decomposed when Dr Spilsbury examined it that he could say little as to either heart or brain.

In the case of Alice Burnham, very little water was found in the body by Dr Billing – so little that he even doubted that death was due to drowning. As we have seen, the absence of water is not inconsistent with death from drowning. The Blackpool bath measured five feet three inches long; the width at the sloping end was two feet three inches at the top and one foot two inches at the bottom; at the tap end the width was one foot three and a half inches, and one foot at the top and the bottom respectively. The depth at the centre was eighteen inches; and the bath was full to within one and a half inches of the top, even after the head was raised out of the water. The body was quite limp when Dr Billing saw it; he opined that death was due to drowning, but we are without any description of the post-mortem appearances in this case. From the absence of anything about the colour of the face or of a bloody froth about the mouth and lungs, and from the small quantity of water found, it is a legitimate inference that death in this case was not brought about solely by asphyxiation, but that there may have been an early loss of consciousness before the efforts to breathe had become very distressing.

As to the theory of epilepsy in this case – and it was hardly maintained by Mr Marshall Hall – not only was there no suggestion of the monitory scream, but a history of an alleged fit at nine years of age, followed by no more at the critical period of puberty, and only succeeded by one after a will just made in favour of an impecunious husband about seventeen years later, may justly be dismissed as of no importance, as Dr Bertram Stone dismissed it, 'because the history is so indefinite'.

The post-mortem appearances in Margaret Lofty's case point to asphyxiation as the main cause of death. The lips were blue and swollen, the whole of the face was congested and the eyelids swollen, and there was froth exuding from the mouth and nostrils. Of violence the only traces were one externally visible bruise above the left elbow on the outer side, and other bruises, recent, beneath the surface. Dr Bates perceived no blood near or about the body; some bloodstains on an undergarment were susceptible of a very obvious explanation, and indicated neither violence nor the existence of a period at the time of death. Evidence of old pleurisy and peritonitis was noticed by Dr Bates, but no suggestion was made that either disease had any bearing on the death. There was no evidence as to the position of this body in the bath. When first seen after the murder by Miss Blatch the corpse was being held up by Smith over the bath, the legs being still in the bath, and whether she had faced the sloping or the narrow end was not made clear. The bath was five feet six inches long at the top, four feet two inches along the flat bottom; at the top of the sloping end it was two feet one and a half inches, narrowing down to one foot six inches. At the tap end the width was one foot six inches, narrowing down to eleven and a half inches. There was no evidence as to the height of the water in the bath.

A view remains to be examined, which may serve to explain the extraordinary sexual familiarity which established itself so early and so easily in the relations of Smith with his brides – the last in particular. It was brought to my notice by a correspondent that hypnotic suggestions might have played a part in causing these three women, not only to place themselves in the very singular situations in which they did, but even, without physical effort on the part of Smith, to drown themselves! Sir Edward Marshall Hall, whom his conspicuous and my more modest public engagements prevented my conferring with until a late stage in the preparation of this essay, in a letter states: 'I am convinced he [Smith] was a hypnotist. Once accept this theory, and the whole thing – including the unbolted doors – is to my mind satisfactorily explained.' Little is known to professors of legal medicine in England of the power of hypnotic suggestion to cause a person to do an act morally or otherwise repugnant to him or her.

Arbert Moll, as quoted by Georges du Bor, states that hypnotic suggestion plays no part in the seduction by a man of a woman. That woman would have given herself to that man anyhow. A. E. Davis, Professor of Psychotherapy to Liverpool Hospital, in his *Hypnotism*, after ridiculing the sexual psychology of *Trilby*, in which Svengali, by mesmeric art, compels the surrender of the heroine to his revolting person, she being all the while in love with little Billie, proceeds to state that, in his experience, it is quite impossible, by hypnotic suggestion, to compel persons to do an act which is morally, aesthetically, or on grounds of religious or similar scruple repugnant to them.

Such, too, was the effect of the evidence of Dr K—, now a member of the Bar, in a case in which he was plaintiff in a contested probate action, and in which he was alleged to have induced his lady patient to make a will in his favour. His defence succeeded. On the other hand, the authorities collected by Wingfield in his *Introduction of the Study of Hypnotism*, are far more guarded. Moll thinks that, by repeated hypnotic suggestions a person could be 'willed' to commit a crime. Forel proved this by compelling a subject to fire twice at a man with a pistol, loaded, but not to his knowledge, with blank cartridge. Von Eulenberg, von Schrenck-Notzing, and other eminent German and Austrian psychotherapists seem to agree. I think I am correct in stating that in Russia once, and in France twice, a woman has successfully put forward as a defence in homicide hypnotic compulsion by a man. Lord Justice Scrutton informs me that he accepts neither the hypnotic theory nor the theory that poisonous vapour was put in the bath water. Digital pressure *per rectum* on the spinal column is an alternative based on a doctor's personal experience with a violent lunatic.

In my view the simple explanation that the unhappy women were in love with Smith explains all. The respondent, in one of the two famous political divorces of the mid-eighties, said of the co-respondent, 'If Charles had asked me to stand on my head in the middle of Piccadilly, I would have done it.'

Certain definite evidence, moreover, indicates the use of some physical violence by Smith, the hair at the sloping end of the Blackpool bath, the overflowing of water from it, the sound of the wet arms and the sighing, as of one struggling to get breath, at Highgate. Smith's own autograph note to Mr Shearman, which that learned counsel gave to me, to my mind, went strongly to show that he – an ex-gymnasium instructor – knew how to accomplish such murders without bruising the victim. And the experiments of Mr Neil confirm the possibility.

A popular and prolific French author (M. Paul Bourget) has in a work marked by all the vigour of youth and all the enthusiasm for his subject of a good Frenchman, endeavoured to analyse the constituents of a 'lady's man'. Looks count for little. Education for nothing. 'Mais le tact de l'homme à femmes est quelque chose de tout particulier – presque un organe – comme les antennes chez les insectes – presque un instinct, car l'éducation n'y ajoute guère. Cet homme, par exemple, du premier coup d'œil, juge exactement quel degré de chance il a auprès d'une femme à laquelle il est presenté.

Il dira mentalement – Celle-ci est pour moi, celle-là, non.' And after a consideration of typical men he concludes, 'Mais ils avaient tous ce fond de tempérament où gît la force vitale.'

Smith's protective antennae seem to have guided him well enough in the search for likely victims; where they failed him was in the inability to warn him of the women in whom his pronounced sexuality aroused an instant and an enduring antagonism. On men, on the other hand, he produced no impression, but one of insignificance and commonness – 'Just like any butcher,' was Mr Neil's appreciation.

It has long been recognized that two radically different types of men favourably impress women; the type possessing a marked femininity of character enabling its possessor to understand women from their own point of view, and those of a very pronounced masculinity, who succeed by riding rough-shod over the finer feelings of women, and whose success is due to the arousing of woman's primitive desire to be mastered – a desire which is normal within limits, but when abnormal is styled by the professors of sexual psychology masochism, to distinguish it from its counterpart, the abnormal desire to inflict pain (within limits psychological in the male at least), which is known as sadism, each term being derived from the man of letters who stands as a type of the abnormally submissive, and the abnormally masterful and cruel.

George Joseph Smith was undoubtedly a male whose love for mastery over women, including the infliction on them of humiliation (witness the letter to Bessie Mundy of 13 September 1910, the circumstances of each desertion of a robbed bride, and the invariable exposure of the nude corpse of a murdered bride to the gaze of strangers of either sex) approached the pathological limit where the normal masculine desire merges into sadism; but, unlike Neill Cream, Chapman or Jack the Ripper, Smith was not driven to murder through an overmastering impulse of sadism, the pecuniary motive being the all-powerful one, murder being only undertaken where robbery could not be accomplished without it. In Cream's case the motive of pecuniary advantage through blackmail was very unsubstantial, and there is little doubt that the half-crazy doctor was a victim of the most dangerous of sexual perversions, one which accounts for a great deal of what is most unsavoury in the divorce court. As to the physical attractions of Smith, he had, it seems, a certain magnetism about his eyes. A woman writer in a popular morning paper has told of the 'irresistible feline luminosity in the eyes', of the sexually attractive man; and Smith's first bigamously married bride has described him thus – 'He had an extraordinary power over women. This power lay in his eyes. When he looked at you for a minute or two you had the feeling that you were being magnetized. They were little eyes that seemed to rob you of your will.' He was accustomed to indulge in such practices as wife-beating. 'Often,' says the authority quoted, 'he has beaten me black and blue. Once he locked me in a cabinet folding-bed.'

Smith made no pretence of fidelity to this bride; indeed, the occasion of one flogging arose out of an amour. I will give the story in the woman's own words. 'Often he used to brag to me about his numerous women acquaintances. Once I met one of his victims with him and warned her to her face about him. She was greatly shocked, and said she had always regarded him as a good, religious man. That night he came home and thrashed me till I was nearly dead.' Whether or not his various 'victims' were so simple as to believe in his whole-hearted devotion, it remains an everlasting truth that women are not much attracted by want of enterprise in the male. To a wife, at least, to have a roué for a husband is an indirect compliment to herself. As Valera says, 'Even the most moral and religious young woman likes to marry a man who has loved many women; it gives a greater value to his choice of her.' Professor Hans Gross well says, 'Only the very young, pure, and inexperienced girl feels an instinctive revulsion from the real roué, but other women, according to Rochebrune, love a man in proportion to the number of other women who love or have loved him. This is difficult to understand; but it is a fact that a man has an easy task with women if he has the reputation of being a great hand with them. Perhaps this is only an expression of the conceit and envy of women, who cannot bear the idea that a man is interested in so many others and not in themselves. As Balzac says, "Women prefer most to win a man who already belongs to another." The inconceivable ease with which certain types of men seduce women, and at whose heads women throw themselves in spite of the fact that these men have no praiseworthy qualities whatever, can only be so explained. Perhaps it is true, as is sometimes said, that here is a case of sexuality expressing itself in an inexplicable manner.' Johnson's famous dictum falls naturally alongside the Austrian jurist's. 'Ladies set no value on the moral character of men who pay their addresses to them; the greatest profligate will be as well received as the man of greatest virtue, and this by a woman who says her prayers three times a day.' Our ladies endeavour to defend their sex from this charge, but he roared them down: "No, no; a lady will take Jonathan Wild as readily as St Austin, if he has threepence more . . . Women have a perpetual envy of our vices; they are less vicious than we, not from choice, but because we restrict them." '

Havelock Ellis has observed that, 'There is no such instinctive demand on woman's part for innocence in a man,' but he adds by way of qualification, 'This is not always or altogether true of the experienced woman.'[5]

But while, as we have seen, Smith without money, manners, education or even appearance to recommend him, produced invariably an effect on women, though that effect was at times the reverse of favourable, men carried away no distinct impression of him. Mr Burnham did, indeed, dislike him, but so faint was the personal impression that he was unable to pick him out at Bow Street. One witness alone, Mr J. R. Robbins, is shocked by Smith's greed after money – when he claims half-commission on the murdered Blackpool bride's policy; but for the most part the quiet professional men, with whom he comes in contact, see nothing to notice about him. The solicitors, the doctors, the bankers, house-agents, insurance agents – even the coroners, those men of more than ordinary perspicacity – to each and all he appears in no wise out of the ordinary; indeed, upon the bank managers he must have

5. *Studies in the Psychology of Sex*, vi, 44.

produced a mildly favourable impression, for he opens account after account in false names, without references, and in one case to the manager's knowledge has only an accommodation address, 'where they call themselves confectioners. It is a sort of small mixture of milk and groceries.' P.C. Heath, who, as having had a good opportunity to notice him at Bismarck Road, was asked by Inspector Neil to keep watch for him outside Mr Davies's office, was unable to identify him. His eyes with their suggestion of mesmeric powers apart, there was nothing in his appearance or manner that struck Mr Shearman, who had constant opportunities for studying him at Bow Street and at the Central Criminal Court. His main endeavour seemed to Mr Shearman to be to pass for a gentleman of independent means and of culture. To produce such an impression, he went so far as to wear a frock-coat and tall hat at Herne Bay in August, where such raiment would certainly arouse remark.

Yet he had only to be in physical propinquity to a woman, and she at once became aware that she was in the presence of a man of some mysterious powers over her sex. To the wife of a high legal functionary he appeared an attractive man; that acute criminologist, the late H. B. Irving, during the trial was seated next two fashionably attired ladies of pleasure, and these vied with one another in praise of the prisoner's charms. At the police court the eagerness with which women thronged round him in the dock was the subject of indignant comment in the papers; and at the Old Bailey the police had special instructions to make it as difficult as possible for women to be present. On the other hand, even in cold print, the dislike of the man that instantly possessed such witnesses as Mrs Tuckett and Miss Rapley appears unmistakably.

There is one masculine failing which women find it peculiarly difficult to overlook in a man; yet Smith possessed this failing in a marked degree – petty meanness in the matter of money. To Edith Pegler he sends only the smallest sums, and his ideas of a honeymoon jaunt stop short at places which are either free to the public or are to be entered for a modest expenditure; it is Brockwell Park, the National Gallery or a shillingsworth of the White City; and he leaves Alice Reavil to pay for the food!

'In all the transactions of his infamous life,' wrote Mr Sims in *Bluebeard of the Bath,* 'whether he was Jekyll or whether he was Hyde, he was abominably mean. He never squandered a farthing of his ill-gotten gains. He rarely, when absent from his Bristol wife, sent her any money. When he decided to murder Miss Mundy he bargained for the bath, did not pay for it and when he had committed in it the murder for which he had obtained it, he sent it back again, not even paying a small amount for the hire of it, although by using it he had obtained between two and three thousand pounds. He never wasted a farthing on any of the young women whose money he was going to get by murdering them. When arrested, although he had made many thousands of pounds by the most economical form of murder possible, he was wearing a suit of clothes for which he had not paid. They had not been paid for when he was hanged.'

He sells Bessie Mundy's clothing before it has come back from the laundry and does not settle the laundry bill, which Mrs Millgate has paid. He disposes of Alice Burnham's wardrobe and rings, and grudges her remains a pitch-pine coffin when deal would do as well. He takes Miss Mundy away from Weston-super-Mare, and does not settle with Mrs Tuckett the £2 10s. owing. He takes Mr Crabbe, a working man, away from his work to witness his marriage and does not pay him a penny. He promises to remunerate Mrs Crossley for her trouble, and gives her nothing but his address for her to forward him the local papers. And he tries to get out of paying Mr Annesley's bill.

Though he claims half-commission from Mr Pleasance over Alice Burnham's policy, he leaves her mother and brother to pay for their modest lunch at the 'Company House' where he has choked the life out of their dear one. But when he is in danger himself, no considerations of expense restrain him from securing what he deems the best professional aid.

How it came about that such a man was able to impose his will so absolutely on three different women, each coming from a home superior to his, and each boasting a greater degree of education, and to leave on each an impression of kindness, truthfulness and genuineness so absolute that, forsaking the natural ties of the flesh, they surrendered all, to them, that they had in the world – their bodies and their belongings with equal abandon – can best be treated in a study of the criminal himself in some detail.

The fascination which very depraved men exercise over women has long stimulated criminologists to discover – hitherto with little success – what common attribute bad men possess which makes them so ingratiating to the sex. 'Duval, the ladies' pride, Duval, the ladies' joy', in common with the other highwaymen, doubtless owed his success to the false romanticism with which the *Beggar's Opera* and less enduring literary tributes contrived to invest the lives of the knights of the road. But the uncomely Sheppard, the hideous Peace, the commonplace Palmer, those 'two singularly common and ordinary persons', Pranzini and Prado, and many another whose crimes are unsung, were equally, in their day, the objects of passionate adoration, in some cases on the part of women much above them in station, and their shameful and well-deserved ends a fruitful cause of tears and heartaches.

'This former conductor of Pullman cars,' observed M. Bourget of Pranzini, 'is mourned in many a lady's bed.' Smith, however, like Dougal, the Moat Farm murderer, belongs specifically to that small band of criminals, of whom Vitalis is an exemplar, who thrived on the exploitation of feminine weakness, and, so far as is known, avoided forms of crime in which the ability to deceive women would not have availed.

The resemblances between Dougal and Smith are more than superficial. The Moat Farm murderer had also been in the army, and his known relationships with women included (1) Miss Griffiths, whom he married, and who died in Canada under suspicious circumstances, being hastily buried without a death certificate (2) a second wife, a young woman of means whom he married on 14 August 1885. She died in a few weeks in Halifax, Nova Scotia, and was buried beside the first wife in a neglected grave (3) a Halifax girl, with whom he lived and by whom he had a child. He several times threatened to murder her, and abandoned her (4) a widow, by whom he had two children, and whom he then left to take small positions in clubs at Stroud Green and Southend (5) a young unmarried woman of means, with whom he got in touch through a matrimonial agency. He induced her to live with him and to sell her property and give him the proceeds (6) the third Mrs Dougal, a good-looking woman, whom he married against her parents' wishes in August, 1892 (7) an elderly lady, with money, who took a public-house for him at Ware. He was suspected of arson here, and was convicted of forgery (8) his last victim, Miss Camille Holland, an elderly lady of means, whom he met after serving his sentence. She was very musical, artistic, and literary, and also very religious: in point of education and status she was far above Dougal. Yet she lived with him as his wife without scruple.

At the time of the murder of Miss Holland, Dougal was endeavouring to seduce – if that word be not too mild to cover what went to the verge of an attempted crime – their maid, and he was industriously running after several other young women in comparatively humble life. In all cases the women's property was at his disposal equally with their persons. He had the education of an N.C.O. of the old-time Army, but was far from being a man of polish. Educationally, however, he was the superior of Smith. 'Mr Philip Curtin' and others, having represented Smith as a man who affected *belles-lettres* and who could turn out a pretty sonnet or *billet-doux* to a lady, let me here say, once and for all, that a man with smaller pretensions to literary skill one could not come across. He was utterly incapable of writing a grammatical sentence or of spelling the commonest words. In a note before me now he writes 'wader' repeatedly for 'warder', and 'difficulity', 'voilence', and 'brusies' for the familiar words they are meant to represent. In a letter to the secretary of a West End club he writes, 'dissadvantage', 'attatched', obivious', and 'conserned'; and in a letter to Mr Davies he writes 'in fain', 'attemt', and 'solomn'. Like some better educated people, he never could distinguish 'principal' from 'principle'. Though we had been at war with Germany for nearly a year when he was tried, the acquaintance of Mr Smith with public affairs and with history was well evinced by the note in which he speaks of 'several jerman or foreign women'. As for his grammar it was nearly as bad as his heart, and sufficiently appears from his letters put in as exhibits.

What, then, is the explanation of the fascination of Dougal and of Smith? Readers of Havelock Ellis will remember that that shrewd observer has remarked that nowhere does the trained observer meet with more sensual women than are to be found in quiet homes and country vicarages. What to the common eye seems a demure young woman of the middle-class is to the eye of *le vrai homme à femmes* a woman who may worship at the chapel or in her father's church, but in secret she is also a worshipper of the pagan divinity Priapus. 'Those cunning little eyes', which 'blinked uneasily' while Mr Justice Scrutton was lashing their possessor with his tongue, could read very well the mind of a woman, and could see whether in the depth of her eyes could be traced the smouldering fires of passion, all the more ready to burst into flame from the constant repression of desire forced on her by the daily round and common task, be it governess or lady's companion or young lady in business.

And having once gained the sexual mastery, how absolute is the villain's control! He writes to Bessie Mundy – 'I have caught from you the bad disorder; for you to be in such a state proves you could not have kept yourself morally clean.' He decamps with Bessie's money, and apparently with most of her clothes, and when they next meet, at Weston-super-Mare, 'there he was looking over the sea', and despite the remonstrances of Mrs Tuckett, she goes off with him in her shift, not troubling to come back to pack a bag with a nightdress! He takes her to the solicitors, and there, before her, concocts the most unblushing lies – it is he who, through some indiscretion, had supposed himself infected. The man of law writes as instructed. Smith writes to the brother in stilted style reminiscent of poor Aram's compositions – 'I know not how I shall offend in dedicating my unpolished lines to you, nor how you will censure me for using so strong a prop to support so grave a burden' – and Bessie adds, 'My dear Howard I trust you will try and forget the past as I have done' – (she who had written, 'The man came across my path . . . I am very sorry . . . I feel it is a mercy I am rid of him.

I do hope my husband will be caught. I feel I have disgraced myself for life') – 'I know my husband now better than ever before. You will be pleased to know I am perfectly happy.' Perfectly well, according to Dr French when he last saw her alive about 3 p.m. on Friday, she sits down to write that letter, which arrived with the telegram announcing her death. 'I have made out my will and left all to my husband.' What art has the monster practised that deep-rooted loathing and deserved contempt are banished and confiding submission rules this poor creature on whom Death is so soon to lay his icy grasp?

Alice Burnham, though younger in years than either of the other murdered brides, was more accustomed to the ways of men. She had contracted a malady, which was not named in Court, though it was discussed in the evidence of Dr Bertram Stone, under re-examination, and again in the cross-examination of Dr Spilsbury when recalled. It had set up septic peritonitis, and, without lifting the veil, which the Court suffered to remain drawn, it may be added that it was thus alluded to in a letter from Dr Stone to the North British & Mercantile Insurance Company, 'I have obtained leave both from Mrs George Smith and her husband to give full details of the unfortunate episode in her life. Mr George Smith is aware of all that occurred.'

The knowledge so obtained by Smith may account in a measure for the influence wielded by him over the least weak-willed of the victims. How absolute that influence was appears from the correspondence. Alice writes to her father on 22 November, giving him until the first post on 25 November to pay her the £100; but on the 24th of that month she had already instructed solicitors 'to take extreme measures'. It has taken only some two months for Smith to root out all her natural affection and sense of filial duty, and to plant in their stead a boundless belief in himself – 'I have the best husband in the world,' wrote the deluded, doomed bride, a few short hours before she was robbed of life.

If, in reviewing the ghastly sequence of events during the few days at Blackpool, one may permit oneself to indulge in the whimsical method of De Quincey and to recognize that, 'murders have their little differences in their shades of merits, as well as statues, pictures, oratorios, cameos, intaglios, or what not', then the murderer will be seen to have advanced in his dreadful art since the Herne Bay affair. So certain is he of accomplishing his object that he carries out the crime in a room directly over one he knows to be in occupation; having fulfilled it, he descends to that room, and, struggling to appear unconcerned, engages in talk about a fire engine! He must have learned something, too, about the possibility of resuscitating the apparently drowned; alone, at 80 High Street, he can leave his victim submerged for as long as he pleases, but in the Company House every moment is precious. The murderer returns with his bride just before eight; about 8.15 the water is observed to be dripping through the ceiling; at 8.35 Joseph Crossley is summoned back from his work to fetch the doctor to what Smith knows to be a corpse. Immediately Dr Billing sees Alice Burnham he exclaims, 'She is dead.'

Tidy has recorded a case, which must surely be exceptional, of recovery after twenty minutes' immersion. Smith on each occasion was present when artificial respiration was tried. It would need the pen of De Quincey or Edgar Allan Poe to conjure up the scene, if at Regent Road, Blackpool, or Bismarck Road, Highgate, Smith had watched the return of animation and had beheld the awful physical traces of his crime one by one disappear under the doctor's art – the congested blood leave the cheeks, the lips resume their normal hue, the eyes, 'staring full ghastly', take on again the tender look they wore when conscious life was suspended, and then, as comprehension came back, had seen the 'bride' lift her accusing finger, from which he had already snatched the rings, fond emblems as she supposed of hallowed love, to denounce the cold-blooded assassin, who but a few short hours before had held her in his arms and caressed her with all the tenderness with which devotion can mask the impetuous desires of the lover!

When we dwell on the commonplace incidents – the fatal Friday, the tapioca pudding, the inquiry if it had been relished, the evening stroll, the appalling deed while the homely north-country family are enjoying their late tea below, the casual entry of the murderer –

'full of agitation' withal – and realize that every detail of this seemingly insignificant winter's day was part of a well-laid scheme thought out many weeks before, and that the sinewy arms, while they hold the bride in the transports of love are cunningly measuring her powers of resistance to a very different description of attack, we realize how utterly apart from normal men, even from criminal men of other types, the cold-blooded mercenary murderer stands. One would have thought that Nature would have stamped on the lineaments of such fiends some warning of their dreadful characters; yet it has not been found so. De Quincey says of Williams: 'The concurrent testimony of many witnesses, and also the silent testimony of facts showed that the oiliness and snaky insinuation of his demeanour counteracted the repulsiveness of his ghastly face, and amongst inexperienced young women won for him a very favourable reception.'

A correspondent of mine whose father had once travelled with Palmer in a railway carriage, tells me that the father was very favourably impressed by the all-persuasive *bonhomie* of the poisoner. Hideous as Peace was, he was yet ingratiating. Nature seems to have endowed murderers with an extraordinary plausibility; they have a popular facility in lying, which Sir James Stephen noted a generation ago.

Nemo repente venit turpissimus, sang the Roman satirist, and Smith, in his last crime, was destined to transcend even his own performances. From the time Margaret Lofty left Bath (after those untruthful missives to her relations about the mythical old lady) to the time when P.C. Heath was summoned to her dead body at Bismarck Road, was but some thirty hours. The bridegroom, his dreadful purpose locked in his bosom, comes at three in the afternoon of 17 December, to the house in Orchard Row, and is repulsed from the door. There was 'a bath that a person might lie in', in that house, and the man fears he will be baulked of his prey. His rage finds free vent in the street. He drags off his feverish bride to other apartments, then to the doctor's, where she is naturally silent. Next day – and by what endearments he charmed away the vexations and anxieties of that Thursday and smiled away her maiden shame, murder all

273

the while in his heart, my pen shall not essay to set forth in words, our language has no vocabulary in which to record such infamy as man never yet had descended to – next day, any suspicion Margaret might have entertained has vanished. It is nothing to her that he has been afraid to meet her relations; that he has compelled her not only to conceal the approaching marriage, but to lie about it, and to lie to the insurance company. It is nothing to her that at the cheap apartment-house, where he has booked rooms for the honeymoon at 16s. a week, a detective in plain clothes has refused him admittance. Overnight she has written from the second lodging-house, where she was so soon to meet her death: 'He was a thorough Christian man, whom I have known since June. He has been *honourable* and kept his *word* to me in everything . . . I am perfectly happy.'

In the whole rogues' gallery there surely was never a knave so plausible as this, never one who, until detection came and his self-control suddenly gave way, could so completely mask his feelings.

Any man who reads carefully as to what happened at Bismarck Road, about which, as the learned Judge observed, it is difficult to comment, must be aghast at the psychological puzzle this amazing criminal presents. The passionate lover of a single day's wedded life, just a week after the murder, sits down and pens the very bald and businesslike statement. It reads: 'Certificate of birth, certificate of marriage, certificate of death, wife's will, policy, receipt for premium paid, official acceptance, receipt for burial.'

One recalls that page in Palmer's diary, where under the date 21st, Wednesday, is recorded, '. . . Cook died at ten o'clock this morning. Jere and William Saunders dined. Sent Bright a 3 mos. Bill,' and under the date 25th, Sunday – 25 after Trin. 'At Church Hamilton preached – dined Yard.'

And yet superior persons wonder why, since bad people do not take any interest in the lives of good people, good people perversely wish to read about bad people!

But what elevates Smith to the highest pinnacle of infamy is that he played upon the very tenderest and most sacred of all our feelings to accomplish his crimes. Of bigamists and seducers and betrayers of women there have been and will continue to be many notable examples; but, complex as our human nature is, Smith provided the first, as his Judge believed he would also furnish the last, instance of a man caressing in his closest embraces of marital love a woman, the exact moment and manner of whose death at his hands he had in his mind, while his lying lips were uttering to her words of the purest passion. He is wholly apart, from the point of view of sexual psychology, from the lust-murderer or mutilator, whose sexual erethism discharges itself in the commission of an act of homicide, or maiming, or in some form of infliction of pain. Smith plays with every success the part of an uxorious and devoted husband, and all the time the exact cash value of his bride to him as a corpse is present in his mind. The tender words and sighs of passion, fondly believed to be reciprocated, are breathed into ears which will hear unmoved in a few hours' time those same lips sighing and panting for life as the cruel water closes over them and for ever puts them to silence.

It would need more than De Quincey's pen, even, to call up before the shuddering reader that scene in the bathroom at Bismarck Road. The poor bride, her whole being throbbing, with a temperature of 101, the tiring winter's afternoon in which there has been so much to do, a will to make here, money to withdraw there, closed by the fall of night, returns to their modest rooms; at once he soothes her; Miss Blatch enters, and there she is on her knees by the fire and he reading the paper – a picture of domesticity! She would like a warm bath; there are reasons; she would feel more comfortable. Utterly confiding, the bride of a day lets her bridegroom come in and invade her privacy. The natural shame of a woman before a man is gone already. She has given herself to this honourable Christian man, and thenceforth she is his.

It is not decent to speculate – save in the privacy of the individual mind – as to what exactly happened in those few fatal moments round about eight o'clock on the night of 18 December. It is barely possible to hold the pen and in the mind's eye try to visualize the scene.

The muscular arms, that could rend a chair asunder, are wrapped around the yielding body, his eyes look into her eyes, the melting, liquid light of passion shining in each. A last tender kiss seals eternally those words of love. The strong hands grip the unresisting body; a fierce, feline look steals into the cunning eyes that a moment ago beamed so kindly. As her head plunges under the water what thoughts flood the mind of Margaret Lofty? Drowning people, we are told, in the brief space of consciousness left them, pass in review every incident of their lives. What recollections and reflections must have raced through her brain! Each caress, every tender word, those letters, in which were revealed the harmony of their souls – all rushed back to her in that crowded last moment of consciousness. And he?

He is looking with professional concern for the signs, which are the heralds of death. The eyeballs are beginning to project – good! The face is blackening – excellent! She did get her head above water for a second and gave a little sigh; that was disconcerting, but it will pass for nothing, and he has locked the door. All will be over before he unlocks it. He can lift her head out of the water now, and judge the progress of the case. A bloody froth streams from mouth and nostrils – it is finished! Now to steal to the parlour downstairs and play as unconcernedly as he can upon the organ. What notes did it peal forth? Some dirge? Some *marche funèbre*? Then out into the bleak night on an errand to buy tomatoes. And when he comes back there is that knocking on the door which, as in *Macbeth*, transfers our sympathy ('of comprehension by which we enter into his feelings and are made to understand them – not a sympathy of pity or approbation') to the murderer. 'In the murdered person all strife of thought, all flux and reflux of passion and of purpose, are crushed by one overwhelming panic. The fear of instant death smites him with its "petrific maze". But in the murderer ... there must be raging some great storm of passion, jealousy, ambition, vengeance, hatred – which will create a hell within him; and into this hell we are to look.' Thus wrote De Quincey in *Murder Considered as One of the Fine Arts*.

Smith, not being 'such a murderer as poet will condescend to', the hell within him provided no material for sublime tragedy;

merely materials for one of the longest and costliest murder trials these islands have ever known.

And if we could look into that hell within him, after he heard the fatal words, 'this appeal is dismissed', the only torments we should find him suffering from would be 'chagrin at the mistake in not securing immunity'. The mercenary murderer, without exception, can find no contrition. The learned Judge in passing sentence must have realized this. 'An exhortation to repentance would be wasted on you.' And in the two last letters from Maidstone, the one to his solicitor, the other to Edith Pegler, the usual canting and hypocritical expressions are mingled with the usual invectives against his Judges and the unjust world which has consigned an innocent man to his doom.

The history of crime, like other history, 'With all her volumes vast, hath but one tale.' His end was like the end of all others, except that he met it abjectly.

'The world contains,' wrote Sir James Stephen, 'an appreciable number of wretches who ought to be exterminated without mercy when an opportunity occurs.'

Though

> Fate will use a running noose
> For the best man and the worst,

I do not think the most ardent advocate of the abolition of capital punishment will deny that fate, through the instrumentality of Messrs Pierpont and Ellis, made a most proper use of her running noose on 13 August 1915.

Ronald True
1922

RONALD TRUE was born in Manchester in 1891. His parents were very young, his mother being a mere child of sixteen – a fact which becomes significant in the light of his mental history. The circumstances of his birth seem to have been unfortunate, but his nurture was in no way prejudiced. He was well cared for from birth; and when he was about eleven years old his mother made an exceedingly advantageous marriage, and was thenceforth enabled to make a provision for him that was not only adequate, but generous. He had every provision that affection, backed with money, could afford. His childhood was healthy and remarkably free from illness, and he grew up into a powerfully built young man, well above the average height. Sound bodies, however, do not necessarily contain sound minds. Even in early childhood True's conduct was peculiar and disquieting. That a boy of five or six years should tell lies, play truant, and be cruel to his pets is in itself no great matter. Such incidents often constitute a phase, ugly but transient, in the childhood of perfectly normal individuals. They may indeed be interpreted as no more than the first crude attempts of the self-conscious being to assert himself against the world. The normal individual, having a capacity for social education, is quick to recognize their futility, and the ugly phase passes. But where the phase does not pass – but develops and deepens – where the lying becomes extravagant, the truancy persistent, the cruelty insensate – there is a presumption of congenital defect which at the crucial periods of adolescent and adult life, will manifest itself in clearly defined neurosis and even insanity.

So it proved with Ronald True. When he was entering his teens, his aunt, Mrs Angus, who had not seen him for several years, found that the abnormality he had evinced at the age of six had noticeably increased. Her evidence on the point is couched in very general terms, but there is no reason to doubt its veracity. One may quite well have a clear impression of a person's character and yet be able to give few illustrations or particulars. Demeanour, as every lawyer knows, is eloquent to him who observes it, but what it tells is well-nigh incommunicable, particularly after the lapse of many years. One curious incident, however, remained engraved in Mrs Angus's memory. True's mother fell seriously ill, and Mrs Angus informed the boy of the fact. He was not at all distressed, but merely remarked, 'Oh, well, if she dies all her property will be mine, and I'll give you her two best rings straight away, and you can have anything you like of her things and jewellery.' This remark was made, apparently without any consciousness of impropriety, by a boy of fourteen, who, as far as can be judged, had always been on affectionate terms with his mother.

True was at this time at Bedford Grammar School, where he remained until he was nearly eighteen. Although it does not appear that he was guilty of any outrageous conduct, his reports were consistently bad, and indicated incapacity for sustained mental effort. In the circumstances it is not surprising that his family made no attempt to put him into a profession, but took the conventional way of disposing of a stupid youth. They shipped him off to the Colonies. It was thought that farming in New Zealand might suit him, so to New Zealand he went. Within a year he was back in England. New arrangements had to be made. A Yorkshire farmer was induced to take him as a pupil. That lasted a month. The Yorkshire farmer could do nothing with him. The next move, in 1911, was to the Argentine. In 1912 he was again on his mother's hands in England. Then Canada was tried. He served in the North-West Mounted Police, but not for long. Subsequently he seems to have drifted to Mexico, but not much is known of his movements until the middle of 1914, when he turned up in Shanghai. He was there when the outbreak of the war in Europe gave him the best of pretexts to return home once more.

Let us pause here. To the casual glance True's career up to this point suggests no more than a born wastrel with possibly some indications of mental defect. But, while no detailed information is available as to his behaviour between 1909 and 1914, three facts were ascertained that are full of significance to the alienist, viz., that during the critical years of adolescence (eighteen to twenty), he was leading a vagabond life, incapable of acquiring any settled mode of livelihood; that during the same period (as will appear) he had acquired the morphia habit; and that on his return to England the peculiarities of his demeanour had noticeably increased.

In the early years of the war, when recruiting methods were still very imperfect, it was inevitable that many unsuitable persons should have been accepted for service. But even when all allowances have been made, it is hard to understand how this weak-minded narcomaniac should have had no difficulty in joining (of all branches of the service) the Royal Flying Corps, and getting a nomination to a flying school with a view to a commission. Of course, he would never have been accepted had his drug addiction been known. That his own family should have been unaware of his habit is, perhaps, not very surprising, but it is curious that the medical men who passed True should have had no suspicions. In due course True became a cadet at Gosport Flying School. His career there was not encouraging. He failed repeatedly in the simplest examinations, and how in the end he managed to pass no one who knew him then has ever been able to imagine. In the air he was not only reckless but incompetent, and during a cross-country trial flight he crashed badly at Farnborough. A month later he had another but less serious accident at Gosport, escaping with a few cuts and bruises. The Farnborough crash, however, was undoubtedly a bad one. No bones were broken, but he suffered concussion of the brain, from which he lay unconscious for two days. It is said that subsequently True had at least two more accidents – one at Yeovil and one in America. If he did have an accident at Yeovil, which is doubtful, it was not a serious one. On the other hand, he did have *one* bad crash in America. True's own statements about his flying mishaps were extremely confused and inconsistent.

From the time of the Farnborough crash, True's malady developed rapidly. His abnormality had always been notorious in Gosport; but after the Farnborough accident, according to the testimony of former cadets, he was regarded as little removed from a madman. His general demeanour is described as feverish, nervous and imbecile. On being awarded his wings, he appeared at mess wearing a pair that he had had specially made of extraordinary design and three times larger than regulation size. He could hardly ever be induced to wear his cap, alleging (probably the truth) that it hurt his head. To meet the requirements of military discipline he went about with his hat in his hand, putting it on, only for saluting purposes, whenever a superior officer appeared.

The Gosport accident in March 1916, may be said to mark the end of True's military career. Shortly afterwards he was invalided out of the Air Force. As the official medical records are not available, the precise circumstances of his discharge cannot be stated. All we know is that, in a Southsea theatre one night, shortly after the crash, he had a sudden and violent seizure of pain in the right hip. Of their charity True's family spoke of the attack as a result of his accident, but all the indications point to a syphilitic condition. The Wassermann test showed a negative result, but True's own statement was that he had suffered from syphilis. Syphilis is admitted to be a prolific cause of mental derangement; but it is doubtful if it had much bearing on True's case. The medical witnesses called in his defence obviously did not attach much importance to it. He was taken into the Alexandra Military Hospital at Cosham, where, by his refractory and often offensive conduct, he made himself such a nuisance that there was general relief among the staff when his mother managed to arrange for his transference to a private nursing-home at Southsea. It was at this time that his drug addiction was discovered. The pain in his hip was so severe that morphia had to be prescribed. The ordinary dose had no effect whatever. The patient would not respond except to doses that proved his long experience of the drug. Naturally, what he got by prescription was quite insufficient for his craving, which he endeavoured to satisfy by all sorts of surreptitious methods – bribing orderlies and cajoling chemists in the town. Generally, his moods alternated between childish exaltation – as when he went about in a bath-chair with a hooter and a doll – and depression with sudden fits of violence. In addition, the chauffeur, Sims, who is the principal authority of True's behaviour, during this period, states that he had frequent and serious lapses of memory and occasional terrors of a delusive nature such as that an assassin was lurking at the back of the theatre box.

After this, which brings us down to the end of 1916, it is distinctly surprising to find a Southsea lunatic turning up in Yeovil early in 1917 as a test pilot at the Government Control Works! Also it is not surprising to hear that the works officials found him utterly unsuitable for the job. He had lost nerve badly, complained constantly of headaches, was noticeably 'moody', and his incompetence as a pilot was manifest and pitiful. He did not stay long at Yeovil, and in June 1917, we find him in New York, very much at a loose end, but posing quite successfully as a war-broken English pilot. It should be said here that, while everyone who came into regular intimate contact with True regarded him as a lunatic, in casual social interest he was capable of creating an excellent impression. His manner was plausible and even engaging. He was, according to some standards, very good company. And in the circumstances of the moment he had no difficulty in being taken at his own valuation. The United States had just entered the war, and no one was disposed to inquire into the antecedents of an invalided English Flying Officer, who spoke with assurance (albeit without a vestige of truth) of his service in France, his honourable wounds and the German airmen who had met their doom at his hands.

Among those who heard True's fairy-tales was a young actress, named Frances Roberts, who was so deeply impressed that before the year was out she married him. She never suspected that her hero had never been to France, that he was unfit to be trusted with an aeroplane, and that his discharge from the Air Force, so far from being due to 'honourable' wounds, was caused by injuries brought about by his own incompetence, aggravated by morphia. It was a foolish and disastrous marriage, but one can hardly blame Mrs

True when we consider that the same year True was able to per-
suade the United States War Department that he was a suitable
person to be employed as an instructor in their flying school at
Mineola. When the school was transferred to Houston, Texas, True
went with it. His wife, having to fill a theatrical engagement, did
not accompany him, and did not see him again until June 1918,
when he returned to New York in poor health. His history during
the intervening months may be stated quite briefly. His employment
at Houston, as might be expected, came to a speedy end. He thereupon wandered down to Mexico, where he developed a chest complaint that kept him in hospital for a considerable time. From
Mexico he crossed over to Cuba, and thence returned to New
York, once more at a loose end. The usual thing happened. Within
a month he was back in England with his mother, and this time the
prodigal had added to the problems of his return by bringing a
young wife with him.

True's mental condition was now serious enough to justify drastic
measures. The evidence of Mr Morgan, a flying officer, leaves no
doubt on the point. Mr Morgan had known True at Gosport in
1916, and regarded him as deranged then. He did not see him
again until shortly after the Armistice, when he met him in London
several times, and found that he was in a distinctly worse condition,
and not accountable for his actions at all. But True's family took no
action, and that is not surprising. Nothing is more difficult than to
try to get a lunatic's relatives to admit he *is* a lunatic. Often nothing
short of the dire realization that the wretch's neck is in danger will
make them face the ugly fact; for, bad as it is to have a near relative
in a lunatic asylum, it is worse to have had one hanged. But at the
end of 1918 there was nothing to suggest that True would be
dangerous to anyone but himself, and so, instead of consulting a
medical specialist, his family were once more trying to find him
suitable employment, at a comfortable distance from England. As
usual, a job was found. In February 1919, accompanied by his wife
(who was shortly expecting a baby) he sailed for the Gold Coast, to
take up an appointment with the Taquah Mining Company.
Within a few weeks of starting his duties as assistant manager in the

native compound he was under suspension. From the moment of his arrival his conduct had been intolerable. His extravagances of talk and behaviour made him the laughing-stock of the station, and even natives summed him up as 'the massa what live with him mammy [wife] and is sick by him head'. There could only be one outcome – dismissal; and so True was packed off home, having been on the Gold Coast less than six months. The ostensible reason for his discharge was that the climate did not suit him. The real reason was that the company had no time for a notorious drug-addict who hobnobbed familiarly with the blacks, and behaved like an imbecile Munchausen among his fellow whites. But True does not seem to have been at all downcast by the circumstances of his departure. He assured the people of Taquah that they would soon see him again, as he intended to form a transport company for the Gold Coast trade. His return to the Gold Coast would be by aero-plane, *via* France, the Mediterranean, and the Sahara! When it was objected that this was a bad route for petrol supplies, True did not agree. There were many places, he said, where oil and petrol could be had, but he omitted to give particulars.

Taquah was the last job True ever had. His family seem to have realized the futility of trying to put him to work. It was less troublesome to leave him alone, and make him an allowance suffi-cient to support his wife and child. Indeed, his condition when he returned from the Gold Coast was such as to put employment of any kind out of the question. Thenceforward, to the time of his arrest, his life was a long dismal history of morphia debauches, punctuated by periodical 'cures' in nursing-homes, rapidly increas-ing mental deterioration, and developments in behaviour that caused his family first anxiety and then genuine alarm. When he returned from West Africa, he was taking morphia in great quan-tities, and so continued until the beginning of 1920, when his wife and mother decided that something must be done. Accordingly he was persuaded to enter a nursing-home kept by a Dr Parham at Brighton, where he remained for six months. In the home he was allowed, on an average, about twelve grains of morphia a day. As that was quite inadequate to satisfy his craving he sometimes endeavoured to acquire illicit supplies, and when these were not forthcoming, for the Brighton chemists were soon on their guard against the 'madman', as he was called, he was often extremely violent.

Three incidents occurred at this time and are of interest as illustrating a fact of morbid psychology, which, while a commonplace among alienists, does not occur at all in the popular conception of the nature of insanity, viz., that mental disorder is in essence an emotional rather than an intellectual condition. A man may show little or no intellectual derangement, and yet be as mad as a hatter. Usually, of course, there is well-marked intellectual derangement, but it is probably secondary to the emotional disturbance. For emotion and intellect are far from being self-contained entities. A good intelligence without the appropriate emotional quality will soon cease to be 'good' just as a plant will languish in improvised soil.

It is not in the intelligence, but in the emotional and instructive activities of the mind, that springs of conduct must be sought. (Even the psychoanalysts are agreed with the alienists on that point.) When one comes to think of it, the conduct of any creature can mean no more than the sum of its attempts to adapt itself to its environment, and in the biological history of such attempts intelligence comes as a late and probably, at best, an ancillary device. But it is true of intelligence, as of every *bonus judex*, that its constant aim is *jurisdictionem ampliare*. Thus men, no matter how instinctively they may act, always essay to construct a rational basis for their conduct. This rationalizing takes a more or less comprehensive account of objective fact, but emotion always keeps it within certain limits. Regarded as an adaptive function, conduct may be successful or otherwise. In either case the individual will invariably attempt to state a rational basis for it. Thus the self-made man always feels himself able to explain to the public 'How I succeeded', and the chronic failure is equally ready – though not with the same eager audience – to account for his misfortunes. Both cases are eloquent of the inveterate bias of the ego in favour of itself. The successful man tends to put to the credit of his own wisdom matters that are no more than lucky chances. The unsuccessful man is preoccupied with his consistent bad luck. *He* is all right, but he has never had a fair chance. In prosperity the ego must be given a fair chance. That is human nature.

Now when a man becomes insane he does not cease to be human. The forces that underlie his insane conduct are the same in character as when he was sane, but their equilibrium has been destroyed. An emotional disorganization occurs, with consequent failure of adaptation. The intelligence, though it does not as a rule remain unaffected indefinitely, may not decay *pari passu*. It may continue to function fairly well, in which case it will persist in its task of 'rationalizing' conduct long after conduct has ceased to be susceptible of rational explanation. If his notions do not accord with the facts, they must be altered as may be necessary. Here we have the initial conditions of a delusion. Presently two more factors come into play – sensory derangement (or hallucinations) and a certain decay of the intelligence that seems inevitably to follow the emotional disorder. The latter need not be extensive. It may never amount to any more than an impairment of the critical activities, which, being the latest development of the human mind, are the first to be attacked; but it is enough. All the conditions are now present for an utterly false reconstruction of the external world, which may proceed to the most fantastic and extravagant lengths. The lunatic thereby reaches a new accommodation, which, however embarrassing to the community, is in a measure satisfactory to himself. The emotional disorder which prevents him from adapting himself to his environment has compensating elements, which enable him to fabricate an environment adapted to himself. These considerations afford a clue to Ronald True's conduct during the period he spent in Dr Parham's home.

He was not only unemployed but definitely unemployable – a state of affairs not at all in accordance with his own estimates of his deserts. It was unthinkable that so meritorious a person should be without a job, and as no job was forthcoming the obvious solution was to invent one. Accordingly, he astonished his friends one day by announcing that he had just obtained 'a billet, a wonderful billet, with a large salary from the Portuguese Government'. Asked for particulars, he produced what he called an 'agreement'. This was a sheet of paper which bore some puerile nonsense, obviously written by True himself and a penny stamp cancelled by writing in the style of a receipt. On being told his precious agreement was worthless, True broke into tears of vexation and tore it up.

To the same class of conduct belongs the incident or rather series of incidents which we may describe as the delusion of the 'other True'. While in Dr Parham's home True occasionally backed horses, and got the racing results by telegram. If the telegram announced a winner, good and well – it was his; but if it announced an 'also ran', True was always quite sure it was not for him, but for *another person of the same name*. So with bills. The Ronald True in the nursing-home never owed money, it was always 'the other Ronald True'. When these facts were given in the trial they pointed to no more than common dishonesty. Such an explanation is inadequate. If the story of 'the other Ronald True' was a fraud, it was the fraud of a dement, for no man in his senses could have imagined that anyone would have been deceived by it. Strange to say there was in fact a Ronald *Trew*; but though he came to know of it later there is nothing to show that at the time True knew of his namesake's existence. The point, however, is immaterial. Whether he knew or did not know that there was a person called *Trew*, the device of accepting all agreeable telegrams and referring all the disagreeable ones to a *doppelgänger* was too silly to be regarded as calculated deceit. Psychologically it was of a piece with the bombast which had made him ridiculous in West Africa, and which certainly had not abated when he went to Brighton. His pathological egoism would not allow that he could ever be a loser. His score at golf was always less than the bogey. He could always give anyone 80 in 100 at billiards. All the horses he backed were winners.

We come now to the third significant incident of the Brighton period. True was wholly dependent on his mother, and had not a penny of his own. Nevertheless he must needs make a 'will' by which he purported to leave £100 to Dr Barnardo's Homes and a like amount to the Battersea Home for Lost Dogs, and directed that his child should be brought up, and indeed adopted, by a lady whom he named. *There was no mention of his wife.* Mrs True knew nothing of this singular document till some time afterwards, when lighting on it by accident she asked her husband what he meant by it. His reply was in the nature of a repudiation. People did strange things in mad fits and it was unfair of her to tax him with it. On this Mrs True destroyed the 'will', and said no more. The episode is instructive as showing a new phase in True's mental derangement – an incipient hostility towards his wife, for whom, up to this time, he had never shown anything but the utmost affection. Later this hostility became pronounced, and possibly, had not another victim intervened, would have had a bloody consummation.

In September 1920, True left Dr Parham's home and went with his wife to Portsmouth, where they lived together for the next twelve months. About the end of the year True informed his wife that he must go to London for a few days to see a Mr Harris, who, he alleged, had promised him employment. (The name Harris was apt, for there was no such person.) In a few days he was back in Portsmouth but almost immediately returned to London. Not hearing from him for several days, his wife telegraphed to an address he had given her. He replied by letter. 'By the time you receive this letter,' he wrote, 'I shall no longer be in this world. The man Harris has let me down.' This was not the first time True had hinted that he might kill himself, but never before had the threat been so explicit. In alarm, Mrs True hurried up to London, and, after a prolonged search, ran him to earth in a Soho restaurant – a mental and physical wreck. His urgent business in London had been a morphia debauch. His condition being now worse than ever, he was persuaded to enter a nursing-home in London for another cure in the spring of 1921, but stayed there only a week. Probably the home was glad to be rid of a patient who was not merely troublesome, but extremely alarming. His violence was such that he had to be looked after by two male attendants, and the other Ronald True developed from a fantasy into a homicidal delusion. He would have to meet the other Ronald True one day, he declared, and then there would be a 'how d'ye do'. When he returned to Portsmouth Mrs True presently discovered that her husband had developed a new and very embarrassing habit, viz., pilfering at bookstalls. His thefts were very petty and quite purposeless. He had no use for the trifles he stole. It simply was that, when he bought newspapers or magazines, he must make a point of taking away something – no matter what – more than he paid for. There was nothing impulsive about these thefts, be it noted; for he would with great complacency show his booty to his wife – doubtless to show her what a cunning dog her husband was. He was never detected. When ultimately he did make an appearance in Portsmouth Police Court, it was on a graver charge, namely, obtaining morphia from a druggist by means of forged prescriptions. He was convicted and fined.

At this juncture his relatives decided that another attempt must be made to cure him of the drug habit. An operation for appendicitis intervened to delay matters, and it was not until November that he returned to the London nursing-home for his 'cure'. As before he had frequent fits of violence that called for drastic measures of restraint, but this time his stay was a little longer. He did not leave the home till the end of a month, when, attended by a nurse, he went down to Folkestone, where his aunt had undertaken to look after him and his child during his wife's absence on a theatrical tour. Mrs Angus, his aunt, by painful experience was prepared for a great deal, but this time she found her nephew harder to cope with than ever before. Druggists could be warned not to supply him, but as his movements could not be controlled, there was no guarantee that he was not getting morphia clandestinely. His irregular habits and late hours worried his aunt considerably. She remonstrated and got a reply of sinister anticipation. Three palmists, he told her – one in Buenos Aires, one in San Francisco, and one in Shanghai – had predicted that he would be killed through a woman soon, so he meant to have a short life and a gay one. In his general demeanour there had developed a new and ugly quality, which Mrs Angus tried to describe by saying that his eyes were those of a certified lunatic. His bombast took a repulsive turn. In Mexico, he boasted, he once wrote out his title to a mining claim in the blood of a German whom he had killed for disputing his right.

After the Folkestone visit, which lasted a fortnight, there is a gap of a week or two in True's movements, but he spent Christmas with his mother and his aunt. It was noticed that he was very morose. He spoke little. He took no interest in his child, towards whom he had hitherto been fatuously affectionate. He spent most of his time brooding in obstinate silence over the fire. To Mrs Angus this gloomy preoccupation was more alarming than any extravagance. She was now convinced that her nephew was not only insane but dangerous, and she and her sister had anxious consultations about what should be done with him. While the discussions were going on True suddenly left home, announcing that he had some business to transact in Bedford. He never returned. His wife, who had just finished her engagement, met him by arrangement in London one day at the end of January. On this occasion he was quite affectionate but not very communicative, and when they parted Mrs True took it for granted that he was returning to Bedford. The point of fact is that all through this period he never left London. A week later she met him again. He was no longer affectionate, but distinctly hostile to her. His conversation was rambling and incoherent, but she gathered that a Mr Davenport had promised him some employment or other, and that he was going to leave her for good.

From that day until the tragic 6 March True vanished from his family's ken. The plight of the three women was a distressing one. They now knew that True was a dangerous lunatic, and from such stray information as they could gather, it appeared he was prowling about London with a loaded revolver in his pocket and murder in his mind. It was imperative that he should be caught and put under effective restraint. Mrs True sought the help of Scotland Yard, but as no crime had yet been committed Scotland Yard could only refer her to a competent private detective, and recommended ex-Inspector Stockley. On Friday, 3 March, Mr Stockley took Mrs True's instructions to trace her husband and at once set to work. But it was too late. On Monday, 6 March, True was arrested in a box at the Hammersmith Palace of Varieties for the murder of Olive Young, *alias* Gertrude Yates.

True, when he was arrested, had been absent from home nearly two months, during which time, save for two short meetings with his wife in January and February, he had held little or no communication with his family. What was he doing?

His movements during January can only be conjectured. The only witness who saw him at this time was his wife, who accepted his story that he was stopping at Bedford on important business, and had only come up to London for the day to meet her. This was a pure invention. He had no business at Bedford, and no prospect of work; and there is no ground for believing that during all this time he ever left London, except on crazy 'joy-rides', of which more will be said presently. He was leading a vagrant life about the West End, and no doubt drugging himself heavily. From the beginning of February information about the manner of his life is available in considerable detail. Here is the story disclosed at the trial by the evidence given there.

One evening in the first week in February a Mr James Armstrong, who among other things had been in the motor trade, but who for the first time was out of work, chanced upon a former business acquaintance in the Corner House, Leicester Square, London. Mr Armstrong's friend had with him an affable stranger whom he introduced as 'Major True'. Armstrong and True seem to have taken to each other at once. They arranged to meet again, and the acquaintance ripened rapidly. For the next few weeks they were together nearly every day for hours on end. Armstrong gathered that his friend had been in the Air Force during the war and had done some strenuous service, and that he was now doing civil flying and made several trips to the Continent, often with valuable cargoes. This present employment, he explained, was attended with some risk. There was always the chance of a forced landing in a lonely and dangerous neighbourhood, and therefore he would be glad to buy Mr Armstrong's automatic pistol, if he was disposed to part with it. Mr Armstrong was quite agreeable and let him have it with a quantity of cartridges for £2. The two men went about the West End constantly, visiting restaurants and places of amusement. True did most of the paying and, no doubt, according to the notions of an easy-going, pleasure-loving, and undiscriminating man, proved a most agreeable companion. He had a preference for going about hatless. His stories of adventure in distant lands were often uncommonly tall – but that could only be part of his fun, for they were stories that nobody could be expected to believe. Another pleasantry of the 'Major's' was that he proposed to form a society of enterprising spirits, who would undertake to 'put away' anybody that anybody else found objectionable at the rate of a 'bob a nob'. Armstrong treated this as a practical joke. It may be doubted if he would have viewed it in that light had he known that after purchasing the automatic pistol and ammunition True's first care was to file the nose of every bullet. There was a further peculiarity of the 'Major's' conduct. He was a bit of a vagabond, moving fitfully from one expensive hotel to another, or sleeping in the Savoy Turkish Baths in Jermyn Street. On the other hand his cards bore permanent addresses, a very impressive one in Mayfair. He seemed to have no lack of money and spent it lavishly, and could always command a smart car and a chauffeur. On the whole, Armstrong, who was looking for employment at the time, seemed to have decided that 'Major' True was an acquaintance worth cultivating; and he was encouraged in his belief when at a later stage True proposed a partnership in Civil Aviation in the United States. Armstrong was willing, whereupon without more ado True phoned to the Cunard Company to arrange for berths and the conveyance of a car and an aeroplane by the next convenient boat. This struck Armstrong as a queer way of doing business, and he began to wonder if his friend were to be taken seriously.

It is worth knowing at this point that all of True's friends (*male*), even those who regarded him as quite mad, saw nothing sinister in his conduct. Even his habit of carrying a loaded revolver in his pocket does not seem to have been taken seriously by men. But with women the case was decidedly different. Among the places of amusement visited by True and Armstrong was Murray's, a well-

known dance and supper club. Neither was a member, but on 5
February they went as guests. They were introduced to a Mrs
Wilson, in whom True took immediate interest. At first Mrs Wilson
thought nothing of it, but when he met her at the club she found his
attentions rather embarrassing. He forced himself on her to the
exclusion of everyone else, and there were things about him that
she did not like. Thus in the middle of conversation he would break
off, stare about him wildly, utterly at a loss, like one awaking from
a dream, until recalled to his surroundings. His attitude of possession
towards her became not only offensive but terrifying. Owing to his
hip trouble he could not dance with her and forbade her to dance
with any other man, declaring that if she disobeyed him 'there
would be trouble', and enforcing his threat by displaying a revolver
which he was careful to point out was loaded with split bullets. In
this connection True told a curious story. There was a man, he
said, going about the West End using the name of Ronald True
and passing cheques which his (True's) mother had to take up.
This man, True suggested, was a dangerous criminal who went
about armed, and consequently he, the real True, had obtained
permission from Scotland Yard to carry a revolver lest one day he
should meet his impersonator. Mrs Wilson was far from being re-
assured by this story. She decided that True was a lunatic and must
be humoured if he was not to do mischief.

For a week or more she had to endure him. He imposed himself
on her as *cavaliere servente*, visiting her at her house, and accompanying her to restaurants and Murray's. The loaded revolver was constantly in evidence, and on several occasions when she hesitated to
go out with him she was told that a bullet in the head would be the
penalty for a refusal. She dared not say him nay. All she could do
was to stipulate that Mr Armstrong should always be with them.
True, she thought, was not a safe man for a woman to be alone
with. Apart altogether from his actual menaces, his conversation
was disagreeably preoccupied with the theme of murder. He was
going to kill the 'other Ronald True', or somebody else – it did not
seem to matter who the victim was. And of course, in murder, as in
everything else, he would be brilliantly successful. 'I will murder

someone one of these days,' he remarked casually to Mrs Wilson. 'You watch the papers and see if I don't. I'm perfectly certain I'll get off. Watch the papers. I want to try it out.' Presently the talk of murder passed from the phase of talk into a fantasy.

One day he had promised to telephone Mrs Wilson at five o'clock – presumably about taking her out in the evening – but no message came. At last, about eleven o'clock, the telephone rang. True was speaking, and he had a horrid tale to tell. He said he had called at his mother's house about six in the evening and, getting no answer, had gone round to the back and entered by a window. All the servants were out, and his mother was lying bleeding on the floor with her head battered in. She was not dead, however, and he had had her removed to a nursing-home. An operation was to be performed next day by a surgeon named *Wilson*, but there was little hope for her recovery. Mrs Wilson was naturally rather excited, and carefully scanned the papers next day for accounts of the outrage. She found nothing. That evening she met True and asked him how the affair of his mother had not leaked out. His reply was, 'I'm keeping it dark, there is to be a big case about it.' Mrs Wilson was puzzled and had inquiries made. She found that the story was a pure invention. What the object of it was she could not divine, but she was confirmed in her belief that True was insane. Suddenly, to Mrs Wilson's great relief, he ceased to visit her and Murray's and she saw him no more. This was in the third week of February – a fateful week in True's history, as we shall see. It was just about this time, it will be recalled, that True had a meeting with his wife, at which he announced he was going to leave her for good. Thenceforward he eluded all the efforts of his relatives to get in touch with him.

A curious point emerges here. When he first left home, True must have been fairly well supplied with money, but by the middle of February he had spent every penny he had. Yet this was the moment he chose to cut himself off from his only source of income. Probably he suspected a design to have him put under permanent restraint and accordingly was taking no risks. What need to worry about money so long as he could borrow or steal? He touched his

friend Armstrong for a pound or two. On 17 February the two
cronies visited the Ring in Blackfriars Road, where True seemed to
have no difficulty in persuading the referee to part with £5 in
exchange for his I.O.U. That same evening he saw Mrs Wilson for
the last time. Murray's Club had to be avoided in future. He had
cashed a cheque there that there might be trouble about.

This cheque incident has the interest that it revealed to True's
family what apparently True's family had not realized before, that
there was another Ronald True, who, however, spelt his name
Ronald Trew; and Mr Trew was a member of Murray's. The two
men had never met, but it is tolerably certain that True knew, and
had known for some time, that he had a namesake. It may have
been this knowledge that started the idea of *doppelgänger* in his
mind. Certainly in his excited fits in the London nursing-home, he
used to complain of the scandal there would be if a man was going
about the streets with a name like his own. To a disordered mind
the fact that another person bore the same name would soon suggest
a sinister purpose, whence it would be an easy transition to the
belief that he was an enemy, carried a deadly weapon, and so forth.
True's fraud does not justify us in assuming that the story of the
'other Ronald True' was a criminal device and nothing more.
Among the many circumstances that point to its delusional character is the curious fact that True never once alluded to it in Armstrong's presence, though he was free enough about it to other
people. For some reason he seemed to take pains to conceal it from
his favourite male associate, though if he had invented the story
simply to 'make evidence', to cover up his misdeeds, this is the very
person to whom the story should have been told. Whether in passing
the cheque at Murray's True forged the name Trew or used his
own name and took advantage of the easy confusion is not clear.
The evidence of the club manager is contradictory on the point.
The fraud, of course, was soon discovered. Ultimately the club
authorities got in touch with Mrs True, who made good the
amount.

True's last meeting with Mrs Wilson was on 17 February. The
very next night he found a new victim – the unhappy Gertrude

Yates. It is not known when they first became acquainted, but there are grounds for believing that True and Armstrong had once met her casually in some West End lounge and True had taken her address. Gertrude Yates was an ex-shopgirl, twenty-five years of age, who had drifted on to the streets and assumed the professional name of Olive Young. As far as one can judge, she was of the better sort in her calling. She was healthy, temperate and quiet in her habits. She was fairly prosperous, always had money ample for her obligations and had a balance of over £120 in the Post Office Savings Bank. She lived alone in a basement flat in Finborough Road, Fulham, where she was attended by a daily servant.

On the evening of Saturday, 18 February, Miss Young had a call from her most intimate friend, a married woman named Dent. While the two girls were talking there was a knock at the door, and presently Olive Young ushered in a tall dark man whom she introduced as 'my friend, Major True'. Mrs Dent noticed that Major True had no hat. The newcomer, who was evidently there by appointment, was very polite. If he had only known that Miss Young had a visitor he would have sent her home in his car. Mrs Dent acknowledged his courtesy and presently departed.

This was True's first visit to the flat in Finborough Road. He did not leave a good impression behind, for on the following (Sunday) evening Olive Young told her friend Doris Dent that she had no wish to see Major True again. After he had gone she had missed a £5 note from her handbag, and she strongly suspected him of taking it. He had shown an admiring interest in her jewellery, too, which she had found extremely unpleasant – and he carried a loaded revolver. He was anxious to meet her again but she did not propose to give him a chance. Olive Young, like Mrs Wilson, thought True was not fit for a woman to be alone with. She kept out of his way, and for more than a week True's attempts to see her failed. Realizing presently that the girl was deliberately avoiding him, True tried a new device. Olive Young was on the telephone. He could ring her up, and did so persistently day after day, but still his victim refused to be drawn.

This brings the tale to the end of February, and True's funds were exhausted. This, however, did not prevent him from continuing to drive about town in motor-cars. Much could be done on credit and on worthless cheques. Still, some ready money was necessary. On 28 February True got a few pounds by pawning a gold wristlet watch that did not belong to him. How he came by it is not known, but it is not hard to guess. That evening he and Armstrong visited the Palais de Danse, Hammersmith. There True recognized an ex-flying officer, named Sach, who, like himself, had been employed as a test pilot by the United States War Department in 1917. Sach, though he remembered True as an odd fish, was quite pleased to renew the acquaintance, and invited True and Armstrong to dine with him and his wife on the following evening, which they did. Evidently the proceeds of the gold watch had gone, for he successfully touched Sachs for a sovereign.

What followed was characteristic. A few hours after leaving the Sachs – that is, in the small hours of the morning of 2 March – True turned up at the Victoria Hotel, Northumberland Avenue. A most annoying thing had happened, he told the night porter. He had been locked out of his flat, having forgotten his latch-key, and had knocked and rung without avail. Could he have a room? The story was a likely enough one. He was given a room. In the morning, having had breakfast at the hotel, he slipped out without paying. An ordinary 'bilker' would have got away from that neighbourhood as soon as possible. Not so True. On leaving the Victoria he merely crossed the street and presented himself at the reception bureau of the Grand Hotel in the capacity of a cross-channel pilot who had just arrived at Croydon that morning from Paris. He wanted a room for a few days, and perhaps the hotel management could arrange to have his luggage fetched up from Croydon the next morning. These matters having been satisfactorily arranged, True's next care was to ring up a West End firm of motor-car proprietors. A chauffeur named Luigi Mazzola took the call. Major True, who was staying at the Grand Hotel, wanted a car at once. Could one be sent immediately? Major True mentioned that he could not pay for the car at the moment, as he had just arrived from Paris by aeroplane and had nothing but French money on him, but he would settle up next day. No objection was made to that, and in the evening Mazzola drove down to the Grand Hotel, picked up his customer, and so became the unwitting actor in the tragedy that was at hand.

That evening True dined with his friend, Armstrong, who was an unmarried man living with his mother. Once again it is to be observed how much more sensitive women were than men to True's abnormality. Mrs Armstrong was uncomfortable about her son's boon companion. He had visited the house once or twice already, and from what she had seen of him she was certain that he was not quite right in his mind and might even be dangerous. She had spoken to her son about it, but her warning had been disregarded. After dinner Mazzola called with the car and the two men drove off on the usual jaunt – Armstrong blissfully ignorant of the fact that his mother's purse, which contained, *inter alia*, a cheque for £7, was in True's pocket. Nothing noteworthy happened until about eleven o'clock, when True ordered Mazzola to drive to Fulham. He gave Armstrong no reason, and Armstrong, being now accustomed to True's journeyings up and down town, was not interested enough to ask. The car proceeded along the Fulham Road until, at the corner of Finborough Road, True ordered the driver to stop. He wanted to look up some friends, he said. Armstrong was to wait for him, he said, in the car – he would not be long. He got out and disappeared up Finborough Road, but was only away a few minutes. His friends were not in, he explained, and the car drove off. It will be observed that although Armstrong did not know where Olive Young lived he may have met her in the West End. True knew that he did not know.

On the following evening (3 March) True and Armstrong were again at the Palais de Danse with Mr and Mrs Sach. In the course of the evening, when Armstrong was not within hearing, True told the Sachs the tale of 'the other Ronald True', much in the same way as he told Mrs Wilson a fortnight before. He even pointed out among the dancers a man – not in the least resembling him – as the pseudo Ronald True, who had swindled his mother out of £5,000 by forging cheques and running up bills in his name. He meant to shoot the other man, he said, and the other man meant to shoot him. But that was not all. There was another man, Mr Sachs learned, with whom True was equally if not more anxious to settle accounts – a man who owed him money, and who lived *in a basement flat in Fulham*. This man, like the other, was armed, having a service revolver, but all the same True was going to go to the flat on Sunday to kill him. He had been trying to make an appointment with the man for some days, he said, but so far had failed. However, he expected to manage it on Sunday. 'Look out for it in the papers on Monday morning,' he told Sachs. 'It will be one or the other of us.' To demonstrate his plan of operations, True drew a rough plan of Olive Young's flat on the back of the menu. Sach regarded it all as a tale 'told by an idiot'. He thought his eccentric travelling companion of 1917 must be madder than ever. Still, that did not prevent him from arranging to meet True for lunch the next day. Having departed from the Sachs, True made his second expedition to Fulham. The performance of the preceding night was repeated. At the corner of Finborough Road the car was stopped. True got out, leaving Armstrong in the car, and presently came back. Once more his 'friends were not in'. I have followed Armstrong's account here, but Mazzola gave a slightly different version. On the Friday night, according to Mazzola, True returned in a minute or two and got Armstrong to accompany him on a second trip along Finborough Road. The two men were absent for several minutes. Armstrong in his evidence said nothing of accompanying True, and the point was not put to him. Mazzola also stated that on either Thursday or Friday, he drove *twice* to Finborough Road. On this point also Armstrong is silent.

The morning of Saturday, 4 March, found True penniless. He had Mrs Armstrong's cheque, of course, and had forged an endorsement, but had had no opportunity of cashing it. This he now expected to be able to do when he met the Sachs for lunch, for, as it conveniently happened, Armstrong was not to be one of the party. About one o'clock he met the Sachs at the Strand Corner House. After lunch, Mrs Armstrong's cheque was produced. Could Sach oblige him by cashing it, as, this being Saturday, all the banks were shut? Sach was sorry he could not, but ultimately Mrs Sach managed to cash it at a shop where she was known. Thereupon True paid back the £1 he had borrowed from Sach the previous Wednesday, and the party, driven by Mazzola (who seems to have had a remarkable capacity for giving credit), went off to Richmond to spend a pleasant afternoon. They had tea at the Castle Hotel, where, oddly enough, there happened to be a third person with whom True was at enmity. This, in fact, was an inoffensive stranger who was having tea at a neighbouring table: but True assured the Sachs that he knew the fellow well, having been to school with him at Bedford, that he was a bad man, that he was not treating a girl right, that the girl's name was Olive and she lived in Bedford, and that he (True) had remonstrated with the man about his conduct, though apparently not to the extent of shooting him. Later, after this man had gone, True was called to the telephone – evidently he had asked for a call to be put through – and returned, telling his friends that he had been speaking to 'Olive' at Bedford, and also that he had met the man outside again and had spoken to him about his conduct towards the girl. The Sachs could not take this story very seriously: for they had noticed that although True and the supposed miscreant had been in full view of each other, no sign of recognition had passed between them.

The significance of the Richmond incident is this: that True had now told Mr and Mrs Sach (1) that there was someone in a basement flat in Fulham from whom he wanted money (2) that he meant to get that money even if he had to murder someone (3) that he had been trying, so far without success, to arrange an appointment with the person, but expected to have the critical interview in the basement flat in Fulham on Sunday night (4) that Monday's papers would certainly announce that murder had been committed in that flat (5) that he knew a girl called Olive, who was being persecuted by a man (6) that he had just been telephoning to 'Olive'.

The party returned to London about nine o'clock. True bade good night to his friends, and ordered Mazzola to drive to the

Ring, Blackfriars Road. There he could not help meeting the referee, who naturally took the opportunity of reminding him of his I.O.U. given him on 17 February. True had an excuse ready. He had been flying to Bristol, Paris and Marseilles with films of Princess Mary's wedding, and would pay up as soon as he collected the money that was waiting for him at Croydon aerodrome.

Mr Broadribb, the referee, had to be satisfied with this. True did not wait long at the Ring, but before he left he made a new acquaintance – a Mr Bishop, who managed bachelor suites in Half Moon Street. He insisted on driving Mr Bishop home. *En route* they stopped for some refreshment at the Strand Corner House, where True made some inquiries about the rent of apartments which Mr Bishop was very glad to answer. By the time Mr Bishop was set down at Half Moon Street, it was eleven o'clock. For the third night in succession – but this time alone – True was driven to Fulham. He got out, as before, at the corner of Finborough Road, saying to Mazzola that he had *urgent business* to see to. As before, he returned, grumbling that he could not find anybody, and drove away.

These midnight visits to Fulham were not True's only attempts to see Olive Young. Throughout that week he had been pestering her with telephone calls trying to arrange a meeting, which the girl steadily refused. Rebuffed in his own name, True tried to pass himself off as Armstrong, but Olive Young recognized the voice and demanded that Armstrong himself should speak. True then tried to make her believe that it was Armstrong's chauffeur that was speaking, but she knew who it was and rang off. The ruse had failed, but the fact that it had been attempted filled Olive Young with alarm. She determined to avoid him more sedulously than ever. Up to Sunday, 5 March, she had been quite successful. Mrs Dent was with her all the afternoon of that day, and in the evening the two women went out to dine together, choosing a place where True was not likely to find them. About half past ten, somewhat reluctantly, Olive Young parted with her friend at Piccadilly Circus Tube Station. She booked to Earls Court, whence she had a few minutes' walk to Finborough Road. The whole journey would take about half an hour, so she must have been in her flat at about a few minutes to eleven.

Meanwhile True had been up the river, Armstrong having the use of a bungalow at Reading. The pair had spent an idle day, having done nothing more energetic than firing Very lights from a pistol. The attentive Mazzola drove them back to town and late in the evening there was yet another visit to Fulham, arriving about ten minutes past eleven. Everything happened precisely as before. Once more True's friends were not at home. The next thing was to take Armstrong home. On the way Armstrong noticed a tall man running along Fulham Road, and so apparently did True, but no remark was made on it at the time. Armstrong having been got rid of, True once more ordered Mazzola to drive to Fulham. This time there was no stopping at the corner of Finborough Road. The car was to turn into the road and stop at No. 13A. There True got out and descended to the basement flat. Presently True returned. He would not want the car again that night, he said, but Mazzola was to come back for him at Finborough Road at 11 a.m. on the Monday morning. The chauffeur took his orders and departed. True spent the night with Gertrude Yates.

The question naturally arises here why, at the second visit on this fatal night, True did not, as before, stop at the corner of the road, but drove right up to his victim's door. The inference is that on the previous occasions he had merely been reconnoitring and that on his last visit he had ascertained that the opportunity to strike had arrived. A fact elicited at True's trial cleared the whole matter up. Olive Young was in the habit of leaving a light burning in the entrance passage of her flat till she came home, when she used to turn it out; and this light would be visible to anyone who looked down from street level through the fanlight. It is fairly certain that when True drove to the corner of Finborough Road on Thursday, Friday, and Saturday, he ran up to No. 13A, and on each occasion found the light burning in the passage, which meant that his intended victim had not come home yet. But on Sunday night Olive Young arrived home just about eleven o'clock, so that when True peered down from the street a few minutes later he had the satisfaction of observing that the light was out. That was enough. All that remained was to get rid of Armstrong, and then return with all speed to Fulham. There was always the chance, of course, that he might be refused admittance, but that was unlikely. Girls of Olive Young's class cannot afford to make scenes at midnight and appeal to the police on the slightest provocation – particularly when their landlady is not *supposed* to know what their calling is. It is better to take a few risks. And so when Gertrude Yates found who was knocking at her door, she bowed to her fate. She let him in, and took her chance.

True's demeanour must have been fairly reassuring, for at seven o'clock on Monday morning Gertrude Yates was still peacefully drowsing in her bed, dimly conscious, perhaps, that her companion was up and about at the business of making early morning tea. This, of course, had to be done in the kitchen next door, and then True, rummaging about, found the very thing he wanted in the copper – a stout rolling-pin. He brought in the tea, and 'Olive' sat up sleepily and took her cup. True slipped round the other side of the bed . . .

She gave no trouble. The first blow of the rolling-pin felled her, sending her cup and saucer crashing to the floor, and four more were delivered in swift succession. She was as good as dead, but the murderer was thorough. A towel thrust deep into her gullet, and the girdle of her dressing-gown drawn tightly round her neck, finished the job.

True dragged the corpse into the bathroom and left it lying on the floor. That he should do that and then go to the trouble of arranging two pillows in the bed to look as if someone were asleep there, suggests the distorted cunning of a defective intelligence. Obviously it would have been far better to have tucked the body in the clothes. True's action cannot be ascribed to the confusion arising from haste. The murder was accomplished by half past seven and True well knew that the daily servant, Emily Steel, was not due to arrive before nine o'clock, and would probably be late. That would give him an hour and a half to lay hands on anything of value and clear out. The curious thing is that True, having rifled Gertrude's handbag, which contained £8, and taken the best of the jewellery he could find, chose to remain in the flat until long after Emily Steel's arrival. Steel, when she came in, noticed a man's coat in the sitting-room, but naturally attached no special importance to the fact. She prepared and ate her own breakfast, and then proceeded to tidy up the sitting-room. Suddenly a man appeared from the direction of the bedroom. That did not surprise her. She had seen him before. Major True was very affable. 'Don't disturb Miss Young,' he said, 'we were late last night, and she is in deep sleep. I'll send a car round for her at midday.' Steel was most obsequious to her mistress's friend, and helped him on with his coat, whereupon he tipped her half a crown, reminding her that he owed her something for getting him a taxi on the last occasion that he had been at the flat. And so he left – two hours after murdering Gertrude Yates. Emily Steel saw him hail a cab at the corner of Finborough Road. A few minutes later she discovered what had happened.

If the slaying of a human being was of small account, there would be something almost ludicrous about True's assurance that his crime could not be brought home to him. For the past fortnight he had been boasting to casual acquaintances that he was going to murder someone, even naming the time and place, though not his victim, which doubtless he regarded as a masterly stroke of cunning, and at the same time he was convinced he could cover up his tracks with the utmost ease. And so it may be imagined that as he was borne along the Fulham Road he reflected with complacency on his morning's work. Olive Young was dead. He had eight pounds odd of her money and the best of her jewellery in his pocket. A few precautions, obvious to a man of his superior intelligence, would completely baffle the police. Meanwhile he must countermand his order to Mazzola to bring the car to Finborough Road; so at the first post office in Fulham Road he stopped the taxi and telephoned to the garage, ordering the car to call first for Mr Armstrong and then go on to the Strand Corner House. True was next taken with all speed to Coventry Street, Piccadilly Circus, where he stopped at a men's outfitters, telling the taxi to wait. He had dealt at the shop before and was known by the assistants. The first thing he wanted this morning was a *hat* – which, as he did not ordinarily wear one, he no doubt regarded as an astute disguise. Next he unbuttoned his overcoat and drew the assistant's attention to some fresh blood-stains. These, he explained, were the result of a flying accident he had just had, and he thought he really must have a new suit at once. He was passed on to the ready-made suits department, where, after trying on several, he found a lounge suit to his taste. 'Not a bad reach-me-down,' he remarked pleasantly. The shop had always known Major True as a pleasant and jocular gentleman, and this morning he was as affable as ever. While the assistant was clearing out the pockets of the discarded suit preparatory to making a parcel of it, he came upon a jewel-case. True at once opened it, and displayed the rings – 'little mementoes' he had just picked up in France, he said. A collar and tie completed True's purchases, which ate up £7 of Olive's cash. His next visit was to a barber in Wardour Street, where he discharged the cab. At the barber's he had a shave and brush up, put on his new collar and tie, and deposited the parcel of bloodstained clothes, saying he would return for it in a few minutes. There was one more thing he must do before he met his friend – pawn the stolen jewellery. He went to a neighbouring pawnbrokers, redeemed the watch and cigarette-case he had pledged on the Saturday, and then offered Olive Young's rings. He wanted £70 for the pair, but had to be content with £25. Of course, he did not return to the barber's for his parcel, but hurried off to the rendezvous at Charing Cross.

Mazzola was waiting with the car when True arrived at the Corner House. He noted with some surprise (having regard to the circumstances in which they had parted overnight) that he was wearing a new suit *and a new hat*. True greeted him with his usual affability, and remarked casually that he was sorry he had dismissed him the night before as his stay in the flat had lasted only twenty minutes. A man and a woman, he said, had got into a violent quarrel, so he thought it best to leave them to fight it out. Presently he told the same story to Armstrong. Before he left the Corner House he encountered Sach, who over the weekend had been worrying a good deal about the cheque transaction to which he had been a party on the Saturday. He did not imagine for a minute that it had been stolen, but for all he knew it might be a 'stumer'. He explained his fear to True, who at once handed over £7 in notes in case the cheque should be returned. Sach departed much relieved, and True and Armstrong drove off to Hounslow and thence to Feltham, to see some internal-combustion engines in which they were interested. About four o'clock the party were at Croydon, where they had tea and True bought a newspaper. He first asked for the *Sportsman*, and failing to get that asked for the *Star*. Prominent, with big headings, on the front page, was the first news of the murder of Olive Young. True glanced at the paper and then tossed it aside with the remark, 'Nothing of interest.' The next stop was Richmond, where True must needs buy a new shirt, which he put on there and then. After that they returned to London, dined and drove to the Hammersmith Palace of Varieties, arriving about nine o'clock in time for the 'second house'. Mazzola was sent back to his garage with instructions to return for them at the end of the show.

Meantime the police had been busy. They had been apprised of the murder of Gertrude Yates within half an hour of True's departure from Finborough Road, and they had not the slightest difficulty in identifying the criminal and picking up his tracks. Some significant information was given to them by ex-Inspector Stockley. Thus it was that when Mazzola returned to his garage in Knightsbridge, he found two Scotland Yard men waiting for him, who, learning where he had left True, ordered him to take them at once to the Hammersmith Palace. Their task was an anxious one. A crowded theatre is an awkward place to make an arrest, particularly when your man is, by all accounts, a homicidal lunatic and carries a loaded revolver. The police were lucky, however, for True and his friend, though they had begun by sitting in the stalls, had exchanged to a box, which enabled the arrest to be made with little delay or disturbance. No one on the stage or in the auditorium had any inkling of the thrilling extra turn that had been going on in one of the boxes. True went quietly.

On being charged True denied all knowledge of the crime. Subsequently he made a statement about seeing, on the Sunday night, a tall man running along the Finborough Road. In due course he was committed for trial, and on 1 May he was brought up at the Central Criminal Court before Mr Justice M'Cardie.

Prima facie True's crime was prompted by a perfectly sane motive. He needed money. Gertrude Yates had cash and valuables. He murdered her, took everything that was worth taking, lost no time in turning the jewellery into cash, and used every means that suggested itself in his mind to escape detection. That was the sum and substance of the case against True; and the prosecution submitted that it not only did not support, but negatived the suggestion that the murderer of Gertrude Yates was a madman. The view was calculated to appeal to the man in the street, who is also the man in the jury-box, as the obvious common sense of the matter, with the result that True was convicted. Nevertheless it was based on fallacy, viz., that an act that might well be the act of a sane man cannot be the act of an insane one.

Before proceeding to the medical evidence on True's state of mind, let us consider the net result of the facts related above. At the end of 1921 and the beginning of 1922 he had a prolonged fit of apathy and silent brooding. Then, on the vague pretext of business at Bedford, he contrived to leave home and began to lead a vagrant life in the West End of London. He cut himself off from the family and became markedly hostile to his wife. His casual associates in London regarded him as abnormal. Some thought him dangerous, others merely fatuous, but none found him taciturn or apathetic. On the contrary, he was invariably vivacious – the inference being that he was getting plentiful supplies of morphia. Presently he began to commit frauds and thefts. He bought a pistol and ammunition, and talked freely about committing a murder, mentioning first one, then two, and finally three men, with whom he was at deadly enmity, one of them being a man who had an assumed name of Ronald True.

In taking True into custody the police realized that they were dealing with a man who was undoubtedly deranged and probably insane in the full sense of the term. He was at once sent to the prison hospital at Brixton, and practically from the date of his arrest until he was placed in the dock at the Central Criminal Court he was kept under close observation by the medical officer, Dr East, and his assistant Dr Young. It was characteristic that he was distinctly popular with his fellow prisoners, being, as always, affable and jocular – but a constant source of trouble and anxiety to the warders and doctors. He slept little, was more or less in an excited state, and, in spite of his jocularity, was easily provoked into violence. One of his first acts was to commit a sudden assault on a fellow prisoner, whom he accused, without any justification, of stealing his food. This incident convinced Dr East that sedatives were imperative, for there was every indication that if excitement and insomnia were not abated, another murder would be laid to True's account. It is important to observe that the sleeplessness and excitement were not in any way connected with remorse for his crime, or anxiety about his situation; on the contrary, he appeared to be very well pleased with himself, and, while always denying that he had anything to do with the death of Gertrude Yates, he took obvious pleasure in being the central figure of a *cause célèbre*. He was quite facetious about it. One day, shortly after his admission to hospital, he managed to escape to another ward where he knew there was another prisoner charged with murder. This was Henry Jacoby, afterwards hanged for the murder of Lady White. 'Here's another for our murderers' club,' he shouted. 'We only accept those who kill outright' – the same silly pleasantry that he had often exchanged with his friend Armstrong. He was inordinately boastful, incapable of speaking the truth, even when no conceivable purpose could be served by lying, and appeared to have the delusion that people were going about impersonating him. After prolonged observation, Dr East formed the opinion that True was in a state of congenital mental disorder, aggravated by the morphia habit, and that he was certifiably insane. Dr Young, the assistant prison doctor, came to the same conclusion. The two doctors reported accordingly.

These opinions were confirmed and in some respects amplified by the eminent alienists, Dr Percy Smith and Dr Stoddart, who examined True at the request of his relatives. Their examinations, of course, were separate and independent. Their conclusions were practically identical. To both True boasted about his capacities and achievements, and he seemed elated rather than depressed by his position. There were some signs of confusion and loss of memory. He had well-defined delusions of persecution and the curious stories that he had told Mrs Wilson and Mr Sach were repeated to Drs Smith and Stoddart in considerably greater detail. He carried a revolver, he said, because he had enemies who would shoot him if they got the chance. Among them was a professional gambler, whose name he gave variously as Eaton, Nicholls, or Hobson, who had once 'held him up with a gun' because he (True) had pressed him to pay a large sum of money he owed him. Then there was 'the other Ronald True', quite a different person who was also 'after him with a gun', though why he should persecute him True could not say; all he knew was that people had told him so. Once at Murray's he had caught a glimpse of the 'other' and had tried to draw a pistol, but the 'other' had slipped out before he could do so. But this Ronald True was not to be confused with the other Ronald *Trew* who had been an officer in the army. According to Dr Stoddart, True was vague about the identity of his double. He complained that he had been impersonated and persecuted in New York, Brighton, and London, and seemed to think that he had several persecutors who all used his name, but he admitted the possibility that there might only be one who went from place to place after him.

Such being the medical reports it was obvious that True's defence would be that when the crime was committed he was insane and not responsible for his actions.

Now when a special defence of insanity is put up, it is the right of the prosecution to call evidence in rebuttal. As a rule this presents little difficulty. There are few points on which doctors will not differ to some degree, and none that is so provocative of disagreement as the question of a person's soundness of mind. Further, in considering the policy to be adopted at the trial the prosecution have regard to the reports of the prison doctor, and if they decide to press for a conviction it usually means that they can rely on the prison doctor to support them in the witness-box. When this happens the expert testimony given for the prosecution has a clear advantage in weight over the expert testimony for the defence; for the latter is called *ad hoc*, whereas the former is based on observations which may be faulty but are certainly disinterested. But in the case of True the reports of the two medical officers of Brixton prison were adverse to the prosecution. Dr East, a man of exceptional experience in the examination of criminal lunatics, and his assistant, Dr Young, were emphatic in their opinion that True was insane, and they concurred in every material respect with the two distinguished alienists who examined the prisoner on behalf of the defence. But, notwithstanding their serious tactical disadvantage, the prosecution decided to make every effort to secure a conviction. They had True examined by a fifth medical man, Dr Cole of St Mary's Hospital, an alienist of high standing. Dr Cole reported that his own examination did not disclose anything that would justify him in declaring True insane, but his opinion was given subject to a number of important reservations.

Sir Richard Muir, senior Treasury counsel at the Central Criminal Court, who was in charge of the prosecution, was in a dilemma. There was a heavy array of medical evidence against him to which he was unable to raise any effective opposition. If he put Dr Cole in the box, Dr Cole's evidence under cross-examination might recoil upon the prosecution with deadly effect. If he did not put Dr Cole into the box the defence would not fail to enlarge upon the fact that the prosecution with all their resources were unable to produce a single doctor who would swear that True was a sane and responsible man. Sir Richard decided that the latter course was the less dangerous. He did not call Dr Cole, and relied for achieving his purpose upon cross-examination and the *Rules in M'Naughton's Case*. The event proved the wisdom of his choice. As Dr Cole was never called his report was never made public. There is reason to believe that he regarded True as mentally deficient rather than insane, inasmuch as that was as far as his own observation would take him, but he was not prepared to traverse the conclusions reached by his professional brethren as the result of their own observations.

To appreciate the meaning of this it is necessary to realize that, for the purpose of bringing down a defence of insanity, the English criminal law thoughtfully provides the prosecution with a double-barrelled gun. First, they can say that the prisoner is not in fact insane. Alternatively, and without prejudice to the first contention, they can submit that, even if the prisoner is in fact insane, his insanity is not of such a nature as to free him from responsibility according to the canons of English law. The two barrels are discharged almost simultaneously, to the great confusion of the jury, who are further confounded by the practice adopted by bar and bench of using the term 'insanity' now in the sense of 'mental derangement', and now in the sense of 'irresponsibility by reason of mental derangement'. It was to this confusion of the mind of the jury, and still more in the mind of the public, that most of the heated controversy over True's case was due. Consequently, it is worth while to consider for a moment a problem on which medical men and jurists have expended much time and breath, ink and paper, but which may be stated with comparative brevity once its true nature has been grasped.

When the law decrees punishment it passes a moral judgment. It says that the culprit is 'responsible', that is righteously punishable, for what he has done. It is not the act *per se* that involves the punishment but the wicked state of mind of which the act is the evidence and fulfilment. *Actus non facit reum nisi mens sit rea.* What then constitutes *mens rea*, or wicked mind? Roughly speaking, we may say that if a person knows what he is doing, he is righteously punishable for his act. But that is not enough. The culprit may be fully conscious of the physical nature and moral quality of his act, but he may have done it against his will, having been placed under some severe external compulsion, such as torture and threats of death, that no man of ordinary courage could be expected to withstand. In such a case, obviously there is no wicked mind, for, although he knew what he was doing his mind did not accompany his act. But even when both volition and knowledge are present, the law will still sometimes excuse on the ground of *imperfection of understanding*. Thus a child of six may well be aware that stealing is wrong, but if he does steal the law will not punish him, holding that, despite all appearance of knowledge and intention, a person of such tender years cannot have enough 'understanding' to have a guilty mind. In the case of children under seven the law's denial of criminal capacity is absolute; and even older children, up to the age of fourteen, will be presumed incapable of *mens rea* until the contrary be proved.

We have thus three cases in which the moral sense of the community would not approve of punishment being inflicted on a wrongdoer – (1) when the person did not know what he was doing, as in the case of somnambulism (2) where the person knew what he was doing, but was overborne by *force majeure* and (3) where the person suffered from such a defect of 'understanding' that it would be unreasonable to impute to him a guilty intention, even although it might be said that, in a sense, he knew and intended what he was doing. If the third category were logically applied, the cause of the defect of understanding would be immaterial. It would apply equally to the child, whose defect is due to immaturity, and to the lunatic, whose defect is due to disease. In point of fact, however, the defect of understanding operates as an excuse only in the case of a child. The law, embodying the traditional psychology of action, which assumes that knowledge necessarily implies control, will not allow it in the case of a lunatic. Indeed, it is doubtful if it would be allowed in the case of a child but for two considerations – first, the fact that everybody knows from immediate experience that the traditional psychology breaks down in the case of a child, and, second, that common humanity, as well as common sense, revolts at the idea of inflicting criminal punishment on a child of tender years – a sentiment which is by no means extended to the adult unsound mind. Consequently, the law will not entertain insanity as an excuse, except where the criminal act comes within the first category; that is to say the accused must show that his alienation of mind was such that he did not know what he was doing, or, if he did know what he was doing, did not know that it was wrong. It is assumed that, if a man does wrong, knowing it to be wrong, he could have refrained from doing it, and that in not refraining he elected to take the consequences. To think otherwise, it is conceived, would be fatal to the administration of the criminal law. Such is the legal doctrine laid down in what are conveniently, but not quite accurately, known as the *Rules in M'Naughton's Case*. These were answers given by the common law Judges to a series of questions submitted to them by the House of Lords in the following circumstances:

In the year 1843 much excitement and even alarm was caused by the death, at the hand of an assassin, of Mr Drummond, private secretary to the Prime Minister, Sir Robert Peel. The murderer was one Daniel M'Naughton, a young Glasgow tradesman of respectable antecedents. The rulers of the country were at that time in a bad state of nerves owing to the prevalence of political agitation, and, when it appeared from M'Naughton's statements that he was under the impression that his victim was the Prime Minister himself, the murder was interpreted as the act of a dangerous revolutionary —and certain colour was lent to the belief by the circumstance that M'Naughton came from Glasgow, which was then, as now, regarded as a revolutionary plague-spot. But when the wretched M'Naughton was brought to trial at the Central Criminal Court, it abundantly appeared that he was far advanced in what is now known as paranoia, a form of insanity, progressive and apparently incurable, and characterized by systematized delusions of persecution. The only ground for giving a political complexion to his crime was his expressed belief that his insatiable and invisible persecutors were the 'Tories' and 'Jesuits'. The evidence was so plain that the presiding Judges (Tindal, C. J., Williams, J. and Coleridge, J.) stopped the case and directed the jury to find a verdict of *Not guilty on the ground on insanity*, which being done, M'Naughton was ordered to be detained in Bethlem Hospital.

The result of the trial created even more indignation in high quarters than the crime itself. Queen Victoria herself was particularly incensed. Her correspondence with her Ministers on the subject makes curious reading. There is an excuse for the young

Queen in that she herself shortly before had been the subject of a feeble attempt by the demented youth Oxford, who, like M'Naughton, was acquitted. The House of Lords, on the initiative of Brougham, gravely debated the question, and it was decided to ask Her Majesty's Judges to declare to what extent the law of England allowed unsoundness of mind as an answer to a criminal charge. To that end their lordships formulated a series of hypothetical questions, to which the Judges (Maule, J., dissenting) gave the answers that have come to be known as the *Rules in M'Naughton's Case*. The substance of the Rules has already been indicated, viz., that insanity is no answer to a criminal charge, unless it amounts to such a disorder of mind that the accused did not know the nature and quality of his act, or, if he did know the nature and quality of his act, did not know that it was wrong.

Whether this was an accurate statement of the law as previously administered may well be doubted. Hitherto insanity had been a comparatively rare defence, being put forward only in cases where it was impossible to ignore it; and the law's attitude had never been clearly defined. Everything depended on the prepossessions of the Judge who happened to try the particular case. Some Judges took the 'wild beast' view, viz., that insanity was no excuse unless it amounted to a fury in which the accused had no appreciation of objective fact. Others were content to direct that if a man were manifestly out of his senses at the time of the act, he should be held guiltless. The latter was the more humane and sensible view, though in practice it was very sparingly applied. Judges and juries regarded the defence of insanity with great suspicion, believing – with some justification in an age in which the phenomena of mental disorder had never been scientifically studied – that unsoundness of mind could easily be simulated. This belief is still widely entertained (as the newspaper correspondence upon True's case showed) though nowadays, as a matter of fact, of all forms of malingering feigned insanity is the easiest to detect. On the whole, it may be fairly said that prior to 1843 the question of an insane prisoner's responsibility was left to the jury as an issue of pure fact to be determined by evidence alone and not with reference to any special rules of law.

The answers of the Judges changed all that. Not that that was their intention. Far from it. All the Judges had in mind was to state the conditions which, in their mind, would justify a jury in inferring irresponsibility. Following the psychological conceptions that were then prevalent, they doubtless conceived that where these conditions were not satisfied, there could be no evidence on which a jury could find that a prisoner was not responsible for his actions. At the same time, the answers, being limited to the terms of the questions, could not properly claim to be exhaustive.

The answers served an immediate purpose of some value. Their tenor was sufficiently reassuring to put an end to the monstrous demand – seriously advanced by respectable and eminent persons – that insanity should in no circumstances be accepted as an excuse for crime, and that lunatics should be punished in the same manner as sane offenders. No more was heard of that proposal. But the ultimate effect of the answers was unfortunate. As an eminent Judge once remarked, they are so drafted that on strict interpretation hardly anyone is ever mad enough to come within them, yet the three Judges who concurred in directing M'Naughton's acquittal also concurred in the answers, though certainly Daniel M'Naughton would not have come within them. The inference is obvious. The Judges never intended that their answers should be elevated to the status of rules of law, exhaustive and requiring strict interpretation. That, however, is what they have become. Mr Justice Maule, who dissented from his brethren, foresaw the danger. He returned his answers more or less under protest, pointing out that the principles of English Law were to be extracted from the judicial decisions upon specific cases after argument by counsel, and that answers given to abstract questions without aid of argument might prove embarrassing to the administration of justice.

The embarrassment exists, but thanks to the common sense which, on the whole, animates the administration of English Law, it is less serious than one might suppose. Where the prisoner is a manifest lunatic, he is usually dealt with upon arraignment, being found unfit to plead to the indictment, whereby the necessity for a nice inquiry into his knowledge of the nature and quality of his act is avoided. Where the prisoner is a certified lunatic, who has killed or maimed an asylum attendant, Judges have sometimes refused to proceed to trial, in spite of the fact that as a rule the M'Naughton test would require such a culprit to be held fully responsible for his act. Difficulty arises only when the prisoner is allowed to plead and issue is joined on the special defence that he is insane or was insane at the date of the act *and was not responsible*. It is important to remember these last words. They mean that proof of mental disorder, though essential, is not enough to establish the defence. The mental disorder must be of such a kind as to satisfy the conditions laid down by the M'Naughton Rules. Similarly, the prosecution, in tendering rebutting evidence, is not required to prove that the man is sane, but only that his mental condition satisfies the test of legal responsibility. In practice, however, the prosecution prefers to fight the case on the broad question of fact, viz., the existence of grave mental disorder, for no jury will convict a man whom they believe to be mad simply in obedience to a lawyer's canon. As a rule the accused's mental condition is sufficiently obscure to allow this course to be taken. If the defence submits medical and other evidence of insanity, the prosecution may, in like manner, produce rebutting evidence; and in directing the jury the Judge will invoke the M'Naughton Rules as a ready means of resolving conflict.

To this device, however, there are serious objections. In the first place, it pretends to distinguish, by an infallible rule, those lunatics who are morally guilty from those who are not – a claim that implies an extraordinary, indeed superhuman, knowledge. Secondly, it is extremely confusing to the plain citizens in the jury-box, who hold the sensible view that if a man is mad he cannot be responsible, and conversely that if he is responsible he cannot be mad. Consequently, when the Judge tells them that the medical evidence is insufficient to prove that the prisoner was not responsible for his act, they take it as a direction that he is not mad, and that the doctors called for the defence have merely been putting up an academic case on behalf of a rascal, who for all practical purposes is as sane as anybody in Court.

True's was not the ordinary case, however. There was no conflict to be resolved. The medical evidence as to his insanity was uncontroverted, cogent, and conclusive. But Sir Richard Muir had no difficulty in showing that it did not satisfy the conditions prescribed by the M'Naughton Rules. In cross-examination, argument, and speech he pressed his point with the utmost skill and pertinacity. Had the temper of the jury been different, this insistence would have been useless. But as the case proceeded it became clear that the facts that to the medical men were so eloquent of profound mental disorder, would convey to the jury only the picture of a depraved callous monster, who, being in need of ready cash, thought to raise a few pounds by murdering and robbing a defenceless woman.

Sir Henry Curtis Bennet fully realized all this. He was aware of the fact that, although he had all the evidence on his side, it would be insufficient to counterbalance the jury's will to convict unless it were supplemented by a strong direction from the Judge. Accordingly his main effort was to get such a direction. The difficulty was the M'Naughton Rules. In a long legal argument Sir Henry submitted that the Rules ought not to be strictly interpreted inasmuch as they had been considerably relaxed by judicial interpretation, particularly during recent years. Mr Justice M'Cardie, who always enjoyed debating a novel point, entered sympathetically into the argument, but the desired direction was not forthcoming. And so in the end Sir Richard's argument prevailed, not so much by its logic as by its congruence with the jury's reluctance to believe that they had to deal with a lunatic. The doctors might say he was mad, but the jury did not believe them. On 5 May, after a trial lasting five days, True was found *Guilty* and sentenced to death.

That there should be an appeal against the verdict was inevitable in view of the strength and unanimity of the medical evidence. On 25 May the case came before the Court of Criminal Appeal, consisting of the Lord Chief Justice (Lord Hewart), Mr Justice Greer, and Mr Justice Acton. The ground of the appeal was that Mr Justice M'Cardie had misdirected the jury on the law as to the criminal responsibility of the insane. Sir Henry Curtis Bennett argued, as he had argued at the trial, that the Rules of the

M'Naughton Case, if not superseded, had at least been considerably modified by eighty years of judicial interpretation; and he submitted that these modifications had not been given sufficient weight in the Judge's summing up. Regarded from a strictly legal standpoint, his case was hopeless from the beginning. There was no reported case of the M'Naughton Rules being used to test if an *admitted* lunatic was responsible for his act. This seems strange, seeing that that was the precise point to which the M'Naughton Rules were directed; but it is so. In practice, we have seen, the Rules have only been applied where the prosecution was prepared to contest the allegation of insanity on its merits, and where there was at least *some* evidence on which a jury could find that the accused was not insane in any reasonable sense of the word. They have been maintained, not for their ostensible purpose of determining the responsibility of an insane person, but as a handy rule of thumb whereby in view of a conflict of evidence, a jury could decide whether a person was in fact insane. The effect of this has been that, in so far as the Rules have received judicial discussion, it has always been in circumstances favourable to their maintenance. It is true that there are many judicial *dicta* that are not in harmony with the Rules; but, as Sir Richard Muir, replying to Sir Henry Curtis Bennett, was able to show, they are mostly *obiter*, and in any case have never received countenance from the Court of Criminal Appeal. True's appeal, then, had little support from the authorities. Its substantial ground was that the Court of Criminal Appeal, recoiling from the proposition that an undisputed lunatic was responsible for his acts, might be induced to review the M'Naughton Rules in the light of modern knowledge and to re-state the English Law as to the criminal responsibility of the insane.

Such a hope, however, implied a more comprehensive view of its function than the Court of Criminal Appeal has ever been disposed to take. Rightly or wrongly that Court has always been timorous of judicial adventures; and in the case of a murderer's appeal on the ground of insanity its attitude has always been defined with reference to two questions: (1) What is the law as laid down in the M'Naughton Rules? and (2) Was there evidence on which the jury could return a verdict in accordance with the law? In True's case the answers to these questions were necessarily adverse, inasmuch as, despite the unanimous opinion of the doctors that he was insane, there was substantial evidence that he knew what he was doing and that it was wrong. The Court accordingly, without the least hesitation, dismissed the appeal, and so far from discussing and modifying the *Rules in M'Naughton's Case*, explicitly reaffirmed them in their entirety as the law of the land. As to the objection that it was contrary to the public conscience that a lunatic should suffer the death penalty, the Court accepted the view presented by counsel for the Crown that it was unnecessary to consider that point, as it could be dealt with more conveniently by the Home Secretary. In taking this course the Court merely followed its own precedents, but it is a question whether the circumstances of True's case did not call for a departure from a practice the soundness of which is not free from doubt. According to the ancient maxim, it is the duty of a Court to prefer a wide to a narrow view of its jurisdiction. *A fortiori*, when its jurisdiction is undoubted, it ought not to refrain from dealing with a difficult general problem simply because substantial justice in the particular case can be secured through executive action. Such an attitude is open to the objection not only of impairing the authority of the Court, but of thrusting upon the Executive a responsibility that it ought not to be called upon to bear.

It will be convenient at this point to sum up the position as it now stood. At True's trial there was evidence, uncontroverted and incontrovertible, that he was insane; nevertheless the jury found him *Guilty*. They were justified in doing so by the fact that by the law of England insanity does not necessarily imply irresponsibility. But even if the law had been different, and the jury had been directed that insanity *simpliciter* was a good defence, it is tolerably certain that their verdict would still have been Guilty. In that case, of course, the Court of Criminal Appeal would probably have been obliged to set the verdict aside. But, the law being as it is, the Court of Criminal Appeal saw no ground for interfering with the jury's findings, and turned over further action, if any, to the Secretary of

State. This brings us to the point at which True's case ceased to be merely an Old Bailey sensation and became the occasion of a furious gust of public passion that for the moment threatened to sweep the Home Secretary out of office and even compromised the existence of a ministry that could ill afford to take unpopular courses even in minor matters.

The Criminal Law of England contains a very notable anomaly. It lays down that even a lunatic may, in certain conditions, be held responsible for his act, but it also lays down that if the act be one that involves the judgment of death, judgment is not to be executed so long as he remains a lunatic. The reasons for the latter rule are variously given by the old writers. One says it is because a lunatic, by reason of his lunacy, might be unable to allege some valid bar to execution, and another is because it is against the conscience to execute judgment of death upon a person who is not in a condition to make his peace with God. These reasons are purely speculative, and in effect mean no more than that, for whatever reason, the public conscience recoils from the idea of punishing the insane with death. The rule is far older than the *Rules of the M'Naughton Case*—Coke speaks of it as being well settled law in his time—but no attempt has been made to define the kind or degree of insanity that entitles an insane person to its benefit. It is enough that he should be insane. The rule presents some curious results. Thus a man, who, being sane, commits a murder and is duly sentenced to death, must be respited if he becomes insane while awaiting execution. On the other hand an insane murderer whose insanity is not of the kind to satisfy the M'Naughton Rules, and who, while awaiting trial or execution, recovers his sanity will be hung for it. But such rapid changes of mental condition are uncommon. The murderer who is found to be mad while under sentence was in all probability mad at the time of his crime, and *vice versa*. It may very well happen, therefore, that the same facts that are unavailing to prevent a prisoner's condemnation will effectually prevent his punishment. In such a case the law in theory says to the culprit – 'Your insanity is no excuse for your crime. But we do not like the idea of hanging a madman, so we propose to wait till you recover your reason, in which case you will duly suffer the punishment that the law has justly decreed for the abominable thing you did when you were mad.' That is the theory. The practice is somewhat different. Once granted, a respite on the ground of insanity is never withdrawn. The public conscience once more cannot stomach the monstrous logic of the law. The death sentence is not commuted! it is simply not executed. Meantime the prisoner is removed to Broadmoor to remain there for the rest of his life precisely as if the defence of insanity had succeeded. It is important to understand these matters in view of their bearing upon the last and most notorious phase of the True case.

As the evidence of True's crime was unfolded at the trial, it became obvious to every lawyer that followed it that so far as True was personally concerned it was a matter of indifference what verdict the jury chose to return, and that when the case for the defence had been closed an insurance company would have been justified in covering the ultimate risk of his neck at a nominal premium. Immediately after the trial, Mr Justice M'Cardie, as was his bounden duty, drew the Home Secretary's attention to the nature of the medical evidence that had been given, and as soon as True's appeal had been disposed of the Home Secretary took the action prescribed in such a case by Section 2 (4) of the Criminal Lunatics Acts, 1884. He appointed a commission of three medical men to examine True and report on his state of mind. The medical men were Sir Maurice Craig, lecturer on mental diseases at Guy's Hospital; Dr Dyer, medical member of the Prisons Commission; and Sir John Baker, formerly medical superintendent of Broadmoor. They saw the condemned man, and found what the medical men who gave evidence at the trial had found – an undoubted lunatic. In view of their unanimous report the Home Secretary had no option but to respite the execution and order True's removal to Broadmoor, and public intimation of the fact was given in the usual way.

A Home Secretary's lot is not a happy one. His duties are often disagreeable, and many discretions are vested in him of such a thankless nature that he counts himself lucky if he can exercise a majority of them without incurring odium. An error of judgment may entail unpopularity and even resignation, but that is all in a day's work. What he has the right to expect is that he shall not be blamed for simply obeying the law. Mr Secretary Shortt had no choice as to his course of action in the True case. None the less he had to face a tornado of execration from the Press and the public.

To understand the uproar that ensued upon the respite of True it must be remembered that only a day or so before True's respite was announced, Henry Jacoby, the youth whom True had encountered so facetiously in the Brixton Prison Hospital, had been allowed to go to the scaffold in spite of a strong recommendation to mercy by the jury that convicted him. The circumstances of Jacoby's crime were abominable – hardly less so than True's – but owing to his youth popular sentiment favoured a reprieve. Accordingly, when it appeared that Jacoby having died True was to live, the Metropolitan Press, from the highest to the lowest, fell into a paroxysm of fury. The Home Secretary's head on a charger was demanded in leading articles in which ignorance of the law was equalled, if not surpassed, by disregard of facts. The correspondence columns were flooded with angry protest. The miserable Jacoby was invested with a martyr's halo. He was more sinned against than sinning, but he was only a working man's son and he had killed a knight's widow and therefore had to hang; while a moral monster like True, who happened to be well-connected, and whose victim was only a poor outcast, was sent off to enjoy the amenities with which life at Broadmoor was supposed to be surrounded. Things that could only be hinted at in print were stated and believed in every suburban railway carriage and public-house. True was the illegitimate son of Lady 'This' or Lady 'That' – various names were mentioned with full assurance – who by the potent social influences she could muster had induced the Home Secretary to enter into a flagitious conspiracy with the doctors to save her son's neck. The very Constitution was declared to be in danger. What was the use of a jury saying a man was not insane if the Home Secretary could set aside their verdict? The Courts of Law had been flouted, and trial by jury was being superseded by trial by 'Harley Street'. Even distinguished lawyers moved by professional prejudice and the general outcry were inclined to think that there was something in this last alarm, and wrote letters to *The Times* about it. The pundits of psychological medicine retorted sharply, and the secular feud between the two professions broke out again over the M'Naughton Rules with unprecedented fury. Plenty of sparks flew, but there was not much illumination.

Of course, the Home Secretary was called upon to explain his action in the House of Commons. Members vied with each other in putting down questions on the 'True Scandal', and the general opinion was that Mr Shortt would be humiliated to the dust. He wasn't. He read the House a stiff but lucid lecture on the law of England with respect to insane criminals. When he rose the House was actively hostile. Before he had finished members began to think the least said about True the better, and when he sat down, with that quick generosity and shrewd appreciation of plain facts that characterize the House of Commons, they cheered him heartily. After that not much could be said. The popular Press, having committed itself deeply, had to make the best retreat it could think of. A continuance of the hue and cry against the Minister was impossible and there were some grumblings about the necessity of amending the law, and a half-hearted attempt was made to represent the medical profession as the real villains of the piece. It was suggested that they had a design to undermine the fabric of criminal justice by means of the pernicious doctrine that all criminals were insane. But Mr Shortt's statement had knocked the life out of the agitation, and within a few days the London public had found something else to think about.

The outburst of popular passion was ugly and discreditable, but it was excusable enough. Nobody realized or could be expected to realize the fantastic complexity of the English law as to the criminal lunatic. In the first place the issue decided by the Courts was misapprehended. It was thought that the substantial question of True's alleged insanity had been dealt with and that further inquiry had been precluded. It completely mystifies the plain man when he is told that the Criminal Courts are not concerned to find out whether a man is sane or insane, but only if he is 'responsible in

Law'. To this confusion another was presently added. By a false
analogy with the general exercise of the prerogative of mercy, it
was assumed that the Home Secretary had a discretion and that he
had gone out of his way to order an inquiry into True's mental
condition. Why had he not ordered an inquiry into Jacoby's case?
In fact, the Home Secretary has no discretion. If he has information
suggesting that a prisoner under sentence of death is insane, he is
obliged by the Criminal Lunatics Act, 1884, to order an inquiry. In
Jacoby's case he had no such information. On the contrary all the
information he had was all the other way. No suggestion that Jacoby
was insane had been put forward at the trial or at any other time.
But in True's case both the trial Judge and the Court of Criminal
Appeal had directed attention to the prisoner's mental condition,
and even if the Judges had been silent it would have been impossible
for the Home Secretary and his legal advisers to ignore the evidence
given at the trial, especially the evidence given by the prison doctors. That so far Mr Shortt had no choice the better informed of
critics had been willing to allow, but it was said that the Criminal
Lunatics Act did not require him to take any action on the doctors'
report. This contention, which was seriously urged, even by lawyers,
was based on a complete misunderstanding of the scope and purpose
of the statute. It is not the Criminal Lunatics Act, but the Common
Law, that ordains that an insane prisoner must be respited. All that
the statute does is to prescribe a procedure for ascertaining if a
prisoner is insane, and for dealing with him if he is so found. It in
no way cuts down the Common Law doctrine – indeed, it pre-
supposes it by making specially stringent provision for the examination of prisoners under sentence of death. The confusion was due to
the fact that the statute does not allow the Secretary of State a
discretion as to the removal of the prisoner to an establishment for
the insane; for, if the prisoner's sentence is due to expire at no
distant date and his condition permits, it may be more convenient
simply to keep him in the prison hospital; but obviously such a
course would be inappropriate in the case of a prisoner under
sentence of death. He must be removed.

Such is the history of True's case, which is unique in the clearness with which it displays the welter of paradox into which the English law has fallen in attempting to find a solution of the difficulty of the criminal lunatic. The difficulty is likely to become more acute, and the inadequacy of the English solution – if it can be so described – still more evident with every advance in our knowledge of mental disorders. The English law is defended on the ground that, for all its illogicality, it has worked well, and that in practice no substantial injustice is done. There is a good deal of truth in this though it is not the whole truth. As we have seen, the M'Naughton Rules have been maintained in being by the judicious conduct of the Crown in never pressing for a conviction on technical grounds where they are unable seriously to dispute that the prisoner is, in the ordinary sense of the word, insane. In True's case that sound rule was not observed. Sir Richard Muir, who doubtless had his reasons, evidently thought it important that the principle that a lunatic may be responsible to the criminal law should be affirmed even if it was barren of practical consequences. He had his way, with what result we have seen.

Ronald True remained for the rest of his life in Broadmoor, where he took an active part in the organization and running of social and sporting events. He died in 1951.

Herbert Rowse Armstrong
1922

FILSON YOUNG

THE little town of Hay in Brecon lies pleasantly just over the Welsh border (its railway station is in England) along the right bank of the River Wye, surrounded in the near distance by such wild hills as Hay Bluff, Lord Hereford's Knob, and the Brecon Beacons. It is a sunny, quaint little place, with irregular, old-fashioned houses and a broad High Street pleasantly lending itself to gossip and the observation of other people's affairs; and behind its quiet gardens, with an endless ripple and chime, runs the river in broad and shining reaches.

The legal business of the town and of the farmers in the neighbouring countryside was, in the year 1906, when this story opens, conducted by two firms of solicitors (both of old standing), whose offices faced one another across the main street. The head of one firm was Mr Cheese, and of the other Mr Griffiths. In 1906 came Mr Herbert Rowse Armstrong as managing clerk to Mr Cheese. He was thirty-seven years of age, but had been admitted a solicitor in 1895, and had been in partnership and practising on his own account for over two years in Newton Abbot, his native town, as well as in Liverpool. Although of humble origin, he had been carefully educated by two maiden aunts, who, at some sacrifice, had enabled him to attend the University of Cambridge, where he graduated M.A. He had worked hard in Newton Abbot and in Liverpool, and had saved, or got, enough money to put capital into Mr Cheese's business and to become a partner very soon after his arrival in Hay. And very soon after that Mr Cheese and his wife both died, leaving Armstrong in sole possession of the business. A year later Armstrong married a Miss Katherine Mary Friend, and in 1907 brought her to live in a little house in the delightful coombe called Cusop Dingle, within half a mile of Hay, where many of the inhabitants have villas. Three years later he moved to a larger house a few hundred yards away called 'Mayfield' – a house with a fairly large garden. During these years the three children of this marriage were born. In it they all lived until Mrs Armstrong died, and was carried from it to Cusop Churchyard in February 1921; and until Armstrong was arrested on the last day of the same year.

The war came and brought its changes to the lives of the people in Hay, as elsewhere. Armstrong had been a Volunteer, and had joined the Territorial branch of the Royal Engineers; and when the war came he went away and served in various parts of England. I believe he did not see any actual fighting, being chiefly engaged in depot work, where his experience as a solicitor would prove useful, and where he was still able to exercise some control over his own business. Mr Griffiths was not so fortunate as his brother solicitor. He was getting on in years and was failing in health, and his son, who had passed his final law examination, but had not yet been admitted as a solicitor, was called away to the front. In these circumstances it became necessary for Mr Griffiths to take a partner, and Mr Oswald Norman Martin, who had served and been in-valided out of the Army, came to join him. Mrs Armstrong had called upon Mrs Griffiths on hearing that a partner was coming, and had asked if her husband might not assist them. He had already made some tentative overtures on the subject of the amalgamation of the two firms, but they had not been favourably received, nor had anything come of the suggestion that he should stand by until the son could come home and take charge. After Armstrong had been demobilized and returned to Hay, Mr Martin was in virtual charge of the business over the way. They met each other, of course; everyone of a certain standing knows everyone else in Hay; and they had professional dealings and social associations, but they were, in a sense, rivals. They were both, as the local people would say, foreigners, and in matters connected with his private affairs the

Welsh farmer is not fond of employing strangers. Mr Cheese had been long known in the place, and so had Mr Griffiths. But when Armstrong found himself alone in his business, it undoubtedly began to fall off. It was a pity, from Armstrong's point of view, that Mr Martin was there to conduct actively the business brought to the old-established firm; if he had not been there circumstances might almost have forced them to make some arrangement with Armstrong. Anyhow, when the war was over, and people were beginning to take up the threads again, there were these two solicitors in Hay, their offices facing each other across the street, and there for the moment we will leave them.

Armstrong was a popular man in Hay. On his return from the war he called himself Major Armstrong, and attached much importance to his military rank. He was very active in all the affairs of the place, and secured, among other appointments, that of clerk to the justices, which introduced his finger into many small local pies. Mr Martin was not so popular. It was not in his character to seek popularity, and he suffered, as a result of his services to his country, from a form of paralysis which affected one side of his face, and sometimes gave people the impression that he was smiling when he was not. He was a quiet man, and lived his own life quietly. Armstrong, although he took pains to ingratiate himself with everyone, was not at home the martial figure that his military career and gallant adventures might have led one to expect. It was common knowledge that he was, in fact, henpecked. The late Mrs Armstrong was a person of peculiar character. She was both cultivated and clever, played the piano extremely well, and had earned the reputation with everyone who had any knowledge of her of being a really good woman. She was, however, notoriously cranky, and extremely severe. She brought up her children with devotion, indeed, but with a strict and sombre austerity, and her husband was ruled with a rod of iron. Until the war broke his boundaries and enlarged his horizon little Armstrong (for he was a very little man, weighing only some 7 stone) had no kind of liberty at home, and, except for certain furtive, amorous adventures of which I have heard, he was obliged to live under the strict conditions imposed by his wife. These conditions were of an unusual severity. No wine or alcohol was admitted to the house. If at the table of some neighbour he was offered wine, his wife would interpose with a negative on his account, except now and then when she had been known to say, 'I think you may have a glass of port, Herbert; it will do your cold good.' If he was smoking as he came along the road, and his wife came in sight, the cigar or pipe had to be hastily put away, and he was only allowed to smoke in one room of his house called 'Mayfield'. On one occasion, at a tennis party, she called to him in the middle of a set that it was time to go home. 'Six o'clock, Herbert; how can you expect punctuality in the servants if the master is late for his meals?' On another similar occasion, in publicly summoning him to come home, she reminded him that it was his 'bath night'. Such a state of affairs seems fantastic, but there is no doubt that it existed. For whatever reason, she had him thoroughly under her thumb, and (no doubt for his own good) was determined to keep him there. People liked the little man, and were sorry for him; but, however hard upon him they may have thought Mrs Armstrong was, it did not diminish – who knows that it did not enhance? – that undoubted respect in which she was held by her neighbours.

This, then, was the course of the life of these people in Hay to the outward eye. Local events came and went. Local gossips talked of this or that person's affairs; people attended little parties, came and went as they do in all such places. Illness is always a topic for gossip in small country towns, and among the figures that moved through the busy life of the place none was more universally regarded with interest and affection than Dr 'Tom' Hincks, who had succeeded to his father's practice in the place and was known and trusted and liked for miles around. The big, upright figure with the open countenance and the charming smile was a familiar sight. Whatever he was doing, hunting up on the hills or shooting in the countryside, Dr 'Tom' always put his patients first; and often, if he were going out for a day's shooting, would get up at five in the morning and attend his medical work and be busy on it up till midnight after he had come home. His presence in a house would indicate to the gossips that somebody was ill. It was rumoured in August 1920, that Mrs Armstrong was in indifferent health, and that her eccentricities had increased; and, sure enough, on 22 August 1920, Dr Hincks himself was seen taking her away in a motor-car to Gloucester, where she was placed in Barnwood Private Asylum. Here was food for conversation. It was known that she suffered from acute depression and some kind of nervous affection of the hands which prevented her from playing the piano, and people's sympathy with her husband already increased when this new trial became known.

During her absence the little man enjoyed, it is true, a certain freedom. People were kind to him and asked him out. Heads, if they were wagged, were wagged in secret. Then, six months later, it was known that Mrs Armstrong was much better, and was coming home. And in January 1921, she came home, but began to fail again. A mental nurse was installed, and in February 1921, people heard that Mrs Armstrong was very ill, and that Dr Hincks was calling every day. And on 22 February this poor lady died, and, a few days later, was buried at Cusop Churchyard, near by her home. A friend, who was one of the four who attended the funeral, told me that Armstrong seemed quite unaffected, and was chatting about fishing rights while the coffin was being carried down. And on the following Sunday at the little village church, where the service was made a kind of memorial to the good lady, he read the lessons (so the sexton told me) with great eloquence and feeling.

And so life was resumed once more; Major Armstrong took a new lease of it, and gave little dinner-parties, at which alcohol was no longer banned. People came and went, got ill and got well, and so on. After one of Armstrong's little dinner-parties the local inspector of taxes, who had done justice to the excellent madeira provided by his host, was taken very ill on the way home and had a very bad night; and people who knew of it rather smiled. There was a good deal of illness in the autumn of 1921. Mr Martin, for example, was ill for several days, and had to have Dr Hincks in constant attendance. Now among those people who did not accept

Major Armstrong's invitations were Mr and Mrs Martin. But it was characteristic of the little man that he was not easily rebuffed, and so he gave continued invitations, and appeared to want to be friendly and sociable, but could only on one occasion induce Martin to come to his house, and they had tea together. When further invitations to tea failed, Armstrong tried inviting the Martins to dinner, but even that was refused, and it was thought that business relations must be getting rather strained.

And then, suddenly, a series of bombshells fell. On New Year's Day 1922, the town was dumbfounded to hear that Major Armstrong had been arrested the day before and charged with attempting to murder Mr Martin. This roused the greatest indignation. People went so far as to suggest that it had been engineered by Martin on account of business rivalry. But still more astounding events happened the next day. Strange doctors came to town; it was known that something was happening up at Cusop Churchyard; and then that Mrs Armstrong's body had been exhumed that very morning and was being examined in a little cottage near the churchyard. Reporters descended apparently from the skies. Sensation after sensation was reported. Gossip upon gossip multiplied, and through five long months, until Armstrong was executed, the town was a centre of sensation and excitement such as is rarely experienced in such a place.

That was the outward course of events. Now let us glance at the events a little beneath the surface as they appeared to those two or three intimately engaged with the persons chiefly concerned, so that later we may go deeper still and examine some matters which were known to nobody at the time except possibly Armstrong himself.

When Armstrong was suddenly arrested on 31 December 1921, there were five people only in Hay who were not surprised. They were Dr Hincks, Mr and Mrs Martin, Mr Davies (Mr Martin's father-in-law), and Mr Trevor Griffiths. For the greater part of two months these people had been certain that Armstrong was trying to poison Mr Martin, and that he had poisoned his own wife. They had been in communication with the Home Office, who had enjoined upon them the strictest secrecy and the necessity for not letting Armstrong have a glimmering of an idea that he was suspected. It was a dramatic and eerie situation for these people, and the last three weeks must have been extremely trying.

Consider the facts. Only two months before Martin, after repeated invitations, had gone to tea with Armstrong at his house. There was a business difficulty between them, and he thought that Armstrong wished to discuss it, although, as a matter of fact, he never alluded to it. During tea he had handed Martin a buttered scone with the apology, 'Excuse my fingers,' and Martin had eaten that, as well as some currant loaf. He had hardly got home before he was seized with the most violent pains, with vomiting and diarrhoea, which continued throughout the night and reduced him swiftly to a condition of extreme weakness. Dr Hincks was called in, and saw the usual symptoms of a severe bilious attack, and prescribed accordingly. But, as the sickness continued, he was (fortunately) not entirely satisfied, and he had an analysis made, and found in the sample submitted that there was one-thirty-third of a grain of arsenic. This set him thinking and pondering, and one day, riding on horseback over the hills to visit a distant patient, and revolving in his mind the circumstances attending the death of Mrs Armstrong, the key to the whole situation flashed on him. That neuritis of hers, which they had all regarded as a merely functional disorder, had not been functional but organic; it was peripheral neuritis – one of the symptoms of arsenical poisoning. He remembered all the other symptoms. Vomiting, the peculiarity known as 'high steppage' gait, discoloration of the skin, etc., etc. – all symptoms of arsenical poisoning. What Martin was suffering from, Mrs Armstrong had died of. And if in a small liquid sample taken from Mr Martin one-thirty-third of a grain of arsenic had been found, what might be found in the body of Mrs Armstrong? The more he thought of it the plainer it became. He wrote at once to the doctors at Barnwood Asylum, and they, too, realized that they had been deceived as to the cause of Mrs Armstrong's physical illness. They remembered how the symptoms had diminished during her stay in the asylum and reappeared after her return home; they, too, realized that they had mistaken organic for functional disease, and (in the complete absence of suspicion) missed the diagnosis which would have put them on the right track. The facts were placed before the Home Office, and the slow but certain wheels of the criminal law began to revolve. Stiffly and hesitatingly they moved at first, as the Director of Public Prosecutions began to make his own independent inquiries; but ever increased in pace and smoothness and momentum, until in the dock of His Majesty's Assizes for the county of Herefordshire they flung off Armstrong into the outer darkness of shameful extinction.

The Home Office was, naturally, slow to move at the beginning; it does not do to suspect everyone against whom some private malice or feud may inspire or suggest suspicion. Moreover, in a recent case of poisoning alleged against a solicitor in Wales the defendant had been acquitted. It was probable that the authorities were determined not to set the law in motion on such a charge unless they were absolutely certain that suspicion was properly founded, and that the case would be proved; for if it is a terrible thing that a murderer should escape, it is an equally terrible thing that an innocent man should be put on trial for his life. Therefore, the first steps were taken cautiously; but to Dr Hincks and the Martins, who were convinced of Armstrong's guilt, and certain that he was engaged in a persistent attempt to poison Martin, the machinery seemed to move slowly indeed. One must consider Martin's position. He was afraid of Armstrong. He remembered that sinister occasion when he had yielded to Armstrong's entreaties to go to tea with him, and the agonies that had followed; and here was the same man daily ringing him up and insisting that he should go to tea with him again. The two were solicitors for the vendor and purchaser of some property respectively. Armstrong had failed to complete; Martin was pressing for the return of the deposit – some five hundred pounds – but neither completion nor deposit was forthcoming from Armstrong – only invitations to tea. If it were not such a grim story there would be something comic in this almost furious bombardment of tea invitations across the village street in Hay.

'Will you come to tea this afternoon?' telephones Armstrong.

'Can't come to tea,' replies Martin, 'but I will look in afterwards about six.' 'Oh, never mind,' says Armstrong. 'Any day will do. Come to tea tomorrow instead.' Martin, quaking with apprehension, does not go to tea tomorrow. The telephone bell rings again. 'Why did you not come to tea?' says Armstrong. 'Tea has been waiting for you for half an hour.'

Tea and telephones, these were the weapons with which the sinister warfare was waged. Then, as Martin would not go to tea at Mayfield on his way home through Cusop Dingle, as Mahomet would not come to the mountain, the tea mountain was brought to Mahomet. Tea was started at Armstrong's office; butter was brought from Mayfield, scones sent over from the little café across the road. The telephone now asked Mr Martin to come across and have tea at the office. In vain was the net spread in the sight of poor Mr Martin; but he was hard put to it to find excuses for not crossing the road and taking his tea with Armstrong. So in sheer self-defence, though, I imagine, with poor appetite, he started having tea in his own office, in order to have an excuse for not going across the road. And so one pictures, amid this furious gale of invitations, these two men sitting on either side of the street having their tea, or unable to have it; Armstrong furiously drinking his, when Martin would not come: Martin distastefully not taking his, in order to say that he had had it. Martin confided to Dr Hincks that he could not stand it much longer. 'Whatever you do,' they said, 'keep away from Armstrong's house. And under no circumstances eat or drink anything in his presence.' The police were making secret visits, chiefly at night, to Hay and insisting on the same policy; above all, Armstrong was not to be alarmed. 'All very well,' says poor Martin, 'but he is bombarding me with invitations to tea; every time I see him he darts across the road, "Why not come to tea?" And I have run out of excuses.' 'Hold on a bit longer,' they tell him. And he and Mrs Martin actually took it in turns to keep awake at night, haunted by one knows not what grim, beckoning spectre with a tea-cup in its hand. And so Armstrong was at last put to the necessity of asking Mr and Mrs Martin to dinner. It was expensive, of course, but it need only happen once.

Martin made some kind of temporizing answer, but on the day that the invitation fell due Armstrong was already in the hands of the police, and Mr and Mrs Martin could breathe freely.

The ordeal of Dr Hincks was to last a day longer. He was in a very peculiar position, owing partly to the courage and integrity of his own character. Armstrong was his patient, and he had been attending him and giving treatment for venereal disease periodically for some time; and while he was attending him he was already in communication with the police on the subject of his arrest. In his own opinion (and I think most people would agree) he had no alternative in either case. He believed Armstrong to be a murderer and wished him to be arrested; but every man is presumed innocent until he is proved guilty, and there was no valid reason why he should discontinue his treatment and so drive his patient to the necessity of confiding in another doctor. But, although Armstrong had been arrested on the charge of attempting to murder Martin, the real case against him was that he had murdered Mrs Armstrong, and until her body had been exhumed Dr Hincks must have been in considerable suspense. Had that body been found free from arsenic he would have been in the position of having made unwarranted accusations against his friend and patient; and he might have walked out of Hay, which had been the scene of his work for thirty years, and his home for fifty. But when, on the day following the arrest of Armstrong, Mrs Armstrong's coffin was opened, the first glance told Dr Hincks and Dr Spilsbury that his suspicions were correct. The state of preservation of the remains told them that at once, and the fact was confirmed a little later when the analysis of Mr Webster revealed the actual presence of a greater quantity of arsenic than he had ever found in a poisoned body.

It cannot be doubted that Dr Hincks acted with a courage worthy of the highest traditions of his profession. He had been mistaken about Mrs Armstrong's illness and the cause of her death, as had the other doctors who had attended her; but as soon as his suspicions were aroused he shouldered the burden of the inevitable consequences, and did his duty to society.

*

The reader must now be informed of another cause of suspicion against Armstrong. About a month before the episode of the tea-time attempt, and soon after Martin's arrival in Hay and marriage to Miss Davies, he had one morning received a parcel containing a box of chocolates. Neither he nor his wife was in the habit of eating chocolates, and the box was put away until some days later, when they were having friends to dinner, and Mrs Martin put some into a bon-bon dish. There was no clue as to where the chocolates came from, and after the party those that were left were put back into the box. Someone was taken ill after that dinner-party, and later the chocolates were examined, and it was found that some of them had a small hole drilled in the base and that arsenic had been inserted. The diameter of the hole exactly fitted the nozzle of the instrument that Armstrong afterwards alleged that he used to inject arsenic into the roots of dandelions. Another case which subsequently brought Armstrong under suspicion was that of Mr Davies, an estate agent at Hereford, who had some controversial business with Armstrong; who came to Hay, had lunch or tea with Armstrong, and was taken ill with acute abdominal pain on his return home. He was operated on for appendicitis, and died, the cause of death being (I believe) certified as peritonitis following acute appendicitis. It is possible that in certain circumstances the cause of his death might have been the subject for further investigation.

When Armstrong appeared before the magistrate at his own bench in Hay, his place as clerk was taken by his elderly colleague, the clerk to the bench at Talgarth, to whose office he had himself aspired already. This gentleman had been one of the dinner-party of four after which the inspector of taxes was taken so ill, and it is possible that the inspector had suffered in his stead. It is said that there was a somewhat rich vein of comedy in the way he handled Armstrong at these proceedings. The prisoner himself, not to be outdone, offered to assist his elderly colleague, whose infirmity hampered him in the execution of his onerous duties. Anyhow, the usual depositions were taken, and Armstrong was committed for trial at the next Herefordshire Assizes, the defence being reserved. The trial began on 3 April 1922, before Mr Justice Darling, who was then on his last circuit prior to retirement. The Attorney-General, Sir Ernest Pollock, K.C. (afterwards Lord Hanworth), assisted by Mr C. H. Vachell, K.C., and Mr St John Micklethwait, represented the Crown, and the defence was conducted by Sir Henry Curtis Bennett, K.C., Mr S. R. C. Bosanquet, and Mr E. A. Godson. The Grand Jury, on Mr Justice Darling's advice, had thrown out the bill as to the attempted poisoning by means of a box of chocolates, there being insufficient evidence to connect the prisoner with the sending of the box.

The proceedings began with a long and important argument as to whether the evidence as regards what we may call the Martin case was admissible. Many cases were cited, and Mr Justice Darling finally decided that the evidence was admissible on the ground that it showed that the use of arsenic for poisoning human beings as well as dandelions had occurred to the prisoner's mind. This decision was of the greatest importance. If it had been wrong, and the Court of Appeal had held that the evidence was, in fact, inadmissible, the conviction of Armstrong would have been quashed, and he would have been released. On the other hand, without this evidence it seemed unlikely that there would be a verdict for conviction, and Mr Justice Darling was already of the opinion that the case was of a kind in which it was desirable, in order to get at the truth, to have as much evidence as possible as to the surrounding circumstances. As it turned out, his decision was right, and was upheld by the Court of Appeal. The greater part of the evidence at the trial was of a medical nature, and was of the unsavoury kind usually associated with cases of arsenical poisoning. The suggestion of the defence was that Mrs Armstrong herself had deliberately taken arsenic, that she was of unsound mind and suicidal tendencies, that her husband had no motive for murdering her, and that there was no evidence that he had ever administered arsenic. There was a further medical defence presented by Dr F. S. Toogood that Mrs Armstrong suffered from auto-intoxication when she went into the mental hospital, and that arsenic had nothing to do with her condition, and that there was nothing in the conditions inconsistent with her having had no arsenic whatever up to 16 February, when one poisonous dose was taken which caused her death. To account for the discrepancy of these conditions with the time taken for the arsenic to reach the parts of the body as found at the post-mortem examination, he put forward the ingenious theory that a large part of the arsenic had become encysted, or retained in a kind of capsule attached to the wall of the stomach. He cited in support of his theory the case of the Duc de Praslin, who was alleged to have been poisoned in 1846, but Mr Justice Darling knew all about the Duc de Praslin, and also that the evidence of his case was known to have been falsified and misrepresented, so he was able to dispose of this ingenious theory in his summing up. The only comment to be made on Dr Toogood's evidence was that it was not good enough.

Perhaps the most dramatic thing in the course of a trial that took place throughout in an atmosphere of tense emotion was the disclosure by Sir Henry Curtis Bennett that after Armstrong's arrest a packet of arsenic had been found in a drawer in his bureau which the police had already searched without result. It seems that after Armstrong's arrest he told his solicitor about this packet, which represented the residue of the white arsenic that he had bought at Davies's shop. His solicitor went on his instructions to Mayfield, looked in the bureau and, like the police, failed to find the packet. Then he went again with his clerk, and he described in his evidence how they found the packet of arsenic 'caught up' at the back of a drawer. They applied for a list of the articles found by the police, in order to ascertain whether this packet had been seen by them or not; it had not, and so they did not disclose its presence until Sir Henry Curtis Bennett produced it so dramatically at the trial itself. At first sight there seems something peculiar about the discovery of this packet, and the reader will naturally ask, was it put there by the defence, and, if so, for what purpose? Or was it put there by the agents of the police, and left as a trap, and, if so, for what purpose? It seems a little mysterious; and the importance of it does not seem sufficient to account for the sensation caused by it. But I believe the facts of the matter to be simply those revealed in the evidence; Armstrong did remember it, and told his solicitor about it, and it was first overlooked and ultimately found, and the finding not communicated to the police. It is interesting to see the different use made of such a piece of evidence and the comments of Lord Darling, Sir Ernest Pollock, and Sir Henry Curtis Bennett respectively. Lord Darling treated it as a very damaging piece of evidence, and commented on Armstrong's alleged failure to remember it; Sir Henry Curtis Bennett went so far as to say that it might save Armstrong's life, as accounting for the remainder of the purchase of arsenic, half of which he alleged he used in making up the little packets for poisoning dandelions. Its chief interest now lies in the example it gives of the ingenuity of a clever counsel in interpreting every fact as favourably as possible to his client.

Armstrong gave evidence on his own behalf with the same calmness that he maintained throughout the trial, and was quite unshaken until, after a severe cross-examination by the Attorney-General and a re-examination by his own counsel, he was taken in hand by the Judge, who, in a few masterly and persistent questions, revealed Armstrong's inability either to explain the little packet of arsenic found on him at his arrest, or to conceal the fact that there was another packet hidden in the desk in his bureau which the police did not find when they searched. The Judge's questions also made it difficult for anyone to believe that Armstrong really did, for the purpose of poisoning twenty individual dandelions, make up twenty individual packets of white arsenic. These questions shook the prisoner, and, I imagine, really shattered the case for the defence. Anyone who reads them, and Armstrong's method of dealing with them, can have little doubt that they went to the root of the matter of his guilt far more certainly than the arsenic ever went to the roots of his dandelions. Sir Henry Curtis Bennett made a very effective and eloquent speech for the defence, and the Attorney-General's reply was a masterly example of its kind. Armstrong sat apparently unmoved through everything, with blue eyes staring in front of him throughout the summing up.

Severe as the Judge's summing up was, the general opinion was that Armstrong would be acquitted, and the betting was in favour of acquittal. Sir Henry Curtis Bennett himself was so confident that he went for a walk, expecting to come back either to hear the verdict for acquittal or to meet Armstrong himself and find that he had already been released. As it was, when he got back to Hereford, the newsboys were crying in the streets the paper announcing the verdict 'Guilty'. A regrettable indiscretion on the part of a juryman and a London evening newspaper revealed to the public the fact that when the jury retired to consider their verdict the foreman asked everyone to write his verdict on a slip of paper, and that eleven bore the word 'Guilty' and one 'Not proven'; and when the foreman announced the result the man who had written 'Not proven' said, 'Well, Tom, you know what "Not proven" means. I really believe the man is guilty.' After which the foreman, finding they were all agreed, was alleged to have said, 'We have heard enough of the case, and we needn't discuss it any more. Let's have a quiet smoke before we go back into Court.' This unexpected glimpse into the methods of a jury consisting of ten farmers and two professional men is undoubtedly interesting, and seems to indicate a degree of common sense which should go far to refute the theories of those who think that an ordinary jury is not a satisfactory tribunal for the testing of circumstantial evidence. But the publication of this story was severely censured at the time by several eminent Judges.

In due time the case came before the Court of Criminal Appeal, presided over by the Lord Chief Justice, who sat with Mr Justice Avory and Mr Justice Shearman. The appeal was dismissed, and a fortnight later, on 31 May 1922, Armstrong was duly hanged at Gloucester, having made no confession. His attitude to the religious administrations of his clerical friends was described as being one of 'respectful attention'. He was visited by Mr Matthews, his solicitor, and Mr Chevalier, a Liverpool solicitor who had been trusted and esteemed by Mrs Armstrong, and (no doubt for her sake and the children's) did what he could to arrange Armstrong's somewhat tangled affairs. Death was dealt to him on that May morning, while the birds in Cusop Dingle were singing about the house where his children were awaking, with the swift and merciful efficiency of modern methods; and for the sins that he committed he paid up to the full measure of his capacity to pay.

Armstrong's presence was characterized by neatness and smartness of appearance and alacrity of demeanour. He was very small, but so well proportioned that he did not seem small, unless he was standing beside a person of normal height. He was voluble and egotistical, regarding himself and his affairs as of great importance; his manners were excellent. Some people found him simply a bore; others, among whom were a certain number of women, found him attractive. The most remarkable thing about him was his eyes. They were light blue, the colour of forget-me-nots, and they had a glittering brilliancy, almost as though there was a light behind them. This, it will be remembered, was also a characteristic of George Joseph Smith, the man who had a habit of marrying women with a little money and drowning them in a bath; and, I doubt not, of many other scoundrels.

In cases where so much of the evidence is circumstantial it is generally considered necessary to have ample proof not only of the cause of death, or of the actual giving of poison, but also that the defendant had it in his possession, knew how to use it, and had both motive and opportunity for using it. Armstrong was an old hand with arsenic. He was interested in his garden, waged a continuous warfare against dandelions and plantains, and always had stocks of weedkiller, which is a preparation of arsenic, in hand. In addition to this he bought arsenic himself and made up his own weed-killer; still further, and this was a significant fact, he bought a quantity of white arsenic in the January preceding Mrs Armstrong's removal to the asylum, and bought it from the local chemist, Davies – Mr Martin's father-in-law. It is this white arsenic which he is alleged to have used to poison Mrs Armstrong and Mr Martin. As to opportunity, there was no doubt, and it was not contested, that he often sat with his wife when she was ill and, in the absence of the nurse, gave her whatever nourishment she was having. As to motive, however, there was a difference of opinion. Sir Henry Curtis Bennett was very impressive on this subject of absence of motive; and, indeed, to any ordinary mind there would seem to be no motive great enough to account for so monstrous a crime. But motives which would not be sufficient for ordinary people were, apparently, sufficient for Armstrong. With regard to his wife there was a financial motive – miserable enough, it is true, for the lady possessed only about two thousand pounds in the world; but the incident of the will indicated that Armstrong attached importance to it. While he was away at the war she made a brief will leaving everything she had to her children, with a small legacy to a Miss Pearce, and nothing to her husband. But soon after he came back she signed, or was alleged to have signed, a new will in which nothing was left to her children or Miss Pearce, and everything to her husband. This will was in the prisoner's own handwriting, and, if the signature was not a forgery, it was almost certainly obtained under a mistaken notion as to what the document was, for the will was improperly witnessed, the witnesses signing neither in the presence of the testator nor of each other. Armstrong's story of this will was given in his evidence; its existence, I am afraid we must admit, shows that he had a financial interest in the death of his wife. To that must be added the fact that he was in financial difficulties at the time, and that he died insolvent.

We have seen what kind of a woman Mrs Armstrong was, and that Armstrong's life with her was not what one might call joyful. There is further to be considered the fact that he had contracted an intimacy – of what degree is really of no great importance – with a lady unnamed, who gave evidence at the trial; she came and spent a night at Hay soon after his wife's death – presumably to see his house and the children; and within a month or two of the death he had asked her to marry him, although at the time of the arrest she had, apparently, not decided to do so. These, then, were the motives which induced him to embark on the campaign of cumulative poisoning in minute doses which had been going on for some time before Mrs Armstrong's removal to the asylum. There is a difficulty as to the administration of the large dose which was evidently given within a few hours of her being removed to Barnwood. One may well ask what can have been his object in administering a large and fatal dose to a woman who had just been examined by two doctors and certified as mentally insane, but physically in ordinary health. Supposing, as might well have happened, that Mrs Armstrong, who was taken violently ill just before starting for the asylum, and had presumably got rid of the greater portion of the dose, had died in the motor-car on the way to Gloucester, there would have had to be an inquest; neither Dr Hincks nor the other doctor who certified her would have given a death certificate in such circumstances; and a post-mortem examination would have revealed the presence of arsenic. One may well wonder why Armstrong took such risks. It can only be assumed that, in the case of the dose being successful, his defence would have been that the poor lady, on hearing that she was going to be taken to the asylum, decided to commit suicide. A possible motive (not put forward by the prosecution) for Armstrong's desire that his wife should be discharged from the asylum, and not merely sent home on leave, was that in the latter case she would still have been under a certificate of lunacy, and therefore not qualified to make the new will which he drafted and which she signed.

The delusions from which she suffered were of a sad and pathetic nature. She, whose life was governed by a sense of duty, went about weighed down by the fantastic belief that she did not do her duty by her husband and children, and that she had committed some criminal act for which she could be arrested. She was also under what was certified as the 'untrue delusion' that she was being poisoned; but in the light of later knowledge this appears to have been no delusion but simple fact.

A terrible possibility here presents itself. It was suggested to me, by one who saw her constantly during this period, that she knew she was being poisoned, and that in her strange mental condition she felt that she must not, for the sake of her children, reveal what she knew and incriminate her husband. If there is any possibility of truth in that view (and only those who knew her and were with her can judge), it raises her martyrdom to a point of heroic tragedy such as has surely never been recorded before. I can only say for myself, having pondered the matter considerably, that I have no kind of certainty about it either way, and that I only hope it is not true. Another of her 'delusions' was that Dr Hincks did not know what was the matter with her; and this, as he would be the first to admit, is not entirely baseless. That at this time she took a dislike to and mistrust in doctors generally on the grounds that they 'did not know what was the matter with her' might add some plausibility to the ghastly possibility that I have suggested. I am bound to suggest it, because the person who held that view had a more intimate knowledge of the circumstances than anyone else.

As to the second large dose of arsenic, from which Mrs Armstrong died, and which, according to the defence, was administered by herself, there is no evidence that in her enfeebled condition she could have moved from her bed to get such a dose, even if she knew where to get it, for a period much in excess of the twenty-four hours preceding her death. Although Sir Henry Curtis Bennett did his best to produce medical evidence that the fatal dose must have been taken earlier than twenty-four hours before death, it did not convince the jury; and, in the light of the evidence of Sir Henry Willcox and Dr Spilsbury, it will hardly convince the reader. Presumably, like all arsenic poisoners, Armstrong got tired of the small doses and decided to hasten matters, and to put an end to the situation once and for all.

Mr Justice Darling dealt thoroughly with the prisoner's story of having actually wrapped twenty little packets for the purpose of poisoning twenty dandelions. It seems unlikely, and the jury disbelieved it. These were the kind of little packets that were handy for using at the tea-table; and, as we know, one of them was actually found in his pocket at the time of his arrest, ready, no doubt, for Mr Martin should his reluctance to come to tea be overcome. There is only this to be said, that people who knew Armstrong well say that it was just the kind of thing he would have done. He was a fiddling and pernickety little man, who liked messing about with chemicals and apparatus; and I have had shown to me the little instrument which he said he used for injecting arsenic powder into dandelion roots – a kind of small syringe with a fine nozzle. Indeed, he gave it to Dr Hincks with some other hospital apparatus, after Mrs Armstrong's death, as something he had no more use for. But it is significant that the little nozzle exactly fitted the little hole that was drilled in the chocolates sent to Mrs Martin.

I have sat through a summer morning on a chair on the tennis lawn of the house which used to be called Mayfield. The dandelions were thicker than ever, and the plantains had, at the time of my visit, taken almost complete possession of half of the lawn. The sun shone, the doors and windows were wide open, so that the summer breeze stirred through the house, and the voices of children at play sounded in the precincts. A saner and more normal life, and a happier set of children, had taken possession of the place. But my thoughts were with those little children whose voices, more repressed and not quite so happy, had sounded there at the time of this story. It is the presence of those children that to me at any rate invests this crime with a peculiar dreadfulness. And in considering the endless puzzle of what it is in one man that, side by side with ordinary human qualities, makes him capable of fiendish cruelty and puts him into the class which we call criminal, I am impelled to the conclusion that what makes a poisoner differ from the normal man is not so much a positive as a negative quality. It is the absence of something from his moral make-up, rather than the presence of something, that seems to me to make the difference. And in this case I would say that what Armstrong and people like him lack is imagination. They see things and actions objectively, not subjectively. Otherwise, how would it be possible for a man engaged with life in all its ordinary relationships not to recoil from contemplation of the effect of his conduct on those little lives? There is something innocent in the worst of us; and no one can live in the company of little children without being aware, were it only wistfully, of the morning freshness and beauty of their outlook. It is easier to understand a man murdering his children in insane desperation than cold-bloodedly scheming and contriving actions which could only blot out the sunshine of their lives in darkness and shame. I am driven to believe, therefore, that this man was deprived of the power of realizing or imagining what might happen, or what must happen, to his children as a consequence of his actions.

William Joyce
1945

J. W. HALL

IN a sense this is written for posterity, for to his contemporaries in Great Britain William Joyce – better known by his nickname of 'Lord Haw-Haw' – needs no introduction.

On 3 September 1939 Great Britain and France declared war on Germany. On 18 September, William Joyce, the holder of a British passport, and believed by the British authorities (and possibly by himself) to be a British subject, entered the German Broadcasting Service. Between 18 September 1939 and 30 April 1945 he broadcast regularly in English from German stations, especially Zeesen, Hamburg, and Bremen. There can hardly be anyone in Great Britain who had access to a wireless set during that period who did not at some time tune in, deliberately or by accident, to that irritating voice which proclaimed 'This is Jairmany calling', and proceeded to prophesy – sometimes accurately – the unpleasant things that Hitler and his cronies had in store for us.

Joyce's distinctive accent was a common topic of discussion. There were even those who insulted our senior University by alleging that it was an 'Oxford accent'. But this was an accent such as Balliol had never conceived, nor Magdalen heard; indeed, as an Oxonian, I am prepared to assert that if (which is not admitted) there be such a thing as an Oxford accent, that accent is not – thank Heaven – the accent of William Joyce, which may have been some sort of hybrid between a Yankee twang and an Irish brogue.

William Joyce, as was proved at the trial, was born on 24 April 1906 at 1377 Herkimer Street, Brooklyn, New York, the son of

Michael Francis Joyce and his wife, Gertrude Emily Brooke, formerly of Shaw, Lancashire, whom he had married at All Saints Church, New York, on 2 May 1905. Michael Joyce was born in 1869 or 1870 (his age was given as thirty-six on William's birth certificate) at Ballinrobe, Mayo, Ireland. In 1888 he went to the United States; on 22 July 1892 he filed in the Court of Common Pleas of New Jersey a declaration of his intention to become a citizen of the United States of America 'and to renounce forever all allegiance and fidelity to any and every foreign prince, potentate, state, and sovereignty whatever, and particularly to the Queen of the United Kingdom of Great Britain and Ireland, whose subject he has heretofore been'. On 25 October 1894 this declaration of intention was followed by a petition for naturalization, accompanied by a declaration on oath renouncing all foreign allegiance in the same terms as above, and Michael Joyce thereupon became a naturalized American citizen. It followed that when William was born in New York in April 1906 he was a natural-born American. In 1909 the Joyce family returned to Ireland, and between that year and 1921 they lived at various addresses, first in County Mayo and later in Galway. In 1917 Mrs Joyce visited England and was required to register as an alien at her native place, Shaw.

In December 1921 William Joyce came to England, being then fifteen. His parents, with the rest of their family, followed in 1922, and settled in England; apparently, coming from Ireland, they were assumed to be British subjects, for there is, as far as I have seen, no record of any aliens' registration at this time. It may be that this was the origin of the confusion as to nationality. Be that as it may, in that same year, 1922, William Joyce passed the London matriculation, and began to study science at the Battersea Polytechnic. In the following year he took up English language and literature, and history at Birkbeck College, where he studied for four years, and graduated in 1927.

On 21 October 1922, soon after his matriculation, Joyce formally applied for enrolment in the University of London O.T.C. In a preliminary letter, dated 9 August 1922, he says, 'It is my intention, if possible, to study with a view to being nominated by the Univer-

sity for a commission in the Regular Army. I have served with the
irregular forces of the Crown, in an intelligence capacity, against
the Irish guerrillas ... I have a knowledge of the rudiments of
Musketry, Bayonet Fighting, and Squad Drill. I must now mention
a point which I hope will not give rise to difficulties. I was born in
America, but of British parents. I left America when two years of
age, have not returned since, and do not propose to return. I was
informed, at the Brigade Headquarters of the district in which I
was stationed in Ireland, that I possess the same rights and privileges
as I would if of natural British birth. I can obtain testimonials as to
my loyalty to the Crown. I am in no way connected with the
United States of America ... As a young man of pure British
descent, some of whose forefathers have held high positions in the
British Army, I have always been desirous of devoting what little
capability and energy I may possess to the country which I love so
dearly.' The University of London O.T.C. being a unit strictly
limited by the War Office to British subjects of pure European
descent, the adjutant, on receipt of Joyce's formal application for
enrolment, wrote to his father on 23 October 1922: 'He says you
were never naturalized as an American. Perhaps, therefore, you
would confirm this point, when I shall be able to proceed with his
enrolment and registration.' Michael Joyce replied on 26 October:
'With regard to my son William. He was born in America. I was
born in Ireland. His mother was born in England. We are all
British and not American citizens.' So William Joyce was duly
enrolled, and served till 1926.

Meanwhile, from 1923 to 1925 he was a member of the British
Fascists, a body whose activities at that time were largely anti-
Communist. In the course of one affray between Fascists and Com-
munists Joyce himself was slashed in the face with a razor, which
left him scarred for life. On 24 April 1927 he came of age, and a
week later married Hazel Kathleen Barr at Chelsea Register Office;
that marriage was dissolved in 1936. In 1928 he did a year's post-
graduate course in philology. From 1928 to 1930 he spoke for and
assisted the Conservative party, and from 1931 to 1933 he studied
psychology at King's College, London. From all of which it will be

seen that by the time he embarked on the broadcasts for which he was tried, William Joyce was a man of very high education well qualified for the task he undertook.

On 4 July 1933 he applied for a British passport. On the application form he described himself as a British subject by birth, 'having been born at Rutledge Terrace, Galway, Ireland'. The application was verified by an official of a bank (against whose good faith no suggestion has at any time been made). This rather suggests that the present system of verification is of little value: it is certainly a nuisance to those who belong to the limited classes entitled to verify, who are constantly being put in the position of offending their acquaintances or risking the making of serious statements on inadequate evidence. And what real value is it as a safeguard? If one of His Majesty's Judges, or an intimate friend at the Bar, came to me and said: 'I'm going abroad: do you mind verifying my passport?' I should no doubt say: 'By all means.' But even in these circumstances I am, in most cases, acting on inference rather than knowledge. What I *know* is that my friend has for a number of years practised at the Bar, or held a judicial office: that he speaks English like a Briton, and, possibly, that he was educated at a British school or University. From which, I *infer* that he is a British subject – an inference probably correct in at least ninety-nine cases out of 100. But one very seldom sees one's friends' birth certificates, and, if one meets them for the first time in adult life, often knows nothing about their parentage. In the hundredth case the inference can easily be mistaken. During the war of 1914–18 there were two ladies, later personally known to me as connections of my wife, for whom I should have had not the slightest hesitation in verifying a passport application. All through the first Great War they lived in England as Englishwomen, doing war work, and I am sure as loyal as any two women could be. After the war they wished to go abroad, and applied for a passport. To their horror they were told: 'It appears from the facts stated that you are, and always have been, German subjects.' What had happened was that they were the daughters of an Englishwoman married to a German, who, at the time of their birth, was British consul at a town in South

America. They were brought back to England in childhood, after their father's death, and had always erroneously assumed that, having been born in a British consulate, they were British subjects (as they would have been if it had been a British *embassy*). If I remember rightly, they were given some sort of temporary document till they could be naturalized.

The list of persons entitled to verify passports is 'a member or official of any banking firm established in the United Kingdom, or a Mayor, Magistrate, Provost, Justice of the Peace, Minister of Religion, Barrister-at-Law, Notary, Solicitor, Physician, Surgeon, etc.'. That 'etc.' in the circumstances is delicious. What on earth does it mean? And what would happen to a person who stated his qualification as 'etc.'? In these democratic days it is difficult to see the reason for so narrow and, if one may say so, so snobbish a list. One might have supposed that a man's employer would be far more reliable as a sponsor than a doctor, parson, or bank official, who sees him only occasionally, and for a limited and special purpose.

But, compared with some documents which one is asked to vouch for, a passport application is a model of sound sense. During the war I was staying in a hotel in Scotland for some weeks. A fellow guest, whom I did not for a moment doubt, asked me to sign an application for permission to enter a 'protected area' to visit her brother who was the local laird. I said: 'Well, I don't doubt for a moment that you are who and what you claim to be, but three weeks' hotel acquaintance is hardly enough to justify me in signing you up as a fit and proper person to enter a protected area in wartime: still, let me see exactly what has to certified.' She produced the form, and all I was asked to state was that 'I have no reason to doubt the truth of the foregoing particulars', or words to that effect. I told her that I did not mind signing that, as it did not pledge me to any personal or affirmative knowledge. But what earthly use it was from a security point of view I have never discovered. But I award the prize for idiocy to the form which I was asked to sign for someone who had lost clothing coupons or ration book (I forget which). I had solemnly to declare – under fearsome penalties for false declarations – that I had put to the applicant the question 'Have you lost your coupons?', and that I had received the answer 'Yes'!

Is it unreasonable to suggest that the system of 'verification' of applications – including passport applications – needs overhaul or abolition?

At all events, a passport was duly issued to Joyce, valid for five years; it was renewed for one year in pursuance of an application dated 24 September 1938, and for a further period of one year from 1 July 1939 in pursuance of an application dated 24 August 1939 only ten days before the outbreak of war. That renewal became a matter of crucial importance at his trial.

Meanwhile, from 1933 to 1937 he was a member of Sir Oswald Mosley's 'British Union of Fascists'. In December 1934, with Sir Oswald Mosley and others, he was charged before Mr Justice Branson and a jury at Lewes Assizes with riotous assembly at Worthing. The defendants were acquitted. On 13 February 1937, his first marriage having been dissolved in the previous year, he married Margaret Cairns White at the Kensington Register Office.

In March of the same year he formed his own organization, the 'National Socialist League'. I am informed by friends in Bristol that this body had an office in Park Street, Bristol, with a shop at which one could buy, without restriction, such useful and necessary articles as rubber truncheons and daggers. One of these daggers is now in my possession, having been acquired by my friend for some perfectly innocent and lawful purpose. During the career of the National Socialist League, Joyce was twice charged before Metropolitan Magistrates with assault, but on both occasions the charges were dismissed. In September 1937 he wrote *National Socialism Now*, and he also wrote articles and pamphlets in support of Fascism.

The final renewal of his passport having been granted on 24 August 1939, on the 27th Joyce ordered the National Socialist League to be dissolved, and at some date before the actual outbreak of war he went with his wife to Germany, and a fortnight later he started the broadcast propaganda which ultimately brought him to the dock. The events affecting Joyce between September 1939 and his arrest on 28 May 1945 can be briefly stated. In September 1940 he was granted German nationality, and on 12 April 1941 a German military passport was issued to him. On 26 June 1942 he was appointed chief commentator on the German Radio for the English Group, and on 1 September 1944 the Kriegsverdienstkreuz 1st Class (a civilian award) was conferred on him by Hitler. On 3 November 1944 a German passport was issued to him in the name of Wilhelm Hansen – the acquisition of passports showed signs of becoming a habit; possibly by that time the progress of the Allies in the west suggested the advisability of building up an *alias*, as William Joyce had every reason to think that it would be bad for his health to fall into British hands. The certificate, issued on 21 December 1944, that he was a member of the Volkssturm may have had a similar object, but if so, why the reversion to his own name? It may be that lack of manpower compelled everyone, including foreign broadcasters – and he was now a German citizen – to enrol in the Volkssturm. Be that as it may, it is not without interest to note that 'Wilhelm Hansen' was said to have been born on 11 March 1906, in Galway, Ireland, while on the Volkssturm certificate the date and place of birth are correctly stated. On 30 April 1945 Joyce delivered his last identified broadcast. On 28 May 1945 he encountered two British officers near Flensburg on the Danish frontier, one of whom shot him in the leg, and they arrested him. I trust it does not sound cynical to say that if the officer had aimed higher much trouble would have been saved.

Both Joyce's parents had died in England during the war: his father, Michael Joyce, on 19 February 1941, and his mother, Gertrude Emily Joyce, on 15 September 1944. In 1940 Joyce wrote and published in Germany a book, *Twilight over Europe*, of which 100,000 copies in German and English editions were sold on the Continent. It has never been published in England or obtainable here.

Such, in barest outline, was the career of the prisoner down to his arrest. We may now consider more closely the nature of the treasonable acts which brought him to the dock.

*

When Joyce first began to broadcast from Germany, just a fortnight after the outbreak of war, the British authorities, it is believed, were not a little perturbed as to the possible effect on morale, and they were far from displeased when a journalist almost immediately christened him 'Lord Haw-Haw', and the name stuck. Usually the inventor of popular nicknames is unidentifiable, but the 'onlie begetter' of Lord Haw-Haw was undoubtedly Mr Jonah Barrington, then of the *Daily Express*, who kindly gave me his own account of how he came to invent the name.

He was working at that time on the collation of foreign broadcasts at a wireless receiving station in Surrey, and had come across Joyce's broadcasts several times, and realized that they had a certain 'nuisance value'. It occurred to him that the most effective counter was ridicule, and he wrote an article about these broadcasts in which he referred to the broadcaster as 'Lord Haw-Haw', and gave an imaginary pen-picture of him as a brainless idiot of the type of 'Bertie Wooster' in Mr P. G. Wodehouse's books. The name caught on; it was taken up by the press generally, and Mr Barrington records with joy that on 17 October 1939 the French newspaper, *Paris-Midi*, in a burst of enthusiastic inexactitude, reported that there was a new radio traitor called 'Lord Ah! Oh!' whose real name was Jonah Barrington!

Thenceforward, it is probably true to say, William Joyce's hope of exercising any real influence on British morale was at an end. From being a sinister bogey-man, he had to many people, if not to most, become a figure of fun, about whom comedians sang songs on the wireless. The Western Brothers, for instance, had a song called 'Lord Haw-Haw the Humbug of Hamburg', which was one of many in similar vein.

Early in 1940 the listener-research department of the B.B.C. prepared a report, at the request of the Ministry of Information, on the effect of Joyce's propaganda in this country. It will be remembered that at that date the war was still in the 'phoney' stage, before the invasion of Norway and Holland, and that many of Joyce's broadcasts were directed to attempts to make people dissatisfied with conditions at home, and to comparing them unfavourably with life under the Nazi régime in Germany. Curiously enough, this was the peak period of listening to Joyce, which fell to insignificant proportions when the 'Phoney war' ended, and never revived. The report covers most of the period in respect of which Joyce was convicted.

Before receiving this official report, I had made personal inquiries (for what they are worth) among the particular section of the community with which I happened to be mainly in contact – the legal profession, members of my club, and so forth – and the answers showed several different reactions to Lord Haw-Haw. My own, which apparently was not a very common one, was: 'By listening to Lord Haw-Haw I am doing precisely what the enemy wants me to do. They do not put him on the air for fun, or with any goodwill to this country, but in the hope that people will listen, and be filled with "alarm and despondency". I should not believe him, anyway, so why gratify the enemy by listening?' And I never did listen, unless I got him accidentally in tuning in to something else. Others took a different view: 'Oh, I always tune in to Haw-Haw and have a good laugh. He's the funniest turn on the air. One can't take him seriously.' Yet others said: 'It is disquieting to find how much information he seems able to get, and some of his forecasts seem to have been unpleasantly true.' On the whole, my impression was – and it is gratifying to find it is in agreement with the official report – that those who regarded him as a joke, if a joke in a very bad taste, probably outnumbered those who paid him serious attention. He was, no doubt, responsible for a certain amount of distress to persons residing, or having relatives and friends residing, in the places he mentioned as intended targets, but since his purpose was undoubtedly the more serious one of causing alarm and despondency among the population generally, he must go down to history as not merely a knave, but an unsuccessful knave. His influence overseas seems to have been still more negligible, even where it can be said to have existed at all.

One may perhaps sum up the general British attitude to Joyce's broadcasts in the words: 'If our people ever catch Lord Haw-Haw, he'll "get it in the neck".' Probably thousands of people used this slang expression without giving a thought to its grim and precise accuracy in the case of William Joyce.

For if the substance of Joyce's broadcasts was regarded by many people as a joke, the fact that he should deliver them was not. Treason is an ugly thing, especially in time of war, and a traitor does not redeem his treachery because his methods make him a laughing-stock – though actually his technique of building an elaborate structure of prophecy of allied disaster on a foundation of quarter-truths was a dangerous one and skilfully worked out, if only he could have induced sufficient people to take him seriously.

Hence there was no doubt whatever that if Joyce – being, as everyone then believed, a British subject – fell into British hands he would stand his trial for treason by 'adhering to the King's enemies'. That was also the crime of Sir Roger Casement[1] in the war of 1914–18, and it is almost inevitable that one should compare and contrast the two cases. Both turned on questions of law; in neither were the main facts seriously in controversy: nevertheless, the contrast soon becomes more striking than the resemblance.

Casement was tried at Bar, in the King's Bench Division, before a Court of three Judges and a jury, under the old and highly technical procedure in the cases of treason. This procedure bristled with formalities, such as the delivery to the prisoner, ten days at least before the trial, of a copy of the indictment, a list of the witnesses, and a copy of the jury panel. These things may have been necessary safeguards in periods of our history when treason sometimes meant little more than finding oneself on the wrong side politically; they are merely troublesome snares for the prosecution in days when Judges are, happily, above suspicion, and the packing of juries an impossibility. But the case of Joyce came under a new act, the Treason Act, 1945, a Statute nominally purely procedural, to assimilate the procedure on a trial for any form of treason in all respects to that on a trial for murder. This had already been done

1. See *Trial of Sir Roger Casement*, edited by G. H. Knott, Notable British Trials series.

in the case of treason consisting of a direct attempt on the life of the Sovereign by the Treason Act, 1800.

The new act is a very clear example of 'legislation by reference'. One might have supposed that all that was necessary was to say that: 'The procedure in all cases of treason and misprision of treason (whether alleged to have been committed before or after the passing of this Act) shall be the same as in trials for murder', and to repeal the old Acts prescribing special procedure, including the Act of 1800, which would now be covered by the general provision. That is far too simple for Parliamentary draftsmen. Sec. 1 of the New Act begins: 'The Treason Act, 1800' – so the first four words necessitate reference to a Statute nearly 150 years old; then, with unusual generosity, we are told in general terms what the Treason Act, 1800, is about – '[which assimilates the procedure in certain cases of treason and misprision of treason to the procedure in cases of murder] shall apply in all cases of treason and misprision of treason whether alleged to have been committed before or after the passing of this Act'. In other words, the Act of 1800 is treated as (though not called) the 'principal Act', and the practitioner or Court must turn to it to find out *precisely* what the new Act effects. He has, even then, to read it subject to five separate repeals of specific words, and to a saving clause in sec. 2, sub-sec. (2) of the new Act, the effect of which is completely unintelligible without further research into the provisions of two still more ancient Statutes of 1695 and 1708 respectively. This saving clause is said to be 'for the removal of doubt', which could, one imagines, never have arisen if the Act of 1800 had simply been repealed and re-enacted in the wider terms now desired. That there may be cases where 'legislation by reference' is unavoidable or even convenient I am not concerned to deny, but to complicate a completely simple matter by enacting something which no mortal can possibly understand without going back 250 years through the Statute Book shocks the conscience of the ordinary person.

There is, however, a more serious criticism of the new Act. It was

WILLIAM JOYCE

introduced into the House of Lords as a purely procedural Statute[2] merely designed to eliminate archaic provisions in treason trials, among which was mentioned, quite incidentally, the necessity for two witnesses. The possible importance of this seems to have escaped attention, though Lord Maugham did comment on the possible danger of abolishing the rule that no evidence should be given of overt acts not charged in the indictment. Under sec. 2 of the Treason Act, 1695, it was necessary to have at least two witnesses, either both to the same overt act, or one to one overt act and the other to another overt act of the same kind of treason. The Treason Act, 1800, had abolished that safeguard in cases falling within it, namely attempts on the life of the Sovereign; and now sec. 2, sub-sec. (1) of the Treason Act, 1945, provides that: 'The enactments set out in the Schedule to this Act are hereby repealed in so far as they extend to matters of procedure in cases of treason or misprision of treason, that is to say, to the extent specified in the third column of that Schedule.' Among the Acts so repealed is the Treason Act, 1695, except secs. 5 and 6. So the protection afforded to the accused by sec. 2 of the Act of 1695 is taken away – probably, even without sec. 2, sub-sec. (1) of the Act of 1945, that would have resulted from the application of the Act of 1800. In the Joyce case, *one witness only*, Detective-Inspector Hunt, connected Joyce directly with the broadcasts. If the Act of 1695 had been in force, possibly other witnesses might have been available, but that is not self-evident, for he was not definitely identified by the B.B.C. till 2 August 1940, after the last date alleged in count three. Admitting that the line between matters of procedure and matters of substance is sometimes a narrow one, to include a statutory requirement of corroboration in the former category is rather startling.

The main issue in the Casement case was whether a person could be convicted of treason in respect of acts committed outside the

2. See *Hansard* (H.L.), 30 May 1945, vol, 136, col. 265: 'Its provisions are absolutely confined to matters of procedure, and it does not make any change whatsoever in the law as to what constitutes treason.' That is strictly accurate, if an important change in the law of evidence is correctly described as a 'matter of procedure'. If so, all the law of evidence is 'procedure'.

King's dominions. That case definitely settled the law on that point, and it was no longer open to Joyce's counsel. But Casement was a British subject, and the first question in the present case was: 'Is Joyce a British subject?' That question of mixed fact and law was decided in his favour, and two further questions remained which were the important issues in the trial. These questions were:

1. Can any British Court try an alien for a crime committed abroad (with the sole exception of piracy, which by the *jus gentium* has always been justiciable anywhere, on the basis that a pirate is an enemy of the human race, to be eliminated by whoever has the good fortune to catch him)?

2. Assuming that there was jurisdiction to try him at all did the fact that Joyce had applied for and obtained a British passport impose on him a duty of allegiance during its currency even when he was outside the British dominions? The determination of this question involved a consideration of the condition in which an alien may owe allegiance to the British Crown, and the circumstances which may put an end to such temporary or local allegiance.

On these questions Mr Justice Tucker ruled against Joyce, after which the verdict of the jury on the question whether he had, in fact, assisted the enemy, was inevitable, for no attempt was or could have been made to deny the facts.

The Joyce case is essentially one of legal interest. *Rev* v. *William Joyce* will certainly rank among the leading cases on that branch of the law of treason which deals with the doctrine of allegiance, and it will probably be found of historical as well as legal importance as the first occasion on which the House of Lords, in its judicial capacity, has pronounced on certain statements of the law based on a somewhat mysterious resolution of the Judges in 1707, in the reign of Queen Anne.

Joyce was brought to England on 16 June, and on 18 June he was charged before the Chief Magistrate, Sir Bertrand Watson, at Bow Street. The terms of the charge were as follows:

'William Joyce is charged for that he in the County of London,[3] within the Metropolitan Police District and within the jurisdiction of the Central Criminal Court, committed High Treason between the 2nd day of September, 1939, and the 29th day of May, 1945, in that he, being a person owing allegiance to His Majesty the King, adhered to the King's enemies elsewhere than in the King's realm; to wit, in the German realm, contrary to the Treason Act, 1351.'

After formal evidence of arrest, he was remanded to 25 June. On that occasion the Crown was represented by Mr L. A. Byrne, Senior Prosecuting Counsel to the Treasury (now Mr Justice Byrne), and Mr H. A. K. Morgan, of the Department of the Director of Public Prosecutions, while Mr C. B. V. Head, of the firm of Ludlow & Co., solicitors, appeared for Joyce. Joyce reserved his defence, and after a further formal remand to avoid committal to the current session of the Central Criminal Court, which would have been inconvenient for want of time to prepare the case, he was, on 28 June 1945, committed to the July Session.

At the July Session of the Central Criminal Court, Mr Derek Curtis-Bennett, K.C., applied for the case to be sent over to the next session. He told Mr Justice Charles that, looking at the indictment, the first fact for the Crown to prove was that Joyce was a person owing allegiance to our lord the King. There had been investigations in the United States as to the nationality, not only of Joyce, but of his father, and the defence had documents from the State of New Jersey concerning a man who might or might not prove to be Joyce's father. It was necessary that someone should go to the United States to see the original documents and signatures, and it might be necessary for the latter to be seen by persons who knew the handwriting of Joyce's father, so that sworn evidence in an admissible form might be before the Court. That would take time, and could not be done in that session. One matter absolutely vital in the case was Joyce's nationality. There was also a record of the birth of William Joyce in New York in 1906, and it would be

3. The curious allegation that treason committed 'in the German realm' was committed in the County of London, etc., is due to the statutory provisions as to venue in the case of treason committed abroad in the Treason Act, 1543, 35 Hen. VIII, ch. 6.

the submission of the defence that if Joyce was born in the United
States he could not owe allegiance to the British Crown.

MR JUSTICE CHARLES: I express no view about it at all.

MR BYRNE [for the prosecution]: We do not desire to put any
obstacles in the way of the defence. It is our desire to render any
assistance of which we are capable.

MR JUSTICE CHARLES: There being no opposition by the Crown,
I am prepared to accede to the request. This case will be adjourned until the September Session, 11th September.

At the September Session the presiding Judge was Mr Justice
Tucker, who fixed 17 September for the opening of the trial. On
that day Joyce was arraigned, and pleaded not guilty to an indictment containing three counts. The first count charged that being a
person owing allegiance to our lord the King he adhered to the
King's enemies elsewhere than in the King's realm, by broadcasting between 18 September 1939 and 29 May 1945; the
second, that being a person owing allegiance to our lord the King
he adhered to the King's enemies elsewhere than in the King's
realm by purporting to become naturalized in Germany. During
the trial these two counts were amended by substituting 'being a
British subject owing allegiance' for 'being a person owing allegiance', thereby emphasizing that in these counts the prosecution
were relying on British nationality. The evidence of Joyce's American nationality being, as Mr Justice Tucker said, 'really overwhelming', the Attorney-General intimated that he was not going
to invite the jury to say that he was British, and therefore the jury
were directed to return formal verdicts of 'Not guilty' on those
counts. The real issue was fought out on the third count, which
alleged that Joyce being a person owing allegiance to our lord the
King adhered to the King's enemies elsewhere than within the
realm by broadcasting between 18 September 1939 and 2 July
1940. The latter was the date on which Joyce's British passport
expired. It will be more convenient to deal separately with the
important legal questions involved, the nature of which has already
been indicated, and to say here that Mr Justice Tucker ruled as a

matter of law that Joyce did owe allegiance to the British Crown, and left to the jury the question whether he had adhered to the King's enemies. To that there could be only one answer, and Joyce, on 19 September 1945, was convicted and sentenced to death.

On 27 September he gave notice of appeal to the Court of Criminal Appeal against his conviction,[4] on four grounds:

1. The Court wrongly assumed jurisdiction to try an alien for an offence against British law committed in a foreign country.
2. The learned Judge was wrong in law in holding, and misdirected the jury in directing them, that the appellant owed allegiance to His Majesty the King during the period from 18 September 1939 to 2 July 1940.
3. There was no evidence that the renewal of the appellant's passport afforded him or was capable of affording him any protection, or that the appellant ever availed himself or had any intention of availing himself of any such protection.
4. If (contrary to the appellant's contention) there was any such evidence, the issue was one for the jury, and the learned Judge failed to direct them thereon.

The appeal was heard before the Lord Chief Justice (Viscount Caldecote), Mr Justice Humphreys, and Mr Justice Lynskey on 30 and 31 October and 1 November 1945. After reserving judgment till 7 November, the Court dismissed the appeal. The Criminal Appeal Act provides that one judgment of the Court shall be delivered, and this was given by the Lord Chief Justice, but its language makes it clear that the decision was unanimous.

No further appeal could be brought unless the Attorney-General was prepared to certify that the decision 'involved a point of law of exceptional public importance, and that it was desirable in the public interest that a further appeal should be brought'. On 16 November Sir Hartley Shawcross, Attorney-General, issued his certificate to that effect.

4. It is a 'vulgar error', beloved of the more popular organs of the press, and occasionally perpetrated even by the B.B.C., to describe a prisoner as appealing 'against the sentence of death', which, being fixed by law, cannot be appealed against. This is carefully provided by the Criminal Appeal Act, 1907, which refers to 'appeal against sentence (not being a sentence fixed by law)'. The appeal in capital cases is, and must be, against conviction. In practice, leave, when necessary, is always granted in capital cases.

The appeal was heard by the House of Lords on 10 to 13 December, the noble and learned Lords sitting being the Lord Chancellor (Lord Jowitt) and Lords Macmillan, Wright, Simonds, and Porter. On 18 December they announced their decision dismissing the appeal (Lord Porter dissenting), and intimated that they would give their reasons at a later date, which they did on 1 February 1946.

It may be useful to the reader to give some account of the law relating to nationality, of the history of passports, and of the conception of allegiance.

At common law, nationality depended on place of birth – a person born within the King's dominions was a subject, a person born outside them was an alien. On this simple doctrine various statutory modifications were grafted, of which the most important was the rule that the children and grandchildren (but not remoter issue), wherever born, of a natural-born British subject, were also British subjects, provided that the father had not before the date of the birth divested himself of British nationality. Before 1870, when the Naturalization Act was passed, a British subject could not divest himself of British nationality. Such divesting could only happen, if at all, by operation of law, e.g. by outlawry.

Thus, if Michael Joyce, the prisoner's father, being a British subject, had gone to America and William Joyce had been born there before his father acquired American citizenship, he would have been a British subject by birth. But as soon as it was proved that Michael Joyce completed the formalities of naturalization in the United States in 1894, while William Joyce was not born till 24 April 1906, it became clear that William was an American and not a British subject.

As regards persons born since 1 January 1915, British nationality has been governed by the British Nationality and Status of Aliens Act, 1914, which defines natural-born British subjects in sec. 1, sub-sec. (1) as follows:

The following persons shall be deemed to be natural-born British subjects, namely:
(a) Any person born within His Majesty's dominions and allegiance; and

(*b*) Any person born out of His Majesty's dominions whose father was a British subject at the time of that person's birth and either was born within His Majesty's allegiance or was a person to whom a certificate of naturalization had been granted; and

(*c*) Any person born on board a British ship, whether in foreign territorial waters or not.

Provided that the child of a British subject whether that child was born before or after the passing of this Act shall be deemed to have been born within His Majesty's allegiance if born in a place where by treaty, capitulation, grant, usage, sufferance, or other lawful means, His Majesty exercises jurisdiction over British subjects.

(This proviso would cover persons born in British embassies and legations abroad.)

The reader will notice the recurrence of the expression 'born within His Majesty's allegiance', and much turned at the trial of William Joyce on the meaning of allegiance. Until this case was decided, any lawyer called on to explain what was meant by 'allegiance' would probably have considered that he had given a correct definition if he had defined it as the duty of loyalty and faithfulness owed to a Sovereign by a person within his protection, and had gone on to say that allegiance might be of two kinds: (1) natural and permanent, which is the allegiance owed to the Sovereign by his own subjects at all times, and in all places, so long as the relation of subject and Sovereign subsists. It is because of this natural and permanent allegiance that a British subject can be guilty of treason even outside the British Empire. (2) The second kind of allegiance is local and temporary, being that owed to a Sovereign by an alien so long as he remains within the dominions of the Sovereign and under his protection. Until the Joyce case it was supposed that such allegiance automatically terminated when the alien left the realm. That must now be recognized as subject to qualification where any alien has, whether by mistake or fraud, applied for and obtained a British passport.[5]

5. It was never established, nor in these proceedings was it material, whether Joyce in applying for the passport, or for its renewal, was mistaken or fraudulent in stating his nationality. It may be said that if he honestly believed himself to be British, it makes his treason all the worse, since he was morally as well as legally a traitor to 'the country he loved so dearly'.

The reason for the temporary and local allegiance of an alien is clear: no country can be expected to admit foreigners within its borders except on the terms that while they enjoy its hospitality they will conduct themselves in accordance with its laws, and refrain from activities subversive of its security or political institutions. Hence it is clear that a man may be subject at the same time to two allegiances. For instance, a British subject who goes on business or pleasure to the United States does not lose, or even suspend, his allegiance to the British Crown, but he has in addition a temporary allegiance to the American Constitution. He must not plot against America, but neither must he engage in activities which would be treason in Britain. This overriding natural allegiance is recognized in the principle of international law by which a subject of a belligerent in enemy-occupied territory may not be required to bear arms against his own country. So far as ordinary law is concerned, the alien is subject to the law of the country where he is temporarily residing, to the exclusion of the law of his own country; thus the Englishman in Switzerland may, if he will, add to the pleasure of drinking a glass of beer in the middle of the afternoon by thinking of his thirsty compatriots at home with two hours to wait before opening time.

It will be noticed that in defining allegiance I have brought it repeatedly into relation with the word 'protection'. They are, indeed, correlatives. It was said by Blackstone, and quoted by the Attorney-General in opening the Joyce case, that so long as the Prince affords protection to his subjects, so long that subject owes a debt of allegiance to the Prince. And long before Blackstone in *Calvin's* case (1608), 7 Co. Rep. Ia; 77 E.R. 377, Lord Coke refers to the maxim '*Protectio trahit subjectionem et subjectio protectionem*', and much of the Crown's argument in the present case was based on the proposition that by deliberately applying for and obtaining a British passport, Joyce had placed himself under the protection of the Crown, and had thereby undertaken the correlative duty of allegiance so long as the right to claim the protection of the passport continued.

Up to a point, both sides in the Joyce trial agreed on the effect of the authorities. In Foster's Crown Law (1762[6]), p. 183, sec. 1, it is stated: 'With regard to natural born subjects there can be no doubt. They owe allegiance to the Crown at all times and in all places. That is what we call natural allegiance in contradistinction to that which is local. The duty of allegiance, whether natural or local, is founded in the relation the person standeth in to the Crown and in the privileges he deriveth from that relation. Local allegiance is founded in the protection a foreigner enjoyeth for his person, his family or effects during his residence here, and it ceaseth whenever he withdraweth with his family and effects.' And on p. 185, sec. 4, he says: 'And if such alien seeking the protection of the Crown and having a family and effects here should during a war with his native country go thither and there adhere to the King's enemies for purposes of hostility, he might be dealt with as a traitor. For he came and settled here under the protection of the Crown, and though his person was removed for a time his effects and family continued still under the same protection. This rule was laid down by all the judges assembled at the Queen's command, 12 January 1707. It is to be observed that the judges in the resolution last cited laid a considerable stress on the Queen's declaration of war against France and Spain, whereby she took into her protection the persons and estates of the subjects of those Crowns residing here and de-meaning themselves dutifully and not corresponding with the enemy. King William and Queen Mary did the same in their declaration of war against France, and so did his present Majesty (George III). These declarations did in fact put Frenchmen residing here and demeaning themselves dutifully, even in time of war, upon the foot of aliens coming hither by licence of safe conduct. They enabled them to acquire personal chattels and to maintain actions for the recovery of their personal rights in as full a manner as aliens may. But as I said before all enemy aliens residing here under the protection of the Crown, though possibly not favoured as the persons last mentioned, yet they in case they commit crimes

6. 1762 is the date of the first edition of Foster. The edition used at the trial was the third, of 1809, but there appears to be no material change in text or pagination.

which in a subject would amount to treason may be dealt with as traitors. For their persons are under the protection of the law, and in consequence of that protection they owe a local temporary allegiance to the Crown.' That resolution of the Judges was also referred to in East's Pleas of the Crown (1903) but in somewhat different terms; the original is apparently not extant, nor are the circumstances in which it was passed known.

The Crown sought to rely upon it as authority that in some circumstances an alien could be prosecuted for treason committed outside the realm, if he was still receiving the protection of the Crown for his family and effects. In the present case Joyce had not left his family and effects in England – for 'family' clearly must be limited to wife and children over whom he can be presumed to exercise some control, and does not include parents and brother and sisters who are in no way responsible to him. But in the Attorney-General's picturesque phrase, by obtaining a British passport he had 'enveloped himself in the Union Jack' and put himself in a position to claim British protection. That protection involved the corresponding duty of allegiance. By broadcasting for the enemy Joyce acted in breach of that duty, and was thereby guilty of treason, for which he could be tried and executed in this country. Such, in the briefest outline, was the case for the prosecution. Against it the defence urged (in addition to the argument that there was no jurisdiction at all to try an alien for a crime committed abroad) that a resolution of the Judges had no binding authority as such; it did not appear that it was a decision in any case then before a Court. In any event, it did not support the Crown's contention, for the exception suggested in the case of the alien leaving his family and effects was due – if it was the law, which, in the submission of the defence, it was not – to his still receiving protection *within the realm*. The protection necessary to attract the duty of allegiance was the protection of the law, and it could arise only where the British law ran, that was to say, within the King's dominions. It must, in other words, be *de jure* protection, and not mere *de facto* protection; not that there was any evidence that Joyce had ever in fact used his British passport to claim protection from any British authority anywhere.

A passport, it was submitted, was not a document granting any right to protection: it was merely recognition of the status of the holder as a British national, and a request to foreign governments to give the holder such rights as flowed from that status. Like other documents certifying status, it was not conclusive, but could be displaced by proof that the status did not in fact exist, and was then a mere nullity. Just as two persons going through a form of marriage were entitled to obtain an official certificate of marriage, so a British subject intending to go abroad could, and in most cases nowadays must, obtain a British passport. The rights and duties of the spouses did not flow from the certificate, but from the relation of husband and wife; and the rights and duties of the traveller did not flow from the passport but from his British nationality. The marriage certificate could be displaced by proof that the marriage was in fact bigamous on the part of one of the spouses, or that they were within the prohibited degrees; so the passport could be displaced by proof that it had been issued to an alien whether he had obtained it fraudulently or under an honest mistake as to his true national status.

Moreover, it was submitted, to say that Joyce, having wrongly obtained a British passport, thenceforth owed allegiance, even though he proved that he was in fact an alien, was the introduction into our law of 'crime by estoppel'. He could not, in a criminal case, be debarred from setting up the defence that he was an alien because he had, for the purpose of obtaining the passport, previously alleged that he was British. (For the benefit of the lay reader, it may be explained that 'estoppel' is a rule of evidence whereby, if a man has made representations as to a matter of fact, on the faith of which someone else has altered his position, the maker of the representation will not be allowed, in *civil* proceedings, to rely on the true facts – in so far as they differ from his representation – against the person who has so altered his position. But this doctrine has never found a place in *criminal* proceedings, in which a defendant can always rely on any defence open to him, notwithstanding previous contradictory statements, which may, of course, be material for cross-examination.)

The *Shorter Oxford English Dictionary* attributes the word 'passport' to the beginning of the sixteenth century. It seems originally to have been a licence to leave the realm, which was otherwise prohibited at common law, possibly because it deprived the King of a man's military service. This sense, with the analogous sense of a licence to enter or pass through a country, is said to be obsolete from the early seventeenth century. The definition given of the modern sense, dating from 1536, is 'a document issued by competent authority, granting permission to the person specified in it to travel, and authenticating his right to protection'. It will be noted that the passport is only said to *authenticate*, not to *confer* the right to protection. The first mention of passports in the Statute Book is in 1548, 2 Ed. VI, c.2, sec. 10, where it is applied to what would now be called a soldier's leave-pass.

There appears to be no steady or consistent development of the system of passports. They seem to have been required or not required of individuals according to the state of contemporary politics in various countries. In *Reg.* v. *Bernard* (1858), 8 St. Trials (N.S.) 887, Orsini was stated to have travelled in France and Belgium under a false passport, six years old, issued by the British Foreign Office under the name of Allsop. Sixty years later, before the war of 1914–18, passports were not necessary for visiting most European countries other than Russia and Turkey, but they were not infrequently carried as a convenient means of identification, and an assistance in claiming the help, in case of need, of diplomatic or consular representatives. Since the First World War they are generally necessary for travel, and British regulations state that 'British subjects travelling to foreign countries must be in possession of valid passports bearing, when required, the visa of the consular representatives of the country or countries to be visited.'

In 1887 Lord Salisbury sent a circular asking British representatives abroad to supply information as to the laws of their respective countries regarding the admission of aliens as residents. The result, published in Parliamentary Papers, 1887, No. 81, contains factual information, but no general statement as to the nature of a passport. But from the various replies, it appears that a passport was regarded as a document required by the country in which the traveller found himself as a formal reference, as a safeguard to that state. In Austria-Hungary the state authorities could grant a traveller a provisional passport, if his own was not in order, provided that he was not a suspicious character. So at that time a British subject might lawfully have entered Austria, with not a British, but an Austrian passport.

In 1872 the British Government apparently regarded it as an inconvenience that British subjects should be required to carry passports, and made representations to France with a view to their abolition. The French Government gave two reasons for retaining them: (1) Security to France. (2) They were a valuable source of revenue which she could not at the moment afford to forgo. There was no suggestion that the passport was a document ensuring the holder British protection; it was rather represented as an unreasonable requirement of the French Government, resented by the British Government, and acting as a deterrent to travel. As a result of this correspondence passports were abolished between Britain and France, but the right of a British subject in France to claim protection cannot have been diminished or affected, which seems rather to support the view that the passport is merely evidence of rights, not their source.

Of judicial authority on passports there is very little. Apart from *Reg.* v. *Bernard* (*supra*), in *Rex* v. *Brailsford and M'Culloch*, [1905] 2 K.B. 730, a conspiracy to obtain a false passport for use in Russia was involved. The gravamen of the offence, as set out in the indictment, was the endangering of the relations between this country and Russia, not a wrongful claiming of protection, and in his summing-up Lord Alverstone, the Lord Chief Justice, thus defined a passport: 'It is a document, issued in the name of a Sovereign, on the responsibility of a Minister of the Crown, to a named individual, intended to be presented to the governments of foreign nations and to be used for that individual's protection as a British subject in foreign countries, and it depends for its validity upon the fact that the Foreign Office, in an official document, vouches the respectability of the person named. Passports have been known and recognized as official documents for more than three centuries, and, in the event of war breaking out, become documents which may be necessary for the protection of the bearer, if the subject of a neutral state, as against the officials of the belligerents, and in time of peace, in some countries, as in Russia, they are required to be carried by all travellers.' There appears to be no more recent judicial criticism or amplification of that definition, which does suggest that the protection of the bearer is the object of a passport, but not that the right to protection springs from the passport, which seems to have been a novel doctrine in the present case, though one which found favour in all three Courts, and must therefore be accepted as the law.

The reasons for their lordships' decision were delivered on 1 February 1946, nearly a month after Joyce's execution. It is perhaps worthy of passing comment that the Home Secretary, before allowing the law to take its course, did not think it necessary to wait and see whether any passages in their lordships' opinions might afford some ground for the exercise of clemency. It may well be that they would not have done so, and that delay would merely have been a prolongation of Joyce's ordeal.

The Lord Chancellor said that the question of law, of far-reaching importance, was whether an alien who had been resident within the realm could be held guilty and convicted in this country of high treason for acts committed by him outside the realm.

The Statute of 1351 was wide enough to cover any man anywhere: 'If *a man* do levy war', etc. But the question whether the act was treasonable depended on the relation in which the actor stood to the King to whose enemies he adhered. Attention had naturally been concentrated on the question of allegiance. To say that an act was treasonable if the actor owed allegiance, and not treasonable if he did not, left undecided the question by whom allegiance was owed. New considerations might demand a reconsideration of the scope of the principle. It was not an extension of a penal law to apply its principles to circumstances unforeseen at the time of its enactment, so long as the case was fairly brought within its language.

It was implicit in the argument for the appellant that, however brief his absence from the realm, he could not during that absence, in any circumstances, by giving aid and comfort to the King's enemies outside the realm, be guilty of a treasonable act. That statement was not only at variance with the law, but was inconsistent with authority which could not be disregarded. The passage in Foster's Crown Law (already cited) had been repeated without challenge by numerous authors of the highest authority, nor had it been challenged in any judicial authority.

In the present case there was no question of vicarious protection. But was there not such protection still afforded the appellant by the Sovereign as to require his continued allegiance? It would be strangely inconsistent with the robust and vigorous common sense of the common law to suppose that an alien quitting his residence in this country, and adhering and giving aid to the King's enemies abroad, could do so with impunity.

The appellant had long resided here, but he (the Lord Chancellor) made no assumption one way or the other about his intention to return, and treated as immaterial the fact that he made a false statement as to his status. When he first made it, it might be that he thought it was true.

The possession of a passport by a non-British subject gave him rights and imposed on the Sovereign obligations which would otherwise not be given or imposed. He was enabled to obtain in a foreign country the protection extended to British subjects. The question was whether by the receipt of the passport he extended his duty of allegiance beyond the moment when he left the shores of this country. As one owing allegiance he sought and obtained the protection of the King for himself while abroad.

The argument that, since the protection of the law could not be given outside the realm to an alien, he could not, outside the realm, owe any duty had no substance. At the time when the common law established between Sovereign and resident alien the reciprocal duties of allegiance and protection, it was to the personal power of the Sovereign rather than to the law of England that the alien looked. It was not therefore an answer to the Sovereign's claim to fidelity from an alien without the realm who held a British passport that there could not be extended to him the protection of the law.

He was of opinion that so long as an alien held the passport he was, within the meaning of the Statute, a man who, if he adhered to the King's enemies in the realm or elsewhere, committed an act of treason.

He did not dissent from the general proposition that an alien could withdraw his allegiance on leaving the realm. But there was no suggestion that the appellant had surrendered his passport, or done any other overt act to withdraw from his allegiance, unless, indeed, reliance was placed on the act of treason itself, which in his opinion could not be done. Such an act was not inconsistent with the appellant still availing himself of the passport in other countries, and even in Germany.

With regard to the question of jurisdiction, a proper regard of the State for its own security required that all who committed the crime of treason, whether within or without the realm, should be amenable to its laws. There was no principle of comity to the contrary.

It was further urged for the appellant that there was no evidence that the renewal of his passport afforded him or was capable of affording him, any protection, or that he ever availed himself or had any intention of availing himself of any such protection; and that if there was any such evidence the issue was one for the jury, and that the Judge had failed to direct them thereon. That point also failed.

Lords Macmillan, Wright, and Simonds concurred with the Lord Chancellor.

Lord Porter dissented. He agreed that the renewal of the passport on 24 August 1939 was evidence from which a jury might have inferred that he retained that document for use after 18 September 1939, when he was first proved to have adhered to the enemy. If an alien was under British protection he occupied the same position when abroad as he would occupy if he were a British subject. But the question of continued allegiance depended on the circumstances of the case, and was a matter for the jury. In the present case a jury properly directed might well have considered that the allegiance had been terminated. He would have allowed the appeal.

It will be observed from the above summary that their lordships have expressly decided that a passport is not merely an evidential document, but one which gives rights and imposes duties; and that an alien in possession of a passport may be tried here for crimes committed abroad. Those matters may well be thought amply sufficient to justify the Attorney-General in granting his certificate. Even so, it is easy to underestimate the significance and importance of the Joyce case. *Directly*, its importance may well be small, for only in the infinitesimal number of cases in which an alien obtains, by fraud or mistake, a British passport, and then goes abroad and commits treason, can it be directly in point. A British subject is covered by his general duty of allegiance, and the passport is immaterial.

But *indirectly*, the case may well prove of vast importance. It has introduced into our jurisprudence, for the first time, the doctrine that a British Court has, in certain circumstances, the right to try an alien for a crime committed abroad. It does not need much imagination to see that, unless those circumstances are very precisely and narrowly defined, this may be the thin edge of a very large wedge indeed.

Secondly, it has introduced, or at least declared, the doctrine that the holder of a British passport *ipso facto* owes allegiance to the British Crown. This may have far-reaching repercussions in British mandated territories, and among 'British protected' persons, where persons who are not British subjects may be entitled to hold British passports.

It is also possible to envisage a perfectly honest person being involved in a conflict of allegiance where it is completely impossible for him to avoid committing treason! Suppose, for instance, that Joyce, instead of being American, had been German by birth, but had lived here and honestly believed himself to be British, and went abroad with a British passport. On the outbreak of war he is claimed as a German subject, liable to military service. If he obeys, he is (under this decision) liable to be hanged by the British; if he refuses, he will certainly be shot by the Germans.

The decision is no longer open to argument: the reasoning

underlying it is a legitimate subject of legal discussion, and it would be untrue to pretend that it meets with unanimous acceptance among lawyers, many of whom thought the appeal would succeed.

On 3 January 1946 William Joyce was hanged at Wandsworth, the Home Secretary, Mr J. Chuter Ede, having intimated a few days earlier that he was unable to find any reason which would justify him in interfering with the course of law. A morbid-minded crowd of some 300 persons gathered outside the gaol, and according to the evening papers police had to control the crowd which surged forward to read the official notice that the execution had been carried out. Two men, it was reported, had travelled from Glasgow to be present. But the most scandalous aspect was the presence of young children brought by their parents.

The statutory inquest produced the inevitable verdict. One may be pardoned for some scepticism as to the value of these formal inquiries after an execution; we have never read of one which failed to record that execution was carried out expeditiously and without a hitch. There is no reason to doubt that everything possible is done, and was done in this case, to ensure the minimum of suffering to the victim, but there are some grim stories in the history of executions, even in modern times, and there is considerable reason to doubt whether, if a hitch did occur, the regulations would permit any news of it to reach the outer world via the coroner and his jury. When Major Wallace Blake was tried in 1926 for a breach of the Official Secrets Act, by disclosing details of a recent execution in a newspaper article, an official of the Home Office was cross-examined as to the instructions issued on 10 January 1925 by Sir Ernley Blackwell, K.C.B., Permanent Legal Under-Secretary to the Home Office, to Prison Governors with regard to their conduct at executions, and the form of their evidence at inquests, which was to be confined to as few words as possible, e.g. 'it was carried out expeditiously and without a hitch'. If pressed for details, 'the Governor should say he cannot give them as he did not time the proceedings, but "a very short interval elapsed", or some general expression of opinion to the same effect'. Questions were asked in the House of Commons by Mr Pethick-Lawrence as to these instructions, but the Home Secretary (Sir W. Joynson Hicks) said: 'It is undesirable to give the exact terms of the instructions . . . the less said at the inquest either by Governors or anyone else, the better.' (See Hansard, 23 June 1927, vol. 207, No. 85, cols. 2022–2023.) One is left sharing Mr Pethick-Lawrence's doubts whether it can possibly be proper to give a witness instructions as to the form and content of the evidence he is to give *on oath* before a judicial tribunal entitled to hear 'the truth, the whole truth, and nothing but the truth'. Whether any alteration has been made in the instructions since 1926 it is impossible for a private individual to know: the regularity with which the phrase 'expeditiously and without a hitch' occurs in the reports of these melancholy occasions suggests that it is improbable.

At an inquest at Lincoln Prison on a man executed on 4 January 1928, the Governor's answer to the question how long elapsed between Pierpont entering the cell and the drop was: 'I am not allowed to say anything except that a very short interval elapsed.'

The Coroner: 'Are you allowed to say how long the body remained hanging?' – 'No, sir, I am not.'

Perhaps one day a jury will have the courage to return a verdict, 'That the deceased met his death by judicial hanging, but the jury have not been allowed to receive sufficient evidence to enable them to say whether the execution was properly carried out.'

In writing this I wish to make it emphatically clear that I am not for one moment suggesting that anyone concerned with the execution of Joyce failed to carry out his duty with complete propriety. My criticism is directed at the system, not at individuals or individual cases. One cannot help wondering whether the American system of summoning a certain number of respectable and responsible citizens (not the type who voluntarily gather outside a gaol to stare at a sheet of paper) as witnesses of the execution is not a greater safeguard, provided that they are not muzzled if there is anything that should be disclosed in the public interest.

For Joyce's crime one can have no sympathy whatever. Though in law an alien, he had lived many years in England, had deliberately served in the O.T.C., and had referred to her as 'the country I love so dearly'. But the question remains, for many thoughtful people: What useful purpose have we served by hanging Joyce, or John Amery about a fortnight earlier? Treason, it is true, is the greatest of crimes, but there are degrees even in treason, and the crime of treason by broadcasting propaganda is hardly comparable to that of treachery in the field. On the day after Joyce's execution a man named Schurch was hanged at Pentonville. He had been convicted on nine charges of giving information to the enemy, and of desertion with intent to join the enemy. Still less, one might have thought, was Joyce's crime, detestable though it was, deserving of the same punishment as the mass murders and torture of prisoners of which the Belsen criminals were convicted.

If it be said, 'There would have been a public outcry if Joyce had been reprieved,' my answer would be that the first function of a legal system is to substitute the reasoned and dispassionate judgment of the law for the clamour of popular prejudice. It may, however, be doubted whether there would have been any popular clamour, for much to my surprise I have found, with a universal reprobation of Joyce's conduct, a very considerable feeling, shared by lawyers and laymen, servicemen and civilians, that (with the utmost respect to the eight out of nine learned Judges) the decision was wrong, and that an unmeritorious case has made bad law. The feeling is not so much that Joyce, having been convicted, should have been reprieved, but that he should not have been convicted.